Theoretical Issues in Language Acquisition

Continuity and Change in Development

Theoretical Issues in Language Acquisition

Continuity and Change in Development

Edited by

Jürgen Weissenborn
Max-Planck-Institut für Psycholinguistik,
Nijmegen, The Netherlands

Helen Goodluck
University of Ottawa, Canada

Thomas Roeper
University of Massachusetts–Amherst

LEA LAWRENCE ERLBAUM ASSOCIATES, PUBLISHERS
Hillsdale, New Jersey   Hove and London

Lawrence Erlbaum Associates, Inc., Publishers
365 Broadway
Hillsdale, New Jersey 07642

Library of Congress Cataloging-in-Publication Data

Theoretical issues in language acquisition : continuity and change in
  development / edited by Jürgen Weissenborn, Helen Goodluck, Thomas
  Roeper.
       p.   cm.
  Includes bibliographical references and index.
  ISBN 0-8058-0379-3. — ISBN 0-8058-0380-7 (pbk.)
  1. Language acquisition.   I. Weissenborn, Jürgen.   II. Goodluck,
Helen.   III. Roeper, Thomas.
  P118.T46   1992
  401'.93 — dc20   91–23938
                                                               CIP

Printed in the United States of America
10   9   8   7   6   5   4   3   2   1

Contents

Preface

A central aim of the study of language acquisition is to explain the development of the child's linguistic knowledge over time. In recent linguistic theory, there has been an explosion of detailed studies of language variation. "Parameter theory" has thrown new light on both fundamental differences (such as those distinguishing languages as different as English and Chinese) and on subtle variations between genetically related and/or similar languages (e.g., variations that characterize differences in the grammars of French and Italian). The studies described in this book apply such recent analyses to the study of child language, using the theory to develop new approaches to change and variation in child grammars. The studies reveal both early knowledge in several areas of grammar and a period of extended development in other areas. Topics dealt with in the book include question formation, 'subjectless' sentences, object gaps, rules for missing subject interpretation, passive sentences, rules for pronoun interpretation, and argument structure. The chapters in the book show how linguistic theory can help define and inform a theory of the dynamics of language development and its biological basis, meeting the growing need for such studies in programs in linguistics, psychology, and cognitive science.

This book contains in-depth studies of the source of errors and the mechanisms of change in the child grammar. Chapters by Clahsen and by Felix take radically different positions ("continuity" vs "maturation") concerning the source of errors in, for example, the interpretation of pronouns by children. Randall's chapter details mechanisms for the attainment of adult knowledge of verbal argument structure.

The book contains much new data and many new analyses. The chapter by Roeper and de Villiers contains new experimental evidence concerning the development of knowledge of constraints on wh-movement. The chapter by Goodluck and Behne contains new experimental evidence on the development of control (PRO) constructions, including previously untested constructions (purpose clauses). The chapter by Weissenborn presents new data on subjectless sentences (pro-drop) from the acquisition of French and German. The chapter by Hyams uses recent linguistic theory to develop new analyses of existing data on the same topic. The chapters are accompanied by commentary chapters written by scholars from a range of disciplines: linguistics, psychology, and computer science.

This volume grows out of a roundtable session at the XIVth International Congress of Linguists, East Berlin, 12 and 14 August, 1987. Most of the papers were presented there in preliminary form; an exception is the chapter by Hyams, which was presented at the 12th Annual Boston University Conference on Language Development, October 1987.

We thank Ken Wexler, who presented a paper at the Berlin workshop, and all the participants in the workshop, for their comments.

Jürgen Weissenborn
Helen Goodluck
Thomas Roeper

List of Contributors

Dawn Behne, Speech Research Laboratory, Indiana University, Bloomington, In 47408.

Harald Clahsen, Allgemeine Sprachwissenschaft, University of Düsseldorf, Universitätsstrasse 7, 4000 Düsseldorf, Germany.

Sascha Felix, Department of Linguistics, University of Passau, Instrasse 40 (Nikolakloster), 8390 Passau, Germany.

Jill de Villiers, Department of Psychology, Smith College, Northampton, MA 01063.

Helen Goodluck, Department of Linguistics, University of Ottawa, 78 Laurier East, Ottawa, Ontario, Canada K1N 6N5.

Nina Hyams, Department of Linguistics, University of California Los Angeles, 405 Hilgard Avenue, Los Angeles, CA 90024-1543.

Charles Jones, Department of English, George Mason University, 4400 University Drive, Fairfax, VA 22030.

Diane Lillo-Martin, Department of Linguistics, University of Connecticut, 341 Mansfield Road, Storrs, CT 06269-1145.

James Pustejovsky, Department of Computer Science, Brandeis University, Waltham, MA 02254.

Andrew Radford, Department of Language & Linguistics, University of Essex, Wivenhoe Park, Colchester CO4 3SQ, United Kingdom.

Janet Randall, Linguistics Program, 282 Nightingale Hall, Northeastern University, 360 Huntington Avenue, Boston, MA 02115-5097.

Thomas Roeper, Department of Linguistics, South College, University of Massachusetts, Amherst, MA 01003.

Rosemary J. Stevenson, Department of Psychology, Human Communication Research Center, University of Durham, Durham DH1 3LE, United Kingdom.

Jürgen Weissenborn, Max-Planck-Institut für Psycholinguistik, Postbus 310, Wundtlaan 1, NL-6500 AH Nijmegen, The Netherlands.

1 Introduction: Old and New Problems in the Study of Language Acquisition

Jürgen Weissenborn
Max-Planck-Institut für Psycholinguistik
Nijmegen, The Netherlands

Helen Goodluck
University of Ottawa, Canada

Thomas Roeper
University of Massachusetts–Amherst

Four questions define the core concerns for a theory of language acquisition:

1. What is the adult grammar? That is, what is the end state of development?
2. What assumptions about language does the child bring to the task of language acquisition?
3. What developmental stages are exhibited?
4. How is language development possible in principle and in fact? That is, what are the conditions for successful learning?

We will briefly comment on these questions and the way they are addressed in the different contributions in this volume.

I. ADULT LINGUISTIC KNOWLEDGE

The authors in this volume share a number of common assumptions concerning adult linguistic competence; these assumptions underlie much work in current generative linguistic theory. Adult languages are assumed to be characterized by cognitive-particularity and modularity. By cognitive-particularity we mean the independence of linguistic constructs from other systems of knowledge; that is, we subscribe to the belief that linguistic knowledge cannot be reduced to principles governing nonlinguistic aspects

1

of human ability, although the latter may influence linguistic systems. By modularity, we refer to the assumption that linguistic knowledge itself comprises a number of highly specialized subsystems of rules and principles, each with its own function.[1]

Differences between adult languages provide some of the most telling evidence in favor of the assumption of cognitive-particularity. For example, English and Italian differ with respect to the grammaticality of questions of the type illustrated by the English question:

(1) Who do you think that came?

In English such questions are ungrammatical although the equivalent sentence without the complementizer *that* is perfectly good:

(2) Who do you think came?

In Italian, questions equivalent to (1) are grammatical, as shown by:

(3) *Chi credi che è venuto?*

These facts cannot be related to any general, nonlinguistic aspect of human cognition. No candidate principles for a nonlinguistic explanation exist and such an explanation would entail the odd assumption that adult speakers of Italian and adult speakers of English differ in their general cognitive makeup. The kind of explanation that has been put forward in the linguistic literature in the past decade or so depends on intricate, system-specific, properties of linguistic rules (see, e.g., Rizzi, 1982).

Most of the chapters in this collection assume the basic correctness of a particular version of the modular approach to linguistic knowledge, that is, the "principles and parameters" approach of Chomsky (1981) and subsequent works. In this approach, languages vary along a number of particular dimensions and a given adult language can be characterized by its "parameter-settings"—the choice of values for a particular rule system, which then affects the applicability of particular principles of grammar. To take an elementary example, languages differ in the position of heads of phrases. A language may be head-initial (such as English) or head-final (such as Japanese and German); the verb as head of the verb-phrase will be realized

---

[1]It is an empirical question which of two alternative views is correct: That linguistic knowledge is autonomous and modular, and that it is acquired through task-specific learning mechanisms, or that there is a close interelation between other cognitive domains and the structure of linguistic knowledge, acquired through domain-unspecific general learning mechanisms.

as phrase-initial in English and phrase-final in Japanese and German (the latter showing the base order in subordinate clauses only). This division between language types can be characterized as the setting of a parameter in the phrase structure module of the grammar (X-bar theory). We will return to other examples of modules of the grammar that exhibit significant variation between adult languages, and which have received considerable attention in both theoretical research and language acquisition research.

II. The Child's Linguistic Abilities

The authors in this volume not only share fundamental assumptions concerning the nature of adult linguistic knowledge (cognitive-particularity and modularity), they also share some basic assumptions concerning the nature of language acquisition. Specifically, they share the assumption that language acquisition could not be achieved unless the child were endowed with a substantial component of innate linguistic knowledge. In other words, children are assumed to acquire language with the aid of principles of Universal Grammar: the set of principles that define the range of possible human languages.

One motivation for assuming the innateness of Universal Grammar is "Plato's problem" (Chomsky, 1986b): How can we know so much on the basis of so little evidence? The fact that there are innumerable errors that one would expect children to make, but that, in fact, never show up, argues for strong constraints on the learning process. For example, children appear to follow structure-dependent syntactic rules from the outset. This may be illustrated by the fact that there is no evidence that children ever consider a rule for forming yes–no questions along the lines: invert the first noun (phrase) with the first auxiliary verb, producing (erroneous) forms such as "*Is the man who tall is rich?" (from "The man who is tall is rich"), although many of the question forms the child hears would be compatible with such a rule.[2] A rich, innate component of linguistic knowledge will help explain the absence of many logically possible errors. Other powerful arguments for an innate basis of linguistic knowledge are the fact that language learning takes place in childhood without effort or a need for special instruction, and proceeds in a comparable manner under both normal and special conditions such as deafness and blindness (see Mills, 1983; Gleitman, Gleitman, Landau, & Wanner, 1989).

III. CURRENT ISSUES

The latter part of the 1970s and the early 1980s saw a burst of work in language acquisition that enhanced the plausibility of the view that lan-

---

[2]See Crain and Fodor (1989) for evidence on this and other points.

guage acquisition proceeded quite rapidly and under constraints imposed by (presumably innate) principles of grammar. For example, a number of studies have argued that at a very early stage a child develops a system that reflects the head-parameter setting for his or her language. By the third year, English-speaking children are sensitive to the fact that in their language the verb phrase is head-initial, and Japanese-speaking children to the fact that in their language it is head-final (Lust & Chien 1984; Lust & Wakayama 1979). Even in languages such as German, in which the basic head-final position of the verb phrase is not reflected in the surface word order of main clauses (but in subordinate clauses only), the system is acquired early on (Clahsen, this volume).

Other studies have successfully probed for knowledge of structure-based principles of grammar, such as the principle that precludes a definite pronoun from coreferring with an NP that it is structurally superior to (Principle C of Chomsky's [1981] binding theory). Thus preschool children are sensitive to the fact that the pronoun *he* and the NP *the dragon* can refer to the same individual in (4) but not in (5),

(4) Before he left the cave the boy stretched

(5) He left the cave before the boy stretched

(see, e.g., Solan, 1983; Crain & McKee, 1985), although errors of interpretation do occur. The total array of data makes sense if children are aware of principles such as Principle C and apply the principle to adult-like structures. To put it another way, evidence for sensitivity to a structure-based principle is also evidence for knowledge of the structures that condition its application and we have good reason, as a result of studies from the late 1970s and early 1980s, to suppose that not merely the basics of language-specific word order are in place by the third year, but also fairly detailed specifications of phrasal configurations.

Accepting the correctness of these observations, the way is open for the study of subtle, nonobvious questions concerning language development. The second and third questions with which we began: (2) what stages of development are observed and (3) what are the conditions for successful learning, are now beginning to be the focus of intensive work in language acquisition, some of which is represented in this volume.

III.i Stages of Development

Plainly, language development exists: The child must get from an initial state of absence of knowledge to knowledge of a grammar more or less identical to that of the adult language(s) he or she is exposed to. We can sketch three possible views concerning the form a child's grammar can take during development. They differ from each other with respect to how much they assume the child's linguistic representations to be constrained by principles of Universal Grammar. They are: (a) the Strong Continuity Hypothesis, (b) the Weak Continuity Hypothesis, (c) the Discontinuity Hypothesis.[3]

The Strong Continuity Hypothesis.   From the onset of language acquisition, all principles of Universal Grammar are available to the child and at each point in time the grammar of the child allows only for structures that are also structures of the target language. As far as we know, this strong position has not been explicitly taken, although work by Crain and Fodor (1987) comes close to it.

The Weak Continuity Hypothesis.   During development, the grammar of the child permits structures that are impossible or only marginally possible in the target language but are possible structures in other languages, that is, they obey principles of Universal Grammar. Moreover, the principles are used in such a way that each non-adult grammar corresponds to a "possible human language." This position seems to be the most popular in the literature. (It is assumed and/or discussed under various names in, inter alia, Borer & Wexler, 1987; Clahsen, this volume; Finer, 1989; Goodluck, 1986; Goodluck & Behne, this volume; Hyams, 1986, this volume; Nichigauchi & Roeper, 1987; Wexler & Manzini, 1987; Pinker, 1984, 1989; Randall, this volume; Roeper and de Villiers, this volume; Weissenborn, this volume; White, 1982.)

The Discontinuity Hypothesis.   There are stages of language development that are not constrained by Universal Grammar (Felix, 1987, this volume). The Discontinuity Hypothesis assumes that principles of grammar mature. Maturation itself does not necessarily imply discontinuity as we have defined it here, that is, systems that violate universal grammar. Borer and Wexler (1987, 1988) assume maturation without any violation of principles of Universal Grammar.

While the distinction between the three hypotheses is quite clear in principle, it is often a difficult matter to tease out evidence for one type of analysis rather than another for any given grammatical stage. For example, we have mentioned that by the third year there is quite firm evidence that

---

[3]Goodluck (1991) gives a slightly different taxonomy, based on a pre-final version of this chapter; Wexler (1990) also sketches three positions with respect to continuity and maturation. The basic problems are clear though the labels may differ somewhat in these various presentations.

children have arrived at an adult-like setting of the head-parameter for their language; that is, they have acquired a knowledge of basic phrase structure configurations appropriate to their language. But what about the very earliest stages, when children are just beginning to put words together into multiword utterances? Are the first multiword utterances governed by phrase structure specifications appropriate to the language being acquired (a Strong Continuity position)? Or are they governed by a phrase structure system that is a full-fledged system, but one that is not correct for their language (a Weak Continuity position)? Or do they altogether lack levels of phrasal structure and types of syntactic category that characterize adult systems (a Discontinuity position)?

The recent literature contains a variety of positions that are, in effect, Discontinuity analyses: for example, Lebeaux (1988), Radford (1988a, 1990), and Guilfoyle and Noonan (1988), have all argued for a version of the hypothesis that early syntactic systems are characterized by an absence of functional categories. In the X-bar theory of phrase structure, a distinction is made between lexical categories such as Noun, Verb, and Preposition, and the phrasal categories that they head on the one hand, and functional categories and their phrases, on the other. The latter are closed-class categories[4] which serve, inter alia, to express and assign various (often morphologically realized) syntactic and semantic properties such as tense, aspect, and agreement for person and number on verbs and case, gender, and number on nouns, and to provide some of the structural positions utilized in sentences with word orders other than the normal order of declarative sentences.[5] For example, the word *that* in a sentence such as "John said that Bill left" is a member of a functional category (complementizer), which heads its own phrase type, the complementizer phrase. In the adult grammar, a sentence-initial question word (such as *what* in "What did John eat?") occupies a position inside the complementizer phrase. On the assumption that all languages exhibit a system of functional categories, the hypothesis that early speech lacks such categories is in effect a discontinuity hypothesis.[6]

Such a Discontinuity assumption is not mandated by the data, however. It should be kept in mind that almost all of the evidence for a restricted system, that is, for a system without functional categories, is the absence of

---

[4]Closed-class categories are categories the membership of which cannot be increased by productive word-formation processes.

[5]Which are the actual functional categories is an open question. It has been argued, for instance, that instead of a general category Inflection, one has to assume different phrasal categories for Tense, Aspect, and Agreement (Chomsky 1989; Pollock 1989).

[6]It has been proposed that there may be languages that lack certain functional categories at S-structure (Fukui 1986).

positive evidence for a more highly articulated one, and that while certain studies may not allow us to decide, there are other pertinent studies that are not compatible with the absence of functional categories. For example, Weissenborn (this volume, 1990) and Weissenborn, Verrips, & Berman (1989) argue that children learning French and German make distinctions at an early age that mandate the presence of some functional categories. A similar conclusion is reached by Lillo-Martin (1986, this volume) in her study on the acquisition of American Sign Language. Moreover, even where there is an apparent absence of functional categories, one may hypothesize that the child has functional categories, but that these, for whatever reasons, are not realized by lexical items, such as the complementizer *that* at an early stage, or features of the INFL-component (Pierce, 1989; Radford, this volume; Valian, 1990). In some ways this current debate revives in new terminology the sort of debates about the nature of early grammars that have been going on since the early 1970s (cf. McNeill, 1970; Bowerman 1973) and illustrates the extreme difficulty of accurately determining the nature of very early grammars. Similar problems are to be found in the literature on children's knowledge of the possibility of sentences without an overt subject (Hyams, 1986, this volume; Valian, 1989; Roeper & Weissenborn, 1990; Weissenborn, this volume).

We do not wish to give the impression, however, that the indeterminacy surrounding the exact nature of the child system in some areas of grammar is a sign that the field of linguistically driven language acquisition research is doomed to rehearse forever old problems with no new breakthroughs. The problems that recur (such as the syntactic nature of very early speech) are central and difficult and progress is being made. One important way in which recent linguistic theory has opened new vistas for the study of child language is through the growth of cross-linguistic research. This is well illustrated by recent research and ongoing work on the development of syntactic movement rules, particularly question movement. In the Chomskyan framework, the formation of questions and other sentence types involves movement of the questioned element to the front of the sentence (to a position in the complementizer phrase, as has been mentioned). Languages differ in the manner in which they "use" movement. In some languages, such as English or German, the question word moves "in the syntax," that is, movement is an operation linking deep structure (D-Structure) and surface structure (S-structure); in others, such as Chinese, movement occurs as an operation between S-structure and logical form (LF); still other languages, such as French, show both possibilities. Thus movement is parameterized, in terms of the levels of grammatical representation that are linked by the movement operation. This parameterization, together with other principles (see Huang, 1982; Lasnik & Saito,

1984; Rudin, 1988) defines a range of language types. Recent studies in acquisition have drawn on this theoretical research to begin to map a picture of the development of movement rules.[7] It seems clear that while children learning languages of the English type have movement as a formal operation quite early on (de Villiers, Roeper, & Vainikka, 1990; Goodluck, Foley, & Sedivy, 1990; Goodluck, Sedivy, & Foley, 1989) the full development of the grammar of movement for a particular language type may be an extended process (Goodluck & Behne, this volume; Roeper & de Villiers, this volume).[8]

To summarize, we can define three positions with respect to the developing grammar of children: Strong Continuity, Weak Continuity, and Discontinuity. The choice between a Continuity versus Discontinuity analysis is often difficult; moreover, the distinction between learning and maturation that partly distinguishes the two approaches is not completely clear-cut (see Stevenson, this volume). Many researchers have adopted Weak Continuity as a framework for formulating hypotheses and evaluating child language data because it seems a sensible compromise between the view that children's developing grammars always conform to the rules of the language they are exposed to and the Discontinuity view that does not put any linguistic constraints on the early grammars of the child, thus predicting more serious deviations from the target in early grammars than can actually be observed. How to account for developmental sequences without necessarily assuming maturation is the topic of the next section. Regardless of how successful any account of transitions in the child's grammar is, the recent work in linguistic theory on parametric variation based on the comparative study of languages provides new possibilities for evaluating conflicting developmental claims that result from continuity and discontinuity views of language acquisition.

---

[7]Movement of interrogative pronouns does not exhaust the range of possibilities but is only one type of movement, namely movement of a maximal projection to a non-theta-marked position, that is, A-bar movement. Other types of movement are movement to a theta-marked position, (A-movement), for example, the movement of the direct object in passives to the subject position, and "head-to-head," for example, movement of the finite verb to INFL or COMP. It has been assumed that these different types of movement develop differently, with A-movement being last (Borer & Wexler 1989; see Demuth, 1989, for a different point of view), whereas A-bar movement and head-to-head movement seem to be acquired quite early.

[8]The issue of the acquisition of movement is partially dependent on a conception of Universal Grammar, which assumes different levels of representation related by an operation, namely move-alpha (Chomsky 1981, 1986). An alternative conception assumes only one level of representation, where move-alpha is a structural relationship between an antecedent and its (coindexed) trace (Koster, 1987). Both points of view have been considered variants of each other (Chomsky, 1981). This may not be so, if Lebeaux (1988) is correct in arguing that acquisition data provide evidence for only the former point of view.

III.ii The Conditions for Successful Learning

There are two main factors to consider in thinking about change in children's grammar: the nature of the input and the nature of the mechanism that works on the input. A basic premise of almost all work on language acquisition in a generative framework is that learning must progress without the aid of overt correction—that is, the learner will not receive "negative evidence," in the form of adult feedback telling the child that his or her utterances do not conform with those of the adult grammar (Brown & Hanlon, 1970). Whatever mechanisms account for the development of grammars over time must be powerful enough to accommodate learning without explicit feedback. Here we will first mention two nonmaturational sources of change: triggering by the input and learning principles.

A long-standing idea with respect to grammar development is that change in the grammar may be "triggered" by properties of the input, that is, the speech the child hears.[9] That is, if the child, by virtue of knowledge of Universal Grammar, knows certain facts about the way human languages are constructed, then his or her realization that the grammar he or she is learning has some property or other may trigger knowledge of a range of other rules whose effects may or may not be directly represented in the input. This type of deductive learning has been quite extensively discussed with respect to null-subject phenomena. Whether or not a language has null subjects, that is, sentences without an overt (lexical) subject, has been linked to a number of grammatical properties (see Jaeggli & Safir, 1989a; Rouveret & Sauzet, 1989). In Romance languages, these include the absence of expletive subjects, the presence of postverbal subjects, subject extraction from complements with an overt complementizer (cf. example (3) earlier; Rizzi, 1982) and clitic climbing (Kayne, 1989). Such properties can potentially be used by the learner to settle on a grammar that permits null subjects, or, alternatively, the existence of null subjects can be used by the learner to predict other less accessible facts (such as the grammaticality of the equivalent of 1). Whether these potential triggers are in fact used by the child is an empirical question. Apparently simple input data do not always lead the child to a predicted developmental step. This "triggering problem" has been one of the main reasons for proposing a maturational account for developmental changes. Under such an account, potential triggering data are ignored by the child because the corresponding grammatical structures cannot be generated in the child's grammar. The potential triggering data will become available only after the biological development of the linguistic principles necessary for its use (Borer & Wexler, 1987).

---

[9]See Lightfoot (1989), together with the peer commentaries, for an extensive discussion of the "triggering problem."

French provides an example of such a triggering paradox, since in that language children continue to use subjectless sentences even after they have already analyzed tense, agreement, expletives, and have found out that French (unlike Italian), is not a clitic climbing language. Any one of these phenomena should have indicated to the child that French is not a null-subject language (Weissenborn, this volume).

Maturation is one answer to the problem of timing in development. A crucial question is whether it is maturation of linguistic capacities (Felix, 1987, this volume; Borer & Wexler 1987) or of nonlinguistic capacities such as short-term memory or computational ability (e.g., Crain & Fodor, 1989) that is involved. Although on an individual level, biological programs can be affected by the environment, systematic cross-linguistic variations in rate of development constitute a potential problem for maturational accounts. Whether a viable nonmaturational alternative can be formulated, one based on the interaction of linguistic input, Universal Grammar, and learning mechanisms, is a question that needs further investigation.[10]

The concept of a trigger is a grammar-internal method of accounting for development. The learner uses knowledge of Universal Grammar together with the input to project hypotheses concerning rules for which he or she may have had no direct evidence. Other sources of explanation for real or projected stages of development have been principles that do not directly follow from the structure of Universal Grammar. An example of such a principle is the Subset Principle (Berwick, 1985; for discussion, see, for example, Crain & Fodor, 1987; Bowerman, 1987, 1988; Kapur, Lust, Harbert, & Martohardjono, 1989; Goodluck, 1991).[11] The basic idea behind the Subset Principle is that the learner will project the grammar that produces the smallest possible output language (smallest set of grammatical sentences) compatible with the sentence forms he or she hears. Essentially, the child is hypothesized to be a conservative learner, avoiding rash postulation of rules. Whether or not there is a conflict between the sort of grammar formation process envisaged under the Subset Principle and that

---

[10]In the context of this discussion, Slobin's (1967, 1985) idea of using children acquiring different languages as subjects in a natural experiment on language development has lost nothing of its interest. Cross-linguistic studies are a test case for developmental predictions of different kinds. They can help, inter alia, to evaluate maturational claims, claims about the default setting of specific parameters, or about the effect of language-specific input data on the developmental schedule. Thus, with respect to the latter point, certain elements, such as clitic pronouns or negation, may indicate to the child in a particular language that certain syntactical positions have to be assumed or that certain elements have been moved (Lebeaux 1988; Roeper 1972; Weissenborn 1988, Weissenborn & Verrips 1989). This may lead to differences with respect to the moment at which certain operations, such as chain-formation and its corresponding restrictions, become available to the child.

[11]Other such principles are the Uniqueness Principle (Wexler, 1981), the Principle of Contrast (Clark 1987), and the Unique External Argument Principle (Borer & Wexler 1988).

envisaged under the concept of grammatical triggers is a complex issue. Basically, a conflict will arise only to the extent that principles of Universal Grammar allow ambiguous projection of rules from data. The main point here is that one way to account for and predict stages in development is to build a model of the learner in which rule projection is done conservatively; the Subset Principle ensures a conservative learner.

III.iii The Implementation of Change

Triggered change, that is, change originating from an interaction between the child's innate knowledge of grammar and the input, and principle-guided learning, that is, the choice between a number of possible analyses compatible with the data, are conceptually simple notions whose actual implementation may be quite intricate. Two related factors seem to us particularly pertinent in accounting for the complexity in learners' paths of development: item-to-rule mapping and input ambiguity. Item-to-rule mapping refers to the process of deducing a general rule system from particular items, which may be sentences, sentence fragments or individual words. With respect to item-to-rule mapping, one question that has been prominent in the recent literature is: To what degree can the acquisition of grammar and the explanation of stages be reduced to "lexical learning," that is, the learning of which phonetic forms map into pre-existing categories in the system provided by Universal Grammar?

The idea of reducing development to lexical learning is particularly appealing, in view of the current interest locating all or most parametric variation in the lexicon (Borer, 1984; Chomsky, 1986b; Clahsen, this volume; Lebeaux, 1988) and has been argued to have some support in the acquisition literature. For example, Jakubowicz (1989) suggests that difficulties children have with the principles of the binding theory may be related to difficulties they have in figuring out which pro-forms have to be categorized as anaphors (reflexives or reciprocals) and which must be categorized as pronouns (see also Solan, 1987). However, there do exist cases of error in children's grammar that have no obvious locus in individual lexical items, for example, children's errors with long-distance wh-movement (Roeper & de Villiers, this volume) or with some control structures (Goodluck & Behne, this volume); such cases place a limit on the potential of lexical learning to explain development (Jones, this volume).

A second, more particular, mapping question that has received considerable attention is: What causes a child to postulate incorrect subcategorization frames for particular lexical items? (as when a child says "She said me the answer"; see Bowerman, 1982, for many examples). And how are such forms eliminated? Whatever the source of the overgeneralizations, several types of solutions have been offered for their elimination, ranging from the exploitation of semantic and morphological subregularity (Mazurkewich & White, 1984; Pinker, 1989), to the use of principles and/or new input to revise the grammar, (Randall, 1985, this volume; Pustejovsky, this volume), to atrophy arising from computational devices that are partly independent of the grammar itself (Goodluck, 1991).

That errors exist at all, and may do so at the level of both lexically restricted and lexically unrestricted phenomena, is not surprising, given that the language-learning child in quite a number of cases receives ambiguous input. Universal Grammar provides a system of sufficient intricacy that the learning mechanism must be able to deal successfully with input in which there is more than one possible analysis for a given input string. For example, in some dialects of English the word *what* (a question word/ relative pronoun in the standard language) acts like a complementizer in relative structures (Radford, 1988b, pp. 522–523) and in that dialect, relative clauses do not exhibit a property characteristic of movement constructions. Thus the learner faced with mastering such a dialect must deal with two related ambiguities: He or she must decide whether a particular lexical item, surely familiar from simple questions such as "What is he eating?", is acting as a moved constituent, that is, a relative pronoun, or as a complementizer, and he or she must decide whether or not relative clauses are formed by a particular operation (movement). There are other examples of ambiguous input: the occurrence of null subjects of otherwise non-null-subject languages such as English, French, or German; the simultaneous existence of moved and in situ wh-phrases in French. Data of this type constitute a potential problem for a parameter-setting account, since they prevent the learner from deciding on a definite setting of the parameter (Valian, 1989, 1990). This ambiguity has led to the assumption by some researchers that for every parameter there must be unambiguous evidence (Roeper & Weissenborn, 1990; Weissenborn, this volume).

To sum up, the ambiguity of the input suggests that the learner needs an efficient data-sorting device if he or she is to use either principles of Universal Grammar or learning principles effectively. One component of such a device we assume to be a processing mechanism similar or identical in form and organization to the adult language-processing device. Indeed, the fact that input is filtered through the learner's sentence-processing mechanism, which may operate in accord with principles, constraints, and biases that are not part of the grammar per se, is another potential source of explanation for developmental stages (Stevenson, this volume; Goodluck, 1991). This type of explanation has been applied, for example, in the case of errors children make in applying the Binding Theory (Goodluck, 1990).

IV. SUMMARY: CONTINUITY VS. DISCONTINUITY

In the preceding sections we have mentioned several ways in which developmental stages may be explained without recourse to maturation: The sentences the child hears, together with knowledge of Universal Grammar and/or learning principles, may trigger new rules or cause the revision of old ones; rules may atrophy; the limited capacity of the immature processing device may produce developmental stages that are only a partial reflection of the nature of the child's grammar. The central question from the grammatical point of view is that of triggering based on input data versus maturation as a cause of change, and for none of the examples we have considered is that issue settled. Beyond the continuity question lies the issue of whether we can provide an account of acquisition stages that links development to the structure of the grammar in a coherent way. One recent analysis that provides such a link is that of Lebeaux (1988), who suggests that stages in development correspond to different levels of representation, starting at the level of lexical structure and subsequently projecting onto the levels of D-structure and S-structure. Children's errors in various modules of grammar are accounted for in terms of the inaccessibility of the levels crucial to the application of the modules. Although it is an important point of fact whether the relevant levels are completely absent from the child's linguistic abilities (i.e., they must mature) or whether they are only temporarily inaccessible (by virtue of, for example, processing difficulty), what seems to us especially interesting is the model's ability to make predictions about what a child should and should not have difficulty with an a certain stage.

V. SUMMARIES OF THE PAPERS

In his chapter, "Language Acquisition as a Maturational Process," Felix addresses the question of how principles of Universal Grammar interact with the child's linguistic experience in shaping and controlling the various aspects of the developmental process. Felix distinguishes two main hypotheses of how this interaction is conceived, "perceptionism" and "maturationism." Perceptionism that is identical to the continuity hypothesis holds that principles of UG are active from the beginning of language acquisition and that the structures that children produce will never violate principles of UG. Developmental changes are essentially data-driven, that is, the result of the child's changing perception of the linguistic input and/or of increasing lexical knowledge. Felix argues that such a view of language acquisition is deficient in a number of ways. First, he argues that child grammars, do, in fact, generate structures that violate principles of UG in different domains, for example, X-bar theory, Theta-theory, Case theory, and Binding theory. In addition, data from the development of negation and interrogation are presented as evidence that children produce structures that are not permissible in adult languages. Second, Felix argues that neither perception nor lexical knowledge can explain how the child finds out at each stage-transition period that the current grammar is incorrect. As an alternative to these theories, Felix suggests that the stage-transition problem can be resolved by assuming that the principles of Universal Grammar are subject to biological maturation, that is, these principles emerge successively in a specific order that is determined by a maturational schedule. That is, maturation tells the child what to do at what time and which input data to attend to at which developmental stage. Under this view, Universal Grammar is seen not only as a constraint on the class of possible languages, but at the same time as a constraint on the class of possible developments.

In his chapter on learnability theory, Clahsen argues for a continuity view of language acquisition and against a maturational theory. He first discusses a number of theoretical arguments in favor of the continuity hypothesis. Second, he presents alternative accounts for maturational schedules that have been proposed for UG principles from different areas, for example, X-bar theory, move alpha, the Theta criterion, and syntactic chains. The specific developmental domains that are discussed concern (a) the development of verb placement in German, (b) the omission of obligatory elements in children's speech, and (c) the development of passives. For (a) and (c) Clahsen proposes an explanation based on lexical learning, whereas for (b) the possible interaction of pragmatic, processing, and grammatical factors is discussed.

In her commentary on Felix and Clahsen, Stevenson points out that the continuity view and the maturational view do not exhaust the possibilities for explaining the developmental problem. It may well be the case that both maturation and lexical learning are involved simultaneously. Discussing examples from the development of Binding theory, Stevenson argues that children's performance should not be taken as the direct reflection of their linguistic knowledge. That is, children's knowledge of principles of grammar may not be visible in their linguistic behavior, due to discourse-level factors and the fact that the integration of linguistic and nonlinguistic processing is limited. Stevenson proposes that, as an alternative to maturation, developmental changes in the processing system may explain the child's changing sensitivity to the input over time that in turn would account for the developmental problem.

The logic underlying parameter theory is the topic of the chapter, "The Catapult Hypothesis," by Randall. She argues that the same logic that allows learners to retreat from early "parametric" errors (those that result from an incorrectly or not yet set parameter) also applies to errors in the domain of the lexicon. This view challenges the classic assumption that the lexicon is the repository of wild and crazy facts about words. She claims that lexical items are related by systematic principles, the result being that theories proposed for learning the lexicon need not be so very different from those proposed for learning the syntax. Randall's Catapult Hypothesis claims that there is a set of lexical principles of the form "If A then not B." These allow learners hearing primary data, A, to use the grammar to deduce "not B." The model alleviates a need for negative evidence and, along the way, solves a number of long-standing learnability puzzles. The focus is on two principles of X-bar theory — The Order Principle and the Attachment Principle — which limit how lexical argument structures can be syntactically realized. Randall shows how these principles, together with primary data, can trigger learners to retreat from their overgeneralizations of several nonalternating verb classes to alternating classes. *Fill* and *spill*-class verbs are typically overgeneralized to the alternating *spray/load* class; *deliver*-class to the double object *give*-class; and for-benefactive and -goal phrases to the alternating *for*-dative class. A section of the article is devoted to contrasting the Catapult theory to "criteria-based" theories of how the lexicon is learned (Pinker; Mazurkewich & White) and then, to discussing it in the context of the Syntactic Bootstrapping view (Gleitman and collaborators) whose basic assumption it shares, namely, that invisible verb semantics can be learned from the observation of verbs in syntactic structures, because of the mediating principles that link them, which learners know.

In his commentary on Randall's Catapult hypothesis, Pustejovsky finds the proposal attractive in that it abandons specific mechanisms for retreating from overgeneralizations in favor of basic principles of X-bar theory, needed in any case. But he argues that it is necessary (a) to examine how the principles are instantiated in the child's grammar and (b) to see how the relevant data are recognized with respect to the principles. He argues that we can interpret these principles of grammar as consistent with other (perhaps independent) mechanisms that permit overgeneralizations at one point, followed by a retreat from these forms at a later stage, and attempts to show that, in making this particular step explicit, we come close to what is essentially one argument put forward by Pinker (1989). Following this view, Randall's theory of principles is strongly consistent with the idea that discriminants become available in the child's data set, such that when the forms are implicitly expunged from the lexicon, overgeneralization is reduced. This can be viewed as a result of recompiling the rules and running them over the data again. Opting for this interpretation of Randall's "principles theory," Pustejovsky thus links it to Pinker's proposal. Catapults can then be seen as instances of inferential reasoning over positive data. What Pustejovsky finds important about Randall's chapter is that it forces us to consider the general mechanisms operative in the grammar, and to realize that any independent criterion for discrimination between lexical forms must be consistent with global principles in the grammar in order for it to be learnable.

In their chapter, "Development in Control and Extraction," Goodluck and Behne report an experiment on the acquisition of control and operator movement. They find children 4–6 years old have an adult-like rule for the interpretation of the PRO subject of purpose clauses, such as that in "John chooses Bill to sing." In the case of temporal adjuncts, such as that in "John hits Bill before singing," children's performance is not adult-like. Goodluck and Behne assume that temporal adjuncts are obligatorily controlled by the main clause subject in the adult grammar; they argue that the varied patterns of performance with this construction in their own and other studies indicate that temporals are nonobligatory control constructions for young children. The pattern of performance on sentences with active versus passive main clauses on Goodluck and Behne's experiment argues that, at least in their experiment, children use a strategy based on thematic structure (the controller is agent) to interpret temporal adjuncts. Goodluck and Behne also tested children's interpretation of purpose clauses with object gaps ("John chooses Bill to sing to"), and whether there is overgeneralization of the possibility of an object gap to temporal clauses. They assume an analysis of the adult grammar in which object gaps in purpose clauses result from covert wh-movement (operator movement), and propose that the absence of an object gap in temporals in the adult grammar follows from the combination of attachment of temporals to the S (as opposed to VP) node, the adult control rule for temporals, and a general c-command restriction on coindexation of an operator (the operator must be coindexed by a c-commanding NP). The results of their test suggest children obey the block on object gaps in temporals, but are not strong, since the presence of an object gap was largely not recognized, even in purpose clauses. Goodluck and Behne discuss their results in the context of a general picture of development whereby details of syntactic configurations for various complement and adjunct types are known to children early on and development is a matter of acquiring the rules that apply to those structures, a process that is constrained by principles of universal grammar.

In his commentary on Goodluck and Behne, Jones develops an analysis of the theory and the acquisition data that differs from that of Goodluck and Behne in several ways. First, temporal adjuncts are assumed to be nonobligatory control constructions in the adult grammar, with the child and adult grammars differing by the fact, that the latter uses a set of interpretive strategies for nonobligatory control that are not used by children. The nonobligatory control analysis of temporals is tied to a structural analysis of temporals in which the adjunct clause is outside the strict c-command domain of the subject of the main clause. Second, Jones proposes that, contrary to the assumption of Goodluck and Behne, there is a period in which the point of structural attachment for adjuncts and certain complements is not fixed; temporals may be reanalyzed from conjunct status to VP-complement/ adjunct status. Jones supports his analysis by pointing to parallelism between the interpretation of PRO by children and strategies for pronoun interpretation, taking the latter to be characteristically applicable to conjunction structures. In the final part of his commentary, Jones discusses ways in which facts concerning the development of control structures may limit the power of acquisition theories that focus on lexical properties as the prime movers in development.

Taken together, the chapters by Goodluck and Behne, and Jones, provide a good example of the way in which differences in detail concerning the analysis of constructions in the adult grammar can lead to substantial differences in our conception of the processes involved in the acquisition of those constructions.

In their chapter, Roeper and de Villiers show how triggers cross modules, and UG interacts with particular grammars in acquiring complex structures for which there is little input. They examine how children learn a particular contrast, the difference between noun phrases and small clauses: (a) "how did she see him riding?" (how-ride = backwards); (b) "how did she see his riding?" (how-see (only) = with telescope). Until children learn that the higher verb gives case to the lower verb, they allow only upper clause extraction of "how" (while adults go equally in both directions). This view is supported by naturalistic data: Children will say "help my dress up" and "my dress up" but not *"help my." This indicates that when children are allowing "my" to substitute for "I," they are not getting case-assignment from the verb. The case-assignment involved is a form of "exceptional case-marking" and therefore emerges, predictably, later. In contexts where there is a full complementizer phrase, the children will allow long-distance extraction much earlier: "When did he say that he hurt himself." This shows how UG, as a collection of particular modules, poses particular problems for acquisition. The result is that the parametric decisions must occur in a certain order.

Radford's commentary on Roeper and de Villiers focuses on two ways in which they claim that the child's case system differs from the adult's: (1) the case rule that assigns objective case to the subject of nonfinite complements is a structural one; and (2) (objective) case-marking obeys an exceptionless strict locality condition. He objects to (1) because he sees it as violating the UG principle, which assigns case under directional government, and he doubts that, as in (2), children first expect government to be an intrinsically local relation when in the adult system it is not. Radford develops an alternative account aimed at avoiding "developmental discontinuity" and bolsters it with data from his naturalistic corpus of children of 2 years and up. Assuming that 2-year-olds' nonfinite sentences are "covertly" inflected (Aldridge, 1990) he suggests that they use the same government-based, case-marking principle in nonfinite structures as in finite. His explanation of children's apparent obedience to a locality condition is based on the Minimality Condition, which holds in child grammar as well. As for Roeper and de Villiers's finding that preschoolers resist adjunct extraction from gerund complements (which his account does not explain), Radford wonders if these structures are within their competence, and suggests examining adjunct extraction elsewhere.

In her chapter, Hyams provides a parameter setting analysis of the null subject phenomenon in early child language which departs in crucial respects from her previous analysis, in particular, that of Hyams (1986). She bases her new analysis on the theory of morphological development proposed in Hyams (1989), and on the notion of "morphological uniformity" proposed in Jaeggli and Safir (1989a). Morphologically uniform languages have null subjects if the additional conditions on the identification of empty categories are fulfilled, whereas morphologically mixed languages do not. Hyams assumes that morphologically mixed languages, such as French or English, are initially analyzed as morphologically uniform by their learners thus allowing for null subjects. Thematic null subjects in early German as opposed to adult German are made possible through differences in the possibilities of identification. The change from a null-subject grammar to a nonnull-subject grammar in the case of languages such as French and English takes place when the mixed inflectional system of the verbs in these languages is acquired, "telling" the child that null subjects are not licensed. Null subjects in German are abandoned when after the development of verb-second the condition on identification is no longer fulfilled. The fact that the child initially adopts morphological uniformity follows from the subset principle. Hyams proposes that the identification of null subjects in early French and English is realized through a topic as they are in languages that uniformly lack morphology (Huang, 1984). The existence of an asymmetry in the use of null subjects and null objects, even in languages that have null objects is explained by the absence of variables in the child's grammar. An account of the development of subjects along these lines is extended to ASL. Finally Hyams rejects Mazuka et al.'s claims that the use of null subjects in English is the result of the interaction of performance constraints and a language's principal branching direction.

In his contribution, Weissenborn discusses a number of problems that result from a pro-drop account of missing subjects in early child language. As shown by much recent work on the null subject parameter in linguistic theory, most languages are not simply [+/− null subject] but they display rather varying patterns of obligatory and optional thematic and expletive subjects. This creates a learnability problem: How does the child determine the value of the null-subject parameter for his or her language if the input presents ambiguous evidence? Based on data from French and German, Weissenborn shows that views that rely primarily on the development of the INFL-component and its related properties (e.g., tense, agreement, case assignment) for the (re)setting of the null-subject parameter do not make the right predictions. He then proposes a solution that, while retaining the necessity for unambiguous primary data as a prerequisite to parameter setting, assumes that it is through parameter interaction that the triggering data for the setting of the null-subject parameter become available to the child.

In her commentary on Hyams and Weissenborn, Lillo-Martin points out certain problems with the assumptions made in these contributions concerning the licensing and identification of null subjects. Following Huang (1984) she suggests that, given the clustering of certain properties of "discourse-oriented" languages (i.e., languages that allow topic binding of arguments), it may be more economical to maintain "Discourse-oriented" versus "Sentence-oriented" as a parameter separate from the "Morphological Uniformity" parameter. This would make the child's reanalysis of English as a nonnull subject language independent of the acquisition of verbal inflection. Lillo-Martin presents arguments against the assumption, also made in Weissenborn's chapter, that thematic null subjects in languages such as English or French are identified by topic binding. On the basis of the analysis of null subjects in ASL as well as in other morphologically rich languages, she comes to the conclusion that the identification requirements on null subjects in each language need to be learned.

REFERENCES

Berwick, R. C. (1985). *The acquisition of syntactic knowledge.* Cambridge, MA: MIT Press.

Borer, H. (1984). *Parametric syntax.* Dordrecht, The Netherlands: Foris.

Borer, H., & Wexler, K. (1987). The maturation of syntax. In T. Roeper & E. Williams (eds.), *Parameter Setting.* Dordrecht, The Netherlands: Reidel.

Borer, H., & Wexler, K. (1988). *The maturation of grammatical principles.* University of California, Irvine, and MIT, Cambridge, MA.

Bowerman, M. (1973). *Early syntactic development: A crosslinguistic study with special reference to finnish.* Cambridge, England: Cambridge University Press.

Bowerman, M. (1982). Reorganization processes in lexical and syntactic development. In E. Wanner & L. Gleitman (Eds.), *Language acquisition: The state of the art.* Cambridge, England: Cambridge University Press.

Bowerman, M. (1987). Why don't children end up with an overly general grammar? In B. MacWhinney (Ed.), *Mechanisms of language acquisition.* Hillsdale, NJ: Lawrence Erlbaum Associates.

Bowerman, M. (1988). The "no-negative-evidence" problem: How do children avoid constructing an overly general grammar? In J. A. Hawkins (ed.), *Explaining language universals.* Oxford, England: Blackwell.

Brown, R., & Hanlon, C. (1970). Derivational complexity and order of development in speech. In J. Hayes (Ed.), *Cognition and the development of language.* New York: Wiley.

Chomsky, N. (1981). *Lectures on government and binding.* Dordrecht, The Netherlands: Foris.

Chomsky, N. (1986a). *Barriers.* Cambridge, MA: MIT Press.

Chomsky, N. (1986b). *Knowledge of language. Its nature, origin, and use.* New York: Praeger.

Chomsky, N. (1989). Some notes on economy of derivation and representation. *MIT Working Papers in Linguistics, 10.*

Clark, E. (1987). The principle of contrast: A constraint on language acquisition. In B. MacWhinney (Ed.), *Mechanisms of language acquisition.* Hillsdale, NJ: Lawrence Erlbaum Associates.

Crain, S., & Fodor, J. D. (1987). Simplicity and generality of rules in language acquisition. In B. MacWhinney (Ed.), *Mechanisms of language acquisition.* Hillsdale, NJ: Lawrence Erlbaum Associates.

Crain, S., & Fodor, J. D. (1989). Competence and performance in child language. *Haskins Laboratories Status Report on Speech Research,* SR 99/100, 118–136.

Crain, S., & McKee, C. (1985). Acquisition of structural anaphora. In S. Berman, J. W. Choe, & J. McDonough (Eds.), *Proceedings of the 16th Northeastern Linguistics Society Meeting.* Amherst, MA: Graduate Linguistics Student Association.

de Villiers, J., Roeper, T., & Vainikka, A. (1990). The acquisition of long-distance rules. In L. Frazier & J. de Villiers (Eds.), *Language acquisition and language processing.* Dordrecht, The Netherlands: Kluwer Academic Publishers.

Demuth, K. (1989). Maturation and the acquisition of the Sesotho passive. *Language, 65,* 56–80.

Felix, S. (1987). *Cognition and language growth.* Dordrecht, The Netherlands: Foris.

Finer, D. (1989). Binding parameters in second language acquisition. To appear in L. Eubank (Ed.), *Point-Counter: universal grammar and second languages.* Philadelphia: John Benjamins.

Fukui, N. (1986). *A theory of category projection and its application.* Unpublished doctoral dissertation, MIT, Cambridge, MA.

Gleitman, L., Gleitman H., Landau, B., & Wanner, E. (1989). Where learning begins: Initial representations for language learning. In F. Newmeyer (Ed.), *Linguistics: The Cambridge survey.* Cambridge, MA: Cambridge University Press.

Goodluck, H. (1986). Language acquisition and linguistic theory. In P. Fletcher & M. Garman (Eds.), *Language acquisition* (2nd ed.), Cambridge, England: Cambridge University Press.

Goodluck, H. (1991). *Language acquisition: A linguistic introduction.* Oxford, England: Basil Blackwell.

Goodluck, H. (1990). Knowledge integration in processing and acquisition: Comments on Grimshaw and Rosen. In L. Frazier & J. de Villiers (Eds.), *Language processing and language acquisition.* Dordrecht, The Netherlands: Kluwer Academic Publishers.

Goodluck, H., Foley, M., & Sedivy, J. (1990). Adjunct islands and acquisition. In H. Goodluck & M. Rochemont (Eds.), *Island constraints: Theory, acquisition and processing.* Dordrecht, The Netherlands: Kluwer Academic Publishers.

Goodluck, H., Sedivy, J., & Foley, M. (1989). Wh-questions and extraction from temporal adjuncts: A case for movement. *Papers and Reports on Child Language Development, 28,* 123–130.

Guilfoyle, E., & Noonan, M. (1988). *Functional categories and language acquisition.* Paper presented at the 13th annual Boston University Conference on Language Development.

Huang, J. (1982). Move WH in a language without wh-movement. *Linguistic Review, 1,* 368–416.

Huang, J. (1984). On the distribution and reference of empty pronouns. *Linguistic Inquiry, 15,* 531–574.

Hyams, N. (1986). *Language acquisition and the theory of parameters.* Dordrecht, The Netherlands: Reidel.

Hyams, N. (1989). The null subject parameter in language acquisition. In O. Jaeggli & K. Safir (Eds.), *The null subject parameter.* Dordrecht, The Netherlands: Kluwer Academic Publishers.

Jaeggli, O., & Safir, K. (1989a). The null subject parameter and parametric theory. In O. Jaeggli & K. Safir (Eds.), *The null subject parameter.* Dordrecht, The Netherlands: Kluwer Academic Publishers.

Jaeggli, O., & Safir, K. (Eds.) (1989b). *The null subject parameter.* Dordrecht, The Netherlands: Kluwer Academic Publishers.

Jakubowicz, C. (1989). Maturation or invariance of Universal Grammar principles in language acquisition. *Probus, 1,* 283–340.

Kapur, S., Lust, B., Harbert, W., & Martohardjono, G. (1989). Universal Grammar and learnability theory: The case of binding domains and the subset principle. To appear in E. Reuland & W. Abraham (Eds.), *Knowledge and language: Issues in representation and acquisition.* Dordrecht, The Netherlands: Kluwer Academic Publishers.

Kayne, R. (1989). Null subjects and clitic climbing. In O. Jaeggli & K. Safir (Eds.), *The null subject parameter.* Dordrecht, The Netherlands: Kluwer Academic Publishers.

Koster, J. (1987). *Domains and dynasties. The radical autonomy of syntax.* Dordrecht, The Netherlands: Foris.

Lasnik, H., & Saito, M. (1984). On the nature of proper government. *Linguistic Inquiry, 15,* 235–289.

Lebeaux, D. (1988). *Language acquisition and the form of the grammar.* Unpublished doctoral dissertation, University of Massachussetts, Amherst.

Lightfoot, D. (1989). The child's trigger experience: Degree-0 learnability. *Behavioral and Brain Sciences, 12,* 321–375.

Lillo-Martin, D. (1986). Effects of the acquisition of morphology on syntactic parameter setting. *NELS, 16,* 305–321.

Lust, B., & Chien, Y. C. (1984). The structure of coordination in first-language acquisition of Mandarin Chinese: Evidence for a universal. *Cognition, 17,* 49–83.

Lust, B., & Wakayama, T. (1979). The structure of coordination in children's first language acquisition of Japanese. In F. Eckman & A. Hastings (Eds.), *First and second language acquisition.* Rawley, MA: Newbury House.

Mazurkewich, I., & White, L. (1984). *The acquisition of the dative alternation: Unlearning generalizations.* Cognition, 16, 261–283.

McNeill, D. (1970). *The acquisition of language: The study of developmental psycholinguistics.* New York: Harper & Row.

Mills, A. (Ed.). (1983). *Language acquisition in the blind child: Normal and deficient.* London: Croom Helm.

Nishigauchi, T., & Roeper, T. (1987). Deductive parameters and the growth of empty categories. In T. Roeper & E. Williams (Eds.), *Parameter setting.* Dordrecht, The Netherlands: Reidel.

Pierce, A. (1989). *On the emergence of syntax: A crosslinguistic study.* Unpublished doctoral dissertation, MIT, Cambridge, MA.

Pinker, S. (1984). *Language learnability and language development.* Cambridge, MA: Harvard University Press.

Pinker, S. (1989). *Learnability and cognition: The acquisition of argument structure.*

Cambridge, MA: MIT Press.

Pollock, J. Y. (1989). Verb Movement, UG and the structure of IP. *Linguistic Inquiry, 20,* 365–425.

Radford, A. (1988a). Small children's small clauses. *Transactions of the Philological Society, 86,* 1–43.

Radford, A. (1988b). *Transformational grammar: A first course.* Cambridge, England: Cambridge University Press.

Radford, A. (1990). *Syntactic theory and the acquisition of English syntax: The nature of early child grammars of English.* Oxford, England: Blackwell.

Randall, J. (1990). Catapults and pendulums: The mechanics of language acquisition. *Linguistics, 28,* 1381–1406.

Rizzi, L. (1982). *Issues in Italian syntax.* Dordrecht, The Netherlands: Foris.

Roeper, T. (1972). *Approaches to a theory of language acquisition.* Unpublished doctoral dissertation, Harvard University, Cambridge, MA.

Roeper, T., de Villiers, J., & Vainikka, A. (1990). The acquisition of long-distance rules. In L. Frazier & J. de Villiers (Eds.), *Language processing and language acquisition.* Dordrecht, The Netherlands: Kluwer Academic Publishers.

Roeper, T., & Williams, E. (Eds.), (1987). *Parameter setting.* Dordrecht, The Netherlands: Reidel.

Roeper, T., & Weissenborn, J. (1990). How to make parameters work. In L. Frazier & J. de Villiers (Eds.), *Language processing and language acquisition.* Dordrecht, The Netherlands: Kluwer Academic Publishers.

Rouveret, A., & Sauzet, P. (1989). Présentation: L'approche paramétrique et les langues romanes. *Revue des Langues Romanes, 93,*. v–xi.

Rudin, C. (1988). On multiple questions and multiple wh-fronting. *Natural Language and Linguistic Theory, 6,* 445–501.

Slobin, D. (1967). *A field manual for cross-cultural study of the acquisition of communicative competence.* Berkeley, CA: ASUC Bookstore.

Slobin, D. (1985). Crosslinguistic evidence for the language making capacity. In D. Slobin (Ed.), *The crosslinguistic study of language acquisition.* Hillsdale, NJ: Lawrence Erlbaum Associates.

Solan, L. (1983). *Pronominal reference: Child language and the theory of grammar.* Dordrecht, The Netherlands: Reidel.

Solan, L. (1987). Parameter setting and the development of pronouns and reflexives. In T. Roeper & E. Williams (Eds.), *Parameter setting.* Dordrecht, The Netherlands: Reidel.

Valian, V. (1989). Children's production of subjects: Competence, performance, and the null subject parameter. *Papers and Reports on Child Language Development, 28,* 156–163.

Valian, V. (1990). Null subjects: A problem for parameter-setting models of language acquisition. *Cognition, 35,* 105–122.

Weissenborn, J. (1988). *The acquisition of clitic object pronouns and word order in French: Syntax or morphology?* Paper presented at the Third International Morphology Meeting, Nijmegen, The Netherlands: Max Planck Institut für Psycholinguistik.

Weissenborn, J. (1990). Functional categories and verb movement: The acquisition of German syntax reconsidered. In M. Rothweiler (Ed.), *Spracherwerb und Grammatik. Linguistische Untersuchungen zum Erwerb von Syntax und Morphologie. Linguistische Berichte,* Sonderheft 3.

Weissenborn, J., Verrips, M. & Berman, R. (1989). *Negation as a window to the structure of early child language.* Nijmegen, The Netherlands: Max Planck Institut für Psycholinguistik.

Wexler, K. (1981). Some issues in the theory of learnability. In C. L. Baker & J. McCarthy, (Eds.), *The logical problem of language acquisition.* Cambridge, MA: MIT Press.

Wexler, K. (1990). On unparsable input in language acquisition. In L. Frazier and J. de Villiers (Eds.), *Language acquisition and language processing*. Dordrecht, The Netherlands: Kluwer Academic Publishers.

Wexler, K., & Manzini, R. (1987). Parameters and learnability in binding theory. In T. Roeper & E. Williams (Eds.), *Parameter setting*. Dordrecht, The Netherlands: Reidel.

White, L. (1982). *Grammatical theory and language acquisition*. Dordrecht, The Netherlands: Foris.

2 Language Acquisition as a Maturational Process

Sascha W. Felix
University of Passau, Germany

1. INTRODUCTION

In recent years it has become increasingly clear that language acquisition must be an essentially deductive process in which the child analyzes input data on the basis of a biologically determined set of principles — technically known as Universal Grammar — that narrowly constrain the kinds of hypotheses to be considered vis-à-vis a given set of data (cf. Chomsky, 1980, 1981, 1986; Hornstein & Lightfoot, 1981; White, 1982; Felix, 1987). A major empirical challenge deriving from this insight concerns the question of how exactly principles of Universal Grammar interact with the child's linguistic experience in the course of language acquisition (see, e.g., Pinker, 1984; Hyams, 1986; Lust, 1986a; Roeper & Williams, 1987, among others, for some more recent proposals). It appears that there are currently at least two competing views about the nature of this interaction. One of these views, which I shall call *perceptionism,* holds that Universal Grammar (UG) is exclusively responsible for constraining the types of intermediate child grammars, while developmental progress is essentially data-driven, that is, driven by the child's (changing) perception of the external evidence. The other view, which may be termed *maturationism,* claims that UG is responsible not only for the types of (intermediate) grammars that emerge, but also for the specific temporal nature of the developmental process. Under the maturationist view, language acquisition is therefore seen as a process that is driven primarily by internal, that is, biologically determined mechanisms.

In this chapter I shall argue in favor of a maturationist view of language acquisition by demonstrating that perceptionism is inadequate on both empirical and conceptual grounds. At the empirical level, perceptionism will be shown to make incorrect predictions about UG-dependent properties of child grammars. At the conceptual level, the inadequacy of perceptionism results from its failure to provide a principled solution to the problem of why and how children move from one developmental stage to the next. The chapter is organized as follows: Sec. 2 gives an outline of what appear to be the fundamental tenets of perceptionism and maturationism, followed by a section dealing with the question of whether or not child grammars are fully constrained by principles of UG. Evidence will be presented to show that at specific developmental points in time child grammars do temporarily violate a wide variety of UG principles. Sec. 4 will discuss what may be called the *stage transition problem,* that is, the question of what makes the child restructure intermediate grammars on his or her way toward adult competence. It will be argued that this restructuring process cannot be fully data-driven, but must be triggered by some kind of maturational schedule.

2. PERCEPTIONISM AND MATURATIONISM

Under a strictly formal perspective, Universal Grammar can be conceived of as a set of principles that specify the class of languages that are attainable by the child under normal conditions of language development, one of the crucial conditions being that the evidence available to the child is severely limited in a nontrivial way (cf. Chomsky, 1981, pp. 1–4). UG is thus essentially a theory of what constitutes a possible, that is, humanly accessible grammar.[1]

While perceptionism comes in a variety of different approaches and theories (see White, 1982; Pinker, 1984; Hyams, 1986; Clahsen, 1988, among others), the fundamental assumption common to all versions of perceptionism is that child grammars fall completely under the constraints of Universal Grammar; that is, child grammars are simply a proper subset of the class of languages defined by UG. In standard terminology: *Child grammars are possible grammars.* The empirical claim following from this assumption is that the structures children regularly produce at various developmental stages will never violate any UG principle(s). Perceptionism

---

[1]More importantly, a theory of UG has also a psychological dimension; that is, it is a theory about the innate mental structures that make language acquisition possible. In this context, Chomsky (1987a) points out that equating the class of languages permitted by UG with the class of learnable languages may turn out to be empirically unjustified. It could be the case that the language faculty permits languages that are, however, not learnable and will thus never occur as existing natural languages.

thus holds that principles of Universal Grammar, apart from being innate, are fully available and active from the very beginning of the acquisitional process.[2] Since this view entails the assumption that the innate endowment for language acquisition does not change over time, it is also called the *continuity hypothesis* (cf. Pinker, 1984).

Much like perceptionism, maturationism is not an entirely homogeneous body of theoretical assumptions, but rather a kind of leading idea (in the sense of Chomsky, 1981). Maturationism assumes that UG is not the only (language-specific) component that controls language development, but rather that—in addition to UG—there is an innate maturational schedule which, loosely speaking, determines what the child will do at what time. In this sense, maturationism incorporates an even stronger innateness hypothesis than perceptionism (see also Borer & Wexler, 1987, p. 125). Under the maturationist view originally proposed and defended in Felix (1984, 1987) the object of maturation is Universal Grammar itself (for a somewhat different perspective, see, e.g., Gleitman, 1981; Wexler, 1987; Roeper, 1986). The fundamental idea is then that Universal Grammar is subject to a (biologically determined) maturational process, which makes the various principles emerge in a specific temporal order. One may visualize this temporal order as a sequence of points in time t_1, t_2, . . . ,t_n, where at each t_i a specific principle (or set of principles) P_i emerges and thus becomes available for grammar construction. The most obvious implication of this maturationist view is that child grammars are possible grammars only in a restricted sense. That is, at each developmental stage the child's grammar will be constrained only by those principles that have already emerged, while at the same time it may violate all principles that have not yet matured.

While perceptionism and maturationism both agree that successive child grammars will differ in the range and complexity of structures available at each stage, they disagree on how developmentally different child grammars relate to principles of UG. According to perceptionism, early child grammars—however defective they may be with respect to the structures permitted—will *never* violate *any* principle of UG. Earlier grammars will differ from later grammars only in terms of the number and types of parameters that have already been fixed. In contrast, maturationism predicts that, apart from differences in parameter setting, early child grammars may and, in fact, do temporarily violate a restricted set of UG principles, which becomes successively smaller as the child's competence grows.

---

[2]Principles may, of course, still be "dormant" at early developmental stages, because the child has not yet mastered the relevant structures; nevertheless, the principles themselves—so perceptionism claims—are fully available at any time.

It seems to be clear that any adequate theory of language acquisition must offer a principled solution to the *stage-transition problem,* that is, to the question of what makes the child move from one developmental stage to the next. Under the perceptionist view, the child's developmental progress will be triggered by perceptual mechanisms, that is, by the child's changing perception of specific data. In contrast, maturationism holds that developmental progress is essentially a function of the maturational schedule which forces the child to restructure his or her current grammar as soon as a new principle (or set of principles) emerges. In other words, the child restructures the grammar in order to make it compatible with formal requirements of UG.

There are consequently two major domains in which perceptionism and maturationism make different predictions and offer different solutions. The first concerns the question of whether or not child grammars (may) violate principles of Universal Grammar; the second relates to the mechanism — perception or maturation — that is responsible for developmental progress.

3. VIOLATIONS OF UNIVERSAL GRAMMAR

In this section, I propose to show that at various early developmental stages child grammars license structures that violate principles of Universal Grammar and thus do not qualify as *possible grammars* (in the technical sense). There are four major domains in which violations of UG will be shown to occur: X-bar theory, Theta theory, Case theory, and binding theory.

It is important to emphasize that the question of whether or not child grammars are possible grammars is strictly a matter of empirical fact and cannot be answered by appealing to logical considerations deriving from the notion of UG as an innate cognitive module. Nevertheless, it appears that various authors tend to believe that the immediate and complete availability of UG somehow follows *logically* from its innate status. Thus Hyams (1986, p. 2) states that "if UG is a specification of the notion 'possible human grammar,' then it constitutes an empirical hypothesis about the structure of child grammars, insofar as the latter are also products of the human language faculty."[3] Recall that the principal motivation for assuming Universal Grammar derives from the insight that natural languages have properties that are not learnable on the basis of evidence that is commonly

---

[3]A similar view is expressed by White (1982, p. 70), who suggests that "by accepting the principles of the theory of grammar as part of the biological specification of the child, one is including the class of child grammars within the class of possible grammars . . ."

available to the child. By constraining the child's hypothesis space during the acquisitional process, UG thus provides structural information necessary for arriving at the correct adult grammar. The concept of Universal Grammar thus entails that the acquisition process *as a whole* must be UG-constrained; it does not entail, however, that UG constraints must operate at each and every developmental stage.

Note furthermore that the question of whether or not a given child structure violates UG cannot be answered by merely pointing to *some* natural language in which such a structure occurs. Rather, the problem of UG compatibility must be considered vis-à-vis the specific properties of the language to be acquired as they appear in the available input data. Suppose a child acquiring English produces an early structure that looks like Japanese. One might thus assume automatically that this structure cannot be a UG violation, simply because it exists in Japanese. However, it may turn out that such an assumption produces a severe learnability problem: The more we are willing to attribute to the child structures that are extremely remote from those of the target language, the harder it is to explain how the child eventually gets back to the correct language; in this case, how the child eventually finds out that he or she is learning English rather than Japanese. In other words, the question of UG compatibility has to be examined against what is learnable on the basis of the available data. Much the same problem arises in the context of adult languages: A sentence such as *the men believe that John shot at each other* is not a UG violation per se (because the corresponding structure is grammatical in Japanese), but it does constitute a UG violation given the specific structural and lexical properties of English.

3.1 X-bar Theory

X-bar theory constrains the types of phrase structure configurations permissible in natural languages. One of the most fundamental constraints expressed by X-bar theory is that sentences are syntactically structured at all, that is, that natural languages have grammars rather than being purely semantic or pragmatic objects.

Since the inception of modern child language research various authors (e.g., Braine, 1963; Brown & Fraser, 1963; Bloom, 1970, 1973; Brown, 1973) have presented evidence suggesting that the earliest two-word utterances that children produce are structured entirely on the basis of semantic (or perhaps conceptual) categories, that is, the child's earliest rules of sentence formation seem to map directly from semantic relations to surface expressions without any intervening syntactic level.[4] Utterances during this

---

[4]Interestingly, this finding led to a fundamental conceptual controversy in the early days of

stage typically contain a word expressing an inherently relational concept that is then combined with a lexical item denoting an object, action, or property, and so on. Some well-known examples of such early two-word utterances — taken from Brown and Fraser (1963), Braine (1963), Miller and Ervin (1980), and Bloom (1970) — are given under (1):

(1) allgone outside   want up
    bye bye man   there high
    night night hot   off bib
    more write   no down

There is, however, reason to believe that syntax comes in relatively soon in language acquisition, as Hyams (1986, pp. 129ff.) has convincingly shown that developmentally slightly later multiword utterances already show clear syntactic properties. Nevertheless, there appears to be at least a short early stage in which utterances are formed on the basis of semantic rather than syntactic rules or principles. If, however, X-bar theory imposes a strictly syntactical structure on natural languages, then such early utterances obviously violate X-bar theory and thus Universal Grammar.

X-bar theory furthermore requires that a maximal projection have a head. Thus PPs must have a preposition, VPs a verb, and so on. There are at least two well-known early construction types in which children regularly produce headless maximal projections, thus violating the relevant X-bar constraint. The first concerns the phenomenon, widely documented in the literature, that during the early stages children typically omit prepositions. The examples under (2), taken from Brown (1973) and Bowerman (1973), give an illustration of some such utterances:

(2) Mommy bathroom   (Mommy is in the bathroom.)
    slipper doggie   (put the slipper on the doggie.)
    sit lap   (want to sit on M.'s lap.)
    Ben swim pool   (Ben is swimming in the pool.)
    throw Daddy   (throw it to Daddy.)

There are two apparent possibilities for explaining away data such as those in (2) as evidence for UG violations. Thus one might argue that nouns such as *bathroom, doggie,* are not really headless PPs, but rather adverbial

---

acquisition research. Some authors (e.g., Schlesinger, 1974) argued that, since the earliest child grammars are purely semantic objects, the same must be true for adult languages, because the phenomenon of syntactical organization simply cannot be learned. This same learnability consideration led others (e.g., Gleitman, 1981) to argue that, since adult languages are undoubtedly syntactical objects, this must also hold for early child grammars. Note that, whatever the empirical facts may be, the learnability problem behind this controversy disappears completely under a maturationist view.

NPs. Such an assumption, however, would lead to an obvious learnability problem. If the child were to hypothesize that in English adverbial NPs can be freely used in place of PPs, then negative evidence would be required to disconfirm this hypothesis at some later stage. Furthermore, as far as I know, it simply does not seem to happen in natural languages having PPs that prepositions can be freely omitted or that PPs can be indiscriminately replaced by adverbial NPs. Alternatively, one might argue that in a sentence such as *sit lap* the child has mistakenly subcategorized the verb *sit* for an NP rather than a PP. However, it is clear that the child must learn the subcategorization properties of individual verbs on the basis of positive evidence, and there is simply no evidence in the child's input data to motivate the assumption that *sit* allows for an object-NP. In fact, if the child did hypothesize that *sit* takes a direct object, then again negative evidence would be required to disconfirm this hypothesis at some later stage.

Another type of headless maximal projection is found in the examples under (3), taken from Braine (1963) and Gruber (1973), in which a verb is followed by what appears to be a headless NP containing only an adjective:

(3) see pretty
    see hot
    see broke

One might want to point out that NPs with an empty head do, in fact, occur in natural languages. Thus German has NPs with a determiner, an adjective, but no lexical noun:

(4) *Hans hat ein neues gekauft*
    John has a new bought
    "John has bought a new one."

Olsen (1987) has convincingly argued that the NP head position in structures such as (4) is occupied by the empty pronominal *pro*. Crucially, this structure meets the general licensing conditions for *pro* (i.e., a "strong" morphology), in that German adjectives are inflected for number, case, and gender. The claim that *pro* is, in fact, licensed by the adjectival inflection finds additional support through a contrast observed in Muysken (1987). Certain color adjectives may occur in prenominal position in either inflected or uninflected form. If the head noun is missing, however, only the inflected form is possible:

(5a) *Maria hat ein rosa*(uninfl.)/*rosanes*(infl.) *Kleid*
     gekauft
     Mary has a pink dress
     bought
     "Mary bought a pink dress"

(5b) *Maria hat ein *rosa/rosanes gekauft*

Notice that the head of an NP may be empty, that is, *pro,* only under very severely restricted licensing conditions. In the child examples of (3), no such "strong" inflection occurs; rather, what appears to be the case at this developmental stage is that the occurrence or nonoccurrence of the head noun is completely free, that is, unconstrained. If, however, the licensing conditions of *pro* are part of Universal Grammar — as is reasonable to assume — then the sentences under (3) obviously represent a UG violation.

3.2 Theta Theory

Bloom (1970) was among the first to observe that during the early stages children frequently produce *noun + noun* constructions in which the two nouns are in a *subject–object* relation:

(6) baby milk   (the baby touches the milk glass)
    cat more meat   (the cat needs more meat)
    Mommy cottage cheese   (Mommy is eating cottage cheese)
    girl dress   (the girl is wearing a dress)

Utterances of the type in (6) represent essentially declarative sentences with a missing verb and thus violate the *Theta criterion* (cf. Chomsky, 1981), which requires that each argument in a sentence bear a Theta-role, where — in the construction under discussion — Theta-roles are assigned by the verb.[5] Subject–object structures without a verb are ruled out by the Theta criterion, simply because they lack a Theta-role assigner. Even at an intuitive level we would presumably not expect to find a natural language in which the verb of a declarative sentence can be freely present or absent; that is, completely unrestricted subject–object constructions of the type in (6) do not seem to exist in natural languages.

There are, however (in English as well as in many other languages), so-called *gapping* constructions in which an object occurs next to a subject without any intervening verb:

(7a) Bill ordered a beer and *John a glass of milk.*

Note, however, that the occurrence of *gapping* is restricted to very specific structural contexts, essentially certain types of coordination (for details, see Neijt, 1979):

---

[5]Note that these *noun + noun* constructions could also be interpreted as violating X-bar theory, if it is assumed that the second noun is the complement of a headless VP.

(7b) *Bill ordered a beer although John a glass of milk.

(7c) *Bill ordered a beer in order for John a glass of milk.

Furthermore, the Theta-roles of the NPs in the gapped part of the sentence must be identical to those assigned by the verb in the ungapped part; that is, (7a) can only mean *Bill ordered a beer and John ordered a glass of milk,* but not, for example, *Bill ordered a beer and John spilt a glass of milk.* In contrast, at the developmental stage under consideration children appear to leave out the verb in a completely unrestricted way and it is exactly this type of "free deletion of verbs" that is ruled out by the Theta criterion.

Clahsen (1988) has recently argued that sentences such as those in (6) do not at all violate the Theta-criterion, because in almost all cases the thematic roles of the NPs can be unambiguously inferred from contextual clues. While Clahsen's observation is undoubtedly correct, his conclusion is based on a misconception of the criterion. The Theta-criterion is a strictly syntactic principle, which has nothing to say about context or situation. It places certain well-formedness conditions on the phrase structure of a sentence. These conditions must be met at the syntactic level and cannot be replaced by either contextual clues or situational information.

The Theta criterion, in conjunction with Case theory, also accounts for phenomena that are standardly referred to under the rubric of *subcategorization* (see Chomsky, 1986). The basic observation is that different verbs require different types and numbers of complements, as the following examples show:

(8a) John showed it to me.

(8b) *John showed to me.

(9a) John kissed Mary.

(9b) *John kissed Mary to Bill.

Again we find numerous examples in which children produce "incomplete" complement structures and thus violate the Theta criterion. The data in (10) are taken from Bloom (1970) and Bowerman (1973):

(10) me show Mommy   (I'll show it to Mommy.)
     I got   (I've got the vacuum cleaner.)
     put a baby   (I put the baby on the board.)
     no, carry   (carry me up the ramp.)
     Daddy pick up   ("gloss missing.")

One might be tempted to argue that sentences such as those in (10) merely show that the early child has simply missubcategorized the relevant verbs. Such an assumption, however, leads again to a learnability problem. Clearly, the thematic properties of individual verbs must be learned on the basis of positive evidence, since these properties are item-specific and may vary across languages. However, there is nothing in the child's input to motivate such a missubcategorization, since the sentences in (10) are ungrammatical in the adult language. Furthermore, even if the child were to hypothesize — on whatever grounds — that a verb such as *put* allows for a single object, then negative evidence would be required to disconfirm such a hypothesis (see also Baker, 1979, for some arguments along these lines).

3.3 Case Theory

Case theory is a subtheory of Universal Grammar that constrains the linear order of constituents within a maximal projection. The central principle of this subtheory is the Case Filter, which requires that every lexical NP be Case-marked. Universally, Case-assignment is a strictly local process whose domain is defined by the notion of government. This notion has a directional dimension, which is subject to language-specific parametrization. Thus in English or in the Romance languages government goes from left to right, in Japanese or Turkish from right to left (see Kayne, 1984, for details on directionality).

Loosely speaking, Case theory is thus responsible for explaining (certain) word or rather constituent order constraints in natural languages. English is a particularly clear case of what is traditionally called a *fixed-word-order* language. NPs not only have to be within the government domain of a Case-assigning head, but they must also be structurally adjacent to that head (cf. Stowell, 1981). Thus object-NPs have to be adjacent to the verbal head and subject-NPs have to be adjacent to INFL.

Data from the early stages in the acquisition of English show, however, that children — apart from using the adult order — optionally have subjects follow and objects precede the verb. Consider the following examples, which are taken from Bowerman (1973):

(11) V + S   O + V
     hug Mommy   balloon throw
     see Kendall   doggie look-it
                                    Kimmy change
                                    here

     O + V + S
     Mommy hit Kendall
     picture Mommy see Kendall

It thus appears that at this early developmental stage the position of subjects and objects relative to the verb is not fixed, but variable. In principle, the sentences in (11) may be assumed to derive from underlying SVO through movement and thus to be an instance of *scrambling*. However, this view does not seem to be particularly plausible, since there is no further evidence to suggest that children do, in fact, have movement at this early acquisitional stage.

Alternatively, one might want to explain the variable word order of (11) by claiming that—for some reason—the child is not yet sensitive to Case theory, in particular that he or she has not yet fixed the adjacency parameter correctly. Note, however, that in a sense this does not seem to be an explanation at all, because it merely pushes the problem to another level. If sensitivity to case theory is something that may be delayed to some later stage, the question arises what exactly is responsible for this delay. Furthermore, the idea of delayed sensitivity to Case theory appears to be empirically indistinguishable from the view that Case theory matures and thus does not become available until a later developmental stage. The crucial observation is that, while the child does use structures to which Case theory applies, he or she nevertheless ignores the relevant constraints.

Another way of defending an essentially perceptionist account would be to argue that while Case theory is fully available, the child has somehow chosen the "wrong" parametric value, namely [-adjacency], which may be assumed to represent the unmarked option. Under this assumption, subjects and objects can receive Case in both preverbal and postverbal position. This idea, however, leads again to a serious learnability problem. If the child had set the parameter to [-adjacency], then only negative evidence, namely the ungrammaticality of nonadjacent complements, could motivate the child to reset the parameter to its correct value at some later stage. Learnability considerations thus indicate that it must be the most restricted value that is unmarked, in our case [+adjacency] (see also Manzini & Wexler, 1987).

3.4 Binding Theory

Binding theory constrains the occurrence of anaphors, pronouns, and R-expressions under coindexation. Principle A of the binding theory requires that anaphors such as reflexives (e.g., *himself*) and reciprocals (e.g., *each other*) be bound in their minimal governing category, while Principle B requires pronouns to be free in this domain.[6] By Principle C, R-expressions have to be free within the domain of the entire sentence. Binding crucially involves the configurational notion of *c-command*, that

---

[6]For a more elaborated version of the binding theory, see Chomsky (1986).

is, a binding relation is only established if the antecedent c-commands the anaphor with which it is coindexed.

The question thus arises whether or not children are immediately sensitive to these constraints once they have properly identified reflexives/reciprocals, pronouns, and R-expressions in their language. Let us first consider the case of Principle A, the binding requirement for anaphors.

Matthei (1981) conducted a series of experiments in which he tested children's sensitivity to Principle A constraints. A group of 17 children ranging in age from 4.2 to 6.6 were asked to act out two-clause sentences containing the reciprocal *each other*. Example (12) illustrates the type of test sentence Matthei used:

(12) The chickens said that the pigs tickled each other.

It is clear that under Principle A the reciprocal can only be coreferential with *the pigs,* but not with *the chickens.* The results of Matthei's experiment show, however, quite clearly that children do violate Principle A in structures such as (12): "64.4% of the total number of responses were ones in which the children chose the matrix clause subject as the referent for *each other*" (p. 107). This result does not seem to be unique or unusual. Matthei mentions an unpublished paper by Read and Hare (1977) in which it is reported that children's early interpretation of reflexives shows similar effects, that is, the reflexive is bound to an element outside of its clause.

Of course, one might hypothesize that the children simply had not identified *each other* as a reciprocal yet, but rather treated it as an ordinary pronoun. Note, however, that children interpreted *each other* correctly in sentences such as (13):

(13) The cows$_i$ were kicking each other$_i$.

If *each other* had the status of a pronoun in the children's grammar, then, of course, a coreferential reading of (13) would be ruled out by Principle B. While it is thus clear that children do violate binding principles, Matthei's data do not permit us to determine uniquely whether Principle A or B is being violated.

With respect to Principle B, Nishigauchi and Roeper (1987) observe that "a large body of experimental acquisition evidence indicates that children do not obey Principle B. Otsu (1981), Jakubowicz (1984), Wexler and Manzini (1987), using a wide range of experimental designs, all provide evidence that children do not initially know that *John likes him* cannot be coreferential" (p. 102). Jakubowicz (1984), for example, found that at a certain age children allow pronouns to be bound within their minimal governing category as illustrated in the following:

(14) John believes that Bill$_i$ will defend him$_i$.

While the coindexation in (14) appears clearly to violate Principle B, Jakubowicz argues that at this age children might simply treat pronouns as anaphors finding out about the pronominal status of *him* only at a later stage. However, as Wexler and Manzini (1987) correctly point out, there is a serious problem with this analysis. If adult pronouns are just anaphors in the child's grammar, then they should always be bound, that is, never occur free. In other words, a sentence such as *it's gone* should be ungrammatical, because it — being an anaphor in the child's grammar — is not bound. As far as we know, however, free (=unbound) use of pronouns is quite frequent in early child language. It thus seems clear that at certain early developmental stages child grammars do violate Principle B.

Let us finally turn to Principle C. In the context of the present discussion this principle is above all responsible for ruling out certain types of so-called *backward pronominalizations,* that is, structures in which the pronoun precedes the coindexed noun. Thus in (15a) the R-expression *John* is c-commanded and thus bound by the pronoun *he* so that the sentence is ungrammatical. In (15b), however, there is no c-command relation between the two coindexed NPs; hence the sentence is grammatical.

(15a) *He$_i$ believes that John$_i$ will pass the exam.

(15b) After he$_i$ passed the exam, John$_i$ got drunk.

Various studies have investigated children's sensitivity to these constraints (for a detailed survey, see Lust, 1986a). The general picture that emerges from these studies is, first of all, that children's interpretation of the relevant structures is subject to what Lust (1981, 1986a) calls a *directionality constraint,* that is, children appear to find backward pronominalizations as in (16a) far more difficult than forward pronominalizations as in (16b), in which the pronoun follows the coindexed NP:

(16a) After he$_i$ had dinner, John$_i$ read the newspaper.

(16b) John$_i$ read the newspaper after he$_i$ had dinner.

Lust (1981) conducted a series of experiments in which a group of children ranging in age from 2.6 to 5.7 were asked to imitate sentences such as those in (16). Lust found that "sentences with forward pronominalization were significantly easier for children to imitate than sentences with backward pronominalization. Means were 0.61 and 0.21, respectively, for the young children, and 1.77 and 1.18, respectively for the older children" (p. 84).

Tavakolian (1978) conducted a number of experiments whose results suggest that children's interpretation of empty subjects is, in fact, constrained by linear precedence. Tavakolian had children act out sentences such as those in (17).

(17a) To kiss the lion would make the duck happy.

(17b) For him to kiss the lion would make the duck happy.

The interesting aspect about these sentences is that the interpretation of the subject of the embedded sentence is more restricted in (17a) than it is in (17b). In the former sentence the empty subject must be *pro* which—under its most natural interpretation[7]—is coreferential with the *duck*. In (17b), however, the pronoun *him* can be coreferential either with *the duck* or with someone not mentioned in the sentence. Tavakolian found that two-thirds of the children she tested chose a sentence-external referent for the subject of the embedded sentence in (17a). She continues to argue that "these responses . . . indicate that children are considering only the linear relationships between a missing subject and a potential antecedent in determining the antecedent of an implicit subject and are ignoring the command relationship between them" (p. 149).

It should be clear that these results do not tell us anything about whether or not early child grammars violate Principle C, since both forward and backward pronominalizations of the type exemplified in (16) are fully grammatical. Note, however, that if children's interpretation of pronominals is indeed subject to a linear or structural precedence constraint, then the question arises why children observe precedence even if UG "tells" them that the relevant notion is c-command, not precedence. In other words, early child grammars seem to violate UG in the sense that they choose the "wrong" type of constraint.

More direct evidence on children's early sensitivity to Principle C is provided by Solan (1981). He conducted a series of experiments primarily designed to test the availability of the notion of c-command in developing grammars of pronoun reference. Children ranging in age from 5 to 7 were asked to act out sentences such as these:

(18a) He told the horse that the sheep would run around.

(18b) He hit the horse in the sheep's yard.

---

[7]In principle, it could, of course, also be PRO_{arb}.

(18c) The horse hit him after the sheep ran around.

(18d) The horse hit him after the sheep's run.

While the results of Solan's experiments suggest that "children are aware at a very young age of . . . structural relationships (that is, c-command), complement type (that is, noun-phrasal or clausal) and linear order of the pronoun and the intended antecedent" (p. 72), some of the children's responses are also relevant with respect to the availability of Principle C. Notice that in (18a) and (18b) the pronoun *he* cannot be coreferential with either *horse* or *sheep,* since this would be a Principle C violation. In (18c) and (18d), however, *him* can be coreferential with *sheep,* since *sheep* is not in the c-command domain of the pronoun. Even though in only 20% of the responses the children interpreted the pronoun as coreferential with the NP — more crucially — a considerable number of children offered a coreferential interpretation not only for (18c) and (18d), but also for (18a) and (18b) where, in fact, coreference is ruled out by Principle C.[8] This indicates that those children were not sensitive to the constraint that requires R-expressions to be free.

Roeper (1986) reports on an experiment in which 5- and 7-year-old children were tested for their ability to distinguish between coreference possibilities in cross-over and non-cross-over constructions. The relevant contrast is given in (19) (Roeper's (4) and (5)):

(19a) Who$_i$ does he$_i$ think t$_i$ wears a hat.

(19b) Who$_i$ t$_i$ thinks he$_i$ wears a hat.

(19a) is ungrammatical because the pronoun *he* A-binds the wh-trace, which by Principle C must be free. In contrast, (19b) is grammatical since the pronoun is free in the embedded finite clause and the wh-trace is not A-bound by any element.

Roeper observes that the children's responses can be split up into two groups. Group B had essentially the adult grammar, while Group A offered a coreferential interpretation of (19a) in about 50% of the cases. This result indicates quite clearly that a substantial number of children in Group A were obviously not sensitive to the constraints expressed by Principle C.[9]

---

[8]Strictly speaking, this is only true for the 5- and 6-year-olds. The 7-year-old children never offered a coreferential interpretation for (20a) and only 6% for (20b).

[9]Roeper himself proposes to account for the Group A responses by assuming that that *pronoun* is an unmarked empty category that "can be used to fill any NP position required by the lexicon without application of language-particular constraints" (p. 195). Consequently, Roeper assumes that the children treat the embedded subject position as *pro* rather than

It thus seems to be fairly clear that the experimental results in the domain of binding theory are not much different from those that we observed in the domain of X-bar, Case, or Theta theory. There are, in fact, early developmental stages in which children do violate the relevant principles. On the other hand, if the observations concerning *linear precedence* relate to facts about competence, then children observe instead principles and constraints that are *not* part of Universal Grammar.

3.5 Some Further Evidence

It has frequently been observed in the literature that in children's earliest multiword negative utterances the negator (usually *no* in English) appears in sentence initial-position (see, e.g., Bellugi, 1967; Klima & Bellugi, 1973; Bowerman, 1973). The examples in (20) (taken from Klima & Bellugi, 1973) are typical of this developmental stage:

(20) no the sun shining
      no Mom sharpen it
      no Fraser drink all tea

Similar structures have been noted by Wode (1977) for a variety of other languages. It thus seems that at the developmental stage under discussion children's negated sentence structures take the form *Neg + S*. Interestingly, natural languages never seem to express sentential negation by means of placing the negator in sentence-initial position, that is, the structure *Neg + S* does not seem to occur in natural (adult) languages. In his survey of sentence negation in 240 languages representing some 40 language families and genetically isolated languages Dahl (1979, p. 93) observes that "the only examples of sentence-initial Neg placement that I have found are verb-initial languages, where this position is identical to immediate pre-FE [= finite element] position."

If Dahl's observations are correct and the phenomenon itself is nonacci-

---

wh-trace. The relevant structure of the sentence would thus be something like (19a'): *who_i does he_i think [pro_i wears a hat]*. This solution, however, creates a host of other problems. First, if children did, in fact, use *pro* indiscriminately for any empty NP, then this would in itself constitute a violation of UG, because the choice of a specific empty category is not free, but rather depends on the structural properties of the relevant position. Furthermore, (19a') would be ruled out at LF by the requirement that every operator (*who* in our case) must *locally* A-bar-bind a variable. Finally, G. Fanselow points out to me that (19a') is possible only if (early) English has resumptive pronouns; i.e., children should use structures such as *who_i did John like him_i*. As far as I know, such structures are not documented in the literature. It thus seems clear that a coreferential interpretation of (19a) does violate UG, even though it might be a matter of debate exactly which principle(s) is/are being violated.

dental, then it seems reasonable to assume that there is a principle (or possibly set of principles) of Universal Grammar that rules out the possibility of *Neg* + *S* structures in natural languages, although I am not aware of any principle proposed in the literature that would have this effect (see Felix, 1987, pp. 127ff., for a discussion of some possibilities). In this case, a grammar generating structures such as those in (20) does not qualify as a possible grammar in virtue of violating the relevant principle(s). At a more general level we may simply observe that children produce structures that do not seem to be permitted in natural languages (see also Chomsky, 1987b, for some comments on this fact).

Another productive child structure that does not occur in adult languages can be found in the development of interrogation. Felix (1980) describes the acquisition of question words by a German-speaking child. Interestingly, the child under observation produced a large number of *wh*-questions without an overt *wh*-pronoun. The examples in (21) illustrate the relevant structures with the glosses indicating the intended meaning:

(21a) *macht du denn*
       make you then
       "What are you doing?"

(21b) *kann das nicht; geht das denn*
       can that not; works that then
       "I cannot do this; how does it work?"

(21c) *kommt der Papi denn*
       comes the Daddy then
       "When does Daddy come home?"

The same structures were also observed by Wode (1976), who studied the acquisition of German by four children. Furthermore, there is some evidence in Weeks (1974) suggesting that also English children pass through a developmental stage in which *wh*-questions without *wh*-pronouns appear. She observes that "extending over a period of time to almost 4.0 Leslie often avoided asking *where*-questions by rephrasing her question to make it a *yes/no* question" (p. 123).

I am not aware of any natural language in which *wh*-pronouns may be freely left out. If such languages, in fact, do not exist, then again it seems reasonable to assume that the relevant structures are ruled out by some principle of Universal Grammar. In this case, however, structures such as those in (21) clearly violate these principles.

The data from the development of negation and interrogation thus provide further evidence for the claim that children do, in fact, produce structures which are not permissible in adult languages and which therefore do not fall within the class of possible human languages.

4. THE STAGE-TRANSITION PROBLEM

Quite clearly, any adequate theory of language acquisition must offer a principled solution to the *stage-transition problem,* that is, the problem of what forces the child to move from one developmental stage to the next. Under a perceptionist view, the mechanism responsible for the child's developmental progress has, of course, to be found outside of Universal Grammar, since — by hypothesis — *all* child grammars are equally possible options within the limits imposed by UG. Perceptionism thus assumes that developmental progress is caused by perceptual mechanisms. The basic idea is that during the developmental process the child's perception of the input data changes, so that he or she is forced to restructure his or her grammar in order to accommodate these newly perceived data. White (1982, p. 43) is particularly explicit in this respect: "the major cause of change in the children's grammars will be their changing view of the data, their realization that a particular grammar is too limited to cover the facts."

In contrast, maturationism claims that developmentally successive grammars differ with respect to (among other things) the number and kinds of UG-principles by which they are constrained. As soon as a new (set of) principle(s) emerges, the child will realize that his or her current grammar violates these newly emerged principles and will thus be forced to restructure the grammar in order to bring it in line with UG. The mechanism that "pushes" the child through the sequence of developmental stages is thus the successive maturation of UG principles (for details, see Felix, 1984, 1987).[10]

---

[10]Wexler (1987) points out an apparent conceptual problem with this type of maturationism. If principles of UG emerge according to a maturational schedule, then child grammars are less constrained than adult grammars and earlier grammars are less constrained than later grammars. Such a view of child language development might appear to be at least counterintuitive, since the impression we get from child data is that early child competence is more rather than less restricted than late child competence. While it is true that there is an intuitive sense in which earlier grammars are more restricted than later grammars, it is far from obvious that this intuitive notion of *restrictedness* is equivalent to the technical notion *UG-constrained.* In fact, there is also an obvious intuitive sense in which just the opposite holds, i.e., in which early grammars are "wilder" (=less restricted) than late grammars; e.g., in the domain of word order variability child grammars partly permit structures that are ungrammatical in the respective adult grammar (see the section on case theory for examples). Again, nothing specific seems to follow from this intuitive notion with respect to the question of whether early grammars are more or less UG-constrained than late grammars.

At a more general level, developing a capacity may be viewed as being equivalent to moving

There seem to be two—largely uncontroversial—facts about language development that make the stage-transition problem a theoretically interesting issue that might be relevant for deciding between perceptionism and maturationism.

First, it appears to be well established that language acquisition is *not* a purely additive process; that is, during the developmental process the child does not merely add more and more structures to his or her existing competence. Rather, a child grammar may generate structures at some early stage, which are then given up and replaced by others at a later stage. For illustration, consider the following data from the acquisition of negation (for details, cf. Bloom, 1970; Klima & Bellugi, 1973; Wode, 1977):

(22) Kathryn no like celery.
     I no taste them.
     He no bite you.

(23) You didn't caught me.
     This can't stick.
     I don't want cover on it.

The examples of (20), discussed in Sec. 3.5, represent the earliest way in which children form multiword negative sentences. In these structures the negator *no* appears in sentence-initial position. At the following stage these structures are abandoned and replaced by those in (22) in which the negator *no* now appears regularly in preverbal (or possibly pre-VP) position. Still later, these structures are again supplanted by those in (23) in which the negator is no longer *no* but rather *didn't, can't,* and so on (presumably still unanalyzed units at this developmental point).

These data show quite clearly that stage-transition is not only a matter of *expanding* the current grammar to cover new structures, but also a matter of *changing* it in such a way that certain old structures will no longer be generated. This, however, implies that a child moving to a new developmental stage has to realize somehow that there is something "wrong" with his or her current grammar in the sense that it generates structures that turn out to be ungrammatical in the adult language. Consequently, an adequate

---

from a less restricted to a more restricted state. Suppose that to play perfect tennis is to be able to perform a narrowly constrained set of arm/body movements called *P*. Any less-than-perfect player can then be characterized as regularly performing movements that fall outside the limits imposed by *P*. Learning to play tennis would then be to move from a (relatively) *P*-unconstrained state to a more and more *P*-constrained state. This view can easily be extended to the development of other physical and cognitive capacities. While for each domain the developmental question is a matter of empirical fact, there is nothing a priori implausible about the idea that development may proceed from a less to a more restricted state.

solution of the stage-transition problem must provide a principled answer to the question of what exactly makes the child realize that structures he or she has regularly used in the past should be ruled out as ungrammatical in developmentally subsequent grammars. Turning again to the negation data for illustration we need to explain what exactly "tells" the child that sentence-initial negation must be abandoned in favor of preverbal negation.

At a general level we can observe that stage-transition crucially involves the child's discovery of ungrammaticalities, or more precisely, the discovery that something previously held to be grammatical is not a possible structure in the target language after all. Note, however, that discovering *ungrammaticalities requires negative evidence which — by standard assumption — is not available to the child. It follows that stage-transition insofar as it involves replacing one structure by another cannot be entirely data-driven, simply because the input doesn't contain any (positive) evidence indicating that a specific structure is ungrammatical and therefore needs to be abandoned. On the other hand there is, of course, positive evidence motivating the child to adopt the new structure. In this process the child might, in fact, be led to conclude that the old *and* the new structure cannot coexist in the same language. Using again the negation data for illustration, once the child has realized (on the basis of positive evidence) that in English the negator has to appear in a pre-VP position, he or she may conclude something like "if it's pre-VP negation, it can't be sentence-initial negation."[11] But, plainly, this conclusion itself cannot be data-driven; that is, there is nothing in the input to suggest that this conclusion rather than some other is valid.

Notice that the theory of Universal Grammar is precisely a theory to explain how children discover ungrammaticalities in the absence of any relevant external evidence. That is, UG provides information necessary for arriving at the correct grammar that is not available in the input data. Since stage-transition involves the discovery of ungrammaticalities, it seems natural to assume that this discovery is, in fact, triggered by principles of UG. If, however, UG is responsible for ruling out certain structures, for

---

[11]This idea is behind Randall's (1988) *Catapult Hypothesis*. She assumes the *Uniqueness Principle* (as a principle of grammar), which roughly states that if there are two conflicting structures with essentially the same meaning, then only one of these structures can be correct. Consequently, if the child decides that it is pre-VP negation, then the earlier (sentence-initial) negation will be "catapulted" away. There are two problems with Randall's account. First, the *Uniqueness Principle* cannot be a principle of grammar because, quite clearly, natural languages do permit alternative structures with essentially the same meaning. Therefore the principle can at best be an acquisitional principle. But if this principle rules out the earlier structure in favor of the later structure, the question arises why the earlier structure was ever adopted in the first place. Either the *Uniqueness Principle* is subject to maturation in the sense that it was not yet active at the earlier stage, or data presentation is ordered, an idea that is standardly assumed to be false.

example, sentence-initial negation, the question arises how the child could ever come to use these very structures in the first place. An obvious answer to this question seems to be that the relevant UG information was simply unavailable prior to the transition point at which the child replaces one structure by another. But this view of the matter amounts exactly to the maturationist claim that principles of UG are subject to a maturational process in the sense that they will emerge and thus become available for grammar construction in a specific temporal order.

The second fact about language development that calls for an explanation relates to a phenomenon that Newport, Gleitman, and Gleitman (1977) have termed *selective attention*. As Hyams (1986, p. 94) notes: "It is well-known that children do not analyze all of the available data. . . . Rather, they select certain data for analysis and ignore others. These other data may then be analyzed at a later point." I will first illustrate the phenomenon of selective attention again with the negation data, turning then to a more complex case.

Note that the available input data are quite unambiguous with respect to the fact that—ignoring irrelevant details—in English sentence negation the negator appears in pre-VP position. Nevertheless, even though the evidence is fully available, the child apparently ignores the relevant data at the earliest developmental stage coming up instead with sentence-initial *neg*-placement, which is ungrammatical in English (or in any other language; Sec. 3.5). At the subsequent developmental stage, however, the child appears to use precisely the data previously ignored to switch from sentence-initial to pre-VP negation. Consequently, the question arises why certain available data are ignored at some early stage, but then lead to a restructuring of the grammar at a later stage.

The usual perceptionist account of these facts is that selective attention is essentially a matter of the child's changing perception. That is, there is some perceptual mechanism that "filters out" (cf. Hyams, 1986) the relevant input data at the early stage, but brings them to the child's attention at some later stage. Note, however, that this view of the matter is not an explanation, but merely a restatement of the facts as long as the exact properties of the perceptual mechanism in question are not made precise. Furthermore, even if we were to assume—for the sake of the argument—that selective attention is a matter of the child's changing perception, the question remains what causes the child's perception to change; that is, why does the perceptual mechanism responsible for drawing the child's attention to the relevant input data not operate earlier than, in fact, it does. Note that the alleged perceptual changes cannot be explained as being caused by the input data, because such an explanation would obviously lead to circularity: The child's perception changes as a result of specific input data becoming available, and these data become available, because the child's perception changes.

Let us now consider a more complex case which relates to Hyams's (1986) proposal of how children fix the *pro-drop* parameter (cf. Chomsky, 1981). Hyams's initial observation concerns the (largely uncontroversial) fact that at an early stage in the acquisition of English children frequently omit the subject of a sentence. In this respect early English thus looks very much like, for example, Italian, a typical null-subject language. Hyams therefore hypothesizes that English children initially choose the positive value of the *pro-drop* parameter. She continues to observe that at this stage children also never use modals such as *can, must,* and so on. Hyams then proposes an analysis — whose details are irrelevant for the present discussion — in which the *pro-drop* properties of a language are systematically related to the structural status of modals. More specifically she shows that — given certain assumptions — it follows that in a null-subject language such as Italian, modals have essentially the status of main verbs, while only in a *non-pro-drop* language such as English modals can have the status of auxiliaries being generated under INFL. It thus becomes clear why children don't use modals at exactly the stage at which they optionally omit subjects. If children initially take English to be a *pro-drop* language, then the resulting grammar does not permit the presence of auxiliaries. Of course, the question arises why in this case children don't simply treat the English modals as main verbs *à l'italienne*. Hyams suggests that English children are sensitive to the defective morphology of English modals, thereby recognizing that they cannot possibly be main verbs. Hyams thus concludes that modals are simply "filtered out" by the early child grammar by virtue of being incompatible with the [+]-*pro-drop* choice.

The obvious problem is, of course, to account for the fact that at some later stage children reset the *pro-drop* parameter to the (correct) negative value. First, Hyams observes that lexical subjects appear to become obligatory at exactly the same stage at which auxiliaries start to emerge. She therefore concludes that the children's resetting of the *pro-drop* parameter is data-driven, that is, triggered by the emergence of modals as auxiliaries. More specifically, the child realizes that modals — again by virtue of being morphologically defective — cannot be main verbs, but have to be auxiliaries generated under INFL. Having realized this, the child is forced to restructure his or her grammar in such a way that the *pro-drop* parameter will now be set to its negative value, because — by hypothesis — only a *non-pro-drop* language permits INFL-generated auxiliaries.

I will accept Hyams's structural analysis as essentially correct. The fundamental problem with this account is that exactly the same type of data — the defective morphology of English modals — leads to different, and, in fact, conflicting conclusions. At the early stage the defective status of modals leads to their being filtered out, whereas at the later stage it is precisely their defective status that makes the child choose the negative value of the *pro-drop parameter*. It seems to be obvious that there is a logical problem with this argument.[12] If the child is already sensitive to the defective status of English modals at the early stage, then the only conclusion that he or she can draw from the relevant observation is that English is *non-pro-drop*. Hence null subjects should never arise in the first place. If, in contrast, the child chooses the positive *pro-drop*-value despite the defective status of modals and, in fact, filters them out as a consequence of this choice, then it is difficult to imagine how data that are filtered out can lead to a restructuring of the grammar at a later stage.

The basic problem is, of course, that exactly the same data do different things at different times, or—to put it differently—if specific data do, in fact, trigger changes in the child's grammar, then they do so only at a very specific time. It is this fact that needs to be accounted for. Following the standard assumption that data presentation is not ordered, it must therefore be some internal mechanism that is responsible for the child's selective treatment of data. In the absence of any alternative proposal in this domain the most likely candidate for this internal mechanism seems to be maturation. In other words, whatever principles—perceptual, grammatical, or acquisitional—eventually turn out to be responsible for the restructuring of child grammars, there must be some additional (biological) mechanism that makes sure that the relevant principles become active at exactly the right time, that is, that they do not operate earlier than, in fact, they do.

Given these considerations I do not see how any adequate theory of language acquisition can do without a strong maturational component. But even if this conclusion is correct, the question still arises what the object of this maturation is. There are, in principle, at least three possibilities: it could be principles of grammar (=UG), principles of acquisition, or principles of perception.[13] Quite clearly, it is an entirely empirical question which of these three possibilities turns out to be true. In other words, it seems to me that the question is not maturation or nonmaturation, but rather what is it that matures.

I have argued in this chapter that the object of maturation is, in fact, principles of UG. There are two considerations that lend at least some plausibility to this view, or more modestly, that make it reasonable to pursue this idea before considering any alternatives.

The first consideration is of an empirical nature. I have tried to demonstrate in Sec. 3 that child structures do temporarily—that is, at specific developmental stages—violate principles of Universal Grammar. Since, by definition, UG principles are innate, the only way of reconciling the innateness of UG principles with their temporary violation in child

---

[12]Hyams does notice this logical problem, but leaves its solution to future research.

[13]Of course, it could also be any combination of these principles.

grammars is to assume that they are subject to maturation. The second consideration relates to general principles of theory construction. Under this perspective the assumption that it is UG principles that mature seems to be the most parsimonious approach. That is, in this case an adequate theory of acquisition needs to consider three components: the data, the principles of UG, and the maturational schedule. In contrast, if we assume that the object of maturation is either perceptual or acquisitional principles, then an additional component — on top of UG — is introduced into the theory. Of course, the principle of parsimoniousness does not say anything about what is empirically true, but it helps to structure a research program in a reasonable way.

5. DISCUSSION

I have tried to show essentially two things: First, a theory of language acquisition that incorporates nothing more than a UG component and a data component may be able to account for how children add new structures and regularities to their current grammar, but it cannot explain in a principled way how they discover that certain structures of their current grammar are ungrammatical in terms of the target and thus need to be abandoned. Consequently, some third component must be incorporated into the theory. While it is basically a purely empirical question what exactly this third component is, I have argued that it must be maturation. The fundamental observation behind this argument is that, whatever principle "tells" the child that a given structure must be abandoned, the availability of this principle (or set of principles) is developmentally constrained. That is, the relevant principles cannot operate until a specific developmental point in time, because otherwise the ungrammatical structure should have never emerged in the first place. Maturation in this sense implies that the principles that constrain the child's hypothesis space are developmentally ordered. Loosely speaking, maturation tells the child what to do at what time and which input data to attend to at which developmental stage.

Secondly, I have argued that the object of maturation is UG itself. Apart from considerations of parsimoniousness (see Sec. 4), the relevant evidence concerns the fact that at various developmental stages children temporarily violate principles of UG. If this is the case, then UG principles must be developmentally, that is, maturationally, ordered. At the empirical level, this version of maturationism crucially depends on whether or not it can be shown that consecutive developmental grammars differ in that the earlier grammar violates a specific principle or notion of UG that the immediately following grammar no longer violates. In Felix (1984, 1987) I have tried to demonstrate that this is exactly what frequently happens in language development.

It seems that a number of interesting consequences follow from this view. First, the interaction between Universal Grammar and the child's linguistic experience is likely to be much more complex than has standardly been assumed. More specifically, this interaction appears to be under the control of a maturational schedule that essentially determines which module or submodule of Universal Grammar interacts with which data at which time. Furthermore it appears that acquiring a language is truly a process of language growth. Knowledge of language grows in the child's mind as a result of innate principles interacting with external evidence; and just as any other process of biological growth, language growth is maturationally controlled with respect to when and how the innate principles operate.

REFERENCES

Baker, C. L. (1979). Syntactic theory and the projection problem. *Linguistic Inquiry, 10,* 533–581.

Bellugi, U. (1967). *The acquisition of the system of negation in children's speech.* Unpublished doctoral dissertation, Harvard, Cambridge, MA.

Bloom, L. (1970). *Language development: Form and function in emerging grammars.* Cambridge, MA: MIT Press.

Bloom, L. (1973). *One word at a time.* The Hague: Mouton.

Borer, H., & Wexler, K. (1987). The maturation of syntax. In T. Roeper & E. Williams (Eds.), *Parameter setting* (pp. 123–172). Dordrecht, The Netherlands: Reidel.

Bowerman, M. (1973). *Early syntactic development: A cross-linguistic study with special references to Finnish.* Cambridge, England: Cambridge University Press.

Braine, M. (1963). The ontogeny of English phrase structure: The first phase. *Language, 39,* 1–13.

Brown, R. (1973). *A first language: The early stages.* London: Allen & Unwin.

Brown, R., & Fraser, C. (1963). The acquisition of syntax. In C. Cofer, & A. Musgrave (Eds.), *Verbal behavior and learning: Problems and processes* (pp. 158–197). New York: Holt, Rinehart, & Winston.

Chomsky, N. (1980). *Rules and representations.* Oxford, England: Blackwell.

Chomsky, N. (1981). *Lectures on government and binding.* Dordrecht, The Netherlands: Foris.

Chomsky, N. (1986). *Knowledge of language: Its nature, origin, and use.* London: Praeger.

Chomsky, N. (1987a). *Language and other cognitive systems.* Paper presented at the Sophia University, Tokyo.

Chomsky, N. (1987b). *On the nature, use and acquisition of language.* Unpublished manuscript, MIT.

Clahsen, H. (1988). *Normale und gestörte Kindersprache* [Normal and pathological child language]. Amsterdam: Benjamins.

Dahl, O. (1979). Typology of sentence negation. *Linguistics, 17,* 79–106.

Felix, S. (1980). Cognition and language development: A German child's acquisition of question words. In D. Nehls (Ed.), *Studies in language acquisition* (pp. 91–110). Heidelberg, Germany: Groos.

Felix, S. (1984). Maturational aspects of Universal Grammar. In A. Davis & C. Criper, & A. Howatt (Eds.), *Interlanguage* (pp. 133–161). Edinburgh University Press.

Felix, S. (1987). *Cognition and language growth*. Dordrecht, The Netherlands: Foris.

Gleitman, L. (1981). Maturational constraints of language growth. *Cognition, 10,* 103–114.

Gruber, J. (1973). Correlations between the syntactic constructions of the child and the adult. In C. Ferguson & D. Slobin (Eds.), *Studies of child language development* (pp. 440–445). New York: Holt, Rinehart, & Winston.

Hornstein, N., & Lightfoot, D. (1981). *Explanation in linguistic theory (Introduction)*. London: Longman.

Hyams, N. (1986). *Language acquisition and the theory of parameters*. Dordrecht, The Netherlands: Reidel.

Jakubowicz, C. (1984). *On markedness and binding principles*. NELS, *14*.

Kayne, R. (1984). *Connectedness and binary branching*. Dordrecht, The Netherlands: Foris.

Klima, E., & Bellugi, U. (1973). Syntactic regularities in the speech of children. In C. Ferguson & D. Slobin (Eds.), *Studies of child language development* (pp. 333–354). New York: Holt, Rinehart, & Winston.

Lust, B. (1981). Constraints on anaphora in child language: a prediction for a universal. In S. Tavakolian (Ed.), *Language acquisition and linguistic theory* (pp. 74–96). Cambridge, MA: MIT Press.

Lust, B. (1986). Introduction. In B. Lust (Ed.), *Studies in the acquisition of anaphora* (pp. 3–103). Dordrecht, The Netherlands: Reidel.

Manzini, R., & Wexler, K. (1987). Parameters, binding theory, and learnability. *Linguistic Inquiry, 18,* 413–444.

Matthei, E. (1981). Children's interpretations of sentences containing reciprocals. In S. Tavakolian (Ed.), *Language acquisition and linguistic theory* (pp. 97–115). Cambridge, MA: MIT Press.

Miller, W. & Ervin, S. (1980). The development of grammar in child language. In U. Bellugi & R. Brown (Eds.), *The acquisition of language* (pp. 9–34). Chicago: University of Chicago Press.

Muysken, P. (1987). *Against percolation*. Paper presented at the World Congress of Linguistics, Berlin.

Neijt, A. (1979). *Gapping*. Dordrecht, The Netherlands: Foris.

Newport, E. & Gleitman, L., & Gleitman, R. (1977). "Mother, I'd rather do it myself": Some effects and non-effects of maternal speech. In C. Snow & C. Ferguson (Eds.), *Talking to children: Language input and acquisition* (pp. 109–149). Cambridge, MA: Cambridge University Press.

Nishigauchi, T., & Roeper, T. (1987). Deductive parameters and the growth of empty categories. In T. Roeper & E. Williams (Eds.), *Parameter setting* (pp. 91–121). Dordrecht, The Netherlands: Reidel.

Olsen, S. (1987). Zum "substantivierten" Adjektiv im Deutschen: Deutsch als eine pro-drop Sprache [On nominalized adjectives in German: German as a pro-drop language]. *Studium Linguistik, 21,* 1–35.

Otsu, Y. (1981). *Universal grammar and syntactic development in children*. Unpublished doctoral dissertation, MIT, Cambridge, MA.

Pesetsky, D. (1982). *Paths and categories*. Unpublished doctoral dissertation, MIT, Cambridge, MA.

Piattelli-Palmarini, M. (Ed.). (1980). *Language and learning: The debate between Jean Piaget and Noam Chomsky*. London: Routledge & Kegan Paul.

Pinker, S. (1984). *Language learnability and language development*. Cambridge, MA: Harvard University Press.

Randall, J. (1988). *The catapult hypothesis: grammars as machines for unlearning.* Unpublished paper, Max-Planck-Institut, Nijmegen, The Netherlands.

Read, C., & Hare, V. (1977). *Children's interpretation of reflexive pronouns in English.* Paper presented at the sixth annual University of the Wisconsin–Milwaukee Linguistics Symposium.

Roeper, T. (1986). How children acquire bound variables. In B. Lust (Ed.), *Studies in the acquisition of anaphora: Defining the constraints* (pp. 191–199). Dordrecht, The Netherlands: Reidel.

Roeper, T., & Williams, E. (Eds.). (1987). *Parameter Setting.* Dordrecht, The Netherlands: Reidel.

Schlesinger, I. (1974). Relational concepts underlying language. In R. Schiefelbusch & L. Lloyd (Eds.), *Language perspectives: Acquisition, retardation and intervention* (pp. 129–151). Baltimore: University Park Press.

Solan, L. (1981). The acquisition of structural restrictions on anaphora. In S. Tavakolian (Ed.), *Language acquisition and linguistic theory* (pp. 59–73). Cambridge, MA: MIT Press.

Stowell, T. (1981). *Origins of phrase structure.* Unpublished doctoral dissertation, MIT, Cambridge, MA.

Tavakolian, S. (1978). Children's comprehension of pronominal subjects and missing subjects in complicated sentences. In H. Goodluck & L. Solan (Eds.), *Papers in the structure and development of child language.* University of Massachusetts Occasional Papers in Linguistics, *4,* Amherst.

Weeks, T. (1974). *The slow speech development of a bright child.* Lexington, MA: Heath.

Wexler, K. (1987). *On maturation in language development.* Paper presented at the World Congress of Linguistics, Berlin.

Wexler, K., & Manzini, R. (1987). Parameters and learnability in binding theory. In T. Roeper & E. Williams (Eds.), *Parameter setting* (pp. 41–77). Dordrecht, The Netherlands: Reidel.

White, L. (1982). *Grammatical theory and language acquisition.* Dordrecht, The Netherlands: Foris.

Wode, H. (1976). Some stages in the acquisition of questions by monolingual children. *Word, 27,* 261–310.

Wode, H. (1977). Four early stages in the development of L1 negation. *Journal of Child Language, 4,* 87–102.

3 Learnability Theory and the Problem of Development in Language Acquisition

Harald Clahsen
Universität Düsseldorf, Germany

INTRODUCTION

The theory of learnability is essentially concerned with the following questions:

(1) a. How can linguistic competence be attained, given the limited data available to the child?

b. Why does the course of linguistic development take the form that it actually does?

The first question addresses the *problem of learnability,* also called the logical problem of language acquisition (Baker & McCarthy, 1981), and the second question is devoted to the *problem of development.* With regard to (1a), it seems now generally accepted in learnability theory that the child is equipped with a set of innate formal principles (called Universal Grammar), which allow him or her to attain the grammar of a particular adult language on the basis of simple positive data available from the input. In this framework, the notion of UG is meant to contribute (in major ways) to the solution of the problem of learnability. UG alone cannot, however, account for (1b). To solve the developmental problem, additional considerations are required, which are a matter of current debate in learnability theory. Essentially, three ways of dealing with the problem of development have been offered: choice, maturation, and continuity

(2) a. The principles of UG directly map primary linguistic data onto the particular grammar of the adult language.

b. The principles of UG mature.

c. The principles of UG do not themselves change over time. They are, rather, available to the child from the onset of language acquisition.

The first view (2a) is the highly idealized picture of language acquisition that is used in Generative Grammar to achieve explanatory adequacy (Chomsky, 1965). Here, language acquisition is taken to be an instantaneous process, that is, as the choice of a particular grammar from the set of options offered by UG. Under this perspective, only two states of the child's development of language are considered: (1) the initial prelinguistic state characterized by UG (with open parameters) and (2) the steady final state characterized by a specific target-language grammar with parameters fixed at the appropriate values. Clearly, this view does not help to solve the developmental problem, but rather abstracts away from the temporal dimension of language acquisition. This idealization might be justified for grammatical theory; it cannot, however, be maintained in a theory of the child's real-time growth of language. This reduces the set of possible solutions to the alternative between maturation and continuity.

The Maturation Hypothesis (MH)

The second view (2b) attributes observed developmental changes in children's language to a *maturational schedule* according to which the principles of UG successively emerge and become operative in a specific temporal order. Two variants of the MH are presently under discussion: (1) The strong version of the MH (Felix 1984, 1987, this volume) according to which the principles of UG themselves are ordered in terms of an innately specified maturational schedule; (2) The weak MH (Borer & Wexler 1987, 1988), according to which there are UG-external learning constraints that restrict the availability of UG principles to the child up to a certain stage and are then successively lost due to the process of maturation.

The two variants of the MH are similar in many ways. They both definitely claim that the principles are not learned and that they do not depend for their emergence on the child's obtaining evidence. Rather, they are said to take time to develop, just like other instances of biological maturation. The developmental problem is solved here by maximizing the child's genetic programming, because, in addition to specifying the child's initial and final states, an extrinsic ordering (as part of the genetic code) is required so that, in the course of the child's acquisition of language, immature states can be replaced by more and more mature ones. The two variants of the MH differ with respect to the question whether intermediate grammars are inconsistent with UG or not. The strong version assumes inconsistency, particularly at early stages, whereas the weak version assumes that the child's grammar at each stage is consistent with UG. I will come back to that in the next section.

The Continuity Hypothesis (CH)

The third view (2c) has been called the CH by Pinker (1984). It claims that all of the innately specified principles for language acquisition are present at all stages of first language development, even at the earliest stages. The developmental problem is solved in terms of the lexical learning hypothesis, that is, changes occurring in the child's grammar over time are attributed to increases in the child's lexicon, in addition, of course, to increases in the child's memory size and processing capacities. Under this view, the lexical (and morphological) items and their associated properties, which the child has to learn for a particular language, induce restructurings of his or her grammar. Given the lexical learning hypothesis, it is possible that, while all of the UG principles are ready to apply from the start, some must await the acquisition of certain lexical triggers, before they can become operative. A theory which is based on continuity plus lexical learning requires no extrinsic ordering of any kind within the UG principles, *and* it contributes a solution to the problem of development in language acquisition. This is what makes (2c) more parsimonious and more attractive than (2b).

Overview

In this chapter I will argue that the CH should be maintained in learnability theory, on theoretical as well as on empirical grounds. First, I will claim that, on the basis of theoretical considerations, the CH has to be preferred over the maturationist's view. Here, I will also try to refute arguments against continuity which have been made in the literature. In the second part, I will argue that the empirical evidence in favor of the MH available from children's language is fairly weak. Several areas of linguistic development will be discussed, which have been accounted for by other investigators in terms of maturational schedules of UG principles, such as X-bar theory, move alpha, the Theta-criterion, and syntactic chains. It will be shown that an approach based on continuity plus lexical learning can account for the observed developmental changes.

1. MATURATION OR CONTINUITY? THEORETICAL CONSIDERATIONS

Every theory of learnability will have to determine the child's initial prelinguistic state and his or her final steady state, to say the least. As we have mentioned, the initial state may be characterized by UG, or a subset of principles from UG, and the final state by a grammar with parameters appropriately fixed. What is currently under debate is the question, whether or not learnability theory—in order to explain the developmental problem in language acquisition—needs an additional ordering that determines the sequence in which UG principles become available to the child. The answer of the MH to this question is yes, whereas it is no under the CH. Here, the solution to the developmental problem rather follows from independently motivated components of the theory, particularly from the lexical learning hypothesis.

Arguments for Continuity

Within Generative Grammar, the CH has normally been assumed, at least implicitly. It has been explicitly stated in Pinker's (1984) version of learnability theory. Under this view, it is required that the language acquisition device (LAD) is *stationary* and *direct,* that is, it does not change over time, and it does not generate developmental patterns or errors which are impossible in natural language.

The CH was introduced in connection with the computer metaphor, which is one of the basic points of orientation in learnability theory. According to this metaphor, the human brain is conceived of as a computational device for manipulating structural representations, and the LAD is seen as a deterministic input/output system consisting of a set of computational mechanisms, which receive positive data as input and produce a cognitive subsystem, that is, a particular language grammar, as output (Chomsky 1986a). Since a learnability account of a given set of language acquisition data must refer to these computational mechanisms, it holds: The fewer the mechanisms, the more parsimonious the theory and the more explanatory its accounts. This implies that the most explanatory theory will posit the fewest developmental changes in the LAD itself. Thus the CH is theoretically motivated by applying Occam's Razor. Pinker uses the CH as his null hypothesis. It will, therefore, not be rejected, until the data leave no other choice. For the following reasons, I consider such a research strategy to be justified.

First, the CH provides for a strong learnability constraint on acquisition theories. In the absence of empirical evidence to the contrary, it requires that the child's linguistic representations, at each stage of development, fall under the limits imposed by UG principles. This prevents acquisition theory from attributing ad hoc grammars to the child.

Note that this constraint is not available under the strong version of the MH. Felix (1984, 1987, this volume) assumes that the maturational schedule, according to which more and more UG principles become available, forces the child to restructure the grammar and to bring it in line with UG. In contrast to that, the weak version of the MH (Borer & Wexler 1988) assumes that the child's grammar at all stages is consistent with UG. Thus, similarly to the CH, the constraint that children's grammars must be possible grammars is maintained here. Given the framework of learnability theory, I think that this view has to be preferred over the strong maturationist's one. The main reason is that the latter approach is theoretically quite unrestrictive and therefore does not allow one to decide among various alternative ways to account for the data. Under the strong MH it is possible, for example, to come up with arbitrary rule systems or utterance templates for early child language, which would later be expunged by virtue of the maturation of new UG principles. It cannot be excluded a priori that child language development proceeds in such a way, but I think the more constrained approach (continuity, weak maturation) should only be given up if the data forces us to do so.

Second, under continuity plus lexical learning one need only postulate the initial and the final state of language development. Given that lexical learning is used to fix UG principles at the appropriate values, the intermediate stages in development are deducible as the products of the LAD operating on the inputs available to the child. As long as it is compatible with the data, no extrinsic ordering determining the emergence of UG principles is required.

In contrast to this, proponents of maturational change assume an ordering in advance without, however, considering whether or not it is really needed. This is true for both versions of the MH. Felix argues that the principles of UG themselves are ordered (in terms of their maturation), whereas Borer and Wexler (1988) establish special constraints that are said to determine the subset of UG principles the child can make use of. One example is the Unique External Argument Principle (UEAP), according to which every predicative element should have a unique external argument. UEAP is said to hold only up to a certain developmental stage, then it is (maturationally) lost. Borer and Wexler leave open the exact nature of principles such as UEAP. Most probably, they are external to UG, because otherwise the claim that children's grammars are possible grammars would have to be given up, and the same arguments would apply that were brought up against Felix's strong maturationism. In any case, Borer and Wexler also assume an additional maturational component in order to solve the developmental problem.[1]

---

[1]The maturational approach, particularly in its strong version, is conceptually similar to the rule orderings (extrinsic or intrinsic) in transformational theories during the 1970s. These theories contained a separate component in which the order of application of syntactical rules had been fixed. Modern linguistic theory has moved further and further away from ordering.

Discussion

In Borer and Wexler (1987), the CH has been criticized, because it would lead to the following dilemma. The hypothesis it is said does not explain why some constructions develop before others. Therefore proponents of the CH must assume that input data trigger the development of later constructions. But now the question arises why these data do not trigger the constructions earlier. According to Borer and Wexler, the only answer would be that the input data the child receives must be strongly ordered. Most of the scholars in this field, however, (including Pinker) would agree that, for conceptual and theoretical reasons, input data cannot be ordered. From this reasoning, Borer and Wexler conclude that the CH lacks theoretical and empirical justification.

This argument does not appear convincing to me. First, it should be noted that, despite similar inputs at different stages, the child's *intake* may actually vary (White, 1981). Probably, every theory of acquisition has to acknowledge that the child's memory size and general processing capacities increase over time. From this we could infer that the child's intake changes as well. Therefore, it is not necessary to assume ordered input, as is claimed by Borer and Wexler. What changes is the child's perception of the input data. Complementizers, for example, might be present in the input from the onset of language acquisition, but, initially, the child will fail to recognize that one is there. Like other unstressed, monosyllabic, closed-class morphemes, complementizers are perceptually nonsalient, unlikely to be uttered in isolation and not accessible through semantic bootstrapping (cf. Pinker, 1984). For these reasons, it will be difficult for the child to pick them out. At the beginning, complementizers will therefore not be part of the child's intake, and some of the UG principles, although present from the onset of development, must await the child's prior identification of those elements, for example, complementizers, that enter into the principles' triggering conditions (cf. Pinker, 1984, pp. 226ff.).[2]

Second, I believe that Borer and Wexler's reasoning underestimates the

---

In the Government/Binding framework (Chomsky, 1981), for example, there are no longer structural descriptions of transformations, simply move alpha. Due to the fact that the various components of grammar, particularly the lexicon, have been worked out more seriously, the same facts can now be handled in terms of the interaction of modules. This ensures that most of the constraints on order of rule application are no longer required. Similarly, the CH may be regarded as a move away from ordering in learnability theory.

[2]It would also be possible that in early development the input data simply do not contain certain function words, for example complementizers, that the child cannot handle yet. This may be determined by the adults' intuitive knowledge of what is appropriate for the child at this particular stage and what is not. Similarly, those UG principles for which complementizers are required cannot become effective, though they are (latently) available.

role of lexical learning on the shape of the child's grammar. In a lexicalist version of learnability theory, principles of the LAD are closely linked with lexical elements and their properties. In particular, lexical categorizations serve as the triggering conditions for UG principles to emerge. Under this view, the problem of development can in principle be solved, even under the continuity constraint. Moreover, this approach does *not* place the solution to the developmental problem outside the domain of grammatical theory as is suggested in Felix (this volume). It rather takes up the basic idea that clause structure is a projection from lexical categories and predicate-argument structure, a view adopted in most current grammatical theories.

A learnability theory that incorporates the hypotheses of continuity and lexical learning allows us to make specific predictions on the acquisition of grammar that could easily be falsified by empirical evidence. Therefore, the approach contributes to the development of explanatory accounts of children's linguistic abilities. We might think of the predictions in (3), among others:

(3) a. Children's grammars are possible grammars.
    b. UG principles are fixed through lexical learning.

Prediction (3a) follows from the CH.[3] Given that the learning device does not change over time, it could be expected that the intermediate grammars constructed by the child are possible grammars obeying the limits imposed by UG. The second prediction is derived from the lexical learning hypothesis, which requires that restructurings of the children's grammar are triggered by simple (kinds of) positive data, such as particular lexical items and their associated properties, which are readily available to the child. From this we might expect to observe developmental correlations between certain lexical (and morphological) items and syntactical structures. In particular it follows that the range of linguistic phenomena being covered by a certain UG principle should be acquired more or less at once, namely, as soon as the (lexical) triggers for that principle are available to the child. In Clahsen (1988a), I tried to provide empirical evidence from German child language for the predictions in (3). The results will be discussed in some more detail in the next section.

---

[3]This claim can also be derived from the weak version of the MH, but not, however, from Felix's strong version of the MH. As I understand the weak MH, there is no qualitative shift in development, but just an incremental process that adds new principles to existing ones, so that each stage is consistent with UG. Felix, however, explicitly states that UG principles, for example the Theta-criterion, are initially violated and that early child grammars are not constrained by UG. I will come back to that in the following two sections.

2. THE CASE OF VERB PLACEMENT IN GERMAN CHILD LANGUAGE: MATURATION OF X-BAR PRINCIPLES?

In the remainder of this chapter, I will discuss maturational schedules that have been suggested in the acquisition literature. The focus will be on three types of data: (1) verb placement in German child language, (2) certain cases of deletion, and (3) passives. The maturationist's accounts will be criticized and alternative ways of explaining the developmental data will be discussed. As a conclusion, it is claimed that the arguments in favor of the MH are dubious and that the empirical evidence currently available does not force us to reject the CH.

In recent theoretically oriented acquisition studies, the development of verb placement in German child language has been an important focus of research. Several analyses of the acquisition data, mostly from a generative perspective, have been presented (Clahsen & Muysken, 1986; de Haan, 1986; du Plessis, Solin, Travis, & White, 1986; Jordens, 1986; Zobl, 1986). Here, I will not discuss these different approaches; I will rather focus on one interesting study, Felix (1984),[4] in which an explicit maturational schedule for this set of data has been suggested.

Felix (1984, 1987)

In his description of the data, Felix draws on the developmental sequence established in Clahsen (1982). He tries to explain this sequence in terms of the maturation of the X-bar schema and the structure-preserving constraint (Emonds, 1976). Felix sets up three stages of the acquisition of German verb placement:

(4) Stage I: random constituent order
Stage II: SOV and SVO used randomly
Stage III: correct verb-second in main clauses

He suggests that the maturational emergence of X-bar principles explains the transition from I to II. The child is said to know at II, but not at I, that the order of lexical heads and their complements is constrained, so that base rules generating random constituent order are excluded in principle. From this it follows that V is either final or initial in the VP, and that base generated orders can be only those in which the object is directly adjacent to the verb (Felix, 1984, p. 150). He concludes that the transition from random constituent order to more constrained word order can be accounted

---

[4]The same analysis can also be found in Felix (1987).

for by assuming the maturation of the X-bar schema at some time before Stage II.

In Stage III the children acquire the verb-second constraint of German syntax. As required in the adult language, all finite verbal elements now occur in sentence-second or initial position, and nonfinite verbal elements are placed sentence-finally. Felix (1984, p. 153) argues that the child at III has chosen SOV as the base-generated pattern, and further that the child has acquired a movement rule generating the correct placements of finite verb forms in main clauses. These developments are assumed to be due to the maturation of the structure-preserving constraint, which is said to emerge at the transition from II to III. Felix argues that, as soon as this constraint is available, the child can rule out SVO as a potential underlying order, since in this case, an additional movement rule needs to be invoked which would violate the constraint. This leaves the child with the correct structure for German, namely SOV plus the structure-preserving rule of verb-second. Felix's general conclusion from this is that the acquisition of German verb placement is significantly determined by the maturation of UG principles.

I doubt that Felix's account of German L1 development can be maintained, since it does not cover the range of empirical facts that have now become available with respect to German child language. In addition to that, an analysis under continuity can be established for this set of data, so that the maturational schedule suggested by Felix appears to be superfluous as a separate component of the LAD.

Note first that, in Stages I and II, word order in the children's utterances is not completely random. It has been observed for these stages in various empirical studies (cf. Clahsen, 1982; Mills, 1985) that (a) verb-initial patterns with the verb appearing before the subject are practically nonexistent in I and II, and that (b) inflected verbal elements, for example those with the suffix $-t$, and modals are placed in sentence-second or sentence-initial position, whereas infinitives and participles occur sentence-finally. Felix took his claim that word order in Stage I is random from Park's (1974) study with a *bilingual* child. The evidence on monolingual children demonstrates that there is no qualitative developmental difference in terms of the acquisition of verb placement between I and II. Second, under the proposed maturational schedule it is difficult to explain the restrictions on possible word-order patterns that have been observed in the data. Given the analysis suggested by Felix, one would expect (contrary to (a)) that the position of the subject is variable. Further, the child's grammar should allow for all kinds of word-order patterns, even at Stage II, provided that the object is adjacent to the verb. This is at variance with the fact that patterns such as OVS and VOS have not been observed in the data. Finally, the choice between SVO and SOV should be random, according to Felix, which it is not, as mentioned in (b). In addition, his explanation of the transition from II to III does not account for observed developmental correlations between verb placement and verb inflection. For these reasons, Felix's maturational schedule for German L1 word-order acquisition has to be rejected.

An Alternative Analysis

An alternative to Felix's account is the lexicalist analysis of the development of verb placement in German child language suggested in Clahsen (1988a).[5] Here, I will only present a brief sketch of those parts of the analysis that are relevant to the acquisition of the verb-second (V2) constraint in German, that is, the period of development up to Stage III. A more detailed description including the subsequent development of verb placement in subordinate clauses and the empirical justification for the analysis may be taken from Clahsen (1988a).

With regard to the development of V2, the following elements of UG are assumed to be particularly relevant:

(5) a. *X-bar theory*
$$X^2 \rightarrow \text{Spec } X^1, X^1$$
$$X^1 \rightarrow \ldots X \ldots$$

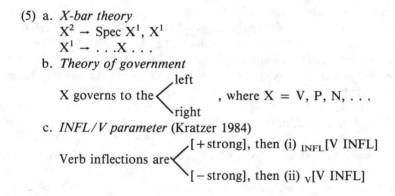

b. *Theory of government*

X governs to the $\Bigg\langle \begin{array}{l} \text{left} \\ \\ \text{right} \end{array}$, where X = V, P, N, . . .

c. *INFL/V parameter* (Kratzer 1984)

Verb inflections are $\Bigg\langle \begin{array}{l} [+\text{strong}], \text{ then (i) } {}_{\text{INFL}}[\text{V INFL}] \\ \\ [-\text{strong}], \text{ then (ii) } {}_{\text{V}}[\text{V INFL}] \end{array}$

Furthermore, it is assumed that the child is confronted with the following word-order data in the input:

(6) a. an alternation INFL . . . / . . . INFL
b. an alternation . . . XV/ . . . VX . . .
c. XVS patterns
d. often Mod . . . Inf patterns

Given (5) and (6), I suggest that the child constructs a phrase structure tree which offers two landing sites for verbal elements: INFL, the head of S, and

---

[5]A similar analysis for early Dutch child language has been suggested in de Haan (1986).

V, the head of VP; the tree may roughly be described as in (7). It is assumed that this tree remains the same throughout Stages I to III.

(7) $[X^{max}[INFL \ldots [_{VP} \ldots V]]]$

The basic idea of the analysis is that the observed developmental stages are due to changes in the morphological categorization of verbal elements, and not so much due to the acquisition of syntactic rules. In the early Stages I and II, the children do not yet have the subject–verb agreement paradigm and make mistakes in choosing the verb inflections required in German. In these stages, we find predominant use of verb-final patterns. Modals, however, are consistently fronted as required in German. In Clahsen (1982, pp. 62f.) it is shown that there are only very few word-order errors with modals throughout the whole developmental process. This suggests that even in I and II the child's grammar has two different positions for verbal elements, as in (7), an initial INFL position and a final V position.[6] The way these positions are filled is determined in the lexicon. I suggest that regardless of their inflections, modals are categorized as INFLs and can thus be placed correctly into the syntactic INFL position.[7] As long as the agreement system has not been acquired, however, main verbs are catego-

---

[6]The syntactical INFL position in (7) is assumed to be created through modals. Given the input (6a), INFL[1] could either be head-initial or head-final. According to (5b), however, the child must choose one of the options in (6a), and for this the input (6d) is relevant. Given that (i) the child can categorize modals easily due to their meanings as INFLs and (ii) the input (6d), the syntactical INFL position is created as in (7).

Crucial for the acquisition of the head-final VP assumed in (7) are (5b) and (6b) in the input as well as the assumption that the verbal elements in structures such as . . . VX . . . occur in the syntactical INFL position. Only on the basis of input (6b) both structures would be possible, (i) $_{VP}[V \ldots]$ and (ii) $_{VP}[\ldots V]$. However, UG principle (5b) forces the child to fix one of the two structures as being the underlying representation. The child chooses the option head-final for the VP, because otherwise movement rules would have to be assumed which would not fall under UG principles. In XVS structures (6c), for example, the movement of the subject to the right would be necessary, a rule which does not fulfill the constraints of "move alpha" (cf. Clahsen & Muysken, 1986). By means of a head-final VP and a syntactical INFL position, such problems do not arise.

[7]Note that the analysis of modals in early German as well as the one presented by de Haan (1986) for early Dutch child language are in contrast to Hyams's (1987) version of the pro-drop parameter and her accompanying analysis of English child language. Hyams argues that children initially develop a [+pro-drop] system which, under her analysis entails that, in the early stages, there can be no lexical material in INFL or AUX. From this we would expect that in German and Dutch modals are initially treated either as main verbs or are simply left out. The available data are against this prediction. De Haan (1986) shows that modals (and auxiliaries) are present early on in Dutch child language, and from the German data it is also quite clear that modals are consistently used before the stage at which the subject becomes obligatory; this might be taken as evidence against Hyams's version of the pro-drop parameter (cf. also Weissenborn, this volume).

rized, in most cases, as Vs rather than as INFLs, and can therefore not be fronted into the INFL position. This is reflected in the predominant use of verb-final patterns in the early developmental phases.

Around Stage III, the children acquire the V2 constraint *and* the correct subject–verb agreement paradigm (Clahsen, 1986). Thus, verb placement is like in adult German, and at the same time, the children use all of the inflections of the agreement paradigm correctly. The decisive feature of this stage is the acquisition of the formative − *st,* which encodes second person singular in German. There are almost no overgeneralizations in the use of − *sti,* as soon as this formative occurs, the previously used verb inflections are integrated into the agreement paradigm required for German. Given these data, I suggest that verb inflections at this stage become "strong" and that, following from this, finite verbs are categorized as INFLs by the word-formation pattern (5ci). This allows the child to bring all finite verbs into the syntactic INFL position of (7) as necessary in German main clauses. Therefore, as soon as AGR features are available, the children no longer have problems using the correct verb-second pattern. This is reflected in the sudden increase in the use of V2 patterns in Stage III.

This analysis covers the range of observed facts. More importantly, no maturation of any UG principle needs to be assumed. Thus, it allows us to maintain the CH. Finally, the results of the analysis are in accordance with the predictions in (3), which were derived from the lexical learning hypothesis and the continuity assumption.

Discussion

Finally, I want to deal with two objections which were brought up against the proposed analysis. First, Manfred Bierwisch (personal communication) pointed out to me that there might be a conceptual problem for the CH with respect to the way the development of *modals* is explained under the present account. I claimed that modals are categorized as INFLs in the early Stages I and II; a similar proposal is made by de Haan (1986) for early Dutch. This, however, is contrary to German (and Dutch), where modals are verbs (V°) in all cases. Thus there does not seem to be much developmental "continuity" here, since modals have to be recategorized from INFL to V at some point. Second, Lisa Travis (personal communication) suggested to me that the proposed account of the acquisition of V2 effects cannot hold in general, since there are V2 languages, for example, Afrikaans, that lack overt agreement. Note that I proposed that in German child language the V2 effects are triggered by a rich morphological agreement paradigm. Obviously, this cannot be applied to languages such as Afrikaans.

Let us first consider the case of modals. I do in fact assume that German children's early categorizations of modals differ from those of the adult language. If, however, it can be shown that the recategorization is triggered by positive data available to the child from the input, this does not pose a problem for the CH. Recategorizations of lexical and morphological items appear to be quite common in the acquisition of a particular language grammar.[8] With respect to modals, the proposed lexical categorization (as INFLs) in Stages I and II is assumed to be due to their meanings. A modal can be conceived of as a modality operator, which takes the whole sentence as its scope. Steele (1981) has argued that this makes modals classical candidates for the category INFL (or AUX in older studies), regardless of their inflections. I suggest that the recategorization of modals in Stage III is triggered by the acquisition of the subject–verb agreement paradigm for both modals and verbs. This allows the child to recognize the overlap between both categories. Since universally INFL elements are morphologically defective (Steele, 1981) and the children at Stage III have discovered that in German modals are morphologically *complex,* the recategorization takes place from INFL to V. This account attributes the changes in development to lexical learning and does therefore not violate the CH.[9]

Consider now the second objection mentioned, which has to do with the range of the analysis proposed for German child language. Given the INFL/V parameter, a correlation is assumed between the strength of inflection and certain word-formation patterns in the lexicon (cf. 5c). If verb inflections are [+strong], INFL can be the head of a morphologically complex verb due to (5ci). This together with the (independently motivated) syntactic INFL position in (7) allow us to derive the V2 effects in German main clauses. Crucially, the analysis does not require the acquisition of any syntactic verb placement rule; the V2 effect is instead acquired through morphological recategorizations. In the development of languages such as Afrikaans, a syntactic INFL position as in (7) is probably available, too. What is clearly missing, however, is the word-formation pattern (5ci). Instead, Afrikaans similarly to English only has (5cii). Therefore, a lexicalist analysis of the V2 effect such as the one suggested for German is not

---

[8]To give just one example, consider the case of separable prefix verbs in German child language (Clahsen, 1988a). Verbs such as *aufmachen* (to open up), *reintun* (to put in), etc., are initially treated by the children like simple verbs. Thus the prefix cannot be separated from the verb as would be necessary in German. Around Stage III, prefix verbs are recategorized and induce an INFL^1-substructure ($_{INFL}$[Pref$_{INFL}$[V INFL]]). This allows the prefix to be a separate constituent in the syntax as required in German.

[9]A crucial test of the proposed analysis would be to study the inflection of modals. From the analysis it can be expected that as long as modals are INFLs, they should be uninflected or at least morphologically simpler than main verbs. The spontaneous speech data on German child language available to me support this claim. Similarly de Haan (1986) found that the auxiliaries and modals in early Dutch are morphologically simple. However, since there are not many chances for clear morphological oppositions in spontaneous speech samples, more data are necessary to establish a systematic analysis of the inflection of modals.

possible. But it is, of course, possible to derive the V2 effect in Afrikaans in the syntax, that is, through head movement from V to INFL (Chomsky, 1986b). Thus the lexicalist analysis proposed for German as well as the one by de Haan (1986) for Dutch can be maintained, whereas the acquisition of the V2 effect in languages that do not have strong verb inflections must be explained in a different way.

THE CASE OF DELETIONS: MATURATION OF THE THETA-CRITERION?

It is a well-known observation from acquisition studies that during the early two-word stage, that is, Stage I, according to Brown (1973), constituents that are obligatory in the adult language are often missing in the children's utterances. Consider the following examples of missing verbs and subjects in English child language:

(8) a. mommy sock
    b. sweater chair
    c. see ball
    d. want baby

In order to explain the transition from Stage I to a more adult-like grammar with obligatory constituents being present, a maturational schedule has been suggested, again by Felix (1984, 1987). He is particularly concerned with missing verbs, such as in (8a) and (8b), and argues that these are due to the fact that in Stage I the Theta-criterion is not available to the child. Basically, this constraint (Chomsky, 1981) requires that arguments bear thematic roles and that thematic roles have to be assigned by the verb or some other predicate. According to Felix (1984, p. 158), this principle emerges at the end of Stage I, thereby forcing the child to abandon the original verbless constructions. Note that Felix's reasoning could easily be applied to missing subjects, as well. Given the UG constraints, thematic subjects should not be deleted, since these are required by predicates. In Stage I, however, all kinds of subjects may be absent (cf. 8c, 8d). Therefore, one might argue that UG principles are not available to a Stage I child, and that the use of subjects as obligatory sentence constituents has to await the maturation of the Theta-criterion.

Under Felix's approach, early child grammars would not fall under the limits imposed by UG and would thus not qualify as possible grammars. If this were correct, the continuity assumption would have to be rejected. In the following, I will argue against this conclusion.

Discussion

Felix's account of deletion phenomena in early child language is hard to accept, for the following reasons.

First, the predictions that can be made from his analysis are not borne out by the empirical evidence available from acquisition studies. Consider, for example, the use of verbless and subjectless sentences by Mathias, one of the children studied in Clahsen (1982).[10]

If, as is claimed by Felix, the Theta-criterion forcing the child to use verbs and subjects matures at the end of Stage I, then we would expect that incomplete sentences disappear from the children's language, as soon as Stage II is reached. However, Fig. 3.1 shows that, against the prediction, there are no substantial differences between I and II concerning the absence of verbs and subjects. In these early stages, subjects and verbs are not obligatory sentence constituents. A clear developmental shift away from this early system takes place between Stages II and III. Given these facts, Felix might possibly claim that the UG principle he considered emerges only after Stage II. But this explanation would be even worse, since a Stage II child has a phrase structure system that falls under the limits of X-bar theory, even under Felix's (1984) account. This would be mysterious under the assumption that projection principles (including the Theta-criterion) are not yet available to the child (cf. also Borer & Wexler, 1987).

Second, Felix's account is highly dependent on theoretical conceptions that are as yet unclear. The exact nature of the Theta-criterion and the level on which it operates is controversial, even within GB theory. Rappaport and Levin (1986) have argued, for example, that arguments can get more than one thematic role provided there are enough predicative elements in the sentence. Felix's account crucially requires that the Theta-criterion can only be satisfied on surface constituent structure. Therefore, he is forced to assume that a thematic role can only be assigned to an object, if a verb is present in phrase structure. However, the Theta-criterion could also be satisfied at other levels, perhaps at the level of predicate-argument structure. This level includes the information necessary for semantic interpretation. Therefore, in a sentence such as (8a), a verb has to be represented at the level of predicate-argument structure, provided that this sentence has the same meaning as it would have had with the verb. Thus we would not have to attribute to the child a violation of the Theta-criterion.

The third argument against Felix's account of deletion phenomena is that

---

[10]The figures for missing subjects have been taken from Clahsen (1986, p. 106); the figures for missing verbs have been calculated in a similar manner. Stages I, II, and III correspond to those of the developmental sequence for word order that has been described in the previous section.

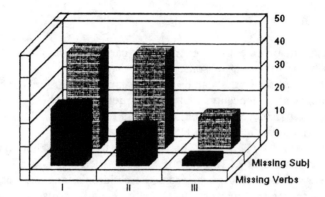

FIG. 1   Percentages of missing subjects and verbs (Mathias).

the facts he is concerned with are probably due to a complicated set of different factors that he does not try to disentangle. The fact that there are verbless and subjectless sentences in early child language can have various reasons. The following three factors might perhaps be most relevant: (1) ellipsis, (2) processing constraints, and (3) the child's grammar. The basic problem with Felix's account is that he quotes some isolated examples from children's speech and argues that all cases of deletions in these utterances are due to (3) without considering the possibility that they might also be accounted for in terms of factors (1) and (2). Felix ignores that he is dealing with spoken language data and that in such data we find many cases of deletions, that is, phenomena of ellipsis (cf. Klein, 1981), even in adult's speech. Moreover, verbal elements as well as subjects are not omitted freely in early child language, as would be expected from Felix's account, but rather depend on contextual factors and lexical restrictions.[11]

Pinker (1984) sketched a processing account of deletion phenomena in early child language. In particular, he argues that the processing mechanism that maps predicate-argument structures to full words occupying terminal nodes in surface structure might be unable to handle more than a certain number (cf. also Weinberg, 1987, p. 175). This would also explain the limitations on length of utterance which have been observed, particularly for Stage I. Consider as an example a situation (cf. Clahsen, 1982) in which one child (= Daniel) is cutting paper into small pieces; a second child looks at him and says:

---

[11]With respect to Stage I in German child language, for example, Miller (1976) showed that in most of the subjectless sentences the child himself or herself can be understood as the subject. Concerning verbal elements, I found that in most cases *sein* (to be) and *haben* (to have) are left out (Clahsen, 1982).

(9) Daniel pier ("D. paper")

In order to account for examples such as (9), Pinker assumes a constraint on production in Stage I that allows only one level of projection. Given such a constraint and ignoring word order for the moment, the child has two options of building up a constituent structure:

(10) a. $_S[_{NP}[$ Daniel $] _{NP}[$ paper $]]$
    b. $_V \cdot [_V[$ cut $] _{NP}[$ paper $]]$

Both types of structures have been frequently observed in Stage I. If the child starts to process the NP_{SUB} (*Daniel*), then the verb has to be left out, because the NP_{SUB} does not belong to the first level of the V-projection. The object, however, can be integrated into the constituent structure of the sentence. The result would be as in (10a). The child could also begin with the predicate *cut*. Then, if the object follows, a V^1-projection, such as (10b), could be established. Note that the foregoing constraint is only one example of a processing constraint that might be relevant at Stage I. It is mentioned here just to illustrate that a processing explanation of children's incomplete sentences could be a plausible alternative to Felix's maturational approach.

In addition to such factors, there is, of course, the possibility that some types of missing elements as well as the development of incomplete sentences can be motivated by the shape of the children's grammar. Consider, for example, the development of missing subjects in German child language. As is clear from Fig. 3.1 and from the description of word-order acquisition in the previous section, there are developmental correlations between (1) the agreement paradigm, (2) correct verb placement, and (3) obligatory subjects. As soon as the agreement paradigm is available to the child in Stage III, finite verbs can be placed correctly, and the frequency of missing subjects significantly decreases. The correlation between (1) and (2) has been explained in terms of the INFL/V parameter (Kratzer, 1984). Similarly, we could argue that in Stage III the presence of subjects in finite clauses is forced by the i(nflectional)-features, particularly AGR, which now, due to the acquisition of the agreement paradigm, are available as part of INFL. According to Borer (1986), these i-features have to be saturated by an argument ($=$the I-subject), just like the (lexical) case features of predicates. This suggests that grammatical factors are also relevant in order to account for such data.

On the whole, I find deletion phenomena in child language hard to evaluate. Detailed analyses are necessary to figure out the contribution of the different factors involved. Felix only presents unanalyzed deletion data. His arguments for the unavailability of the Theta-criterion are therefore dubious.

THE CASE OF PASSIVES: MATURATION OF
SYNTACTIC CHAINS?

A further type of acquisition phenomena which, at first sight, appears to cause problems for the CH are so-called undergeneralizations, in which the child, at certain intermediate stages, applies a rule only in a limited subset from the range of applications possible in adult language. As an example I will consider here the development of passives that has been assumed by Borer and Wexler (1987) to be determined by the maturation of UG principles, particularly by the availability of syntactic chains to the child. In the following, I will first give a brief summary of the Borer and Wexler account and then discuss the evidence for the proposed maturational schedule.

Borer and Wexler (1987)

Borer and Wexler start out from the observation (cf. Horgan, 1978) that in the acquisition of English adjectival passives, such as (11a), are present in early grammars, whereas verbal passives, such as (11b), are not (up to approximately age 48 months):

(11) a. tree is broken
b. John was hit (by Mary)

Borer and Wexler use this evidence to establish a maturational schedule for A(rgument)-chains. They argue that to generate an adjectival passive, the child's grammar has to accomplish the tasks in (12):

(12) a. $[+V, -N] \rightarrow [+V, +N]$
b. Delete the theta-role of the subject.
c. Externalize the internal theta-role.

The categorical change in (12a) results in the elimination of the accusative-case assigning feature. According to (12c) the theta-role that was previously assigned to the object, is now assigned to the external argument, that is, the subject. Moreover, the original theta-role of the subject has been eliminated through (12b). Under this analysis it is assumed that the child knows that all referential NPs must be assigned a thematic role. Thus, contrary to Felix (1984, 1987), the Theta-criterion is claimed to be available to the child even in the early stages. Verbal passives are analyzed by Borer and Wexler as an instance of NP movement. The underlying structure of (11b) is assumed to be something like (13a), and the derivation involves the factors (13b) and (13c), until one gets the surface structure (13d):

(13) a. e was hit John
    b. $[+V, -N] \rightarrow [+V]$
    c. The passive morphology absorbs the external theta-role.
    d. John$_i$ was hit $[e]_i$ (by Mary)

In contrast to adjectival passives, the internal theta-role and the subcategorized (object) position are preserved in verbal passives. In addition to that, Borer and Wexler (p. 143) argue that the recategorization in (13b) guarantees that the accusative case is not being assigned to the object position. Both these factors result in the obligatoriness of NP movement in verbal passive constructions. Since, following from the Projection Principle, the object position in (13a) may not be deleted, a trace must be left behind after NP movement has been applied. This trace forms an *A-chain* with its antecedent in subject position. The objective theta-role is assigned to that chain by the participle *hit,* thus rendering the surface-structure representation in (13d).

Borer and Wexler argue that in the early stages the child is not capable of forming an A-chain, that is, he or she is said to be unable to combine a moved NP and its trace into a nonlocal relation. As a result, the child cannot assign a theta-role to the moved NP and would be driven (due to the Theta-criterion) to rule out the derivation. As long as the ability of nonlocal theta-role assignment (A-chains) does not mature, verbal passives such as (11b) can therefore not be generated by the child's grammar. At the same time, however, sentences such as (11a) can be used by the child, since A-chains are not required to generate adjectival passives.

Discussion

Borer and Wexler's account makes use of a maturational schedule to solve the developmental problem. If their analysis were correct, then the CH would have to be given up. In the following, I will try to argue against this conclusion.[12]

First, the authors' analysis of the acquisition data is hard to accept, because (a) the empirical evidence they have is ambiguous, and (b) their analysis lacks an explanation for certain aspects of the developmental data. Their hypothesis is crucially based on Horgan's (1978) claim that children's early passives lack *by*-phrases and that they are exclusively stative. Pinker, Lebeaux, and Frost (1987) have shown, however, that Horgan's results stem from her data collection technique of having the children describe pictures. Pinker et al. summarize spontaneous speech data from other studies and

---

[12]Some arguments against Borer and Wexler have been made in Weinberg (1987) and in Pinker, Lebeaux, and Frost (1987); they will be summarized herein.

present elicitation data that show that in young children's speech there are passives with dynamic readings, as well as passives containing *by*-phrases. Similarly, Maratsos and Abramovitch (1975) showed that long and short passives are acquired at the same time in development (cf. Weinberg, 1987, p. 176). These observations are in conflict with what is assumed by Borer and Wexler.

With respect to (ii), Weinberg (1987, pp. 180ff.) notes that Borer and Wexler are unable to explain why Hebrew children do not produce verbal passives until school age.[13] Weinberg argues that the authors' account is insufficient, because the Hebrew child could come up with a purely lexical rule for verbal passives, which would not require A-chain formation. Nothing in Borer and Wexler's account excludes this possibility, and thus the fact that Hebrew child language lacks passives is left unexplained.[14]

Second, there are empirical inadequacies in the grammatical analysis Borer and Wexler use to account for the acquisition data (Weinberg 1987, pp. 177f.). Their version of the adjective-forming rule involved in passives (cf. 12) deletes rather than internalizes the theta-role associated with the D-structure subject. Borer and Wexler's argument for that is the assumed inability of *by*-phrases to occur in adjectival passives. This, however, is not quite correct given examples such as (14) (cf. Pinker et al., p. 263; Weinberg, p. 177). These examples show that, in contrast to the Borer and Wexler claim, long passives can be constructed with verbs and with adjectives.

(14) a. This island is uninhabited by humans.
     b. The child was unwanted by his parents.
     c. The problem was unsolved by any linguist.

Third, Borer and Wexler are not able to demonstrate that their maturational schedule is the only way to account for the data. Berwick and Weinberg (1984) argue for a nonmaturational account of the development of passives that may be taken as an alternative to the maturation hypothesis Borer and Wexler argue for.[15] Weinberg (pp. 178f.) demonstrates that the

---

[13]In addition to that, Borer and Wexler cannot explain why English-speaking children loose overgeneralizations of the causative at a certain point in development. I will not go into this here (cf. Weinberg, 1987, p. 180, for further details).

[14]A possible explanation could be that, according to Borer and Wexler, verbal passives are rare in the input addressed to a Hebrew child. This leaves open two possibilities: either that the children do know the verbal passive but fail to utter it for the same reasons that adults do, or that they acquire the verbal passive late due to the infrequency of this construction in the input (cf. Pinker et al., 1987, p. 262).

[15]Basically, the late occurrence of verbal passives is derived here from recategorizations necessary for the *-ed* ending which is involved in the formation of passive participles in

nonmaturational account could explain the developmental patterns in all cases cited by Borer and Wexler, thus suggesting that the proposed maturational schedule is superfluous.

A related problem is that the authors in question assume without further justification that the observations they try to account for can only have grammatical explanations. As is shown in Pinker et al. (1987), long passives including *by*-phrases are indeed rare, though not totally absent, in early child language. Under Borer and Wexler's analysis this would be due to the child's underdeveloped grammar, in particular the unavailability of A-chain formation. However, various other factors seem to be relevant as well. Consider, for example, the fact that long passives including *by*-phrases are also rare in the speech of adults and thus in the input addressed to the child (Weiner and Labov, 1983). Moreover, there might be functional reasons for the dominance of short passives (cf. Pinker et al., pp. 260f.). In the canonical case in which an animate being acts on an inanimate object the arguments are distinguishable from one another by their intrinsic properties; this holds for active and passive sentences. Therefore, in such cases the child might find less need to discriminate the arguments functionally and to specify the identity of the agent-argument explicitly.

Note further that across languages explicitly realized *by*-phrases are rare. Keenan (1982) found that agentless passives are universally preferred even in those languages which, in some cases, permit agent-phrases. This is similar to early child language. Moreover, Keenan established, on the basis of typological analyses, the following implicational universal:

(15) If a language has passives with agent-phrases, then it has also agentless passives, but not vice versa.

Given that (15) can be maintained as a typological universal, *by*-phrases do not belong to the core properties of passives. Rather, the agentless construction appears to be the basic or unmarked passive, and this could contribute to its early use in child language acquisition.

Finally it is important to note that long passives can only be generated, if there is an argument position which could take up the internalized agent-argument. In contrast, short passives do not require additional argument positions, since, in these cases, the agent has simply been deleted. Therefore, short passives can be generated, even by very simple grammars.

English. Berwick and Weinberg argue that *-ed* is initially categorized only as a past tense form and that only later in development the child marks certain verbs as taking an exceptional *-ed* affix that absorbs case. This, however, takes time to develop. The triggers for the assumed recategorization are cases in which past tense forms and passive participles are morphologically different.

The use of adult-like long passives (in English), however, presupposes the prior development of the required argument positions and the syntactic features, such as [p by], to which they are linked. Pinker (1984; pp. 80f.) reports that, in the early stages, children often mark the passive agent with the instrumental prepositions *from* or *with,* thus suggesting that the argument position and its syntactic features in English are not fully available to the child at this stage. This could also contribute to the quantitative preference of short passives in early child language.

To sum up, the evidence for the maturational schedule proposed by Borer and Wexler turns out to be quite weak. They tried to argue that the absence of certain elements (i.e., *by*-phrases) from children's early speech provide such evidence. However, the fact that something is missing from children's spontaneous speech can have several different reasons. With respect to that, the arguments that were made against Felix's (1984, 1987) account of deletion phenomena (cf. sec. 2) apply to Borer and Wexler as well. Neither Felix nor these authors make an attempt to figure out the role of the different factors involved in missing elements. This makes it difficult to evaluate the observed facts and to accept the claim that they can only be due to the unavailability of UG principles.

CONCLUSION

Two ways of dealing with the problem of development in language acquisition were discussed, the maturation hypothesis (MH) and the continuity hypothesis (CH). Both approaches come from the theory of learnability and share a lot of basic assumptions. The crucial difference has to do with the way the developmental problem is solved. The MH assumes a maturational schedule as part of the child's genetic code, according to which UG principles successively emerge during language development. Under this view, the maturational schedule contributes the essential solution to the developmental problem. In contrast, the CH assumes that the learning device of the child is present from the onset of language acquisition, and that it does not change over time. The CH by itself does not offer a solution to the problem of development. Therefore, the additional hypothesis of lexical learning has been introduced. Lexical learning provides the child with a way to fix UG principles at the appropriate values without requiring him or her to learn the principles themselves. In this way the developmental problem may be solved, even under the continuity constraint.

The main conclusion from the previous discussion is that the second approach, that is, continuity plus lexical learning, should be preferred over the MH. The CH establishes a strong learnability constraint and is more parsimonious than the maturationist's view. Therefore, it should not be given up, until the data leave no other choice. This, of course, puts the burden of proof on proponents of the MH. Three areas of child language development, for which maturational schedules have been suggested in the literature, were investigated in this chapter. The evidence in favor of the MH has been shown to be fairly weak, and, in some cases, alternative analyses of the developmental data have been sketched out which did not require any maturation of UG principles. This suggests that the proposed maturational schedules have to be rejected and that the CH can be maintained as a part of the theory of learnability.

ACKNOWLEDGMENT

This chapter is a revised version of a paper presented at a round table on theoretical aspects of language acquisition at the 14th International Congress of Linguists, Berlin, August, 1987.

REFERENCES

Baker, C., & McCarthy, J. (Eds.). (1981). *The logical problem of language acquisition.* Cambridge, MA: MIT Press.

Berwick, R., & Weinberg, A. (1984). *The grammatical basis of linguistic performance.* Cambridge, MA: MIT Press.

Borer, H. (1986). I-subjects. *Linguistic Inquiry, 16,* 375–416.

Borer, H., & Wexler, K. (1987). The maturation of syntax. In T. Roeper & E. Williams (Eds.), *Parameter setting* (pp. 123–172). Dordrecht, The Netherlands: Reidel.

Borer, H., & Wexler, K. (1988). *The acquisition of participle agreement: A maturational account.* Paper presented at the GLOW Colloquium, Budapest, March.

Brown, R. (1973). *A first language. The early stages.* Cambridge, MA: Harvard University Press.

Chomsky, N. (1965). *Aspects of the theory of syntax.* Cambridge, MA: MIT Press.

Chomsky, N. (1981). *Lectures on government and binding.* Dordrecht, The Netherlands: Foris.

Chomsky, N. (1986a). *Knowledge of language: Its nature, origin and use.* New York:Praeger.

Chomsky, N. (1986b). *Barriers.* Cambridge, MA: MIT Press.

Clahsen, H. (1982). *Spracherwerb in der Kindheit. Eine Untersuchung zur Entwicklung der Syntax bei Kleinkindern.* Tübingen; Germany: Narr.

Clahsen, H. (1986). Verb inflections in German child language. Acquisition of agreement markings and the functions they encode. *Linguistics, 24,* 79–121.

Clahsen, H. (1988a). *Normale und gestörte Kindersprache. Linguistische Untersuchungen zum Erwerb von Syntax und Morphologie.* Amsterdam: Benjamins. English translation: (1991). *Child language and developmental dysphasia.* Amsterdam: Benjamins.

Clahsen, H. (1988b). Parameterized grammatical theory and language acquisition. A study of the acquisition of verb placement and inflection by children and adults. In S. Flynn & W. O'Neill (Eds.), *Linguistic theory in second language acquisition* (pp. 47–75). Dordrecht, The Netherlands: Reidel.

Clahsen, H., & Muysken, P. (1986). The availability of Universal Grammar to adult and child learners. A study of the acquisition of German word order. *Second Language Research, 2,* 93–119.

de Haan, G. (1986, March). *A theory-bound approach to the acquisition of verb placement.* Paper presented at the annual meeting of the German Linguistics Association (DGFS), University of Heidelberg, March.

duPlessis, J., Solin, D., Travis, L., & White, L. (1986). UG or not UG, that is the question: A reply to Clahsen and Muysken. *Second Language Research, 3,* 56–75.

Emonds, J. (1976). *A transformational approach to English syntax.* New York: Academic Press.

Felix, S. (1984). Maturational aspects of Universal Grammar. In A. Davies, C. Cripper, & A. Howatt (Eds.), *Interlanguage* (pp. 133–161). Edinburgh: Edinburgh University Press.

Felix, S. (1987). *Cognition and language growth.* Dordrecht, The Netherlands: Foris.

Horgan, D. (1978). The development of the full passive. *Journal of Child Language, 5,* 65–80.

Hyams, N. (1987). The theory of parameters and syntactic development. In T. Roeper & E. Williams (Eds.), *Parameter setting* (pp. 1–22). Dordrecht, The Netherlands: Reidel.

Jordens, P. (1986). *The acquisition of verb categories and word order in Dutch and German: Evidence from first and second language development.* Paper presented at Language Acquisition Research Seminar, Utrecht, March.

Keenan, E. (1982). Passive in the world's languages. In T. Shopen (Ed.), *Linguistic typology and syntactic description* (pp. 243–281). Cambridge, England: Cambridge University Press.

Klein, W. (1981). Some rules of regular ellipsis in German. In W. Klein & W. Levelt (Eds.), *Crossing the boundaries in linguistics. Studies presented to Manfred Bierwisch* (pp. 51–78). Dordrecht, The Netherlands: Reidel.

Kratzer, A. (1984). *On deriving syntactic differences between English and German.* Unpublished Ms., Technische Universität Berlin.

Maratsos, M., & Abramovitch, R. (1975). How children understand full, truncated, and anomalous passives. *Journal of Verbal Learning and Verbal Behavior, 14,* 145–157.

Miller, M. (1976). *Zur Logik der frühkindlichen Sprachentwicklung.* Stuttgart, Germany. Klett (English translation: (1979). *The logic of language development in early childhood.* Berlin, New York: Springer).

Mills, A. (1985). The acquisition of German. In D. Slobin (Ed.), *The cross-linguistic study of language acquisition* (pp. 141–254). Hillsdale, NJ: Lawrence Erlbaum Associates.

Park, T. Z. (1974). *The development of syntax in the child with special reference to German.* Department of Psychology, University of Bern. (Published (1981). Innsbruck: Innsbrucker Beiträge zur Kulturwissenschaft, 45).

Pinker, S. (1984). *Language learnability and language development.* Cambridge, MA: Harvard University Press.

Pinker, S., Lebeaux, D., & Frost, L. (1987). Productivity and constraints in the acquisition of the passive. *Cognition, 26,* 195–267.

Rappaport, M., & Levin, B. (1986). What to do with theta-roles. *Lexicon Project Working Papers II.* Cambridge, MA: MIT Center for Cognitive Science.

Steele, S. (1981). *An encyclopedia of Aux. A study in cross-linguistic equivalence.* Cambridge, MA: MIT Press.

Weinberg, A. (1987). Comments on Borer and Wexler. In T. Roeper & E. Williams (Eds.), *Parameter setting* (pp. 173–187). Dordrecht, the Netherlands: Reidel.

Weiner, E., & Labov, W. (1983). Constraints on the agentless passive. *Journal of Linguistics, 19,* 29–58.

White, L. (1981). *The responsibility of grammatical theory to acquisitional data* (pp. 214–271). In N. Hornstein & D. Lightfoot (Eds.), *Explanation in linguistics.* London: Longman.

Zobl, H. (1986). A functional approach to the attainability of typological targets. *Second Language Research, 2,* 16–32.

4

Maturation and Learning: Linguistic Knowledge and Performance: A Commentary on Clahsen and Felix

Rosemary J. Stevenson
University of Durham, England

The problem of learnability in language acquisition concerns the fact that language is learned from a limited input. The developmental problem concerns the fact that there is a time course to language acquisition during which a consistent pattern of errors occurs before the adult pattern emerges. Borer and Wexler (1987) were among the first (see also Felix, 1987) to observe the benefits of discussing the developmental problem in the context of learnability: Proposed solutions to the combined problem (of development and learnability) increase the range of concepts and data available for solving the learnability problem. Borer and Wexler then proposed that a solution to the developmental problem was the concept of maturation: The innate principles of Universal Grammar mature over time. That is, they are not learned, and—crucially—they do not depend on environmental input. This maturation view contrasted markedly to the continuity view that was generally held at the time. Borer and Wexler pointed out that the established view of workers in the field (including themselves) was the continuity hypothesis (e.g., Hyams, 1986; Wexler & Culicover, 1980). On this view, the developmental problem is solved by assuming that the principles of Universal Grammar are all present from birth but that environmental inputs trigger the availability of these principles during development. These two views are represented in the chapters by Felix and Clahsen in this volume. Felix argues for the maturational view while Clahsen argues for the continuity view.

Both Clahsen and Felix point out that the major empirical claim that distinguishes the two views is whether or not child grammars violate the principles of Universal Grammar. Since the continuity view maintains that all the principles of Universal Grammar are present from birth, then child grammars will not violate those principles. By contrast, the maturational view assumes that the child's grammar is only constrained by those principles that have already matured, hence the grammar may violate those principles that have not yet emerged. The argument, therefore, centers on whether or not there is evidence to suggest that children's early grammars violate principles of Universal Grammar. Felix presents evidence that suggests that they do. Clahsen discusses some of that evidence and argues that it does not hold up under close scrutiny. Consequently, Clahsen argues, the continuity hypothesis can be maintained.

However, both Clahsen and Felix assume that maturation or continuity exhaust the set of possible hypotheses for explaining the developmental problem. But this is not the case. These two hypotheses seem to form extreme cases from a range of hypotheses that could be considered. Here I will introduce two additional ones. One is that the developmental problem may be best solved by assuming that both maturation and lexical learning contribute to language development. The second is that children's errors may be due to a range of nonlinguistic factors and thus may not be relevant to the issues of maturation or continuity at all.

I will suggest here that both the maturational and the continuity hypotheses are biologically plausible. Indeed, there are examples from other biological systems for both of them, but examples of continuity also seem to include maturation. However, I will further suggest that taking child language data at its face value is not sufficient to decide between the two views. This is because the sentences that children produce are not pure reflections of linguistic knowledge. In order to clarify the developmental problem, it is necessary to interpret the experimental data in terms of the nonlinguistic factors that may mask the child's real linguistic ability. More crucially, I will argue that the developmental problem will not be solved until the evidence from child language is considered as evidence for linguistic processing, not for linguistic knowledge. Only in this way is it possible to disentangle the linguistic and nonlinguistic components of performance, and so produce accounts of language development that are not contaminated by nonlinguistic factors. In Sec. 2, I take an example from binding theory to illustrate the way different interpretations can be applied to the same evidence. In the following sections, I will discuss each of the interpretations in turn; maturation, continuity (including continuity plus maturation) and nonlinguistic components of processing.

AN EXAMPLE FROM BINDING THEORY

Principles A and B of binding theory state:

A. An anaphor (e.g., reflexive) must be bound in its minimal governing category (where "bound" means "coindexed with a c-commanding noun phrase").

B. A pronominal (e.g., nonreflexive) must be free in its minimal governing category (where "free" means "not coindexed with a c-commanding noun phrase").

Clearly a knowledge of these constraints is necessary for children both to produce and understand anaphors and pronouns, and a number of people have investigated young children's knowledge of these constraints (e.g., Deutsch, Koster, & Koster, 1986; Jakubowicz, 1984; Lust, 1981; Solan, 1983; Tavakolian, 1978). The general procedure has been to ask children to use toys to act out the sentences containing anaphors or pronouns, and the major observation from these studies is that children use anaphors appropriately before they use pronouns appropriately.

This observation has been interpreted in a number of ways, some of which correspond to different versions of the continuity view. For example, Jakubowicz proposes that children initially assume that pronouns as well as anaphors are subject to Principle A. According to these accounts, the children do know Principles A and B, thus preserving the continuity assumption, but they have not yet learned how pronouns differ from anaphors. Presumably, positive evidence will eventually lead children to reinterpret the lexical items as pronouns, and hence subject to Principle B.

However, the data could also be interpreted in terms of the maturational view. That is, it could be argued, as Felix does in this volume, that Principle B has not yet matured and that is why the errors with pronouns occur.

But there is a third (processing) interpretation of these data (Deutsch et al., 1986; Stevenson & Pickering, 1987). This is that anaphors are acquired more easily than pronouns because the use of anaphors only requires knowledge of Principle A, whereas pronouns are not deterministic in this way. A pronoun may point directly to an object in the situation and have no linguistic antecedent at all, or it may have an antecedent in a prior sentence, or it may have an antecedent in the sentence that contains the pronoun. It is only in the latter case that Principle B applies. Thus, pronouns are acquired more slowly than anaphors because pronouns require the use of nonlinguistic knowledge as well as linguistic knowledge.

MATURATION

The maturation of innate systems irrespective of the environmental input is common in other biological systems. Borer and Wexler (1987) cite the onset of puberty. In the rhesus monkey the corticospinal tract of the nervous system develops throughout the first 6 to 8 months of life. Early on, baby monkeys (up to 2 months) will not execute independent finger movements when picking up food. The adult pattern of picking up is only found after the final neural development of the corticospinal tract. However, young monkeys can still pick up objects, but using the alternative medial brain stem pathways. Indeed, lesions of the corticospinal tract in baby monkeys leads to an adult that has no general motor deficits but which does have an inability to perform fine finger movements (Lawrence & Hopkins, 1972). The point of this example is that the development of fine finger movements is dependent on the anatomical development of a particular neural pathway, which is not completed until some time after birth. Under normal circumstances, this neural system will develop to a more or less set genetic timetable, which is not dependent on environmental triggers.

Thus, a maturational view is certainly a biologically plausible view. However, the data Felix uses to support this position are not particularly convincing. He claims that headless maximal projections at the two-word stage (e.g., "Mommy bathroom" meaning "Mommy is in the bathroom") are due to the late maturation of X-bar theory; that subject–object constructions at the two-word stage are due to late maturation of theta theory; that a variable order of subjects, objects, or verbs in the two-word stage is due to late maturation of case theory; and that errors in producing sentences containing anaphors or pronouns are due to the late maturation of binding theory. Clahsen shows that alternative interpretations are available for much of this evidence. In addition, I would like to make the following points: First, evidence based on two-word utterances can never be decisive. There are many possible ways to interpret two-word utterances, including the possibility that they are based on semantics and not syntax at all (e.g., Bowerman, 1982). Hence, their role as evidence for the use of particular grammars is likely to be weak.

Second, it has already been pointed out that errors in sentences containing pronouns can be interpreted not only in terms of the maturation of binding theory or in terms of continuity, but also in terms of processing demands on the use of pronouns. This point can also be illustrated by considering Principle C of binding theory. Principle C states that R-expressions (e.g., full noun phrases) must be free in the entire sentence. Felix cites data from Solan (1983) to argue that children are not sensitive to the constraint that R-expressions must be free. Solan asked children from 5 to 7 years old to act out sentences, which included the following:

1. He told the horse that the sheep would run around.
2. He hit the horse in the sheep's yard.

3. The horse hit him after the sheep ran around.
4. The horse hit him after the sheep's run.

Felix points out that the pronoun cannot be coreferential with either the horse or the sheep in (1) or (2), because this would violate Principle C. He goes on to point out that a considerable number of children did give coreferential responses to (1) and (2) and not just to (3) and (4). Solan, in fact, argues that the complete set of data (not shown here) supports the idea that the children do have knowledge of Principle C and the c-command constraint, but have not yet learned its exact domain of application. However, if the children do know Principle C, why do they make any errors at all? One likely reason is that the children's performance was affected by factors unrelated to principles of Universal Grammar. For example, the sentences are not ones that would normally be encountered by children, or even adults. Thus it is difficult to interpret the data as support for a maturational view unless it can be clearly shown that adults (who we assume do possess the full grammar) perform very highly on this task.

In an unpublished study, I presented adults (students from Durham University) with Solan's sentences and asked the adults to act out the sentences using toys. The results were clear-cut: The performance of adults was virtually identical to that of the children. For sentence (2) Solan's children produced 16% coreferential responses (Principle C violations), the Durham students produced 33% coreferential responses. For sentences (3) and (4) the results were: (3) Solan's children 31%, Durham students 39%; (4) Solan's children 27%, Durham students 22%, (Sentence 1 was not tested). The crucial observation is that adults produced more Principle C violations than did the children. Solan's own interpretation of his data is that the children avoided an ungrammatical response (in sentence 2) 84% of the time, hence the children indicated that they did know Principle C. Similarly, the adults in the Durham study avoided an ungrammatical response 67% of the time. The adult data would seem to support Solan's interpretation: The children, like the adults, do know Principle C but this knowledge is not always reflected in performance (see also Grimshaw & Rosen, 1990; Stevenson, 1988).

Thus, Felix's evidence in support of maturation is not clear-cut. Furthermore, the analysis of Solan's results, in conjunction with the results from adults, indicates that performance data are not pure guides to underlying grammatical knowledge. This makes the interpretation of the evidence particularly difficult. However, it has been pointed out that maturation is common in other biological systems. For this reason, it cannot be completely ruled out as a plausible candidate for solving the developmental problem, although it does leave open the question of what kind of data could support the hypothesis and of the precise nature of the maturational process, that is, what matures when.

CONTINUITY

Examples of innate principles that require specific environmental triggers are harder to find in other biological systems than are maturational examples. However, in imprinting, there is a genetic predisposition for chicks to follow the mother within a critical period after hatching. If an alternative moving object is seen within this critical period, it can act as a trigger for the subsequent following response. For example, the chick might follow a human experimenter or even a flashing light (Horn, 1979). This is a clear example of how a specific environmental event can trigger a genetically prepared system. However, there are other examples where nonspecific environmental input may be needed for normal development to occur. Such an example is the development of binocular cells in the visual cortex. The development of a cell so that it can respond to input from both eyes follows a clear developmental sequence that requires normal visual input (e.g., Kandel, 1985).

Thus a continuity view is also biologically plausible. Pinker (1984) and Clahsen (this volume) argue that it is also the preferred view on grounds of parsimony and falsifiability. It is a strong hypothesis in that it makes very few assumptions about development. According to Clahsen, the only additional developmental mechanism is the principle of lexical learning, and it is this principle that explains the developmental problem. However, as Clahsen points out, the continuity view runs into difficulties because it does not explain why some constructions develop before others (Borer & Wexler, 1987). That is, it cannot explain why a construction A might appear before a construction B. If the input were strongly ordered, so that the triggering event for construction A occurred before the triggering event for construction B, then this input ordering could solve the problem. But it seems unlikely that the input is strongly ordered in this way. Thus Clahsen appeals to the notion of intake rather than input (White, 1981). Children's sensitivity to the input changes over time.

Clahsen cites Pinker's account of the acquisition of complementizers. Pinker argues that these are acquired late because they are perceptually nonsalient in the input. They are acquired after homophonous prepositions (such as "to"), because the prepositions are in semantically transparent positions. Pinker cites Bloom, Tackeff, and Lahey (1984) to support the view that the same sound is identified as a preposition before it is identified as a complementizer.

But this account is not wholly satisfactory. For example, it leaves open the questions of how and why the child becomes sensitive to prepositions at the relevant time. Why are the triggering data not "noticed" earlier? Pinker's general answer seems to be that sensitivity to the input data depends on increases in the child's knowledge base, increasing access of computational procedures to the knowledge base, and quantitative changes in parameters such as the size of working memory. It is almost certainly the case that these developmental changes will affect children's comprehension of what they hear. But there is still the need to specify precisely the way in which these nonlinguistic developments allow sensitivity to the input to change in ways that are related to changes in the child's use of language.

Furthermore, there is an alternative possibility that may be more parsimonious than the one assumed by Pinker and Clahsen. This is that children are not sensitive to particular features of the input until they have the necessary feature detectors available. That is, the sensitivity to the input might mature. This is certainly the case with imprinting, and also with the development of the visual system. In the examples cited here, a chick's sensitivity to a moving object is confined to a brief critical period. Similarly, the development of binocular cells is only sensitive to the visual input within a highly constrained critical period. The input has no effect until the brain has developed to a certain point. Thus, the biological examples are more compatible with a view that includes maturation rather than one in which innate principles are triggered by lexical learning.

It is certainly the case that the continuity view has produced more detailed explanations of language acquisition than the maturational view. This is because the continuity view has motivated empirical investigations into specific learnability problems. Borer and Wexler (1987) provided a maturation account of the acquisition of passives, which is based on the notion that children are initially unable to form Argument chains. However, their analysis has been queried by Weinberg (1987) and, in addition, the analysis does not address the major learnability question concerning passives. This question, which was originally posed by Baker (1979), concerns the fact that the passive rule does not apply to all verbs. So how do children learn which verbs can occur in passive sentences and which cannot? In fact, Baker pointed out that, for a wide range of constructions, there is no obvious relationship between verbs that occur in those constructions and verbs that do not. The passive construction is one example of this general case, where it has proved particularly difficult to specify exactly what characterizes verbs that can occur in the passive form and verbs that can not.

However, this question has been addressed by Pinker, Lebeaux, and Frost (1987) within the framework of continuity. I will discuss this study in some detail because it illustrates both the merits and the drawbacks of the continuity view. Thus, Pinker et al. point out, for example, that the passive construction involves transitive verbs in English but that not all transitive verbs can occur in the passive form, as the following examples from Pinker et al. show:

(1) The argument escapes many people.
This bottle contains a deadly poison.
John has three bicycles.

(2) Many people are escaped by the argument.
A deadly poison is contained by the bottle.
Three bicycles are had by John.

Obviously, the passive versions in (2) are not grammatical. The problem then, is why and how children do not massively overgeneralize once they discover passive sentences in the language. Baker's solution to this problem was to propose that children are conservative learners. They only use verbs in their passive form if they have already heard them in the passive. Thus, the lexical information in the verbs is learned separately for each verb.

However, if this is the way that children learn passive (among other) constructions, then it makes the learning process a very protracted one. Not only that, it implies that children will only use passives with verbs that they have encountered in the passive form. But this does not seem to be the case. A number of researchers have observed that children do use passives productively. That is, they use passives with verbs that they would not have heard in the passive form. For example, Bowerman (1983) reported one of her daughters saying "If you don't put them in for a very long time they won't get staled," referring to crackers in a bread box. Pinker et al. give other examples from Brown (1973) and other sources.

Given these observations, the problem is not solved, because we still need to know how children grow up to recognize that a sentence like "Three bicycles are had by John" is ungrammatical. The problem seems to have become more difficult with these examples of productivity not easier. Pinker et al. made up novel words to examine how far children from 3 to 8 years old will use them in the passive form when they have not heard them in that form. In particular, Pinker et al. created novel words to test a number of possibilities of how passive verbs might form a coherent set.

For example, Pinker (1982) has suggested that initially children only apply the rule to subjects and objects that are agents and patients respectively. This is the "semantic bootstrapping hypothesis." Children use semantic information to constrain the domain of application of the passive rule. By restricting the passive rule to subjects and objects that are agents and patients the child is able to form some generalizations (to other agent–patient sequences) rather than learning verb by verb. There is evidence to suggest that children comprehend passives containing action verbs, like "hit," more readily than they do passives containing perception verbs, like "see" (e.g., Maratsos, Kuczaj, Fox, & Chalkley, 1979). In addition, such a generalization is possible because all agent–patient verbs do passivize. On the other hand, this is not the correct adult rule, so at some stage the child has to learn that other subject–object combinations can be passivized. Possibly, this is done on a verb by verb basis.

Pinker et al. tested this possibility by creating four novel verbs, two of them action verbs and two of them perception verbs. For example, the nonword "gump" was used to express the action "to rub the back of the neck of," while the nonword "pell" was used to express the perceptual relationship "to hear through an ear-trumpet-like instrument." Children were then taught the meanings of these nonwords in either the active or the passive form. For example, they would be shown two dolls acting together and would hear the sentence "The dog is gumping the elephant." Other children would only hear the passive version: "The elephant is being gumped by the dog." The same procedure was used for the novel perception verbs. The children were then tested on their ability to produce sentences containing these nonwords in either the active or the passive form. They were required to describe the actions of the dolls to the experimenter.

The critical results were those cases where the child learned the active version and produced a passive version of the same verb. These are cases of productivity. The child has generalized from the active to the passive form without ever hearing the verb in its passive form. What Pinker et al. found was that the children were just as likely to passivize the perception verbs as they were the action verbs. Thus, the suggestion that children confine the passive rule to action verbs was not supported. This finding was confirmed in a second study in which the nonwords described either actions or static spatial relationships. Here, too, the children were just as likely to generalize from the active to the passive with spatial verbs as they were with action verbs. It appears, therefore, that children are not conservative learners and that they generalize the passive to new verbs even when they have not heard them in the passive and even when the verbs describe nonactions.

What Pinker et al. propose, therefore, is that children generalize on the basis of the argument structure of the verb. Specifically, they propose that the thematic roles associated with each verb determine whether the verb can be passivized. They argue that Universal Grammar specifies that verbs that can be passivized are those where the underlying subject argument has an agent thematic role and the underlying object argument has a patient thematic role.

To test this proposal, Pinker et al. carried out a third study in which the nonwords described actions that violated this argument structure. For example, they used the nonword, "flooze," in which the argument structure consisted of a theme (or patient) in the subject position and of an agent in the object position. Thus the sentence "The dog floozed the giraffe" meant that the giraffe leapfrogged over the dog. These "anticanonical" verbs were contrasted to canonical verbs with the agent being the subject and the patient the object. In this study, Pinker et al. found that the children were extremely reluctant to passivize the anticanonical verbs when they had only heard them in the active form. This was in contrast to their willingness to passivize canonical verbs in the same situation, and in contrast to their willingness to passivize nonaction verbs in the previous studies.

Thus, there is some support for the notion that children restrict their use of passives to verbs with agent subjects and patient objects. However, as Pinker et al. point out, this does not account for the full range of passives that are possible in English. Neither perception verbs nor spatial verbs could be passivized if this was an absolute rule. Yet children readily passivize such verbs, and these verbs can be passivized in English. Pinker et al. suggest, therefore, that languages vary in the way that these agent–patient thematic roles can be extended to include verbs that do not obviously have this argument structure.

In particular, English defines a large class of verbs that can be interpreted as having an agent–patient argument structure only at an abstract level. For example, some spatial verbs in English are not passivizable at all. These are verbs such as "contain," which cannot be interpreted as having a patient argument. The thing that is contained is not affected by the container in any way. By contrast, some spatial verbs can be passivized. These are verbs such as "surround" or "lined." For example,

The house was surrounded by a moat.

The street was lined by trees.

It turns out that these verbs can also be used in a sense in which the object is affected by the action, and hence can be regarded at one level as having a patient in object position. This can be seen from the following examples:

The landscapers surrounded the house with a lawn.

The planner lined the street with trees.

On the basis of these observations, Pinker et al. suggest that these "abstract" agent–patient verbs have to be learned by young children because the particular range of verbs that can be used in this way is specific to English. However, Pinker also argues that once the child has learned the way the agent–patient verbs can be extended in the language, then the passive rule can be used productively. It can be applied to verbs that have not been heard in the passive form. Thus, Pinker proposes a way out of the problem originally posed by Baker (1979). Children are not conservative learners. Instead, they generalize initially on the basis of "canonical" agent–patient verbs (the action verbs) but rapidly learn the way that these pure agent–patient verbs can be extended to other verbs in the language so that these other verbs can then also be passivized.

This series of experiments shows how the continuity view has been used to address the issue of learnability and illustrates the merits of such an approach. However, the study also highlights the major unanswered question in the continuity view; namely, how do the children come to recognize that some verbs in the language take abstract agent–patient roles? It may be that these verbs are not in the input in the early stages of language acquisition, or it may be that this abstract notion of thematic role is too cognitively complex to be grasped in the early stages. Neither alternative seems particularly likely. The evidence so far does not indicate that the input to the child is strongly ordered, and the child already recognizes the agent–patient relationship in canonical verbs. Thus the question of how sensitivity to the input comes about remains unanswered. It may well be that certain "detectors" in the brain need to mature before the abstract verbs (or argument structures) are detected in the input.

PROCESSING

There is one problem that is common to the arguments of both Clahsen and Felix. This concerns their assumption that inferences about children's grammars can be made on the basis of children's performance. I have already suggested, when discussing Solan's results, that inferences from performance to inferences about knowledge are not straightforward. Studies by Emslie and Stevenson (1981) on the use of referring expressions and by Stevenson and Pollitt (1987) on the use of temporal terms also show that if the task is made simple enough, then children's performance seems to be based on adult-like knowledge. Grimshaw and Rosen (1990) make a similar point in their review of studies on the acquisition of the binding principles. They show that many aspects of performance indicate that children know the binding principles even if they do not obey them. Apart from difficulties associated with particular tasks, Grimshaw and Rosen suggest that children may be complying with a discourse-level constraint that pronouns normally have linguistic antecedents. Rather than violate this constraint, children may violate the binding principles.

The findings of Stevenson and Pickering (1987) also suggest that linguistic knowledge of Principles A and B is intact in young children. They found that the pragmatic plausibility of a context sentence, which preceded the sentence containing the pronoun, had no effect on childrens' selections of sentence-internal antecedents for either pronouns or anaphors. However, the plausibility of the context did affect the frequency of choosing the person mentioned in the context sentence as the antecedent of a pronoun. Thus, (pragmatic) discourse-level processes and (syntactic) sentence-level processes did not interact. Furthermore, Stevenson and Pickering found that the children made very few errors of interpretation with either anaphors (5%) or pronouns (11%). These results suggest that children do have knowledge of Principles A and B. What takes time to develop is the integration of sentence-level and discourse-level processes in the interpretation of pronouns. Goodluck (1990) suggests that the late development of pronouns as opposed to anaphors may be accounted for by the assumption (e.g., Forster, 1979) that the integration of sentence-level and discourse-level factors only occurs at a late stage in linguistic processing.

The use of a performance model to clarify the nature of children's knowledge underlying language use can also be illustrated by a study by Goodluck and Tavakolian (1982). They carried out a series of experiments to investigate the way children interpret relative clauses. They propose that children 4 to 5 do make use of the c-command constraint at the level of competence. They also propose that performance is affected by a language processor that is sensitive to aspects of the sentence that increase the memory load.

Goodluck and Tavakolian presented children with active and passive sentences containing either relative clauses or temporal participial complements, and required them to act out the situations described by the sentences. Examples of their sentences are the following:

Active relative:
The boy hits the girl that jumps over the fence.

Passive relative:
The boy is hit by the girl that jumps over the fence.

Active participial:
The boy hits the girl after jumping the fence.

Passive participial:
The boy is hit by the girl after jumping the fence.

Goodluck and Tavakolian found that the children interpreted the relatives as coreferential with the object of the matrix sentence, regardless of whether the active or passive version was presented. However, only the active temporal participials were interpreted as coreferential with the object. The passive construction led to an increase in subject coreference responses. Goodluck and Tavakolian suggested that the data support the view that children's grammatical knowledge concerning c-command constraints on the interpretation of empty noun phrases was the same as adult knowledge. The fact that performance was never 100% was attributed to the suggestion that the sentence processor is affected by features of the sentence that affect memory load.

For example, children find sentences with animate direct objects more difficult to process than sentences with inanimate direct objects. They showed that this was the case in their first experiment where they asked children to act out the situations described by sentences containing relative clauses containing either an animate object:

The dog kicks the horse that knocks over the sheep.

or an inanimate object:

The dog kicks the horse that knocks over the table.

They found that children were much more likely to act out the sentence correctly when the relative clause contained an inanimate object than when it contained an animate object. Goodluck and Tavakolian explain this additional difficulty with an animate object in terms of Frazier and Fodor's (1978) model of sentence processing. Frazier and Fodor propose that there are two stages involved in processing (or parsing) a sentence. In the first stage, the processor analyzes a restricted range of words as they are heard and attempts to build up a syntactic structure for these words without regard for the overall structure of the sentence being analyzed. The limits on this stage are limits on the capacity of working memory. It is likely that this capacity is limited by features such as time and number of words as well as by structural complexity. Once the capacity of working memory is exceeded, the least current material is passed to the second stage of the parser. In this second stage, the processor can complete the analysis and can revise it in the light of the overall structure of the sentence that has been constructed so far.

Goodluck and Tavakolian suggest that children can analyze the complete relative clause when it contains an inanimate object in the first parsing stage. This allows the relative to be attached to the correct antecedent because it is still in working memory. However, they suggest that an animate object in the relative clause adds sufficient additional difficulty for working memory to be overloaded so that the matrix sentence is passed to the second stage before the relative can be attached to the c-commanding noun phrase. This means that the relative clause has no potential antecedent in the first stage so can only be interpreted in the second stage. They also propose that in the second stage, the children are more likely to attach the relative clause to the Sentence node than to the NP node, which means that the only noun phrase that c-commands the relative is the subject of the sentence. Hence, the children make more (subject) errors when relative clauses contain animate as opposed to inanimate object.

This study suggests that children do know the c-command constraint of Universal Grammar, but the application of this knowledge interacts with the operation of the processor in children's performance. Thus, the data are compatible with the continuity view rather than the maturational view: Children do have the Principles of Universal Grammar available right from the start, but that knowledge may not be revealed in performance. Similarly, with binding theory: The analyses by Grimshaw and Rosen (1988), Goodluck (1990) and Stevenson and Pickering (1987) all suggest that the binding principles are available to the child, but these principles may not be revealed in performance, which is subject to additional discourse-level factors and general limitations on the integration of linguistic and non-linguistic processing.

Overall, then, the evidence seems to support the continuity view. However, the role of the environment in this view remains unclear. Clahsen suggests that children's sensitivity to the input changes with age. But this proposal only begs the question of how these changes in sensitivity come about. One possibility is that sensitivity matures, just as sensitivity to the environment "matures" during the development of binocular vision. Alternatively, it may be that a full account of the development of linguistic processing will render this environmental aspect of continuity redundant, since changes in proposed sensitivity may turn out instead to be due to developmental changes in processing.

REFERENCES

Baker, C. L. (1979). Syntactic theory and the projection problem. *Linguistic Inquiry, 10,* 533–581.

Bloom, L., Tackeff, J., & Lahey, M. (1984). Learning "to" in complement constructions. *Journal of Child Language, 11,* 391–406.

Borer, H., & Wexler, K. (1987). The maturation of syntax. In T. Roeper & E. Williams (Eds), *Parameter setting.* Dordrecht, the Netherlands: Reidel.

Bowerman, M. (1983). How do children avoid constructing an overly general grammar in the absence of feedback about what is not a sentence? *Papers and Reports on Child Language Development, 22,* Stanford, CA: Stanford University Department of Linguistics.

Brown, R. (1973). *A first language: The early stages.* Cambridge, MA: MIT Press.

Deutsch, W. C., Koster, C., & Koster, J. (1986). What can we learn from children's errors in understanding anaphora?, *Linguistics, 24,* 203–225.

Emslie, H. C., & Stevenson, R. J. (1981). Pre-school children's use of the articles in definite and indefinite referring expressions. *Journal of Child Language, 8,* 313–328.

Felix, S. (1987). *Cognition and language growth.* Dordrecht, the Netherlands: Foris.

Forster, K. (1979). Levels of processing and the structure of the sentence processor. In W. Cooper & W. Walker (Eds.), *Sentence processing.* Hillsdale, NJ: Lawrence Erlbaum Associates.

Frazier, L., & Fodor, J. D. (1978). The sausage machine: A new two stage parsing model. Cognition, 6, 291–325.

Goodluck, H. (1990). Knowledge integration in processing and acquisition: Comments on Grimshaw and Rosen. In L. Frazier & J. de Villiers (Eds.), *Language acquisition and language processing.* Dordrecht, the Netherlands: Reidel.

Goodluck, H., & Tavakolian, S. (1982). Competence and processing of children's grammar of relative clauses. *Cognition,* 11, 1–27.

Grimshaw, J., & Rosen, C. (1990). Knowledge and obedience: The developmental status of the binding theory. *Linguistic Inquiry, 21,* 187–222.

Horn, G. (1979). Imprinting—in search of neural mechanisms. *Trends in Neuroscience, 2,* 219–222.

Hyams, N. (1986). *Language acquisition and the theory of parameters.* Dordrecht, the Netherlands: Reidel.

Jakubowicz, C. (1984). On markedness and binding principles. *Proceedings of the Northeastern Linguistics Society, 14,* 154–182.

Kandel, E. R. (1985). Early experience, critical periods, and developmental fine tuning of brain and architecture. In E. R. Kandel & J. H. Schwartz (Eds.), *principles of neural science* (2d edit.). New York: Elsevier.

Lawrence, D. G., & Hopkins, D. A. (1972). Developmental aspects of pyramidal motor control in the rhesus monkey. *Brain Research, 40,* 117–118.

Lust, B. (1981). Constraints on anaphora in child language: A prediction for a universal. In S. Tavakolian (Ed.), *Language acquisition and linguistic theory,* Cambridge, MA: MIT Press.

Maratsos, M., Kuczaj, S. A., Fox, D. E., & Chalkley, M. A. (1979). Some empirical studies in the acquisition of transformational relations: passives, negatives and the past tense. In W. A. Collins (Ed.), *Minnesota Symposium on Child Psychology* (Vol. 12), Hillsdale, NJ: Lawrence Erlbaum Associates.

Pinker, S. (1982). A theory of the acquisition of Pescical interpretive grammars. In J. Bresnan (Ed.), *The mental representation of grammatical relatione.* Cambridge, MA: MIT Press.

Pinker, S. (1984). *Language learnability and language development,* Cambridge, MA: Harvard University Press.

Pinker, S., Lebeaux, D. S., & Frost, L. A. (1987). Productivity and constraints in the acquisition of the passive. *Cognition, 15,* 195–267.

Solan, L. (1983). *Pronominal reference: Child language and the theory of grammar.* Dordrecht, the Netherlands: Reidel.

Stevenson, R. J. (1988). *Models of language development.* Milton Keynes, England: Open University Press.

Stevenson, R. J., & Pickering, M. (1987). The effects of linguistic and non-linguistic knowledge on the acquisition of pronouns. In P. Griffiths (Ed.), *Proceedings of the Child Language Seminar,* York University, York, England.

Stevenson, R. J., & Pollitt, C. (1987). The acquisition of temporal terms. *Journal of Child Language, 14,* 533–545.

Tavakolian, S. (1978). Children's comprehension of pronominal subjects and missing subjects in complicated sentences. In H. Goodluck & L. Solan (Eds.), *Papers in the structure and development of child language.* University of Massachusetts Occasional Papers on Linguistics, Vol. 4, Amherst.

Weinberg, A. (1987). Comments on Borer and Wexler. In T. Roeper & E. Williams (Eds.), *Parameter setting*. Dordrecht, the Netherlands: Reidel.

Wexler, K., & Culicover, P. (1980). *Formal principles of language acquisition*. Cambridge, MA: MIT Press.

White, L. (1981). The responsibility of grammatical theory to acquisitional data. In N. Hornstein & D. Lightfoot (Eds.), *Explanation in linguistics*. London: Longman.

5 The Catapult Hypothesis: An Approach to Unlearning

Janet H. Randall
Northeastern University

PARAMETRIC VS. NON-PARAMETRIC LEARNING: TRADITIONAL ASSUMPTIONS

The "principles and parameters" approach to linguistic theory has spawned a flurry of research in language acquisition linking the source of learners' errors and their eventual disappearance to the setting and resetting of hypothesized linguistic parameters. Under parametric accounts of language, Universal Grammar provides a small number of parameters each with two (or more) settings. When these differently set parameters are combined, the result is the array of innately possible grammars, exhibiting the major structural differences that we see between languages.

The head parameter provides an example of how a single parameter works (Williams, 1981). This parameter determines where the head of a syntactic phrase is positioned, given two possibilities, head-first or head-last. A minimum of primary data allows the learner to set the parameter for one type of phrase and then, assuming uniformity across phrase types, to impose the same structure automatically on other phrases. This parameter setting has consequences for other syntactic choices; the direction of government and the possibility and direction of movement are determined by the location of the phrasal head.[1]

---

[1]Other hypothesized parameters govern the choice of syntactic domain for anaphor and pronoun binding (Wexler & Manzini, 1987) and the possibility for null subjects (Hyams, 1987, 1989). Subparameters have also been proposed (Nishigauchi & Roeper, 1987).

(1) a.

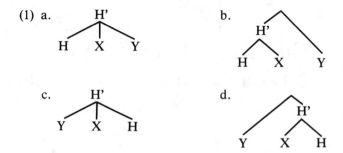

In learning a language under the parametric model, the learner figures out which way her language goes on each parameter by identifying primary linguistic data consistent with one of its settings. And because many syntactic facts follow from a single parameter, many types of input are available to determine each parameter setting and later, to reset parameters that were initially set incorrectly. The parameter setting model, in this way, explains how learners can have the major structural facts of their languages figured out early, and explains how errors in structural properties of the language can be corrected with primary data alone.[2]

For all its success at charting the course of syntactic errors, however, parameter theory has not been applied to another cache of errors: those involving the properties of lexical items. If we divide errors into what we might call "parametric" errors (i.e., those errors made on parametric-ally determined aspects of the language, and hence, correctable through resetting a parameter) and "nonparametric" errors (those not) then it is clear why lexical errors are nonparametric errors. Parametric errors are highly detectable because a parameter is set to allow certain structures while disallowing others, but nonparametric errors are not detectable, because there is no relationship between two elements in the language such that if one is included the other is excluded. To put it another way, parameters allow only **one** ultimate setting, so forms resulting from other settings are ruled out. But forms not determined by a parameter are not limited; **all** options are potentially available, and no form is obviously incorrect.

---

[2]Valian (1990b) rejects the idea that parameters are initially set. She argues that they are initially unset, and that learners weigh the evidence for one setting over another. This version of parameter theory would be compatible with the discussion that follows. Valian also discusses and critiques the parameter-setting literature, in particular the null-subject parameter.

Lexical information fits into the nonparametric category. Verbs with similar semantics have different argument structures (*leave* NP but *depart* PP); adjectives idiosyncratically form nouns in *-ity* or in *-ness* (*curious* + *ity* but *furious* + *ness*); verbs allow either two alternative complement structures, or only one (*give* [NP PP] and [NP NP]; *deliver*[NP PP] but not [NP NP]). So the existence of one form does not exclude the existence of another.

To sum up, whereas a parameter embodies an either/or logic—all the forms it governs either behave this way or that way, but not some mixture of ways—lexical items don't fit the either/or model in any obvious way. This has led to the standard view, under which parametric and nonparametric errors are worlds apart. The assumption is that the behavior of lexical item *x* cannot force lexical item *y* to behave one way or another, and from this it follows that theories proposed for learning the lexicon must be quite different from those proposed for learning the syntax. To see what these differences entail, let us review two theories of how lexical facts are learned.

1.1 Learning from Positive Input

The well-known "learning from positive input" theory (Baker, 1979; Dell, 1981), otherwise known as the "conservative learning" theory, tackles the question of how learners acquire the argument structures of semantically similar but syntactically different verbs. Two verbs just mentioned, *give* and *deliver,* which are indistinguishable on most counts, have different syntactic patterns:

(2) *give* [$_{NP}$a package][$_{PP}$to Mary]   *deliver* [$_{NP}$a package][$_{PP}$to Mary]
    give [$_{NP}$Mary][$_{NP}$a package]   **deliver* [$_{NP}$ Mary][$_{NP}$a package]

If learners construct rules about lexical classes of items based on a small sample of the data, generalizing from the verbs they hear in a context to those they haven't yet heard but consider otherwise similar, then what will prevent them from incorrectly generalizing the NP NP complement possibility available for *give* to *deliver?* The theory argues that with no systematic or guaranteed correction, learners must be conservative, and classify a verb only after hearing it in its syntactic environments. They must wait for positive input for each verb, and register the verb in its attested syntactic frames, in item-by-item fashion.

The "learning from positive input" theory fell down, however, in the face of the evidence. As is now well documented, probably the most visible errors that language learners make are overgeneralization errors (Bowerman, 1982a, 1982b, 1988). *I disappeared it, Erica bringed me a cookie,* and

Don't say me that are hallmarks of early speech, attesting to the fact that learners, finding two verbs similar in certain ways, **do** assume that they are similar in one more. With "learning from positive input" no longer an option, other accounts of lexical learning were needed. In marched the learning mechanisms.

1.2 Learning Mechanisms: A Preview

According to some accounts, (e.g., Braine's, 1971, 1988), learners can only figure out which words behave in what ways by essentially keeping a running tally. Having incorrectly overgeneralized a rule, they can retreat if they have registered and counted the input and kept track of which forms occur in which syntactic (and other) environments. From this record they can surmise which forms do and which forms don't undergo particular rules, and eventually conclude that a word they originally thought obeyed a rule does not.[3] A related model is the "Criteria Approach" (Mazurkewich & White, 1984; Pinker, 1984, 1989), where learners must identify the characteristics of items undergoing a rule. When they do, the rule is checked, and whenever possible, tightened, the characteristics imposed as "criteria" on which items the rule may apply to. Items that fail the tighter criteria are forced out of the rule's domain.

We will look at these accounts with greater scrutiny in Section 5, where we compare them with our own proposal for lexical learning. For now let us just suggest that by requiring the learner to keep track of, count, or weigh the input, or to scour words for similarities and differences along every potential dimension without knowing in advance which ones will be relevant, these proposals seem prima facie difficult to justify. Given their need for additional learning machinery to count and scour, it isn't clear what advantages these accounts have over earlier acquisition models which relied on "negative evidence."[4] Both require something more, something not obviously available, and as such they compare poorly with a model like parameter-setting, in which acquisition—in particular, the sticky problem of retreat from overgeneralizations—follows just from the facts of the grammar itself.[5]

---

[3]A much more detailed discussion of this approach and the following one is given in Bowerman (1987, 1988).

[4]Negative evidence is evidence that certain forms are ungrammatical in a particular language. Although somewhat controversial, the consensus (since Brown & Hanlon, 1970) has been that negative evidence is neither generally nor reliably available as a good source of information for first-language learners.

[5]It must be stressed that we are not ruling out the possibility that the learner may notice distributional regularities in her input. Valian (1990b), citing Valian (1990a) points to "considerable evidence . . . that young children are sensitive to patterns of occurrence and

1.3 Retort: An Unsystematic Lexicon?

The basic obstacle to curing lexical overgeneralizations is the assumption that the lexicon is unsystematic, the warehouse of unruly information about words. However, if one property of a lexical item is predictable from another property or properties of other lexical items, then the problem of acquiring lexical information changes, since there are then many ways to identify lexical classes and relationships. As we will show, a systematic lexicon doesn't require the double-barreled learning mechanisms that an unruly lexicon does. Overgeneralization errors in a rule-governed lexicon will yield to the same parametric logic as syntactic errors, where the learner is guided by a set of exclusive either/or choices. Lexical learning can then be explained with a model of acquisition, which, just like parameter setting, needs no machinery besides the grammar itself.

The claim we will make is that the grammar provides "Catapults," generalizations, which like parameters are structured to exclude certain possibilities while including others. How catapults can solve the lexical overgeneralization problem is the topic of the next three sections.

2. CATAPULTS

2.1 The Logic of Catapults

Consider the simplest parametric system, one with two parameter settings. The learner sets the parameter to be consistent with the data as she perceives them. However, if this choice is incorrect, further data from the input will contradict it and trigger a switch to the other setting. This is the sequence in Hyams's (1986) account of the null-subject parameter. English learners initially choose the null-subject setting, allowing them to produce subject-less sentences such as *ride truck* and *no morning*. Later, they recognize that English contains nonthematic expletive subjects, as in *it's not raining* and *there's no more,* data that show that English cannot be a null-subject language, since languages with null subjects don't have expletives. With this

---

co-occurrence, substitutability, and other types of distributional regularities," and her account of how the null-subject parameter is set relies on the child observing distributional patterns of where subjects are omitted in her language. Valian offers this account, however, because she finds the parametric account for learning about null subjects unworkable. But Valian herself would prefer a parametric account could one be made to work. See Roeper and Weissenborn (1990) and Weissenborn (this volume) for discussion. It is not clear to us which account of null subjects is the correct one, but what is clear is that where possible, we would steer away from learning accounts that rely on the learner continuously registering co-occurrence patterns in her language.

either/or logic about languages built into the child (**either** null subjects **or** expletives, but not both), expletives in the input can trigger a switch from the null-subject value of the parameter to the no-null-subjects value. Thus, by tolerating either setting A or setting B—but not both—the parameter allows positive information to have a negative impact, with the parameter doing the work.

Notice that the parameter permits the learner to go from the initial assumption "null subjects are allowed" to the opposite conclusion "null subjects are not allowed." As is often noted, the data alone could not have triggered this retreat, since although every sentence the English child encountered would have contained a subject, no sentence would have explicitly shown that a null subject is ruled out.[6] It is the parametric connection between null subjects and expletives that gets retreat to happen, the exclusive **either** null subjects **or** expletives.[7]

The logic of parameters follows an ancient formula, **Modus Ponendo Tollens** given in (3a). (3b) is logically equivalent.

(3) MODUS PONENDO TOLLENS

a.　　　　　　　　　　　Either A or B (exclusive *or*)

　　　　　　　　　　　　A

　　　　　　　　　　　　----------------

　　　therefore:　　not B

b.　　　　　　　　　　　If A then not B

　　　　　　　　　　　　A

　　　　　　　　　　　　----------------

　　　therefore:　　not B

In this case, A = the language contains expletives, and B = the language allows null subjects. Once learners find out that the language contains expletives, they conclude that it does not allow null subjects.

Pictorially, parameters work on what we might call the "Catapult Principle." They have the basic shape in (4), the simple mechanical device used in a circus teeter-board or seesaw.

---

[6]As pointed out by Valian (1990a), there is a certain amount of contradictory input, even in non-null-subject languages such as English: "Seems like a good idea." These types of examples, however, may be innocuous. See Roeper and Weissenborn (1990) and Weissenborn (this volume) for discussion.

[7]Note that this sort of retreat is not a case of moving from a larger to a smaller set, which would violate the Subset Principle (Dell, 1981; Berwick, 1982, 1985). The trigger for resetting the parameter is the presence in the data of the expletive pronouns, *it* or *there,* not present *as such* in the initial grammar. So while it is true that the set of grammatical sentences shrinks from those with both null subjects and non-null subjects to those with only non-null subjects, the set at the same time expands to incorporate expletives.

(4) THE CATAPULT

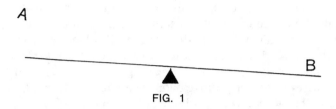

FIG. 1

When incoming data (A) land on the high end, current incorrect assumptions (B) on the low end are catapulted out. The parameter does not accommodate both.

What's important about the fact that parameters are catapults is that there exist catapults that are not parameters. The criticism has been leveled against parameter theory that parameters are proliferating; for every decision the learner makes, we now posit a parameter. But this is not necessary. There are many relationships in the grammar of the form "If A then not B." Wherever these exist, a mechanism that does the job of a parameter is available, even if a parameter is not justified.

2.2 The Catapult Hypothesis

Catapults are a powerful tool in language acquisition. They form the basis of the parameter-setting theory, but they can also operate in domains that are not parametrically governed. We might hypothesize that *wherever* learners overgeneralize, there is a grammatical catapult to dislodge their errors. In other words, we might adopt a "Catapult Hypothesis," (5), as a research strategy for how the lexicon, as well as the syntax, is learned.

(5) CATAPULT HYPOTHESIS:
   For every overgeneralization,
         a) the grammar contains a disjunctive principle, P,
            [either A or B (exclusive)]
   and b) the primary data exhibits A (or B).

The Catapult Hypothesis states that there will be primary data, which together with a principle of grammar, will undo every overgeneralization that a learner makes.

One caveat must be noted about (5). While it gives the possibility for retreat, it has nothing to say about when retreat will occur. In fact, there are at least two reasons why retreat may not be instantaneous. First, the data must be recognized as relevant to the overgeneralization. A learner may in fact have heard the critical piece of triggering data, A, but may have interpreted it incorrectly, in a way which does not threaten the coexistence of the violating B. In this case, B will stay around for a period alongside A, and will not be forced out until it is seen as being in direct conflict with it. Instantaneous retreat would also be delayed if what we might call the "trigger threshold" hasn't been reached — if the learner has not seen a sufficient number of tokens for triggering to occur. The question of threshold arises whenever positive data are invoked in learning (basically, all the time) but we know surprisingly little about it. All one can say for certain is that there is probably a threshold, and noninstantaneity may be the result of its not being reached.

An illustration is in order. One principle with an obvious Catapult structure is the Uniqueness Principle (Wexler, cited in Roeper 1981; see also the Principle of Contrast, Clark, 1987).

(6) **Uniqueness Principle:** In the unmarked case, each deep structure is realized as one and only one surface structure.

If one surface structure (A) is understood as the realization of a particular deep structure form, then the appearance (and persistence) of a second surface structure form with the same function (B) will drive the first one out. The principle has been applied to the unlearning of incorrect inflectional forms. For past tenses, for instance, the sequence of attested forms is generally first the correct irregular *went,* then the overregular *goed,* then back to *went.* The sequence adheres to the Uniqueness Principle: (i) Primary data present *went,* (ii) a rule is learned that supplies *goed* (and rules always take precedence over individual items), but (iii) *went* persists in the primary data, while *goed* does not so (iv) the balance is ultimately changed again, *went* driving out *goed.* There are some learners, however, who seem to allow two past tense forms for one verb, both *goed* and *went* simultaneously, in apparent violation of the Uniqueness Principle. But suppose that in these learners' grammars the forms belong to different paradigms. Then *went* would have nothing to do with *goed* and should not dislodge it. Evidence for this two-paradigm hypothesis comes from the existence of *wented* (Kuczaj, 1977; Clark, personal communication), which shows that *went* is assumed not to be the past tense of *go,* but a verb in its own right, with its own, unique, past tense form. The learner must eventually collapse the two paradigms, and interpret *went* as related to *go,* then the Uniqueness Principle will continue to apply, but this time forcing one to drive out the other.[8] To summarize, delay is the result not of the Uniqueness Principle

---

[8]Pinker (1984) gives an alternative account of the inflectional acquisition sequence based on the learner's limited processing capacity.

not applying, nor to the absence of triggering data, but to the learner's realization that the data and the principle go together.

The Uniqueness Principle provides a neat but limited illustration of how Catapults work, since although it operates in the inflectional system, where the simple "If A then not B" formula holds for virtually all forms, there are few other lexical facts that it governs.[9] But having proposed that there will be a catapult-shaped principle for each lexical error, we now must identify some candidates. In the following section we introduce two principles of X-bar theory, both substantive principles that govern the behavior of lexical items.

3. X-BAR PRINCIPLES

3.1 The Order Principle

The Order Principle (formulated slightly differently in Randall, 1985; 1987) governs the order of obligatory and optional arguments with respect to their phrasal head. Optional arguments must occur outside of obligatory arguments. (7) phrases it as a conditional, revealing its catapult "If A then not B" shape.

(7) **The Order Principle:** If a argument is optional, then it may not intervene between a head and an obligatory argument.

In left-headed languages like English, phrases must have the form in (8a), not (8b). Right-headed languages allow (8c) but not (8d).[10]

(8) a. [H' [H X (Y)]]   b. [H' [*H (X) Y]]

---

[9]However, we will return to the Uniqueness Principle in Sects. 4.2 and 5.1, where it plays a different but crucial role in retreat.

[10]In fact, the Order Principle may follow from other grammatical principles and not be a separate principle of its own. Case Theory requires all NPs to be case-marked; obligatory NP arguments, therefore, will be adjacent to the verb, in order to receive case. No verbs appear to exist in English that take an obligatory oblique object and an optional direct object. Verbs with two obligatory NPs require an additional stipulation, since the second NP must also receive case. There are competing accounts, among them, Chomsky (1981), Kayne (1983), Larson (1988), Baker (1988).

c.

(Y)   X   H

H'

d.

*Y   (X)   H

H'

The Order Principle can be illustrated with English VPs. The cases in (9) require a direct object NP and permit an additional PP argument. The order must be NP (PP).[11,12]

(9) a. Pablo invited [Doris] ([to the art opening]).
Juliet got [directions] ([from Romeo]).
Alice collected [those recipes] ([from her travels]).
Dylan spent [a lot of money] ([on drink]).
    b. Pablo invited (*[to the art opening]) [Doris].
Juliet got (*[from Romeo]) [directions].
Alice collected (*[from her travels]) [those recipes].
Dylan spent (*[on drink]) [a lot of money].

Dative cases like (10), which take a direct object and a *to-* or *for*-PP, obey the principle.[13] So do resultatives in (11), which require an NP followed by an XP maximal projection: NP, AP or PP (Carrier & Randall, 1989).

---

[11]It is possible to violate the Order Principle under special, marked, conditions; for example, when the direct object is a heavy NP:

(i) a. Pablo invited (to the art opening) all the prospective buyers he could find.
    b. Juliet got (from Romeo) directions to their appointed meeting place.
    c. Alice collected (from her travels) many recipes requiring truffles.
    d. Dylan spent (on drink) all of the royalties that he earned on his last two books.

See Rochemont (1986) for a discussion of this and other focus constructions, and Erteschik-Shir (1979) for discourse effects on datives.

[12]This formulation may be too strong for other languages. In French, for instance, adverbs may intervene, and Dutch and German allow certain optional NPs. There are a number of ways that these counterexamples to the Order Principle may be handled. For example, adverbs have been proposed to be invisible in French, otherwise case-assignment under adjacency would not hold. An alternative, also proposed for German and Dutch, is that case is assigned under adjacency but that scrambling subsequently applies (see Pollock, 1989, for discussion). We will not take a position on these possibilities here; but certainly more must be said about the Order Principle in other languages.

[13]The cases in (10) are from Fischer (1971). She observed, "unless the direct object is complex [i.e., heavy], if there is a *to*-phrase or a *for*-phrase, it must come after the direct object in surface structure."

(10) a. John brought a candy bar to Bill.
         Karen got a new tie for Fred.
     b. *John brought to Bill a candy bar.
         *Karen got for Fred a new tie.

(11) a. They danced the sailors dizzy.
         They walked their feet to tatters.
         The gardener watered the tulips flat.
         The jeweler rubbed the gems to a glossy shine.
     b. *They danced dizzy the sailors.
         *They walked to tatters their feet.
         *The gardener watered flat the tulips.
         *The jeweler rubbed to a glossy shine the gems.

Before we see how the Order Principle allows learners to retreat from their overgeneralization errors, we turn to a second principle of X-bar theory.

3.2 The Attachment Principle

The relative attachment of arguments and adjuncts is governed by what we will term the Attachment Principle. Arguments, selected by the head, must be sisters of the head, inside H'. Adjuncts, which are not specified in lexical entries of specific lexical items, attach freely, adjoining outside the lowest H'.

(12)

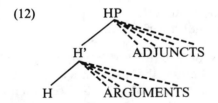

The Attachment Principle is another instance of a catapult. Stated as a conditional, it has the "If A then not B" structure, (13).

   (13) **The Attachment Principle:** If a constituent is an adjunct, then it
        may not intervene between a head and its arguments.

3.3 The Principles as Diagnostics

Before we turn to how the learner uses these two X-bar principles, let us see how they work in the adult grammar as diagnostics for the attachment site of constituents in phrase structure.

3.3.1 Dative for vs. Benefactive for

The Attachment Principle provides syntactic evidence about whether a constituent is an argument or an adjunct. In this way it can be used to distinguish two types of *for*-phrases, those in (14a), usually called "dative" *for*-phrases and those in (14b), BENEFACTIVE phrases. The thematic role that these dative *for*-phrases express is RECIPIENT (Jackendoff 1990), so we will use this term. In contrast, the BENEFACTIVE *for*-phrases mean, essentially "on behalf of".

(14) a. The architect is drawing a plan [for the clients]$_{REC}$.
    The chef is cooking his specialty [for us]$_{REC}$.
 b. The teaching assistant taught the class [for the professor]$_{BEN}$.
    The valet parks the bigwigs' cars [for them]$_{BEN}$.

(15) shows that when both are used, only one of the two possible orders is grammatical: RECIPIENTS must precede BENEFACTIVES.[14]

(15) a.   With the chief architect too busy to draw a plan for the clients, his assistant will draw one [for them]$_{REC}$ [fór him]$_{BEN}$.
 b.   *With the chief architect too busy to draw a plan for the clients, his assistant will draw one [for him]$_{BEN}$[for them]$_{REC}$.

Were they both adjuncts they could be reversed, as (16), with two locative adjuncts, shows:

(16) a. Mary slept [in her car] [in the woods].
 b. Mary slept [in the woods] [in her car].

Therefore, either both are arguments, or RECIPIENTS are arguments and BENEFACTIVES are adjuncts. (17) confirms the latter, since locative and temporal phrases, known adjuncts, may precede BENEFACTIVES but not RECIPIENTS.[15]

(17) a. *The architect is drawing a plan [in his studio] for the clients.
    *The art teacher bought pastels [at Woolworth's] for his class.
    *The chef is cooking his specialty [tonight] for us.
 b. The valet parks the bigwigs' cars [in the garage] for them.
    The teaching assistant taught the class on Wednesday [for the professor].

---

[14]The second *for* must be stressed in (15a); notice that no stress pattern can make (17b) interpretable.

[15]The judgments are relative. The (a) cases are perhaps not totally bizarre, but they are certainly several degrees worse than either the (b) cases or the cases in (c, d).

John's in charge of making the kids their breakfast, but
Mary makes them breakfast [sometimes] fór him.

We can conclude that the attachment sites are as in (18):

(18)

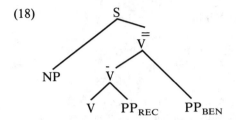

Having established that RECIPIENT *for*-datives phrases like (14a) are
arguments, we can see how they parallel *to*-dative arguments, which also
cannot be separated from their verb by an adjunct.

(19) *Romeo gave those posies [on June 3] to Juliet.
      *Cressida sends poems [sometimes] to Troilus.
      *Hamlet lent this book [tonight] to Horatio.
      *Gertrude showed the recipe [in the garden] to Polonius.

Like *to* forms, RECIPIENTS participate in the double object NP NP
alternation. Note that the double object forms of both types satisfy the
often-noted semantic requirement (see Mazurkewich & White, 1984, and
references cited there). The NP adjacent to the verb must be the "prospective possessor" of the second NP.

(20) a. give   a package *to Mary*
      b. give   *Mary* a package

(21) a. The artist is drawing a picture *for Edie.*
      b. The artist is drawing *Edie* a picture.

Returning, now, to BENEFACTIVES, notice that as adjuncts they don't
participate in the alternation, which is reserved for arguments. Moreover,
the BENEFACTIVE "on behalf of" meaning is incompatible with the
prospective possessor requirement.

(22) *The valet is parking *Edie* her car.

There has been a certain amount of confusion concerning which *for*-
phrases alternate, because verbs which standardly take BENEFAC-

TIVE *for,* such as (23), occasionally surface in a double-object form, (24), suggesting that here the *for* phrase is really a RECIPIENT argument.

(23) a. Jeeves washed the dishes for me.
         The butler opened a cabinet for little Arthur.
         The assistant brushed Hilda's hair for her.
     b. *Jeeves washed me the dishes.
         *The butler opened little Arthur a cabinet.
         *The assistant brushed Hilda her hair.

(24) Jeeves washed me a cup (so I could have some coffee).
      The butler opened little Arthur a bottle of Perrier.
      The assistant brushed the hairdresser a wig (to put on the mannequin).

And, in fact, the first objects in (24) *are* RECIPIENTS. The reason that these verbs only sometimes allow the NP NP alternate form is that in most contexts, like (23), they create no product for a "prospective possessor" to possess. When a possessible product *is* created, as in (24), the *for* NP can be a RECIPIENT and the requirement for the NP NP form is met (Carrier & Randall, in press).

One further fact is relevant to the RECIPIENT double-object alternation. Where the semantic condition is met, the RECIPIENT object can be expressed *either* as an NP **or** in a *for*-phrase, but not both.[16]

(25) *The architect is drawing [the clients] a plan [for the clients].
      *Jeeves washed [me] a cup [for me].

3.3.2 RECIPIENT for vs. Goal for

One more set of *for*-phrases, (26a), can be distinguished from both BENEFACTIVE and RECIPIENT *for.* They do not alternate, and so they are clearly not RECIPIENT arguments.[17]

(26) a. The actors read a few scenes for the director.
     b. *The actors read the director a few scenes.

---

[16]I am assuming some version of the Theta-criterion (Chomsky, 1981), which allows each thematic role that a verb assigns to be realized once and only once in the argument structure of that verb. This is a simplification that suffices for the purpose here; for a more refined version of the Theta-criterion and discussion, see Carrier and Randall (1989, in press).

[17]There is, of course, a double object form for *read* but it corresponds to the *to* PP argument case: *We read the director the message.*

Rather they appear to be adjuncts, as (27) and (28) illustrate. They align with BENEFACTIVES (17b), not RECIPIENTS (17a), in permitting adjuncts to separate them from their head verb. And when they appear with a BENEFACTIVE, they switch positions freely.

(27) The actors read a few scenes [last night/on location] for the director.

(28) a. The understudy read a few scenes [for the director] [for the regular actor].
b. The understudy read a few scenes [for the regular actor] [for the director].

However, these phrases aren't BENEFACTIVES themselves, since they don't mean "on behalf of." We will call these adjunct *for*-PPs "GOAL *for*s." They attach outside V'.

3.3.3 A Question of Representation

Before concluding our discussion of the Attachment Principle, we must solve one apparent problem. It might be claimed that the double-object construction in (21b), in which *Edie* seems to be an optional constituent, poses a counterexample to the first X-bar principle we discussed, the Order Principle, because this optional NP *Edie* precedes the obligatory object NP, *a picture*. If *draw* is represented as either (29) or (30), then this is so.

(29) draw a. THEME (RECIPIENT)
b. (RECIPIENT) THEME

(30) draw a. THEME RECIPIENT
b. (RECIPIENT) THEME

However, there is another way to represent the argument structure of *draw,* which does not violate the Order Principle, and which is better motivated on other grounds.

(31) draw a. THEME (RECIPIENT)
b. RECIPIENT THEME

If parentheses actually encode information about alternate forms of a verb then (31) claims that *draw* with a single postverbal THEME argument is more closely related to *draw* with two-postverbal arguments in the order THEME-RECIPIENT than it is to the double-object RECIPIENT-

THEME version. An equivalent representation is (32), which posits two basic verbs *draw,* a verb with a single internal THEME argument, to which a RECIPIENT can be added, and a double-object verb with the order RECIPIENT-THEME. In both, what is maintained is the grouping: the THEME-RECIPIENT case is a variant of the single THEME object form, and is completely independent of the RECIPIENT-THEME structure.

(32) a. draw   THEME
                THEME RECIPIENT
     b. draw   RECIPIENT THEME

Is there any basis for preferring (31) (or its equivalent (32)) over (29) and (30)? One reason is the semantic difference between the THEME-RECIPIENT and RECIPIENT-THEME versions of verbs of this type. While the RECIPIENT-THEME double object form requires that the RECIPIENT be the prospective possessor of the theme, the THEME-RECIPIENT form does not. And neither does the basic single postverbal THEME argument form. We could explain this semantic distribution if we assumed that (32a) and (32b) correspond to two different semantic structures, and that the THEME-RECIPIENT form is derived from the underlying THEME form by "tacking on" an optional RECIPIENT.[18]

A suggestion along these lines has been made for verbs that participate in the "locative alternation," (33) (Rappaport & Levin, 1984, 1988).

(33) a. load the truck with cartons
     b. load cartons into the truck

Like the dative alternation, the locative alternation exhibits a near but not exact paraphrase. According to Rappaport and Levin, in (33a) the LOCATION (*the truck*) is understood as "wholly affected by the action denoted by the verb. When this argument is realized as the object of a preposition, a partially affected interpretation is also possible. In (33a) [their (9b)] the truck is full of cartons, but this is not necessarily so in (33b) [their (9a)]." Rappaport and Levin argue that for this reason (as well as others which we will not discuss here) the two variants must be independent, with separate lexical semantic representations.[19] In this way, meaning components can be

---

[18]My earlier interpretation of the distinction (Randall, 1987) led me to group the THEME-RECIPIENT variant of verbs like *draw, paint, read, write* with the other three-argument variant of these verbs and not with the single-object case. While this captured the semantic distinction between the double-object (RECIPIENT-THEME) and single-object (THEME) forms, it missed the parallelism between the single-object form and the THEME-RECIPIENT variant, which this analysis achieves.

[19]The proposal is stated in terms of two separate Lexical Conceptual Structures (LCSs), where the meanings of the two forms is encoded. Thematic roles are labels for more primitive

present in one variant but lacking in the other.

Semantic intuitions lead to a similar conclusion for a verb such as *stack,* which takes either a single THEME postverbal argument (*He stacked the books*) or two postverbal arguments in either order (*He stacked the books on the shelf; He stacked the shelf with books*). Here, the form with a single postverbal argument, *stack* with a THEME, is the basic form and the full form with the additional argument in (34a) can be derived from it by adding a LOCATION. (34b), with the arguments reversed, would be a separate case. For *draw,* parallel reasoning would derive the full form in (35a), with a RECIPIENT, from the more basic form without it. (35b) would be independent. This coincides with our choice in (31).

(34) a. stack THEME (LOCATION)
     b. stack LOCATION THEME

(35) a. draw THEME (RECIPIENT)
     b. draw RECIPIENT THEME

One point which will be important in the discussion later on is that the single postverbal argument form of a verb like *draw* (*paint, read, write*) (i.e., *draw* NP) is quite different from the single postverbal argument forms of verbs like *give* or *bring,* which occasionally surface but leave the impression that something is "understood" or "missing" (indicated with a #).

(36) a. The architect drew a plan.
         Pablo painted a picture.
     b. #John brought wine.
        #Susan gave five dollars.

This difference supports distinguishing these cases. *Draw* has a grammatical version with a single postverbal argument, while *bring* or *give,* as we will show, require two postverbal arguments, but may omit one in situations that contextually supply it.[20]

To conclude, we have argued that *draw* cannot be given either of the

---

LCS arguments. We agree that ultimately LCS is the correct level at which verbs are represented (see Carrier & Randall, in press, for explicit arguments); however, in this chapter we will continue to use more abbreviated thematic or categorial notations, since the details of LCS notation are not critical to our arguments.

[20]This possibility for implicit arguments is similar to the omission of the object in cases such as *John ate.* See Rizzi (1986), and Randall (1987), for further discussion.

representations that would violate the Order Principle but must be represented as in (31), or (32), where the optional argument is outside the
obligatory argument, just as the Order Principle requires.

4. PRINCIPLES AS CATAPULTS FOR LEARNING ARGUMENT STRUCTURES

Let us now turn to how the Order Principle and the Attachment Principle
can be used by the learner to retreat from several classes of lexical
overgeneralizations.

4.1 The Order Principle

The errors to which the Order Principle applies involve a head and its
arguments. We will examine three classes of errors in which the Order
Principle forces retreat from overgeneralization: dative verbs, and the
"inverse" verb classes, the *fill* class and the *spill* class.[21]

4.1.1 to- Dative Overgeneralizations

Both spontaneous utterances like (37a) (Bowerman, 1987) and experimental intuitive judgment data (37b) (Mazurkewich & White, 1984) fall into
the category of *to-* dative overgeneralizations.[22] Overgeneralized elicitations
with nonsense verbs are also reported (Gropen & Pinker, 1986), though we
will not discuss those here.

(37) a. *Don't say me that or you'll make me cry. (C, 2;6)
        *I said her *no*. (C, 3;1)
     b. *David suggested Ruth the trip
        *Susan explained Jane the problem
        *John reported the police the accident
        *Cathy described Lisa the movie

The learner's problem with the non-alternating *deliver*-class verbs in (37)
is that she has assumed that they are parallel to verbs of the *give*-class, (38),
which allow both a *to-* dative PP (a) and a double object (b) form.

---

[21]The first argument based on the Order Principle was first published as Randall (1985) and
in more expanded form (1987).

[22]The judgment data were gathered in an intuitive judgment test, in an experiment originally
reported in Mazurkewich (1982). A full report of the experimental design and results is
available in Mazurkewich and White (1984).

(38) a. Romeo gave those posies to Juliet.
   Cressida sent a poem to Troilus.
   Hamlet lent this book to Horatio.
   Gertrude showed the recipe to Polonius.
   Cordelia told the news to her father.
   b. Romeo gave Juliet those posies.
   Cressida sent Troilus a poem.
   Hamlet lent Horatio this book.
   Gertrude showed Polonius the recipe.
   Cordelia told her father the news.

Having overgeneralized the rule which identifies a verb's membership in one class with membership in the other, and hearing nothing in the primary data to indicate otherwise, the learner assumes that the two classes look alike:

(39) a. deliver   NP PP
                   NP NP
     b. give   NP PP
                   NP NP

How can she find out which verbs are miscategorized?

The solution is based on an unnoticed fact about *deliver*-class verbs. Unlike *give*-class verbs, *deliver*-class verbs can appear with just a direct object NP. Except in marked cases, *give*-class verbs cannot.

(40) a. *Romeo gave those posies.
        *Cressida sent a poem.
        *Hamlet lent this book.
        *Gertrude showed the recipe.
        *Cordelia told the news.
     b. Romeo delivered the posies.
         Cressida recited a poem.
         Hamlet described this book.
         Gertrude explained the recipe.
         Cordelia reported the news.

Learners will hear cases of single-object *deliver* but never single-object *give*. At this point the entry for *deliver* can be revised: (39a) becomes (41a); (39b) repeated in (41b), stays as before:

(41) a. deliver   NP (PP)
                   (NP) NP

    b. give   NP PP
               NP NP

But this resulting structure is now subject to the Order Principle, repeated here:

(7) *The Order Principle:* if an argument is optional then it may not intervene between a head and an obligatory argument.

Deliver's optional NP may not intervene between the verb and its obligatory NP. The second *deliver* entry must be discarded, leaving (42). Example (43) restates the principle in Catapult terms.

(42) a. deliver   NP (PP)
     b. give   NP PP
                  NP NP

(43)   If A then not B   [A = NP is optional]
                                     [B = Optional NP may intervene
                                         between *deliver* &
                  A   obligatory NP
                  ----
    therefore   not B

The learner retreats from the overgeneral rule, selectively discarding the NP NP possibility for each verb that he or she encounters with a single NP. *Give*-class verbs will not be affected because they do not occur with a single NP object.[23]

To summarize so far, we have successfully shown how the learner can undo overgeneralizations of her rule for *to*-datives, through the interaction of the Order Principle and specific pieces of data.

Before turning to the next set of errors that the Order Principle can undo, we should discuss what happens if a learner applies the Order Principle incorrectly, to verbs of the *give* class, after having heard one of the pragmatically controlled "understood argument" cases we saw in (36). To a learner trying to assign verbs to subclasses, it is not obvious whether

---

[23]Bowerman (1988) asks why children would overgeneralize in the first place if data with a single NP are available all along. This question assumes that verbs with single objects are more frequent than verbs with two objects, for each learner for each verb. This is unlikely. Rather, the frequency difference may be true overall but violated for particular verbs in each learner's experience. And it may be just those verbs that each learner overgeneralizes. Empirical work, which we are beginning, will test the issue.

sentences like *Susan gave five dollars* actually require the context they're uttered in, or are simply grammatical regardless of context. A learner hearing this sentence would add parentheses to her *give* entry, creating (44), and then drop the second line, leaving (45).

(44) give   NP (PP)
             (NP) NP

(45) give   NP (PP)

Sometimes called benign errors (Baker, 1979) or positive exceptions (Bowerman, 1988), this type of error is not fatal. Double-object primary data like (38b) will always be available for *give,* and will eventually oblige the learner to reinstate NP NP. This double-object line will be added without parentheses, in compliance with the Order Principle. The parentheses will be removed from the NP (PP) line remaining in (45), to prevent the two lines from contradicting one another.[24] She must then conclude that the single NP cases in the input like (36) came about via elipsis, and the correct entry, (46) will result:

(46) give   NP PP
             NP NP

Overretreat, then, is reparable. While *give*-class verbs do sometimes appear with single objects, they show up in their NP NP forms eventually, and force reanalysis. Since *deliver*-class verbs never appear with double objects, they will not be reanalyzed and retreat will hold.

---

[24]Leaving the parentheses in (45) and then reinstating the NP NP line would result in (i).

(i) give   NP (PP)
            NP NP

The contradiction comes from the possibility of a single NP available in the top line, but not in the bottom. I assume that such contradictory situations are unstable, and will be avoided by the learner as she revises her entries. Note that this situation is not parallel to verbs like *draw* and other members of this class, *bake, cook, sketch, peel, write, read,* where as we argued in Section 3.3.3, we have two separate verbs with two separate semantic structures. What would be a contradictory situation for a single verb is allowed to exist here, because the two lines belong to two separate verb entries.

Although I will not explore the possibility here, it is possible that these sorts of contradictions are what lead the learner to set up two separate homophonous verbs in the first place. They would be maintained as long as the semantics continued to justify them.

4.1.2 Fill and Spill Overgeneralizations

A catapult parallel to the one for dative-verb overgeneralizations elimi-
nates two other sets of errors, involving verbs with two postverbal
arguments, like *fill* and *spill*. *Fill* and *spill* are "inverse" verb classes in that
they both take a THEME and a LOCATION, but in opposite orders:

(47) a. *fill   THEME   LOCATION
     b. fill LOCATION THEME

(48) a. spill   THEME   LOCATION
     b. *spill LOCATION THEME

Learners assume that verbs in these classes belong to the class of "*spray/
load*" verbs, whose two postverbal arguments are freely ordered.[25]

(49) a. [THEME] [LOCATION]
         Mary sprayed [paint] [on the wall].
         Mary loaded [hay] [into the truck].
     b. [LOCATION] [THEME]
         Mary sprayed [the wall] [with paint].
         Mary loaded [the truck] [with hay].

Errors reported in Bowerman (1982b) show *spill*-class verbs in the (49b)
structure and *fill*-class verbs in the (49a) form.

(50) errors with *fill*-class verbs
         *Can I fill some salt into the bear? (E 5;0)
         *I'm going to cover a screen over me. (E 4;5)

(51) errors with *spill*-class verbs
         *I don't want it because I spilled it of orange juice. (E 4;11)
         *I poured you with water. (E. 2;11)

We can surmise that both types of nonalternating verbs are represented
schematically in the learner's lexicon like alternating *spray*-type verbs.

(52) a. spray THEME   LOCATION
     b. spray LOCATION THEME

---

[25]Instead of representing the category of the verbs' arguments, as earlier, here we present
their thematic roles: (a) [THEME] [LOCATION] or (b) [LOCATION] [THEME].

(53) a. fill   THEME   LOCATION
     b. fill   LOCATION   THEME

(54) a. spill THEME   LOCATION
     b. spill LOCATION   THEME

The solution, once again, lies in which arguments are optional and which are obligatory. And once again, the Order Principle is relevant. For verbs like *fill,* the LOCATION but not the THEME will occur alone in primary data.

(55) a. Mary filled [$_{LOC}$the jug] [$_{TH}$ with orange juice].
     b. Mary filled the jug.
     c. *Mary filled (with) orange juice.

(55) will lead the learner to parenthesize the THEME argument in her representation, converting the incorrect (47) to (56).

(56) a. *fill (THEME)   LOCATION
     b.   fill LOCATION   (THEME)

(56a), though, violates the Order Principle: An optional argument precedes an obligatory argument. It must be thrown out and the correct (56b) remains.

A similar scenario will eject *spill*-class overgeneralizations like (48b). These verbs allow only (57a, 57b) but not (57c): the THEME but not the LOCATION may appear alone.

(57) a. Mary spilled [$_{TH}$ some water] [$_{LOC}$ on the cat].
     b. Mary spilled some water.
     c. *Mary spilled (on) the cat.

Data like (57b) force the learner to alter (48) by parenthesizing the LOCATION, as shown in (58). But once again an Order Principle violation results. The (b) cases must be dropped; the grammatical (58a) cases will remain.

(58) a. spill THEME   (LOCATION)
     b. *spill (LOCATION) THEME

Having taken care of overgeneralizations of both types of nonalternating verbs, the alternating *spray* class now looks like a problem.

(59) a. spray   THEME   LOCATION
     b. spray   LOCATION   THEME

Here the THEME argument is optional.

(60) Mary sprayed the wall (with paint).

And adding parentheses to (59a) would lead to an Order Principle violation, and force the learner to throw it out as ungrammatical.

(61) a. *spray   (THEME)   LOCATION
     b. spray   LOCATION   (THEME)

Notice, though, that overretreat here is solved just as it was earlier. The (61a) cases will recur in the primary data and can be reinstated in a separate entry specifying both arguments as obligatory. The single postverbal argument version will be represented as a variant of the LOCATION-THEME version, with the THEME optional.

(62) a. spray   THEME   LOCATION
     b. spray   LOCATION   (THEME)

These representations match those we proposed for *draw* in Sec. 3.3.3: one verb has two obligatory postverbal arguments; a second verb has a single obligatory object, and its meaning can — but needn't — be enhanced with an additional argument.[26] Thus, as we argued, it is misleading to think of the THEME-LOCATION and LOCATION-THEME forms of *spray* as "alternating" forms of the same verb. They have different meanings and different syntactic realizations.

In sum, a learner can move from an incorrect grammar, in which a verb is *assumed* to allow two argument structure possibilities when it allows only one, to a correct grammar, in which one of the two possibilities is dropped. What does the work is positive data, by telling the learner that certain elements in her lexical representation are optional, and the Order Principle, which stipulates where optional and obligatory elements must go.

Before leaving these verb classes, there is one other thing to note. We have been able to show how the errors in (50) and (51) are corrected under the assumption that in the learner's grammar, these two classes are understood as verbs with two postverbal arguments, with both THEME and LOCATION obligatory. Another possibility is that the verbs are under-

---

[26]They are the inverse of those for *stack* and *draw,* whose optional argument is LOCATION.

stood as having only one obligatory and one optional postverbal argument, but the verb classes they belong to are reversed. In other words, the learner may have the adult representations for the two classes, but just have assigned each verb to the wrong one:

(63) a. *fill   THEME   (LOCATION)
     b. *spill LOCATION (THEME)

There is support for this in several of Bowerman's examples. *Pour,* a verb of the *spill*-class, occurs first with only a LOCATION.

(64) E (2;11) Pour, pour, pour, Mommy. I poured you. [waving
              empty container near M.]
     M You poured me?
     E Yeah, with water. [= poured water on you]

And the same learner uses *fill* with the THEME alone.

(65) a. E (4;1) I didn't fill water up to drink it, I filled it [=water] up
              for the flowers to drink it.
              [= filling [$_{LOC}$ the watering can] [$_{TH}$ with water]]
     b. E (4;11) And I'll give you these eggs you can fill up
              [giving M beads to put into chicken-shaped container]

Another error with a *fill*-class verb shows that a different child believes the THEME is obligatory.

(66) M Simon says, "Touch your toes."
     C (4;3) To what? [interprets toes as 'figure', is looking now for
              'ground'.
              [a moment later]
     M Simon says, "Touch your knees."
     C To what?

These learners appear to know that there are verbs which take a single LOCATIVE NP, and that there are others which take a single THEME NP. Example (65) reveals that the learner knows the *with*-THEME option. In all cases, the error is simply that the verb has been assigned to the wrong class.

The learner in these examples is obviously not ready to retreat, despite the available data. When she is, though, more examples like *touch your toes* will trigger her representation to change from (67a) to (b). Since this is an unstable Order Principle violation, it will then change to (c).

(67) a. touch   THEME   (LOCATION)
     b. touch   (THEME)   LOCATION
     c. touch   LOCATION

Finally, additional data like *touch your toes with your pinky* can supply the additional optional THEME, resulting in the correct adult representation (68).

(68) touch LOCATION (THEME)

4.2 The Attachment Principle

4.2.1 Benefactive for-Phrase Overgeneralizations

Let us now return to the second principle of X-bar syntax, which can act as a Catapult in dislodging learners' errors (this proposal comes from White, 1986). Recall that the Attachment Principle requires arguments to hang inside of adjuncts with respect to a head in phrase structure. As we saw, the principle distinguishes between the attachment sites of two varieties of *for*-PPs in English, RECIPIENT *for* and BENEFACTIVE *for*.

(69) a. The architect is drawing a plan [for the clients]$_{DAT}$.
       The chef is cooking his specialty [for us]$_{DAT}$.
    b. The teaching assistant taught the class [for the professor]$_{BEN}$.
       The valet parks the bigwigs' cars [for them]$_{BEN}$.

RECIPIENT *for* phrases, as arguments, must hang inside V'; BENEFACTIVE *for*s, as adjuncts, hang outside V'.

(70)   (= 18)

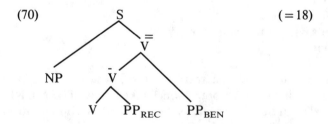

We also saw that *for*-PP arguments that can be expressed alternately in NP NP double object forms impose an additional "prospective possessor" proviso on their indirect object. As a result, a verb cannot participate in the "dative alternation" rule unless it can be interpreted as creating a product that the indirect object can possess.

(71) Jeeves washed me [*the dishes/a cup].
The butler opened little Arthur [*a cabinet/a bottle of Perrier].
The assistant brushed the hairdresser [*her hair/a wig for the mannequin].

Learners mistakenly assume that the rule holds of other verbs that allow a *for*-phrase. Taking alternating verbs like (72) as their model, they create (73). They clearly do not impose the semantic restriction; their verbs appear in contexts that do not result in a transfer of possession.[27]

(72) a. Bake a cake [for the birthday boy].
        I'll draw a picture [for you].
     b. Bake [the birthday boy] a cake.
        I'll draw [you] a picture.

(73) a. Button the rest for me.
        I'll brush his hair for him.
        Mummy, open the door for Hadwen.
     b. *Button me the rest.   (from White, 1986)
        *I'll brush him his hair.
        *Mummy, open Hadwen the door.

It is also clear that the learners' rule is a lexical rule, taking a verb with NP *for*-NP as its input and creating as output a verb with a new, NP NP, argument structure. Since lexical rules operate only inside X', within the domain of a head (e.g., to a verb and its sisters), learners must assume that the *for*-phrases in (73) are arguments, attached inside V'.

(74) a.

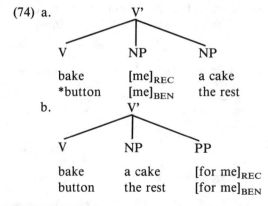

<hr/>

[27]We are dealing here with the three-argument *bake* and *draw,* which, as we have discussed, are represented in different lexical entries from the two-argument forms. The same distinction would hold for (71).

Here is where the Attachment Principle becomes relevant.

The problem is how the learner can figure out that the benefactive *for*s aren't attached in the same place as the RECIPIENT *for*s, but rather outside V'. Data that can trigger this realization are (75), where a locative phrase or time adverbial, each one an indisputable adjunct, precedes the BENEFACTIVE *for*-phrase:

(75) The valet parks the bigwigs' cars [in the garage] for them.
The teaching assistant taught the class [on Wednesday] for the professor.
John's in charge of making the kids their breakfast, but Mary makes them breakfast [sometimes] fór him.

As stipulated by the Attachment Principle, if an adjunct appears inside another constituent such as a *for*-PP then this constituent must also be an adjunct and not an argument. If a phrase is not an argument then a lexical argument-shifting rule such as the learner's dative alternation can't apply to it. Forms like (73b) are dropped.[28]

Before concluding this discussion, two questions arise: First, how radically or conservatively does retreat happen? White (1986) assumes that this procedure happens verb by verb. If so, then for a period of time, a learner could attach BENEFACTIVES in two different places, as an adjunct for some verbs and as an argument for others, depending on whether the particular verb had occurred in her data in a context like (75). However, here, conservative retreat isn't justified. Where BENEFACTIVES attach isn't a lexical fact but a syntactic fact about PPs, which holds regardless of a particular verb's argument structure. Contrary to White's assumption, we must assume that the learner applies the new information to all *for* BENEFACTIVES. Then a single example like (75) will indicate that for *all* verbs — not just *park* or *teach* or *make* — BENEFACTIVE *for*-phrases attach outside V'.[29]

---

[28]This solution, of course, rests on the assumption that *for*-phrases hang in a unique position in the tree. Such a caveat follows from the Uniqueness Principle, discussed in Sec. 1; (or alternatively the Principle of Contrast, Clark, 1987) which requires that each base form correspond to one surface form. When learners discover that *for*-BENEFACTIVES hang outside V' then they must conclude that they do not hang inside, because one position precludes the other. We return to the Uniqueness Principle in Sec. 5.1.

[29]This would be predicted by the following condition on how learners use information.

(i) The Domain Condition: Principles apply by domain.

According to (i), in the domain of the lexicon, learners will behave conservatively; elsewhere, they will take the radical course. It's useful to contrast this radical retreat story with the learners' conservative retreat we traced out earlier for *deliver* class verbs. Recall that for *deliver,* as (iia) illustrates, what the learner discovers from the primary data is a lexical fact,

A second question concerns the learner's confusion between RECIPIENTS and BENEFACTIVES. What is really being confused? Is it really that she differentiates dative from BENEFACTIVE *for* phrases but only attaches both inside V', a pure attachment error, or could it be that she doesn't distinguish between RECIPIENT and BENEFACTIVE *for* at all? Under this second scenario, the *for* phrases in (24)'s, *open a bottle for Arthur* and *open a cabinet for Arthur,* would both be arguments and also both examples of the same thematic role, perhaps some cross between RECIPIENTS and BENEFACTIVES. When "cabinet-*for*" is confirmed as an adjunct via the syntactic trigger, the learner will do one of two things. (1) Look for a meaning difference between "cabinet-*for*" (now a certified adjunct) and the other *fors* (still possibly arguments), to support the syntactic distinction. This would be the correct outcome. (2) Assign adjunct status to all the neutralized *for*-phrases, maintaining their semantic unity. This would be a case of overretreat, but a harmless one. Later-encountered double object cases would mark RECIPIENT *for*-phrases as arguments, forcing the learner to reconsider. She would then look for another feature distinguishing the alternators from the adjuncts, and eventually tease apart the two types of *fors*.

To return to the main point and briefly recapitulate: The Attachment Principle account we have just given is another case of a Catapult, since the Attachment Principle has the "If A then not B" form.

(76)   If A then not B   [A = a constituent C can
                                          be separated from
                                          its head by an adjunct
                                       [B = constituent C is an
                                          argument
                 A
                 ----
      therefore not B

The constituent C in question is a *for* BENEFACTIVE phrase. Since it is not an argument, it must be an adjunct. The learner changes her attachment

---

that a certain verb's argument is optional, thus the domain must be the lexicon and retreat is conservative.

(ii) a. deliver *(NP) NP
     b. [$_V$, makes them breakfast *[$_{BEN}$]] [$_{ADJUNCT}$ sometimes] [$_{BEN}$ fór him]

But with *for* BENEFACTIVES, in (iib) what she learns is a syntactic fact about the attachment site of a kind of PP. What she initially thought was part of argument structure is not. This nonlexical fact allows her to reanalyze her structures en masse, for all cases where BENEFACTIVES occur. For further discussion, see Randall (1990), 1381–1406.

of *for*-PPs which have a BENEFACTIVE reading; other phrases are not affected.

4.2.2 Goal for-phrase Overgeneralizations

We have seen how the Attachment Principle provides the necessary catapult to rescue learners who overgeneralize their dative rule to BENE-FACTIVE *for*-phrases. However, one more set of forms is as yet unsolved, "GOAL *for*" cases, (77), which as we have noted, are semantically distinct from "on behalf of" BENEFACTIVES.

> (77) a. *The actors read the director a few scenes.
>   b. The actors read a few scenes for the director.

Because of this difference, learners' retreat from BENEFACTIVE has no effect on any *for* GOAL overgeneralizations they might make. Reported cases are rare, but these examples with *choose* if not BENEFACTIVES might be GOALS (Bowerman, 1987):

> (78) C (2;6)   I want Daddy choose me what to have. (Re: what kind
>   of juice to have at breakfast)
>   M (5+)   Choose me the ones that I can have.

Can we extend White's benefactive solution to handle cases like these? The answer is yes. Parallel to BENEFACTIVE *for* phrases, GOAL *for* phrases permit intervening adjuncts.

> (79) The actors read a few scenes [last night] for the director.

Again, one piece of positive data will suffice for all GOAL *for* phrases, correctly forcing learners to treat them as adjuncts and not arguments, and thereby getting them out of the scope of the argument-based dative alternation.

4.2.3 Learning the Semantic Restriction

In sum, the syntax provides the learner with a way to recognize and discard all double object violations mistakenly created from adjuncts. And there is an interesting side-effect of this solution: The semantic constraint is now learnable. Notice that once BENEFACTIVE and GOAL *for*- phrases are outside the scope of the dative rule, a correlation crops up between *for*-phrases that have a "prospective possessor" meaning and *for*- phrases that alternate. Observing this correlation, the learner can add a semantic constraint onto her rule and use it to restrict the rule in the future.

4.2.4 An Alternative Account of Spray-, Stack-, Spill- and Fill-class Verbs

Jackendoff (1987) takes the "separate-verb" treatment we gave for *spray* class verbs in 4.1.2 one step further, analyzing *with*-THEME PPs (*with paint* in (49b) and *with orange juice* in (55a)) not as optional arguments but as adjuncts, attached outside the V domain. *Fill*-class verbs would be analyzed the same way, as two-argument verbs, with an added THEME adjunct. If this analysis is correct, then the Attachment Principle is now relevant.

Recall that after retreat from overgeneralizations via the Order Principle, learners' grammars look like (80).

(80) a. spray THEME   LOCATION
        spray LOCATION   (THEME)

     b. stack THEME   (LOCATION)
        stack LOCATION   THEME

     c. spill THEME   (LOCATION)
     d. fill   LOCATION   (THEME)

Hearing primary data like (81) in which an adjunct like *yesterday* is inside a *with*-THEME would trigger the learner to reassign the optional *with*-THEME phrases outside the V' argument level altogether, resulting in the representations in (82).

(81) a. ?She sprayed the truck [yesterday][with red paint].
     b. ?She filled three jugs [yesterday][with orange juice].

(82) a. spray THEME   LOCATION
        spray LOCATION
     b. fill   LOCATION

A similar scenario would apply to the locative phrases in (83), if they also turned out to be adjuncts. Then (80b) and (c) could, with these data and the Attachment Principle, be reanalyzed as (84a) and (b).

(83) a. ?She stacked the magazines [yesterday][on the shelves].
     b. ?She spilled a glass of water [yesterday][on the cat].

(84) a. stack THEME
        stack LOCATION   THEME
     b. spill THEME

It is not clear that these phrases really are adjuncts, however. For many speakers, the examples in (81) and (83) are both questionable. Other intervening adjuncts sound ungrammatical.

(85) a. *She sprayed the truck [on May 1][with red paint].
     b. *She filled three jugs [at 3:00][with orange juice].

(86) a. *She stacked the magazines [on May 1][on the shelves].
     b. *She spilled a glass of water [at 3:00][on the cat].

For these speakers, as for Rappaport and Levin (1988), the *with*-THEME and LOCATIVES that these verbs take are arguments. There are speaker differences, however, and Jackendoff's dialect must be accounted for, too. What we have shown is that either way, via the Order Principle for the argument analysis, or via the Order Principle plus the Attachment Principle for the adjunct analysis, retreat from overgeneralizations is possible.

5. SOME EXISTING ACCOUNTS OF LEXICAL RETREAT: WHERE LEARNING MECHANISMS FALL SHORT

The Catapult model, where the grammar's own principles are the lever in the acquisition machine, contrasts with other accounts of how acquisition works. In this section, two are presented. What is interesting is what they require the learner to do.[30]

5.1 Reinforcement, Data-weighing, and Other Quantitative Approaches

One proposal requires the learner to monitor the input for regularities, both syntactic properties that occur across sentences and lexical properties of individual items. In Braine's (1971, 1988) model, the learner passes this information through a series of intermediate memory stores, until the more frequent properties finally move into permanent memory. This has the effect of a sieve: Properties registered by mistake will drop out for lack of reinforcement, never making it to the final grammar.

Consider how Braine's model would apply to a learner who overgeneralizes the affixation rule for plurals and creates *foots*. Since subsequent data

---

[30]An extremely lucid and complete discussion of approaches to how learners retreat from overgeneralizations is Bowerman (1988). Since we are sacrificing breadth for depth here by concentrating on a small number of problems and an even smaller number of solutions, we refer the reader to that article for a bigger picture.

will provide contain more instances of *feet* than *foots, feet* will stay and *foots* will drop out. What the learner registers from the input depends on her capacities at a particular time. So for example, if she has not yet formulated a general rule, she may first use an incorrect, more specific rule. This would account for the U-shaped curves sometimes found in lexical learning (e.g., *feet — foots — feet*.)

Two complications surface in Braine's model. First, consider the *feet* example. Presumably, during the time that the irregular *feet* is reinforced in the input, the regular rule for plurals is reinforced too, for each regular plural that occurs. So although *foots* itself won't be reinforced, the rule will be, and the learner's ability to use it creatively will allow *foots* to continue to vie with the well-documented *feet*.[31] To solve this problem, something like the Uniqueness Principle, which we have discussed, is required, to force the learner to assume that only one of the two plural forms can be correct.[32]

(87) *Uniqueness Principle:* In the unmarked case, each deep structure is realized as one and only one surface structure. (Wexler, cited in Roeper, 1981)

Applied to the case in question, (87) is understood as (88):

(88) *Uniqueness Principle for plurals:* In the unmarked case, each noun has one and only one plural form.

But now notice that (88), like all instances of (87), is a principle with a catapult "If A then not B" structure.

(89)   If A   [A = *feet* is the plural of *foot*
             then not B   [B = *foots* is the flural of *foot*
             A
             ----
    therefore   not B

Unless such a principle is operating, there is nothing to keep the learner from using the two forms alongside each other; the irregular one reinforced with positive input, the regular one the result of the constantly reinforced general plural rule.[33]

---

[31]The same problem arises for other pre-emption theories (e.g., Bybee & Slobin, 1982; Kuczaj, 1977).

[32]The Principle of Contrast (Clark, 1987) would work here as well. Of course, either case requires an additional assumption: that it is the encountered form and not the self-generated form that is retained.

[33]A reasonable question to ask here is: Why doesn't the Uniqueness Principle operate from

The second issue is that even if we beef up the Sieve Theory with a principle to allow the learner to decide between competing forms, this only works when there is a substitute form to "drive out" the competition. When there is none, the problem remains. Take dative verbs that lack double-object forms. As we saw, these are not blocked by the existence of an alternative form; there is simply a gap in the paradigm. The Sieve solution, even when enhanced by the Uniqueness Principle, seems to leave unanswered the question of how learners can retreat from overgeneralizing "exceptional" rules such as the dative alternation, where the Uniqueness Principle does not operate.[34]

5.2 Finer and Finer Distinctions: Rule-tightening "Criteria" Approaches

A second kind of solution to the overgeneralization problem involves the constraints that are thought to limit lexical rules—those very constraints supposedly violated when overgeneralizations are made. Looked at the other way around, "constraints approaches" are "criteria approaches," since we can think of lexical items as having to meet certain **criteria** in order to undergo a specific rule. The logic of this solution is as follows: As learners acquire the criteria that characterize particular lexical rules, they can impose them as constraints on their early too-loose rules, thereby making them tighter and ruling out overgeneralizations (Mazurkewich & White, 1984; Pinker, 1984).

Criteria-based approaches can be evaluated on two counts. First, what must the learner do in order to identify criteria and incorporate them as constraints on overgeneral rules? Is this procedure realistic? Second, are the criteria correct? As the advocates themselves admit, if counterexamples litter the input from which the criteria are to be extracted, then the criteria will be camouflaged and refinement will be impossible. We address these questions in turn and see that on both counts criteria-based learning is untenable. The discussion will concentrate on one overgeneral rule, the dative alternation, although the objections apply to the other rules as well.[35]

---

the start? The learner eventually has to throw out all but one plural form for each noun. So why doesn't she do so immediately, or as soon as she realizes that both forms express plurality and therefore "compete." Theoretically, this "instantaneous" model is possible, but as we noted, in Section 1, a certain amount of lag time is expected, since it is likely that all of the irregular plurals are not yet stored. Until each one is secure in memory, the rule provides a substitute (but surefire) way to express plural meanings.

[34]See Bowerman (1988) for other, just as difficult, examples.

[35]Bowerman's (1988) cogent survey raises some of the objections included here and others, too, but it may be useful to review them here for readers who are unfamiliar with that work.

5.2.1 Summarizing the Criteria Approach to Dative Overgeneralizations

In Pinker (1989) is a summary of what a learner using the criteria approach must do. In short:

1. Record the argument structures of verbs heard in the input.
2. If a large number of verbs occur in the same two argument structures, create a productive lexical rule with the verb in one argument structure as input and in the other as output.
3. If a large number of verbs then appear which **fail** to occur in one of these argument structure forms, and if those verbs lack a property that the two-form verbs exhibit, use the property to divide the verbs, and allow the rule to apply productively only to the class which has it. Impose the constraint retroactively, to expunge any forms produced by the earlier too-loose rule that violate the new constraint.
4. If a hypothesized constraint is later falsified because a large number of verbs in the input violate it, search for a new property that distinguishes alternating from nonalternating verbs and substitute it for the old criterial property.

The gist of the criteria approach is step 3. And here is where the first difficulty raises its head. What moves the learner to impose criteria when with her current overgeneral rule she can parse all the cases in her input (Fodor & Crain, 1987; Randall, 1987)? Since no trigger in the input will clue her that she hasn't yet heard the verb in a particular argument structure, she must count and compare: the number of occurrences of the verb overall versus the number heard in each argument structure. The troubling aspect of the criteria approach is that it expects the learner to be trying to fine-tune rules that already work without indicating which rule might need tuning. As Bowerman has continually pointed out, if monitoring the numbers is so critical, then the learner can be all too easily thrown off by both positive exceptions, which will lead to rejecting criteria (via step 4), and negative exceptions, which will prevent her from formulating them in the first place.

A second question concerns the nature of the properties. Pinker proposes that phonological, semantic, or thematic properties might all be potentially applicable. How does the learner figure out which one to try where? What tells her to look for say, a phonological constraint on the dative rule but not on the causative or passive?

5.2.2 What are the Purported Criteria and are They Correct?

To see what properties the criteria proponents have in mind, consider Mazurkewich and White's (1984) and Pinker's (1984) two criteria for eliminating overgeneralizations to the learner's "rule for the dative alternation." (Neither draws the distinction between *to* and *for* datives that we argued for in Section 3.3.1 and used in our solutions. The criteria are (a) the morphological condition and (b) the semantic condition.[36] We will show that the morphological condition is incorrect and that the semantic distinction is unnecessary.

5.2.2.1 The Morphological Condition. The purported morphological condition on double-object datives takes a number of formulations in the literature. For a verb to allow NP NP, it must be (a) monosyllabic/one metrical foot; (b) non-Latinate/non-Classical; (c) both (a) and (b), and so on. But even the tightest version, (c), springs leaks. Exceptions exist among well-established verbs, like (90).

(90) assign them some homework
     construct me a proof
     offer John some help
     promise Ernie a cookie

Beyond these, a whole class of double-object forms can be systematically derived from the very class of Latinate, polysyllabic verbs that blocks it. The derivation is in two steps; first, take a nonalternating verb such as *transmit,* (91a), and add the instrumental *-er* noun suffix to form *tránsmitter,* (91b), correspondingly shifting stress onto the first syllable. Second, apply the English noun-to-verb rule (Clark & Clark, 1979; Kiparsky, 1982) to form a new verb, with the same stress as the noun, *to tránsmitter,* (91c). This form is compatible with the NP NP dative, as (91d) illustrates.

(91) a. *We transmítted John the news.
     b.   a tránsmitter
     c.   to tránsmitter
     d.   We tránsmittered John the news.

As (92) shows, the noun-to-verb rule applies quite generally to instrumental nouns regardless of their derivational history and regardless, too, of whether they are instruments for transferring information, *to*-datives, or for creating a product, *for*-datives. These all allow the double-object form.

---

[36]These date back to work by Fischer (1971), Goldsmith (1980), Green (1974), Oehrle (1975), Stowell (1981), Grimshaw (1985), and a host of others.

(92) a. *to*-datives

John *frisbeed/e-mailed* Mary a love letter.

That transmitter *satellites/radios* us the news.

John is *helicoptering/dogsledding* the climbers some supplies.

Mary is *hydroplaning* the divers some lunch.

b. *for*-datives

I think I'll *Shake & Bake/cornflake* the kids some chicken.

Mom is going to *skillet/microwave* John a pork chop.

Fred promised to *wok/convection-oven* Mary some moo-shi pork.

In sum, whatever tendency nonalternating verbs have to be monosyllabic or Latinate, no morphological condition applies, either to established or to new verbs, to prevent them from taking NP NP complements. This is not to say that speakers are not sensitive to phonological properties of the words in their language. On the contrary, adult English speakers enforce a "classicality" criterion (Latin/Greek) on made-up words in the *-ity* suffix (Randall, 1980). It is only that the morphophonological profiles of the possible double-object verbs are too varied for learners to use this kind of criteron successfully. Further, we still have no answer to the question posed here: What signals the learner that a condition like "classicality" or "one-footedness" (Grimshaw, 1985) is what's relevant? Those rules, like *-ity* affixation, that *are* sensitive to morphology are rules that themselves operate in the morphological domain. Among these are rules that add affixes, adjust phonological features, or shift stress. The rule of dative shift is not a morphological rule. So why would a condition of that sort be involved? To conclude, the morphological condition on double-object datives, as far as retreat from overgeneralizations is concerned, is a red herring. Let's look at the other condition.

5.2.2.2 The Semantic Condition.   The semantic condition, as proposed by Fischer (1971), is (93):

(93) "in a sentence containing an indirect object, the indirect object is the direct recipient of or benefits from the possession of the direct object — the indirect object 'gets to keep' the direct object, at least for the period of time under consideration in the sentence." (pp. 21–22)

This condition does seem to be correct, as we saw in Section 3.2. Verbs that ordinarily resist a double-object form (94a) accept one when they can be interpreted as creating a product for someone to possess, (94b).

(94) a. *Jeeves washed me the dishes.
         *The butler opened little Arthur a cabinet.
         *The assistant brushed Hilda her hair.
     b. Jeeves washed me a cup (so I could have some coffee).
        The butler opened little Arthur a bottle of Perrier.
        The assistant brushed the hairdresser a wig (to put on the mannequin).

Metaphorical possession is also included, as cases like *give him a kick* and *dance me a jig* indicate (Green, 1974).

If the "semantic requirement" is a reliable indicator of which verbs allow double-object datives, then presumably it is eligible as a criterion on the rule. But the other reason we have given to reject the criteria approach still applies here. To discover a semantic requirement on NP NP forms, the learner needs to count and tally all the while she is using her rule. Again, this is quite a tax to impose on the learner, especially since it can be avoided, as we saw in Section 4.3, by the Catapult solution, whose trigger is a single piece of positive evidence, available without computation. The *for*-phrases that don't alternate are all adjuncts, therefore, all syntactically detectable. And notice that once the syntactic cutback has been made, the learner can discover the semantic constraint *without* having to count and tally. Every alternating *for*-phrase form that remains exhibits the right semantics. The semantic generalization is now available from positive evidence. There is more to say about the mechanism behind this aspect to the criteria approach. Since it goes beyond the semantic criterion per se, we address it in the next section.

5.2.3 Other Reasons to Question Criteria

The counting requirement that the criteria approach imposes is a form of "Indirect Negative Evidence,"[37] an interesting trapdoor in the language-acquisition device. A learner is using Indirect Negative Evidence when she (a) notices that certain forms expected in her input are continually absent, and (b) takes this as a sign that they must therefore be ungrammatical and should be ruled out. When such absences occur in the output of a learner's rule, this could be evidence that the rule is overgeneral. But how does this story square with overgeneralizations she herself is creating? If the learner must assume that certain double-object forms are ungrammatical if they don't surface within a limited time, it is interesting that the system allows her, at the same time, to be creating these illicit examples herself.

---

[37]Christened by Chomsky (1981) and discussed at length in Valian (1990b). Many proposals in the literature use it in one form or another. See Bowerman (1988) for discussion and references.

Then there is the "eternal wait" problem, raised by Valian (1990b). Under Pinker's scenario, the child tracks the input to see if a sizable number of verbs arise in one form *but fail to arise in another*. Valian muses, "The child is like someone prospecting for gold that isn't there; what will make her decide that she is on a fruitless quest?" The question is one of frequency. How often should a learner expect to hear a specific verb in a particular argument structure? The grammar says nothing about this, since, as Valian notes, frequency of usage of a form is not a grammatical phenomenon.

In sum, the criteria approach seems to pose more problems than it solves. And as we saw for the semantic condition on the dative rule, the criteria that learners must formulate by noting the **absence** of particular constructions under this approach are a natural by-product of the Catapult solution, available from positive evidence alone.

6. THE CATAPULT THEORY AND EVIDENCE

How realistic is the Catapult Hypothesis? Is it reasonable to claim that principles of grammar are all that the learner needs to rescue her from her early overgeneral lexical rules? Catapults only work when the language is not arbitrary. But we have seen that the supposedly idiosyncratic gaps in argument structure alternations are actually rule-governed. It is a principle that tells learners that verbs that take a *to*-PP but not NP NP are exactly those verbs that take a single NP. It is another principle that restricts where adjuncts may be attached.

But how do we find evidence that learners actually have the principles that the theoreticians say they have? The evidence we have given here has been heavily hypothetical and decidedly theoretical. But some empirical data support these claims too. Overgeneralizations cured by the Order Principle require that the Order Principle be present. At the time learners drop their incorrect NP NP structures, we find no reported evidence of Order Principle violations, like **Sue put under her pillow the yoyo* or **Alec bought for Fido a flea collar*. Evidence that the Attachment Principle is present comes from the absence of any reported NP NP forms, (95a), derived from *for*-phrase adjuncts, (95b):

(95) a. *Bill bought five hundred dollars that motorcycle.
        *The Porters visited their vacation Italy.
        *We rode free the ferriswheel.
        *Katy watched an hour a TV special on whales.
    b. Bill bought that motorcycle for five hundred dollars.
        The Porters visited Italy for their vacation.

> We rode the ferriswheel for free.
> Katy watched a TV special on whales for an hour.

These *for* phrases could not be misanalyzed if they are already considered adjuncts by the learner, already correctly hung in the learner's tree.

On the other hand, the lack of certain errors is never as convincing evidence that learners have Principle Such-and-Such as is the presence of certain errors in the learner's own utterances. For the two principles we have discussed, it is hard to see what kinds of ungrammatical utterances these would be. But to see how empirical data can show that a learner has a particular principle of grammar, consider the Case Principle, in (96).

(96) Case is: required by nouns
                assigned by verbs and prepositions
                not assigned by adjectives or nouns

We might claim that it is this three-part principle that is playing a role in how children learn the syntactic categories of ambiguous words.[38]

Suppose Sam, aged 3;9, knows the word *tired* only as a verb (take a nonsense word like *bired* to get the effect of being Sam): *The cowboy's bired (tired) his horses* (with the *'s* standing for *has*). At this stage, he would always analyze *bired* (*tired*) as a verb in *The cowboy's bired* (*tired*) (again, *'s* means *has*). If Sam knows the case principle, he will know that adjectives do not case-mark nouns, but prepositions do. Suppose that he knows, also, that *of* is a preposition. Now he can learn from positive evidence like *The cowboy's tired* (*bired*) *of his horses* that *tired* (*bired*) is either a noun or an adjective. Since the sentence ends after *horses,* it must be an adjective, since calling it a noun would make the sentence an NP (cf. *the cowboy's memory of his horses*).

A subpart of (96) provides an "If A then not B" catapult:

(97) If *of* is inserted between a word, w, and a noun, to case-mark that noun, then w is not a verb.

Now what about independent evidence for (96) in Sam's grammar? Knowledge of (96) should prevent him from using words that he thinks are not verbs as case-markers. And he should also not insert a case-marker between a verb and a noun. In other words, he should not produce examples like (98):

---

[38]The example is not so far fetched when we assume that ambiguous words violate the Uniqueness Principle (or Principle of Contrast), which requires that forms and meanings map one-to-one.

(98) a. I'm not [**adjective**] the dessert.
      She's [**noun**] my banjo.
   b. I'm not [**verb**] of the dessert.
      She's [**verb**] of my banjo.

But alongside the absence of these forms, we should find positive evidence that *of* is understood as a case-marker, and is used with nouns and adjectives. In fact, this is exactly what we do find.

(99) Sam 3;9: *I'm not interested of the dessert.
               *She's interested of my banjo.
               *She's interesting of my banjo.
               *It's a banjo; you are really interesting of it.
               *There's a hole of it.
               [about a banjo case with a hole in it]
     Sam 4;5 *I want to be a scientist of trees.

Although Sam does not yet know which preposition to use with which noun or adjective, his spontaneous use of the default preposition *of* shows his understanding of all three clauses in (96). So (99) supports the hypothesis that this learner has the Case Principle.

7. CONCLUSIONS

We began this study by presenting a commonly held view about language acquisition: Acquiring the lexicon must be quite different from acquiring the syntax. Since the lexicon is arbitrary and idiosyncratic, the behavior of lexical item *x* could never tell us how lexical item *y* will behave. Through the course of our discussion, we have taken issue with this view and shown that it can, that learning the lexicon and the syntax are equally principled tasks. This required demonstrating that supposed "exceptions" to lexical rules are in fact rule-governed. Principles hold in the lexicon. Crucially, the principles we looked at have an "If A then not B" shape, the same shape as syntactic parameters, the shape that allow them to serve as catapults for overgeneralizations.

It might be useful to put this conclusion into the context of other recent ideas about language acquisition. One idea is Syntactic Bootstrapping (Gleitman, Gleitman, Landau, & Wanner, 1989; Naigles, Gleitman, & Gleitman, in press), which claims that learners can derive the semantic properties of lexical items from their syntax. This is indeed what each of our examples has shown. What triggered the learner to question her existing, incorrect, lexical items was always a syntactic fact, and the properties that she altered were at least partly semantic. To review: a verb with a single postverbal NP triggered the Order Principle to eject (a) verbs that take *to* datives but which are mistakenly assigned NP NP; (b) verbs of the *fill* LOCATION THEME class, mistakenly assigned *fill* THEME LOCATION; and (c) verbs of the *spill* THEME LOCATION class, mistakenly assigned LOCATION THEME. The presence of a syntactic adjunct allowed the Attachment Principle to force out (a) BENEFACTIVE and (b) GOAL *for*-PP adjuncts, both mistakenly considered arguments, thereby allowing the verb to participate in the dative alternation. This unmasked a correlation between the remaining *for*-PP RECIPIENTS and the NP NP forms, allowing the learner to master the semantic "prospective possessor" constraint. In the Case Principle example, syntactic elements allow the learner to change the category label on a lexical item from verb to adjective.

In sum, many of the assumptions of the Syntactic Bootstrapping and Catapult theories are shared; it remains to be seen how much of Syntactic Bootstrapping is achieved by Catapult-shaped principles, and which ones these might be.

A second idea that has gained some attention is maturation. In work by Gleitman (1981), Borer and Wexler (1987, 1989), and Felix (1984), the suggestion is made that principles mature. They are not available from the earliest stages, but their shapes are set and it is only a matter of time until they emerge. We have been able to account for the learner's path by assuming that the crucial principles have always been available, but that the data, the correct interpretation of the data, or the lexical identification of particular pieces of data is what is delayed. But one could make the opposite assumption: that the data are there but the principles mature. This question is under debate, however, we would join those who take the view that the invariance of UG Principles plus the lexical learning hypothesis of language acquisition would be preferred on theoretical grounds if it can be maintained on empirical ones (Jakubowicz, 1989; Clahsen, this volume).

Of course, we have only scratched the surface of the research to be done in the framework set out here. There are a panoply of principles relevant to lexical acquisition, at various levels. Some deal with thematic structure, (the Theta-Criterion; Chomsky, 1981), others with Argument Structure (the Unique External Argument Principle; Borer & Wexler, 1988): still others, with phrase structure configurations (the Two-XPs-in-V' Constraint; Carrier & Randall, in press). And there are principles that operate over semantic representations, or Lexical Conceptual Structure (Carrier & Randall, 1989, in press; Jackendoff 1983, 1987; Rappoport & Levin, 1988) and those that assign the mapping between LCS and AS (Carrier & Randall, 1989, in press). It should not be surprising that the learner manages to retreat from her lexical overgeneralizations if even some of these principles turn out to be on the right track. Perhaps by seeing how they might work in language acquisition, we'll find out which ones are.

ACKNOWLEDGMENTS

This article has benefited from discussions with many generous colleagues. I would like to thank Melissa Bowerman, Jill Carrier, Janet Fodor, John Frampton, Lila Gleitman, Steve Pinker, Cliff Pye, Virginia Valian, Maaike Verrips, Ken Wexler and, especially, the editors of this volume. I am also grateful to audiences at the Boston University Conference on Child Language, the University of Connecticut and the Max Planck Institute for Psycholinguistics, where earlier versions of this research were presented. I gratefully acknowledge support from Northeastern University (through a Research and Scholarship Development Fund grant and a Junior Research Appointment) and the Max Planck Institute.

REFERENCES

Baker, C. L. (1979). Syntactic theory and the projection problem. *Linguistic Inquiry, 10,* 533–581.

Baker, M. (1988). *Incorporation.* Chicago: Chicago University Press.

Berwick, R. (1982). *Locality principles and the acquisition of syntactic knowledge.* Unpublished doctoral dissertation, MIT, Cambridge, MA.

Berwick, R. (1985). *The acquisition of syntactic knowledge.* Cambridge, MA: MIT Press.

Borer, H., & Wexler, K. (1987). The maturation of syntax. In T. Roeper & E. Williams (Eds.), *Parameter setting.* Dordrecht, The Netherlands: Reidel.

Borer, H., & Wexler, K. (1989). *The acquisition of participle agreement: A maturational account.* Paper presented at the GLOW annual meeting, Budapest.

Borer, H., & Wexler, K. (1988). The maturation of grammatical principles. Paper presented at the GLOW annual meeting, Venice, Italy.

Bowerman, M. (1982a). Evaluating competing linguistic models with language acquisition data: Implications of developmental errors with causative verbs. *Quaderni di semantica, 3,* 5–66.

Bowerman, M. (1982b). Reorganizational processes in lexical and syntactic development. In E. Wanner & L. Gleitman (Eds.), *Language acquisition: The state of the art.* Cambridge, MA: MIT Press.

Bowerman, M. (1983). How do children avoid constructing an overly general grammar in the absence of feedback about what is not a sentence? *Papers and Reports on Child Language Development, 22,* 23–25. Stanford University Department of Linguistics, Stanford, CA.

Bowerman, M. (1987). Commentary, In J. B. McWhinney (Ed.), *Mechanisms of language acquisition.* Hillsdale, N. J.: Lawrence Erlbaum Associates.

Bowerman, M. (1988). The "no-negative evidence" problem: How do children avoid constructing an overly general grammar? In J. A. Hawkins (Ed.), *Explaining language universals.* Oxford, England: Basil Blackwell.

Braine, M. D. S. (1971). On two types of models of the internalization of grammars. In D. Slobin (Ed.), *The ontogenesis of grammar.* New York: Academic Press.

Braine, M. D. S. (1988). Modeling the acquisition of linguistic structure. In Y. Levy, I. M.

Schlesinger, & M. D. S. Braine (Eds.), *Categories and processes in language acquisition.* Hillsdale, N. J.: Lawrence Erlbaum Associates.

Brown, R., & Hanlon, C. (1970). Derivational complexity and order of acquisition in child speech. In J. Hayes (Ed.), *Congnition and the development of language.* New York: Wiley.

Bybee, J., & Slobin, D. (1982). Rules and schemas in the development and use of the English past. *Language 58,* 265–289.

Carrier, J., & Randall, J. (1989). *From lexical structure to syntax: Projecting from resultatives.* Paper presented at Conference on Knowledge and Language, University of Groningen, Groningen, The Netherlands.

Carrier, J., & Randall, J. (in press). *From lexical structure to syntax.* Dordrecht, The Netherlands: Foris.

Chomsky, N. (1981). *Lectures on government and binding.* Foris, Dordrecht.

Clark, E. (1987). The principle of contrast: A constraint on language acquisition. In B. MacWhinney (Ed.), *Mechanisms of language acquisition* (pp. 1–33).

Clark, E. V., & Clark, H. H. (1979). When nouns surface as verbs. *Language, 55,* 767–811.

Dell, F. (1981). On the learnability of optional phonological rules. *Linguistic Inquiry, 12,* 31–37.

Erteschik-Shir, N. (1979). Discourse constraints on dative movement. In T. Givon (Ed.), *Syntax and semantics. Vol. 12: Discourse and syntax.* New York, Academic Press.

Felix, S. (1984). Maturational aspects of universal grammar. In A. Davis, C. Criper, & A. Howat (Eds.), *Interlanguage.* Edinburgh University Press.

Fischer, S. D. (1971). *The acquisition of verb-particle and dative constructions.* Unpublished doctoral dissertation, MIT, Cambridge, MA.

Fodor, J., & Crain, S. (1987). Simplicity and generality of rules in language acquisition. In B. MacWhinney (Ed.), pp. 35–63.

Gleitman, L. (1981). Maturational determinants of language growth. *Cognition, 10,* 103–114.

Gleitman, L., H. Gleitman, B. Landau, & Wanner, E. (1989). Where learning begins: Initial representations for language learning. In F. Newmeyer, (Ed.), *The Cambridge University linguistic survey* (Vol. 3). New York: Cambridge University Press, pp. 150–193.

Goldsmith, J. (1980). Meaning and mechanism in language. In S. Kuno (Ed.), *Harvard studies in syntax and semantics, III,* Department of Linguistics, Harvard University Press, Cambridge, MA.

Green, G. M. (1974). *Semantics and syntactic regularity.* Bloomington, IN: Indiana University Press.

Grimshaw, J. (1985). *Remarks on dative verbs and Universal Grammar.* Paper presented at the 10th annual Boston University Conference on Language Development.

Gropen, J., & Pinker, S. (1986). *Constrained productivity in the acquisition of the dative alternation.* Paper presented at the 11th Annual Boston University Conference on Language Development.

Hyams, N. (1986). *Language acquisition and the theory of parameters.* Dordrecht, The Netherlands: Reidel.

Hyams, N. (1987). The theory of parameters and syntactic development. In T. Roeper & E. Williams (Eds.), *Parameter setting.* Dordrecht, The Netherlands: Reidel.

Hyams, N. (1989). The null-subject parameter in language acquisition. In O. Jaeggli, & K. J. Safir (Eds.), *The null subject parameter.* Dordrecht, The Netherlands: Kluwer.

Jackendoff, R. S. (1983). *Semantics and cognition.* Cambridge, MA: MIT Press.

Jackendoff, R. S. (1987). The status of thematic relations in linguistic theory. *Linguistic Inquiry, 18,* 369–411.

Jakubowicz, C. (1989). *Linguistic theory and language acquisition facts: Reformulation, maturation or invariance of binding principles.* Paper presented at the Conference on Knowledge and Language, University of Groningen, Groningen, The Netherlands.

Kayne, R. (1983). Datives in French and English. In *Connectedness and binary branching.*

Dordrecht, The Netherlands: Foris.

Kiparsky, P. (1982). Lexical morphology and phonology. In I. S. Yange (Ed.), *Linguistics in the morning calm.* Seoul: Hanshin.

Kuczaj, S. (1977). The acquisition of regular and irregular past tense forms. *Journal of Verbal Learning and Verbal Behavior, 16,* 589–600.

Larson, R. (1988). On the double object construction. *Linguistic Inquiry, 19,* 335–391.

MacWhinney, B. (Ed.) (1987) *Mechanisms of language acquisition.* Hillsdale, N. J.: Lawrence Erlbaum Associates.

Mazurkewich, I. (1982) *Second language acquisition of the dative alternation and markedness: The best theory.* Unpublished doctoral dissertation, University of Montreal.

Mazurkewich, I. & White, L. (1984). The acquisition of the dative alternation: Unlearning overgeneralizations. *Cognition, 16,* 261–283.

Naigles, L., Gleitman, L., & Gleitman, H. (in press). Children acquire word meaning components from syntactic evidence. In E. Dromi (Ed.), *Language and cognition: A developmental perspective.* Norwood, N. J.: Ablex.

Nishigauchi, T., & Roeper, T. (1987). Deductive parameters and the growth of empty categories. In T. Roeper & E. Williams (Eds.), *Parameter setting.* Dordrecht, The Netherlands: Reidel.

Oehrle, R. T. (1975). *The grammatical status of the English dative alternation.* Unpublished doctoral dissertation, MIT, Cambridge, MA.

Pinker, S. (1984). *Language learnability and language development.* Cambridge, MA: MIT Press.

Pinker, S. (1989). Resolving a learnability paradox in the acquisition of the verb lexicon. In R. Schiefelbush (Ed.), *The teachability of language.* Baltimore, MD: Paul H. Brookes.

Pollock, J. Y. (1989). Verb movement, universal grammar and the structure of IP. *Linguistic Inquiry, 20,* 365–424.

Randall, J. H. (1980). *-ity:* A study in word formation restrictions. *Journal of Psycholinguistic Research, 6,* 524–535.

Randall, J. H. (1985). Negative evidence from positive. In P. Fletcher & M. Garman (Eds.), *Child language seminar papers.* Proceedings of the 1985 Child Language Seminar, University of Reading, Reading, England.

Randall, J. H. (1987). *Indirect positive evidence: Overturning overgeneralizations in language acquisition.* Indiana University Linguistics Club, Bloomington, IN.

Randall, J. H. (1990). Catapults and pendulums: The mechanics of language acquisition, *Linguistics, 28,* 1381–1406.

Rappaport, M. B. & Levin (1984). A cast study in lexical analysis: The locative alternation. *Center for cognitive science occasional paper,* Cambridge, MA: MIT.

Rappaport, M. B. & Levin (1988). What to do with theta-roles. In W. Wilkins (Ed.), *Thematic relations.* Syntax and Semantics, (Vol. 21). San Diego: Academic Press.

Rizzi, L. (1986). Null objects in Italian and the theory of *pro. Linguistic Inquiry, 17,* 501–557.

Rochemont, M. S. (1986). *Focus in generative grammar.* Amsterdam: J. Benjamins.

Roeper, T. (1981). On the deductive model and the acquisition of productive morphology. In C. L. Baker & J. J. McCarthy (Eds.), *The logical problem of language acquisition.* Cambridge, MA: MIT Press.

Roeper, T., & Weissenborn, J. (1990). How to make parameters work. In L. Frazier & J. de Villiers (Eds.), *Language Processing and Language Acquisition.* Dordrecht, The Netherlands: Kluwer.

Stowell, T. (1981). *Origins of phrase structure.* Unpublished doctoral dissertation, MIT, Cambridge, MA.

Valian, V. (1990a). Null subjects: A problem for parameter setting models of language acquisition. *Cognition. 35,* 105–122.

Valian, V. (1990b). Logical and psychological constraints on the acquisition of syntax. In L.

Frazier & J. G. de Villiers (Eds.), *Language processing and language acquisition*. Dordrecht, The Netherlands: Reidel.

Wexler, K., & Manzini, R. (1987). Parameters and learnability in binding theory. In T. Roeper & E. Williams (Eds.), *Parameter setting*. Dordrecht, The Netherlands: Kluwer.

White, L. (1986). Children's overgeneralizations of the English dative alternation. In K. Nelson & A. van Kleek (Eds.), *Children's language* (Vol. 6). Hillsdale, N. J.: Lawrence Erlbaum Associates.

Williams, E. (1981). Language acquisition, markedness and phrase-structure. In S. L. Tavakolian (Ed.), *Language acquisition and linguistic theory*. Cambridge, MA: MIT Press.

6 Principles vs. Criteria: On Randall's Catapult Hypothesis

James Pustejovsky
Brandeis University

1. INTRODUCTION

In her chapter, "The Catapult Hypothesis," Randall re-examines the question of overgeneralization of lexical rules for Baker's paradox. Her main thesis is that conventional assumptions about how to analyze the problem, what Pinker has termed the "criteria approach," can be abandoned in favor of a theory of principles, without necessitating specific mechanisms for re-evaluating the status of the child's grammar and lexicon. The principles are those which are already needed to characterize the adult's grammar correctly. This general procedure makes use of a reasoning schema, termed a *catapult*. A catapult is essentially a template for stating a principle of grammar as an exclusive *or*. Randall argues that syntactical representations can be used for the application of lexical rules, and that this obviates more specific criteria for unlearning ungrammatical forms.

What I hope to clarify in this short remark is the following: The attraction of Randall's proposal is that it abandons specific mechanisms for retreating from overgeneralizations in favor of basic principles of X-bar theory, needed in any case. What I would like to argue is that, in order better to evaluate this proposal, it is necessary: (a) to examine how the principles are instantiated in the child's grammar and (b) to see how the relevant data are recognized with respect to the principles. I will show that there are two possible interpretations of the Catapult Hypothesis. Under one interpretation, the very principles used for retreat from overgeneralizations, in fact, *proscribe* the overgeneralizations to begin with, thereby suggesting that the child would never produce such ill-formed sentences. Given the observable data, this interpretation is obviously untenable.

Under the second interpretation, we can interpret the principles as consistent with other (perhaps independent) mechanisms that permit over-generalizations at one point, followed by a retreat (i.e., unlearning) of these forms at a later stage. I will attempt to show that, in making this particular step explicit, we in fact come close to what is essentially one argument put forward by Pinker (1989). Following this view, a theory of principles is strongly consistent with the idea that discriminants become available in the child's data set, such that overgeneralization is then reduced when the forms are implicitly expunged from the lexicon. This can be viewed as a result of recompiling the rules and running the lexical rules over the data again. This position links the principles approach to Pinker's proposal, and I believe it is this interpretation of Randall's theory that should be adopted. The role of catapults can then be seen as instances of inferential reasoning over positive data. What is important about Randall's chapter is that it forces us to consider the general mechanisms operative in the grammar, and to realize that any independent criterion for discrimination between lexical forms must be consistent with global principles in the grammar in order for it to be learnable.

2. THE CATAPULT HYPOTHESIS

Randall argues that lexical learning can be incorporated within a model of language acquisition where no independent machinery is needed besides the grammar itself, including the particular settings of parameters. Thus, for example, the observed behavior of null subjects in English learners suggests that the initial null-subject setting changes when expletives are observed in the data (cf. Hyams, 1986). Let us assume that a parameter is a statement pertaining to some aspect of the grammar that may assume more than one value, or is a predicate assuming binary values (cf. Chomsky, 1981). Randall suggests that the null-subject parameter can be stated as an exclusive disjunction of the following form:

(1) Either null subjects or expletives, but not both.

Examples from Modern Greek and Spanish show, however, that this statement is incomplete at best.[1] Stockwell et al. (Stockwell, Bowen, & Martin, 1965, p. 96) first pointed out that Spanish allows partial pro-drop, as shown in (2):

---

[1]This was brought to my attention by Bob Ingria (personal communication).

(2) a. Los Americanos somos muy afortunados.
    (We) the Americans are (1st-pl) very fortunate.
   b. Nosotros los Americanos somos muy afortunados.
    We the Americans are (1st-pl) very fortunate.

Furthermore, Ingria (1981, p. 126) discusses similar examples in Modern Greek:

(3) a. I aksiomatiki ine δili ma i stratiotes iste yeney.
    The officers are cowards but the soldiers are (2nd-pl) brave.
   b. I aksiomatiki ine δili ma esis i stratiotes iste yeney.
    The officers are cowards but you the soldiers are (2nd-pl) brave.

Examples such as these, however, are ungrammatical in null-subject languages such as Italian. What these data suggest is that an exclusive disjunctive statement of the null-subject parameter cannot adequately describe such partial pro-drop languages. That is, in a Boolean statement of the pro-drop parameter there is no way to characterize languages that can either leave the entire subject null or merely leave the pronominal part empty. However, since this problem is not peculiar to Randall's analysis alone, we will not pursue it here.

Let us return to the form of the exclusive disjunction in (1). Randall suggests that this can be taken as a general template for stating parameters in the grammar. Using this template, she proposes the following hypothesis in (4).

(4) *Catapult Hypothesis:* For every overgeneralization, the grammar contains an exclusive disjunctive principle, P, given as [A *XOR* B], and the primary data exhibit A.

This hypothesis is important because it assumes that for any overgeneralization in the data, there is a general principle of grammar that will expunge the incorrect lexical forms. Assuming that an overgeneralization is a full syntactic expression (i.e., a S or VP), this assumes that the source of the overgeneralization is easily identifiable as the verb,[2] and the incorrect form quickly removed from the lexicon.

Randall explores the role for catapult-like schemata in the solution of Baker's paradox. The two principles that she examines as candidates for

---

[2]This approach to the credit assignment problem is based on a nontrivial assumption, linked to a general verb-centered view of lexical projection and syntactic effects. Cf. Ingria and Pustejovsky (1990) for discussion of alternatives.

catapults are the *Order Principle* and the *Attachment Principle.* These are stated as independently needed principles of X-bar theory, and are then shown to act as mechanisms for lexical unlearning. The Order Principle governs the order of obligatory and optional arguments with respect to a phrasal head:

(5) *The Order Principle:* If an argument is optional then it may not intervene between a head and an obligatory argument.

Such a principle, Randall argues, is needed as a characterization of the adult grammar, as illustrated by the following examples.

(6) a.   Juliet invited Doris to the art opening.
    b.   *Juliet invited to the art opening Doris.

(7) a.   John brought a candy bar to Bill.
    b.   *John brought to Bill a candy bar.

According to this principle, because verbs such as *bring* and *invite* allow optional PP arguments, they will not appear in a position between the verb and the obligatory argument.

The second principle of X-bar theory that Randall discusses is the *Attachment Principle,* a statement on the positioning of adjuncts with respect to arguments.

(8) *The Attachment Principle:* If a constituent is an adjunct, then it may not intervene between a head an its argument.

This will account for the obvious ungrammaticality of sentences such as (9b) and (10b).

(9) a.   Mary ran a mile in the park.
    b.   *Mary ran in the park a mile.

(10) a.   John hit Mary near the TV.
     b.   *John hit near the TV Mary.

If seen as a condition on deep structure, then this principle is essentially a definition of an adjunct, as given in various forms (cf. Jackendoff, 1977, for one). If, however, it is viewed as a condition on surface structure, then it is really better seen as a descriptive statement, conflating perhaps several independent principles from Case Theory, Theta-assignment, and so on.

For purposes of our discussion, however, let us imagine it as a single principle.

How are these principles relevant to the problem of overgeneralization? Randall invokes the Order Principle to solve the false dativizations for verbs such as *deliver* (cf. (12b) in the following way. Both *give*-verbs and *deliver*-verbs have syntactic realizations in the following contexts in the child's grammar.

(11) a. *give* NP PP
     b. *give* NP NP

(12) a. *deliver* NP PP
     b. *deliver* NP NP

Randall points out, however, that *deliver* also appears in single direct-object contexts, such as those shown in (13), while *give*-verbs do not, for example (14). It is this additional syntactic context that distinguishes the two verb classes, allowing the Order Principle to filter the false datives for *deliver*-verbs.

(13) a. Romeo delivered the posies.
     b. Hamlet described the book.
     c. Bill dictated the letter.
     d. Joan contributed six warriors.

(14) a. *Romeo gave the posies.
     b. *Hamlet lent the book.
     c. *Cressida sent the book.
     d. *Joan lent six warriors.

This additional syntactic information informs the learner that the dativized NP is optional, and the revised lexical entry for *deliver* in (15), is now subject to the Order Principle, which deletes (15b) from the lexicon.

(15) a. *deliver* NP (PP)
     b. *deliver* (NP) NP

As Pinker (1989) observes, however, some of these distinctions are difficult to maintain, since many *give*-verbs successfully drop the PP argument.

(16) a. Romeo gave the lecture.
     b. Hamlet sent a letter.

c. Cordelia told a story.
d. Gertrude showed a movie.

In the absence of data that provide a reliable syntactic discriminant to the learner, the catapult hypothesis would act to expunge *V NP NP* forms for *give*-verbs as well.

A similar explanation accounts for the argument structure distinctions between *spill* and *fill,* and Randall's analysis fares much better. The potential problem with *spray* is overcome by positing two verb entries, with distinct semantic representations. This is independently argued for in Rappaport and Levin (1988), who provide evidence for treating verbs such as *load* and *spray* as ambiguous. Although this works here, we will discuss some difficulties with this strategy for the learner.

In discussing how the Attachment Principle acts as a catapult, Randall looks at the syntactic distribution of recipient and benefactive *for*-phrases in the dative alternation. Learners assume that benefactive phrases with verbs such as *brush* and *button* will dativize as do the verbs in (17). Thus, ungrammatical forms such as (18b) are part of the child's grammar.

(17) a. Bake a cake for the birthday boy.
    b. Bake the birthday boy a cake.

(18) a. Brush his hair for him.
    b. *Brush him his hair.

As with the Order Principle, an additional syntactic context is available in the input, which allows the learner to distinguish the two forms, and subsequently expunge the incorrect forms from the lexicon.

These data indicate that there is something right in the generalization Randall is making concerning the filtering effect of general principles of grammar. The analysis, however, is not without its problems, and I will turn to a discussion of these difficulties in the next section.

3. PROBLEMS WITH CATAPULTS

Although the Catapult Hypothesis seems to solve Baker's paradox, it does so by making several questionable assumptions. The first problem is this. There are several counterexamples to the application of the Order and Attachment principles for expunging unwanted lexical forms. For example, the verb *draw,* as Randall notes, poses a counterexample to the Order Principle, since the optional NP may precede the obligatory NP in (19b):

(19) a. Mary drew a picture for John.
   b. Mary drew John a picture.

Thus, the lexical forms for *draw* would appear to be identical to those of *deliver,* and if so, the sentence in (19b) would be expunged since it reflects an ill-formed lexical form according to the Order Principle. Since forms such as (19b) are grammatical, however, Randall proposes that there are two distinct lexical entries for *draw,* as shown in (20).

(20) draw-1 NP   (PP)
             Th   R

      draw-2 NP   NP
             R   Th

By establishing two separate lexical representations, as shown in (20), the forms are not subject to the filtering effects of the Order and Attachment principles.

Randall suggests that there is reason to choose this solution on semantic grounds. As we have mentioned, the variants of *spray/load*-verbs that participate in the "locative alternation" are arguably ambiguous (cf. Rappaport & Levin, 1988), since they exhibit well-known aspectual and affectedness distinctions. The argument is less convincing for verbs such as *draw,* however, since the semantic distinction between the two forms in (20) is exactly that which distinguishes the two forms of *give.* It is not clear, therefore, why the same option would not be available to *deliver*-verbs, as illustrated in (21).

(21) deliver-1 NP   (PP)
                Th   R

      deliver-2 NP   NP
                R   Th

Since no necessary or sufficient conditions are given for how such lexical discriminations are made, it is not clear why the child would not be able to posit dual entries for every verb that gives rise to false dative forms. That is, if the mechanism is available to one verb class, it should be available to all classes uniformly, if appropriate syntactic or semantic discriminants can be found that distinguish them. Yet, it seems as though every counterexample to the filtering effect of the catapults is analyzed as an ambiguous verb, even when such motivation is somewhat difficult to maintain.

Now let me turn to some more general comments on Randall's theory. As mentioned in Sec. 1, I believe there are two interpretations of the Catapult Hypothesis, one strict and the other loose. In the remainder of this section, I will briefly discuss the first of these, and demonstrate how it is inconsistent with the data. The reason I entertain this interpretation at all is because, at times, Randall seems to subscribe to the strict interpretation, while, in general, she advocates the loose interpretation.

The problem can be stated as follows: Most principles of grammar are thought of as consistently operative for adult speakers of a language. Under a strict interpretation of the Catapult Hypothesis, the same would hold for principles throughout the acquisition phase for the language learner. That is, the Order and Attachment principles would always be operative during learning. Assuming this were true, then how would the learner be able to make *any* overgeneralizations in the lexical forms she posits for her verbs?

To illustrate this situation briefly, consider the lexical forms for *deliver*-verbs once more. On the basis of positive evidence, the learner formulates the correct forms, [V NP (PP)], and because of the Order Principle's constant application, he or she will never entertain the dativized form [V NP NP]. Similar lexical filtering would occur with the Attachment Principle as well as with the Uniqueness Principle. The obvious problem with such a scenario is that it contradicts the data, and this is certainly not Randall's intended interpretation.

In the remainder of the chapter, I will discuss how another interpretation of Randall's theory can be seen as a link between the criteria approaches of Mazurkewich and White (1984), Pinker (1989) and others, and the static grammar view inherent in the principles approach.

4. CRITERIA LICENSED BY PRINCIPLES

In this section, I will argue that by making the Catapult Hypothesis more explicit, it comes very close to a criteria-based analysis of lexical unlearning. As has been mentioned, a static view of principles fails to account for the data. Thus, it is necessary to examine how the principles are instantiated in the child's grammar, and to make more explicit the mechanisms for how the relevant data are recognized with respect to these principles.

Implicit in the Catapult Hypothesis is the notion that lexical forms undergo occasional reanalysis according to grammatical principles. Thus, there is a sense in which the principles are *applied* as well-formedness conditions to existing forms, and any incorrect expression is expunged accordingly. This is analogous to recompiling the lexicon by running the lexical rules over the data again.

Let us consider the false datives generated with *deliver*-verbs once again. According to the Catapult Hypothesis, no particular criterion (e.g., phonological, semantic, or thematic) is necessary to account for the retreat from false datives, since the catapults will filter such forms eventually. Yet, strictly speaking, the learner must make use of semantic discriminations even within this principle-based approach. For, recall that there are two possible options for such cases as *deliver:* either to posit one entry with optional arguments, or to posit two entries where the arguments are expressed as obligatory elements in each entry. In order to make such a decision, however, semantic criteria must be available, since lexical ambiguity — and with it, distinct argument structures — is a reflection of a clear semantic distinction between two lexical forms. Thus, the decision to treat *deliver* as a single entry and *draw* as two entries is based on semantic criteria similar to those proposed by Pinker (1989) and Mazurkewich and White (1984).

Another point worth making here is that the syntactic discriminant for *deliver* cases (i.e., the ability to appear with just the *Theme* argument) is itself dependent on semantic criteria. That is, sentences with *give*-verbs are apparently just as grammatical as those with *deliver*-verbs when certain semantic conditions are satisfied. What these conditions are is not as important as the fact that syntactic configurations alone are insufficient to distinguish them. Criteria, therefore, start creeping back into the solution of Baker's paradox.

In examining the argument structures for these verb classes, however, it is interesting to note what role the semantic interpretation of the complement plays in the well-formedness of sentences without a goal argument. Curiously, every counterexample to the Catapult Hypothesis mentioned herein and in Pinker (1989) involves a systematic semantic generalization:

(22) a. Romeo gave the lecture.
    b. Hamlet mailed a letter.
    c. Cordelia told a story.
    d. Gertrude showed a movie.
    e. Mary asked a question.

Namely, the relationship between verb and complement in these cases is what I have referred to elsewhere (Pustejovsky, 1991) as *cospecification.* Cospecification arises when the verb governing the complement is itself "selected" (in a technical sense) by the noun. Thus, letters are typically *mailed,* stories are typically *told,* and questions are typically *asked.* When cospecification exists between two expressions, the argument structure within the phrase is changed. That is, the meaning of the verb *is* systematically distinct in such cases. Thus, there may be some predictive power in Randall's analysis in explaining the overgeneralization data if an analysis such as this is taken into account. That this is plausible is supported by data such as (23), where verbs in the *give*-class do not allow dative drop because of the absence of cospecification with the complement.

(23) a. *Bill told the secret.
    b. Bill told me the secret.

(19) a. *Mary gave a book.
    b. Mary gave John a book.

(20) a. *Cordelia showed the record.
    b. Cordelia showed Mary the record.

In each example, the complement does not select the verb governing it (although there are predicates selected by these nouns; e.g., *keep a secret, read a book,* and *play a record*). If an analysis in terms of cospecification can adequately account for the data, then Randall's argument is strengthened, since this essentially substantiates the separate lexical entry analysis. Because of space, however, we will not pursue this discussion here.

Returning to the problem of emerging discriminants, in Pinker's formulation of how criteria operate over lexical data, discriminants are brought to bear to reanalyze an existing partitioning of the data, giving rise to finer lexical classifications. In our interpretation of Randall's theory, we can think of the specific principles of grammar as providing the raw material for such finer discriminations to be possible. That is, the principles must be adhered to by all mechanisms involved in expunging overgeneralized forms. The semantic representations for a verb (and the accompanying argument structures) are constantly changing for the learner. But the recognition of (or the discrimination of) a certain feature will be part of a maturational process, a spelling out of what is structurally permitted and restricted by grammatical principles.

5. CONCLUSION

In conclusion, I believe that Randall's theory of principles is strongly consistent with the idea that discriminants become available in the child's data set and subsequently act to expunge ill-formed forms. Furthermore, if the analysis of cospecification can provide additional support for what constitutes structural semantic grounds for creating separate lexical entries, then I think that Randall's chapter can be seen as making a serious attempt at applying acquisition-independent principles of grammar to solving the learning paradox of lexical overgeneralization. As stated before, what is important about Randall's proposal is that it forces us to consider the general mechanisms operative in the grammar when discussing criteria-based analyses. Furthermore, it should be remembered that any independent criterion for discrimination between lexical forms must be consistent with global principles in the grammar in order for it to be learnable. In this respect, then, Randall's analysis may act to bridge the approaches in the discussion of Baker's paradox.

ACKNOWLEDGMENTS

I would like to thank Jane Grimshaw, Bob Ingria, and Janet Randall for useful discussion and comments. All errors and judgments are, of course, my own.

REFERENCES

Chomsky, N. (1981). *Lectures on government and binding*. The Netherlands, Foris.
Hyams, N. (1986). *Language acquisition and the theory of parameters*. Dordrecht, the Netherlands: Reidel.
Ingria, R. J. P. (1981). *Sentential complementation in Modern Greek*. Unpublished doctoral dissertation, MIT, Cambridge, MA.
Ingria, R. J. P., & Pustejovsky, J. (1990). Active objects in syntax, semantics, and parsing, in C. Tenny (Ed.), *The MIT parsing volume*. Parsing Project Working Papers 2, Center for Cognitive Science, MIT, Cambridge, MA.
Jackendorf, R. (1977). $\overline{X}$-syntax. Cambridge, MA: MIT.
Mazurkewich, I. & White, L. (1984). The acquisition of the dative alternation: Unlearning overgeneralizations, *Cognition, 16*.
Pinker, S. (1989). *Learnability and cognition*. Cambridge, MA: MIT Press.
Pustejovsky, J. (1991). The generative lexicon, in *Computational linguistics, 17*(4).
Rappaport, M., & Levin, B. (1988). What to do with Theta roles, in W. Wilkins (Ed.), *Thematic relations,* Syntax and Semantics (Vol. 21). San Diego: Academic Press.
Stockwell, R., Bowen, D., & Martin, J. (1965) *The grammatical structures of English and Spanish*. Chicago, London: University of Chicago Press.

7 Development in Control and Extraction

Helen Goodluck
University of Ottawa, Canada

Dawn Behne
Indiana University

This study concerns the development of rules for the interpretation of the missing (PRO) subject of embedded clauses, both with and without an empty object position. We will argue that clauses attached within the VP are distinguished from adverbial (adjunct) clauses, which attach to the S node in the adult grammar, both in terms of the rules for interpreting PRO and (less conclusively) the possibility of an object gap. Our results argue against previous accounts of children's treatment of S-attached adjuncts, in which it was proposed that children misattach such adjuncts to the VP node. In common with some previous studies, we will argue that significant aspects of the grammar of control rules (rules for PRO subject interpretation) and extraction (for object gaps) may be late to develop. First we describe our experimental work; then we sketch a picture of development for the constructions we deal with within the framework of current linguistic analyses.

1. AN EXPERIMENT

There are two parts to our experiment. The first part tests children's interpretation of the PRO subject of three types of embedded clause: complements to *tell,* purpose clauses, and temporal adjuncts. It also tests the interpretation of an object gap in purpose clauses. The second part tests whether the possibility of an object gap in purpose clauses is overextended to temporal adjunct clauses.

151

Part 1: Interpretation of PRO subjects and object gaps

Sentence Types Tested. Examples of the sentence types tested in the first part of the experiment are given in (1–7):[1]

1. Active main clause; complement to *tell*
   Daisy tells Pluto$_i$ [PRO$_i$ to do some reading]
2. Passive main clause; complement to *tell*
   Daisy$_i$ is told by Pluto [PRO$_i$ to do some reading]
3. Active main clause; purpose clause
   Daisy chooses Pluto$_i$ [PRO$_i$ to do some reading]
4. Passive main clause; purpose clause
   Daisy$_i$ is chosen by Pluto [PRO$_i$ to do some reading]
5. Active main clause; temporal adjunct
   Daisy$_i$ hits Pluto [before PRO$_i$ doing some reading]
6. Passive main clause; temporal adjunct
   Daisy$_i$ is hit by Pluto [before PRO$_i$ doing some reading]
7. Active main clause; purpose clause with object gap
   Daisy$_i$ chooses Pluto$_j$ [PRO$_i$ to read to e$_j$]

Sentence types (1, 2) contain infinitival complements to the verb *tell*. As the coindexing in the examples shows, the PRO subject of the complement is interpreted in the adult grammar as referring to the main clause direct object when the main clause is active (1) and to the main clause surface subject when the main clause is passive (2). Sentence types (3, 4) contain purpose clauses; these clauses are constituents of VPs headed by verbs such as *choose*. The facts for the interpretation of the PRO subject of purpose clauses are the same as for complements to *tell;* the PRO subject refers to the main clause direct object when the main clause is active and the surface subject when the main clause is passive. The control (coreference) facts in (1–4) can be summarized by saying that the PRO subject of an infinitival complement to *tell* or a purpose clause refers to the main clause NP with the thematic relation *goal* (or *theme*). Sentence types (5, 6) contain temporal adjunct clauses, introduced by the preposition *before;* temporal adjuncts, unlike complements to *tell* or purpose clauses, which are VP constituents, are attached to the main clause S node. Regardless of whether the main clause is active (5) or passive (6), the PRO subject of the temporal adjunct refers to the surface subject. Temporal adjuncts thus contrast to comple-

---

[1]The trace of a moved object (coindexed with PRO) is omitted from the representations for passive main clauses in sentences (2, 4, and 6); this is not critical to any of the points to be taken up.

ments to *tell* and purpose clauses in that control of the PRO subject for temporal adjuncts always involves the same grammatical relation (*subject*), which may have different thematic roles (*agent* in (5), *theme* in (6)), whereas control of complements to *tell* and purpose clauses involves the same thematic role (goal/theme), which has different surface grammatical realizations (*object* in (1, 3); *subject* in (2, 4)).[2]

The final sentence type tested in this part of the experiment is (7), in which there is a purpose clause with an object gap. As the coindexing in (7) shows, for this sentence type the PRO subject must be interpreted as referring to the main clause subject (in contrast to 3), and the object gap is taken to refer to the main clause object. (The object gap in (7) is designated [e]; the derivation of such sentences is discussed later.)

Materials, Subjects and Procedure.   Our test used a toy manipulation task of the type familiar in child language studies, beginning with C. Chomsky (1969). The child was introduced to a set of three animals (a cow, horse, and dog) to be used as subject and object of main clauses in the experiment and taught their names (Daisy, Champion, and Pluto). The child was also introduced to some other, smaller animals and objects to be used as props (a small book, a flower, a chicken, a turtle, and a pig). The child sat opposite the experimenter; the animals and other props for the experiment were arranged in front of the experimenter. Between the animals and the child, there was a wooden block. The child was taught that whenever an animal did any reading or singing, the animal was to stand on the block; this made clear who the actor was for the verbs *read* and *sing*.

Before beginning with the test sentence types (1–7), the child was taught how to act-out reading and singing, as just described, and also acted out two simple active sentences (with direct object), two simple passive sentences, and three simple sentences with prepositional objects. The prepositions used were those that occur in the subordinate clause of sentence types (1–7) in the test sentences. Finally, before beginning with sentence types (1–7), the experimenter pointed out to the child that he or she would have to make the animals do two things, and had the child act-out a conjoined sentence ("Daisy kisses the pig and kicks Pluto").

The test sentences in Part 1 of the experiment comprised four tokens of each of the sentence types (1–7), arranged in four blocks of one token of

---

[2]General assumptions we make concerning the grammar of control are that control of clauses in the VP requires reference to thematic relations whereas control of adjuncts that are attached to the S-node does not (at least for temporals) require reference to thematic relations. For some pertinent recent discussion of the grammar of the constructions we deal with (not all in agreement with the analyses we adopt/propose in this chapter), see Manzini, 1983; Mohanan, 1983; Nishigauchi, 1984; Jones, 1985; Jaeggli, 1986; Roeper, 1987; Williams, 1987, and references therein.

each sentence type. For each of the sentence types (1–6) there were two tokens in which the subordinate clause contained a prepositional object (e.g., ". . . read to Pluto") and two tokens in which no object was specified (e.g., ". . . do some reading"). The complete set of test sentences is given in Appendix 1. Three different orders of presentation of the test sentences were used.

The child was given up to two repetitions of each sentence if he or she did not respond at once or asked for the sentence to be repeated. The child's responses were scored according to which main clause NP was made coreferent of the PRO subject of the subordinate clause and (for sentence type 7) which NP was made object of the subordinate clause. Other pertinent aspects of the child's responses were noted, including whether the main and subordinate clause actions were correctly performed in all respects other than PRO/gap interpretation.

Thirteen 4-year-olds, sixteen 5-year-olds and thirteen 6-year-olds were tested.

Results.   Table 7.1 gives the results for sentence types (1–6), in terms of the mean percentage of responses in which the PRO subject of the embedded clause was made coreferential with the main clause surface subject. Subject coreference is the correct response to the PRO subject for sentence types (2, 4, 5, and 6) and incorrect for types (1) and (3). Two sets of figures are given in Table 7.1. The first is the mean percentage of subject responses calculated for those responses in which the action of the main and subordinate clauses was correctly performed; that is, the first set of figures represents the percentage of choice of subject as opposed to (direct or

TABLE 7.1
Interpretation of PRO: Mean Percentage Coreference with Surface Subject

	4 years n = 13	5 years n = 16	6 years n = 13	Overall mean
1. *Tell*-ACT*	11%	2%	6%	6%
	(10%)	(2%)	(6%)	(6%)
2. *Tell*-PASS	72%	71%	71%	71%
	(56%)	(61%)	(60%)	(59%)
3. Purpose-ACT*	24%	5%	4%	11%
	(17%)	(5%)	(4%)	(8%)
4. Purpose-PASS	63%	74%	86%	74%
	(49%)	(66%)	(66%)	(60%)
5. Temporal-ACT	89%	92%	81%	88%
	(73%)	(77%)	(77%)	(76%)
6. Temporal-PASS	48%	52%	71%	55%
	(38%)	(50%)	(58%)	(49%)

*Subject reference = incorrect response.

prepositional) object of the main clause as subordinate subject, when the main and subordinate clause actions were correctly acted out. The second set of figures (in parentheses) is the mean percentage of responses in which the main clause subject was made referent of PRO and the main and subordinate clauses were acted out correctly, calculated as a percentage of the total number of responses (including incorrect act-outs, failures to respond, etc.). The figures were calculated in these two ways since there was a fairly high level of incorrect act-outs and other responses not scorable for subject or object reference of the PRO subject of the subordinate clause, particularly for the conditions with a passive main clause (the percentages of such unscorable responses for the three age groups combined are 25, 19, and 19 for conditions 2, 4, and 6, respectively), and the first set of figures (although of most interest with respect to the point of this experiment) do not give a complete sense of the nature of the data. In calculating the first set of figures, the mean for the condition for the child's age group was used in two instances in which a child had no responses scorable for subject or object response for that condition.

The overall pattern of results can be seen from the means in the right-most column of Table 7.1. For complements to *tell* and purpose clauses, the general pattern is adult-like, with avoidance of control by the subject when the main clause is active (1, 3) and a switch to subject control when the main clause is passive (2, 4). With temporal adjuncts, children do not do as well. Although there is a high percentage of correct, subject-coreference, responses when the main clause is active (5), there is a drop in subject coreference when the main clause is passive (6). For each of the paired conditions (1, 2), (3, 4), and (5, 6) an anova comparing the proportion of subject responses is significant at a probability level lower than .000, for both sets of figures reported in Table 7.1. The differences between the conditions reflect adult-like performance for the *tell* complement and purpose clauses and error on the temporal complement conditions, for which the adult grammar predicts no difference in proportion of subject responses. The only significant effect of age is for purpose clauses, where there is a significant sentence type $\times$ age level interaction ($p < .01$, for the first set of figures; $p < .05$ for the second set of figures), reflecting the rather poor performance of the youngest children with the active purpose clause condition (see Table 7.1).

The primary error for the passive temporal condition (6) was to interpret the object of the passive *by*-phrase as subject of the temporal clause. Table 7.2 gives the distribution of children according to whether they had a greater proportion of subject responses to condition 5 (the active temporal condition) than to condition 6 (the passive temporal condition) or vice versa. As in Table 7.1, the first figures are based on responses in which the main and subordinate clause were acted out correctly and the alternative to subject response is a (direct or prepositional) object response and the second set of figures is for the total number of responses (main and subordinate clause acted out correctly and subject chosen as controller vs. any other response). Table 7.2 shows that the majority of children had more subject responses to the active condition (5) than to the passive condition (6), although the difference is small for 6-year-olds. This pattern of results will follow from a tendency to make the PRO subject of a temporal adjunct coreferential with the main clause NP with the thematic role *agent*. That will account for children's adult-like performance with sentence type (5) and poor performance, involving choice of the prepositional object as referent of PRO for sentence type (6).

The remaining sentence type in this part of the experiment is sentence type (7), containing a purpose clause with an object gap. With this sentence type, children do poorly. Table 7.3 gives a breakdown of responses to type (7) sentences. The percentage correct (i.e., main clause subject made subject of the subordinate clause and main clause object made object of the subordinate clause) is low for all age groups. Two types of error occurred with some frequency. One (error type 2) was to ignore the preposition at the end of the sentence and interpret the sentence as if it were a sentence of type (3) (i.e., a sentence such as "Daisy chooses Pluto to read to" is interpreted as if it were "Daisy chooses Pluto to read"); this error type accounts for 32% (37/117) of all errors, and is most frequent among 6-year-olds. The second frequent type of error (error type 3) was to assign the matrix clause object as subordinate subject (PRO) and the matrix clause subject as subordinate object (e); this error type accounts for 41% (43/117) of all errors, and is (by a small margin) commonest for 5-year-olds. It is not completely clear to us whether this response should be interpreted as a response in which the subordinate clause is treated as transitive; on occasion

TABLE 7.2

Sentence Types 5 and 6: Distribution of Children by Relative Proportion of Subject Responses

	More subject responses to type 5	*More subject responses to type 6*	*No difference*
Number of children			
4 years	7 (8)	3 (3)	3 (2)
5 years	11 (11)	1 (2)	3 (3)
6 years	5 (7)	4 (4)	4 (2)
Total:	23 (26)	8 (9)	10 (7)

Note: The number of children for the first set of figures totals 41; one child had no correct main clause interpretations for condition 6.

TABLE 7.3
Breakdown of Responses Purpose Clause with Object Gap (Sentence type 7)

Response type:	Correct	1 Error	2 Error	3 Error	4 Error
4 Years (*n* = 13)					
Total number	15	4	12	12	9
Mean percentage	29%	8%	23%	23%	17%
5 years (*n* = 16)					
Total number	24	3	8	19	8
Mean percentage	38%	5%	13%	31%	12%
6 years (*n* = 13)					
Total number	12	0	17	17	8
Mean percentage	24%	0%	34%	34%	8%

Error responses: 1 = main clause subject is made PRO (subordinate clause subject); no object assigned in the subordinate clause (the subordinate clause is treated as if it were intransitive)
2 = main clause object is made PRO; no object assigned in the subordinate clause
3 = main clause object is made PRO; main clause subject is made object of the subordinate clause.
4 = other errors (includes incorrect act-outs of main clause; use of nonmentioned animals as object; use of both mentioned animals as PRO)

children used the subject or another animal as recipient of the subordinate clause action, when no object was specified (for example, when acting out ". . . to do some reading") and this type of error could be a response along those lines, perhaps promoted by awareness of the transitive nature of the preposition. The ambiguity in interpreting this error type is clearly an uncomfortable one, if one wants to make claims about when knowledge of an object gap emerges and whether the possibility of an object gap is overextended to temporal clauses, as we show in the next section.[3]

Part 2: Overgeneralization of Object Gaps?

Temporal adjunct clauses, unlike purpose clauses, do not permit object gaps. Thus (8) is ungrammatical, in contrast to sentences of type (7), tested in the first part of the experiment,

8. *Daisy hits Pluto [before PRO reading to e]

---

[3]As Larry Solan points out to us, this error is an interpretation that yields a nested rather than intersecting dependency, in the sense of Fodor (1978). We would be more inclined to accept this response type as a genuine transitive interpretation if there exist languages that admit purpose clauses with this interpretation; we do not know what the facts are.

The second part of our experiment was designed to test whether children would overgeneralize the possibility of an object gap from purpose clauses to temporal adjuncts. We will describe the results of this part of the experiment briefly, since they are suggestive but not strong.

We presented children with sequences such as those in (9) and (10).

9. Daisy loves running and jumping
   Daisy chooses Pluto to júmp around

10. Daisy loves running and jumping
    Daisy hits Pluto before júmping around

The child had to act out the second sentence of the sequence. In (9) the second sentence contains a purpose clause, in (10) the second sentence contains a temporal adjunct. In both, the embedded clause VP contains the preposition *around,* which can be either transitive (*John jumped around Bill*) or intransitive (*John jumped around*).

There is ordinarily a stress clue to transitivity, with the preposition in the subordinate clause receiving relatively greater stress when it is intransitive. Both the purpose and temporal clauses in (9) and (10) were read with primary stress on the verb, yielding the stress pattern normally associated with transitivity of the preposition. The function of the first sentence in the sequences of two sentences (9-10) is to neutralize the stress clue to transitivity. The first sentence creates a context, such that stress on the subordinate verb of the second sentence has the discourse function of picking out one of two actions mentioned in the first sentence. Stress on the verb thus sounds natural, even when the preposition is treated intransitively, as it must be according to the adult rules for temporal clauses, which do not permit object gaps. Notice that in neutralizing the stress clue to transitivity of the preposition in this way, the pattern presented is the one normally associated with the transitive interpretation of the preposition; any avoidance of a transitive reading of the preposition thus cannot derive from stress.

If children are aware of the fact that purpose clauses, but not temporal adjuncts, can contain an object gap, it should be possible for them to treat the preposition as transitive in sentences such as (9), but not in sentences such as (10).

Children went on the Part 2 of the experiment immediately after completing Part 1. The experimenter began Part 2 by telling the child that he or she was going to act out a few more sentences about things the animals especially liked doing. Six sequences of sentence pairs such as (9) and (10) were then presented, containing three examples with purpose clauses and three with temporal adjuncts. The materials are given in Appendix 1. Three different orders of presentation were used.

The critical question with respect to sentence types (9) and (10) is whether the preposition is interpreted transitively. Many children (19/42) gave no transitive responses for either condition. If we take as transitive interpretations of the preposition only those responses that correspond to the adult transitive reading of sentence type (9), with the main clause subject as controller of PRO and the main clause object as subordinate object, the percentage transitive interpretation is 28% for type (9) and 17% for type (10). This difference in transitive interpretations for the two sentence types falls short of significance ($p < .10 > .05$). Only if such responses are combined with responses in which the main clause object is made referent of PRO and the main clause subject is made subordinate object (error type 3 in Table 7.3) does the difference between transitive readings for (9) and (10) become substantial enough to reach significance (36% vs. 18%, $p < .002$).[4, 5]

Two aspects of the data suggest that this study did not tap the question of whether children distinguish purpose clauses from temporals in terms of the object gaps as well as it might have done. First, throughout the experiment (Parts 1 and 2) there was a preference for interpreting the subject of an active main clause as PRO for temporal clauses, which we suggest in Sec. 3, may have resulted in part from the experimental design. The largest proportion of responses for both sentence types (9) and (10) consists of responses in which the preposition was treated intransitively, and for the intransitive interpretations the difference in proportion of subject interpretations for PRO is large (14% for sentence type (9) versus 95% for type (10)). This suggests that even if we accept responses in which the main

---

[4]The pattern of results with respect to transitive readings of conditions (9) and (10) is similar for 18 children for whom stress reading was checked and established at 98% accurate; the difference in proportion of transitive readings does not reach significance for these children, however transitivity is calculated (24% vs. 15% for transitive readings with the object as subordinate object ($p > .10$ by t-test, 1 tail); 26% vs. 15% for all transitive readings ($p < .10 > .05$), not surprisingly, given the large proportion of intransitive interpretations for both conditions).

[5]After completing the sequence of sentences of types (9) and (10), children were presented with three tokens of a sentence with a purpose clause such as that in (9), but with stress on the preposition ("Daisy chooses Pluto to jump aróund"). These three sentences are listed at the end of Appendix 1; they were interspersed with three simple declarative sentences. Performance on these purpose clause sentences was similar to that for purpose clauses with stress on the verb (type 9); there was no significant effect of stress on proportion of transitive readings, however transitivity was calculated, for either the complete set of children or the stress-checked children (footnote 4). For both the stress-checked children and the complete set of children, there was a small trend (maximum difference 7%) in the direction predicted by sensitivity to the stress clue to transitivity. (A similar nonsignificant trend was found also for the 10-year-olds who took part in the shortened version of the experiment described in sec. 2).

clause object is made PRO and the main clause subject is made object of the preposition as genuine transitive responses for sentence type (9), the relative absence of such responses for (10) could derive from an experimentally induced bias toward making PRO refer to the main clause subject for temporals as much as from any knowledge of the difference in possibility of an object gap in the two sentence types (although such a bias in and of itself cannot explain why there were few responses in which the main clause object was made subordinate object for type (10)). Second, an item analysis revealed a lexical bias that may have reduced the number of transitive responses to sentence type (9). One of the tokens of type (9) had the matrix predicate "take along." With this predicate, children tended to make both main clause actors perform the action of the subordinate clause. There were 62 such responses in the complete experiment (Parts 1 and 2 combined, including purpose clauses with stress on the preposition, see fn. 5), of which 40 were for sentences with the main clause predicate "take along"; this response type was much more prevalent in the second part of the experiment (49 responses, of which 32 were with "take along") than the first, and in the second part of the experiment only occurred for sentence type (9) and purpose clauses with stress on the preposition, suggesting that this response is a reflection of the combination of matrix predicate with a potentially intransitive preposition in the subordinate clause.

Thus for two different reasons related to particulars of the experimental design and materials, we believe that the second part of the experiment may not have been as revealing as it might have been with respect to whether children obey the block on an object gap in temporal clauses.

In sum, Part 2 of the experiment shows a trend in the direction of sensitivity to the distinction between purpose clauses and temporal adjuncts with respect to the possibility of an object gap; however, the most convincing difference (in terms of proportion of responses corresponding to the adult transitive reading of purpose clauses) is not significant.

2. TEN-YEAR-OLDS

Part 1 of the experiment points up two gaps in children's knowledge. Children do poorly with respect to the interpretation of the subject of temporal adjuncts and with respect to purpose clauses with an object gap. Previous work suggests that the adult rule for temporals may be mastered quite soon after age 6 (see Hsu, Cairns & Fiengo, 1985). Purpose clauses have not been tested previously, but we suspect that knowledge of the adult rules for positing and interpreting an object gap in purpose clauses may not be acquired until well into the school years, at least for some children. One of us (Goodluck) tested eight 10-year-old children with an abbreviated version of the experiment reported here, as part of course in linguistics for school children at the University of Wisconsin. Each child acted out one token of sentence types (3–7) and two tokens of sentence types (9, 10). For the sentences of types (3–6), these 10-year-olds' performance was just as predicted under the adult rules as we have described them, with the exception that one child permitted the object of the *by*-phrase to control the PRO subject of the subordinate clause for the example of sentence type (6). For the sentence of type (7), six children acted out the sentence ("Pluto chooses Champion to run up to") in the way dictated by adult rules and without comment. But two children (different from the child who made the error with sentence type (6)) did comment on the sentence, and one acted it out incorrectly. The first child said "to run up to what?" and then acted out the sentence according to the adult interpretation. The second child acted out the sentence incorrectly and also provided some plain verbal evidence that he was unfamiliar with the construction involved, as the following extract from the interview shows:

Helen: Pluto chooses Champion to run up to.
Child: Can you repeat that please?
Helen: Pluto chooses Champion to run up to.
Child: . . . to run up to.
　　　　[acts out the sentence with Champion running away, toward
　　　　no one]
Helen: Pluto chooses Daisy to do some singing.
　　　　[child acts out the sentence correctly]
Child: That second to last one said, Pluto chooses Champion to run
　　　　up to . . . *what?*
Helen: Yeah, OK, you've to decide.

In the second part of the experiment, neither of these two children gave a transitive interpretation of the subordinate clause for purpose clause sentences of type (9), while the other six 10-year-olds each gave at least one transitive reading. Two of the six children who permitted a transitive reading for type (9) also gave transitive reading(s) for the temporal clauses of type (10). For these 10-year-olds, all transitive readings involved the main clause subject as referent of PRO and the main clause object as subordinate object. The percentage transitive interpretation for sentence type (9) was 62% (10/16 responses), compared with 19% (3/16 responses) for sentence type (10) ($t(7) = 3.17$, $p < .01$, one tail).

3. DISCUSSION

In this section we will first summarize the results of this and previous studies and then give an interpretation of these results in terms of the child's developing grammar.

The Facts

In our experiment, children clearly distinguish between complements that are attached to the VP (complements to *tell* and purpose clauses) and temporal adjuncts, which are attached to the main clause S node in the adult grammar.

With respect to the interpretation of the PRO subject of complements to *tell* and purpose clauses, the overall pattern of children's performance is adult-like, with selection of the NP with the thematic role *goal* or *theme* as controller of the PRO. With respect to adjuncts, children show a nonadult tendency to make the NP with the thematic role *agent* controller, in contrast to the adult rule, which requires reference between the PRO subject of a temporal clause and the surface subject of the main clause, regardless of the thematic role it occupies.

Success in interpreting the PRO subject of complements to *tell* with both active and passive main clauses has been found in several other studies (Goodluck 1981; Hsu et al., 1985; Maratsos 1974). Control of VP-attached purpose clauses has not previously been tested, to our knowledge.

Errors with S-attached adjuncts has also been typical of previous studies. However, the pattern of errors in this study is different from that in other studies. Goodluck (1981), Goodluck and Tavakolian (1982) and Hsu et al. (1985) found that children aged around 4–5 permitted a direct object to be controller of a temporal clause, but eschewed control by the object of a PP. In these studies, control by the object of a passive *by* phrase (as in sentence type (6)) was in general not permitted; nor was control by a locative/directional PP, as in sentences such as,

11. Daisy $\begin{Bmatrix} \text{stood near} \\ \text{walked by} \end{Bmatrix}$ Pluto [before PRO doing some reading]

Thus children in this study chose as controller of the PRO subject of a temporal adjunct a main clause NP (*by*-agent) that they largely if not entirely avoided as controller in previous studies (cf. Goodluck & Tavakolian, 1982, note 5).

Errors of coreference between a direct object and the PRO subject of a temporal adjunct are also found by Smith and van Kleeck (1986), Lust, Solan, Flynn, Cross, and Schuetz (1986) and Cairns and McDaniel (1988).

A different type of error for temporal adjuncts was found by Goodluck (1980, 1987), who found in one experiment that the large majority of children aged 5–6 preferred to make the PRO subject of a preposed adjunct, such as (12), refer to an entity not mentioned in the sentence, an interpretation that is not permitted in the adult grammar,

12 Before jumping the fence, the princess kissed the woman

This result with preposed adjuncts contrasts to the findings of Goodluck (1981), Hsu et al. (1985) and Lust et al. (1986) for the same clause type, where there was little evidence of external reference for the PRO subject of a temporal adjunct and where (in the study by Goodluck, 1981) choice of main clause subject or object as controller of the PRO correlated highly with choice of controller in the corresponding sentences with sentence-final adjuncts (sentence type 5).

In sum, with respect to PRO subject interpretation, children under age 7 appear to do well with complements attached within the VP, but they do poorly with respect to S-attached adjuncts, although how they go wrong may differ from experiment to experiment. It should be noted that across the experiments in which children are treating adjuncts in quite different ways, rather consistent patterns of responses are found for other constructions. For example, there is no comparable fluctuation across experiments in responses for complements to *tell;* and in Goodluck (1987) the same children who commit the error of external reference for adjuncts show an adult-like pattern of discrimination with respect to other sentence types involving structural restrictions on definite pronoun interpretation, replicating Solan (1983). Thus variation in performance with temporal adjuncts cannot be put down to some kind of general inattentiveness or failure of the experiments to tap children's grammatical knowledge.

In the present experiment we have identified another construction in which children do not appear to master the adult grammar until into the school years: purpose clauses with object gaps. The 4–6-year-olds did poorly on this construction in part 1 of the experiment, and two of the 10-year-olds we tested also had trouble with this construction.

In Part 2 as well as Part 1 of the experiment, children draw a distinction between VP complements and temporal adjuncts, permitting an object gap in purpose clauses more frequently than in temporal adjuncts, although the evidence for 4–6-year-olds is not clear-cut, as we have discussed.

Grammatical Interpretation

We propose the following picture of children's grammar of control constructions. From the earliest stages, children assign approximately the correct phrase structure analysis to the complement types we have tested. That is, complements to *tell* and purpose clauses are treated as constituents at (levels of) the VP, and temporal adjunct clauses are attached at some higher level. We assume these constituent structures to be invariant for languages of the English configurational type, and to be essentially written into Universal Grammar; particular semantic values of complements and adjuncts will be automatically assigned to certain positions on the tree.[6] Children's grammar of control will differ from the adult grammar in that temporal adjuncts, which we assume are obligatorily controlled by the main clause subject in the adult grammar will be free (arbitrary) control complements (Goodluck, 1987). As such, any pragmatically suitable entity in the environment may be construed as subject of a temporal, including NPs in the main clause and entities not mentioned in the sentence.[7]

Children's choice of a particular NP as subject of a temporal may be determined by particulars of the experimental situation. For example, in the experiment reported here, the NP with the thematic role *agent* may be favored as subject of the temporal because the experiment contained a high proportion of passive main clauses in the test sentences and (unlike previous experiments) there were simple passive sentences in the training session. The training sentences and concentration of passive sentences in the test sentences may have somehow focused the child on the thematic role agent, making that role salient and so promoting its choice as subject of temporals. Similarly, the high proportion of external interpretations of the subject of sentence-initial temporals such as (12) in Goodluck (1987) (in contrast to Goodluck, 1981, and Hsu et al., 1985) may derive from the fact that in that experiment there was a high concentration of sentences with infinitival and gerundial subject clauses with null or pronominal subjects (e.g., "(His) jumping quickly over the fence scares the pirate"), for which external interpretation of the subject is possible, and in some cases preferred, in the adult grammar.

On this account of children's performance with temporal clauses, what the child will have to learn is that temporal adjuncts are obligatorily controlled by the main clause subject in the adult grammar; the child will not have to learn that temporal adjuncts are immediate constituents of the main clause S node (or some higher level).

Our analysis contrasts to the account of children's treatment of temporal adjuncts given in Goodluck (1981) and Hsu et al. (1985), where it was proposed that this phrase type is misattached to the VP in early stages. This proposal had some explanatory force, for the results reported in those papers. As mentioned earlier, a basic finding of Goodluck and Hsu et al.

---

[6]We recognize that although this statement may be correct for the VP-attached purpose clauses and temporals we deal with in this study, the general picture may be more complex, as witnessed in particular by the fact that English permits clauses with a purpose-type reading to attach to the S node ((*in order*) *to* clauses; see Faraci, 1974, for an early discussion of the distinction between VP-attached purpose clauses and (*in order*) *to* clauses).

[7]Lust et al. (1986) and Goodluck (1980, 1987) also suggest that this clause type is a free control complement for children. The proposal is enhanced by the finding of Lust et al. that pragmatic context affects interpretation of the subject of a temporal.

was that children allowed subjects and direct objects, but not the object of prepositional phrases, to be made controller of temporal adjuncts. This pattern of results could be explained under a c-command condition on control of PRO, provided that temporal adjuncts were misattached to the VP; the subject and direct object c-command elements within a VP-attached clause, the object of a preposition does not,

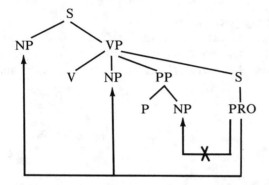

The results of the present experiment provide two arguments against the misattachment analysis. First, in the first part of the experiment, children allow the object of a passive *by*-phrase to be made controller of a temporal adjunct. This cannot be reconciled with a surface structure c-command condition on control without positing intuitively crazy structures, in which the temporal adjunct is attached within the *by*-phrase. Moreover, to attempt to account for control errors by misattachment would not explain why in this experiment children avoid control by a direct object. Second, Part 2 of the experiment showed that to some extent that children draw a distinction between purpose clauses and temporals with respect to object gaps; an explanatory account can be given of this distinction (albeit a weak one) if children know that temporals are attached outside the VP, contrary to the misattachment analysis.

The contrast between purpose clauses and temporal adjuncts with respect to the possibility of an object gap (7 vs. 8) can be explained as follows. We assume as a general grammatical constraint that all the elements to which a (nonparasitic) gap is linked must c-command that gap. In current transformational analyses, the object gap in purpose clauses will be derived by movement of an abstract operator (O) from object position to presentential position (see, e.g., N. Chomsky, 1986), and coindexing of the operator with a main clause NP. Under the c-command constraint just mentioned, such an operator must be linked to a c-commanding NP, a requirement that is met for purpose clauses by coindexing with the object,

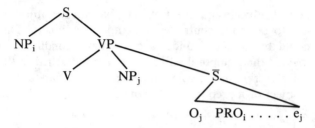

The absence of (nonparasitic) object gaps in temporal and other S-attached adjuncts will then follow from their structural position. The PRO subject of the adjunct is coindexed with the subject, leaving only the matrix object as the potential coreferent for the operator O; but the object does not c-command O,[8]

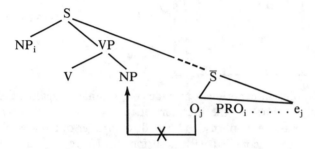

The c-command condition on gaps is one that we take to be an invariant property of Universal Grammar, plausibly available to children from the outset. On this (rather uncontroversial) assumption, failure to overgeneralize object gaps from purpose clauses to temporal adjuncts is to be expected, *provided* that children know that temporals are constituents of the main S node, not VP constituents.[9]

3. CONCLUSION

The results of this experiment fit with the growing conviction that although children 4 and younger have highly developed grammars that conform in

---

[8] A maximal-projection definition of c-command will be needed, given that purpose clauses are at a higher V-bar level than direct objects.

[9] There is some literature that argues that temporal adjuncts are constituents of the projection of V (see, for example, Andrews, 1982). If such arguments are correct, the first argument given here against an erroneous low-attachment of temporals by children (in terms of the inability of misattachment to account for control by a *by* phrase or relative absence of control by a direct object) will remain unaffected. The second argument (based on c-command of O, plus the lack of overgeneralization of object gaps to temporals) may be invalidated, although we have not worked the details through.

essential ways with the dictates of Universal Grammar, grammatical development is nonetheless a process that may extend well into the school years. Children must learn that S-attached adjuncts are obligatory control constructions.[10] It is not difficult to think of data that might in principle initiate such a change in their grammar (for example, "The dog bit the boy after scratching itself," in which knowledge of the binding theory plus the gender of reflexives will point to the correct control rule, although it will not uniquely determine that rule). How such change actually does take place is an empirical question, not yet addressed in either the experimental or observational literature. Our results also argue that object gaps in purpose clauses are acquired relatively late.[11] The difficulty children have with object gaps in purpose clauses invites comparison with the finding of several studies (Crain, 1988, notwithstanding) that object gaps in constructions of the *easy*-type ("John is easy to please") are frequently not mastered until the child is well into middle childhood (see Cromer, 1987, for one recent study and some refreshing commentary on pertinent learnability issues). Both object gaps in the *easy* construction and purpose clauses have been analyzed as involving covert (Operator) movement. On such an analysis, these studies fit with recent proposals that (components of) the grammar of movement may be acquired at different points in development (see Borer & Wexler, 1987; Nichigauchi & Roeper, 1987).

The deficiency of the data presently available on the development of gaps and the rules for deriving them is worth stressing. Child language studies characteristically do not provide evidence with respect to the standard diagnostics for whether a gap results from movement (in particular, we generally lack knowledge concerning children's sensitivity to subjacency). The nature of rules associated with gaps is thus very much an open question. In Part 2 of this experiment there was a degree of error in positing object gaps in temporal clauses. That is, although Part 2 of the experiment provided some evidence that children distinguish between purpose clauses and temporals with respect to the possibility of an object gap, the error of positing an object gap in temporals did occur (and was committed by two

---

[10]In the adult grammar an arbitrary reading can be assigned to the subject of a temporal where there is no suitable controller in the main clause (as in "After skiing quickly, hot chocolate tastes good"). However, where the surface subject is a suitable controller, control by the subject has the force of a rule, not simply a preference.

[11]Nishigauchi and Roeper (1987) give some examples of a 2–3-year-old child's spontaneous production of clauses with an object gap and a purpose-type interpretation. In none of the examples they give, however, does the purpose-type clause occur as complement to a verb such as *choose*, leaving open the possibility that object gaps within clauses with a purpose-type interpretation may develop at different times, depending on the host construction. Nichigauchi and Roeper suggest object gaps in early grammar may involve a pronominal element (pro) rather than movement.

10-year-olds). There is a burgeoning literature on object gaps that do not lend themselves straightforwardly to a movement analysis (see, e.g., Xu, 1986; Rizzi, 1986). The existence of some degree of object gap interpretations in this experiment for a construction (temporals) that solidly resists extraction via overt movement ("*What did John hit Bill before eating?"), at least suggests that there may be quite an extended period in which the child experiments in matching rule types to the input that he or she receives; object gaps in temporals may present themselves as a possibility via a mechanism other than movement.

Overall, basic structural configurations may be present in child grammars virtually from the outset, but the rules and operations that apply over those configurations may take years to develop.

Finally, we note the oddity of the findings with control of temporal adjuncts. It seems that control of this clause type by the subject of the sentence is the norm in languages of the world, including languages without a surface structure VP (for which subject control cannot be read off the surface structure by virtue of a c-command condition, unlike in English and similar languages; see Mohanan, 1983; Goodluck, 1985).[12] The case of control of S-adjuncts is thus a case in which children consistently fail where adult languages do not vary; as such it runs contrary to the commonly held view that the most frequent situations in languages of the world represent basic, unmarked situations that will govern child grammars from the outset.[13]

ACKNOWLEDGMENTS

This chapter was completed in early October 1988, and is a revised and expanded version of presentations given at the 61st Annual Meeting of the Linguistic Society of America, New York, 30 December 1986; the fourth International Congress for the Study of Child Language, Lund, Sweden, July 23, 1987; the 14th International Congress of Linguists, East Berlin, August 12, 1987; and McGill University, February 8, 1988. We are grateful to persons at those talks and also to Rita Manzini for helpful comments. The LSA presentation is published as Goodluck and Behne, 1988. A brief report on more recent experiments that continue the research reported

---

[12]The claim that control is by the subject may be correct only in the sense that when the subordinate subject is controlled by an NP inside the sentence, that NP will be the subject NP (cf. Goodluck, 1987; Lust et al., 1986).

[13]In Goodluck and Behne (1988), we suggest that failure with control of S-attached clauses may arise from a general inability to pick out the grammatical relation subject, or external argument. As Lydia White has pointed out to us, this idea clearly needs some working out, given that children reliably assign the right thematic roles to subject position of a verb from a very early age.

here is given in Goodluck, 1990. The work reported here was supported in part by funds from the Graduate School of the University of Wisconsin (project no. 170668, to Helen Goodluck).

REFERENCES

Andrews, A. (1982). A note on the constituent structure of adverbials and auxiliaries. *Linguistic Inquiry, 13,* 313–317.

Borer, H, & Wexler, K. (1987). The maturation of syntax. In *Parameter setting,* E. Williams & T. Roeper (Eds.). Reidel: Dordrecht, The Netherlands.

Cairns, H., & McDaniel, D. (1988). The processing and acquisition of control structures Paper presented at University of Massachusetts Conference on Language Acquisition and Parsing, May.

Chomsky, C. (1969). *The acquisition of syntax in children from 5 to 10.* Cambridge, MA: MIT Press.

Chomsky, N. (1986). *Barriers.* Cambridge, MA. MIT Press.

Crain, S. (1988). *Easy acquisition.* Paper presented at University of Massachusetts Conference on Language Acquisition and Parsing, May.

Cromer, R. (1987). Language growth with experience without feedback. *Journal of Psycholinguistic Research, 16,* 223–231.

Faraci, R. (1974). *Aspects of the grammar of infinitives and FOR-phrases.* Unpublished doctoral dissertation, MIT, Cambridge, MA.

Fodor, J. D. (1978). Parsing strategies and constraints on transformations. *Linguistic Inquiry, 8,* 427–473.

Goodluck, H. (1980). *Backward anaphora in child language.* Paper presented at the annual meeting of the Linguistic Society of America, New Orleans.

Goodluck, H. (1981). Children's grammar of complement subject interpretation. In *Language acquisition and linguistic theory,* S. Tavakolian, (Ed.). Cambridge, MA: MIT Press.

Goodluck, H. (1985). Deficits in sentence comprehension: Are they syntactic? *Applied Psycholinguistics, 6,* 1981–1989.

Goodluck, H. (1987). Children's interpretation of pronouns and null NPs. In *Studies in the acquisition of anaphora* (vol. 2), B. Lust (Ed.), Dordrecht, The Netherlands: Reidel.

Goodluck, H. (1990). Flashbulb effects in the development of operator movement. *Cahiers Linguistiques d'Ottawa,* 19, 91–101.

Goodluck, H., & Behne, D. (1988). External argument, thematic roles and control of adjuncts: A case of late-acquired knowledge. *Cahiers Linguistiques d'Ottawa, 16,* 103–113.

Goodluck, H., & Tavakolian, S. (1982). Competence and performance in children's comprehension of relative clauses. *Cognition, 11,* 1–27.

Hsu, J., H. Cairns, H., & Fiengo, R. (1985). The development of grammars underlying children's interpretation of complex sentences. *Cognition, 20,* 25–48.

Jaeggli, O. (1986). Passive. *Linguistic Inquiry, 17,* 587–622.

Jones, C. (1985). Agent, patient and control into purpose clauses. *Proceedings of the annual meeting of the Chicago Linguistics Society.*

Lust, B., Solan, L., Flynn, S., Cross, C., & Schuetz, E. (1986). A comparison of null and pronominal anaphora in first-language acquisition. In *Studies in the acquisition of anaphora* (Vol. 1), B. Lust (Ed.). Dordrecht, The Netherlands: Reidel.

Manzini, M. R. (1983). On control and control theory. *Linguistic Inquiry, 14,* 421–446.

Maratsos, M. (1974). How preschool children understand missing complement subject. *Child Development, 45,* 700–706.

Mohanan, K. (1983). Functional and anaphoric control. *Linguistic Inquiry, 14,* 651–674.

Nishigauchi, T. (1984). Control and the thematic domain. *Language, 60.*

Nishigauchi, T., & Roeper, T. (1987). Deductive parameters and growth of empty categories. In T. Roeper & E. Williams (Eds), *Parameter setting.* Dordrecht, The Netherlands: Reidel.

Rizzi, L. (1986). Null objects in Italian and the theory of *pro. Linguistic Inquiry 17,* 501–557.

Roeper, T. (1987). Implicit arguments and the head-complement relation. *Linguistic Inquiry, 18,* 267–310.

Smith, C., & Van Kleeck, A. (1986). Linguistic complexity and performance. *Journal of Child Language, 13,* 389–408.

Solan, L. (1983). *Pronominal reference: Child language and the theory of grammar.* Reidel: Dordrecht, The Netherlands.

Williams, E. (1987). Implicit arguments, the binding theory and control. *Natural Language and Linguistic Theory, 5,* 151–180.

Xu, L. (1986). Free empty category. *Linguistic Inquiry, 17,* 75–93.

APPENDIX

Test sentences — Part 1

1. Active main clause; complement to *tell*
   Daisy tells Pluto to sing to Champion.
   Champion tells Daisy to do some dancing.
   Pluto tells Champion to do some reading.
   Daisy tells Champion to dance around the chicken.
2. Passive main clause; complement to *tell*
   Champion is told by Pluto to run around Daisy.
   Pluto is told by Champion to read to the pig.
   Daisy is told by Pluto to do a somersault.
   Champion is told by Daisy to do some singing.
3. Active main clause; purpose clause
   Pluto takes Champion along to read to the turtle.
   Daisy picks Pluto to do a somersault.
   Champion chooses Daisy to do some singing.
   Pluto picks Champion to hop around Daisy.
4. Passive main clause; purpose clause
   Pluto is chosen by Daisy to do a somersault.
   Champion is chosen by Pluto to do some singing.
   Daisy is picked by Champion to read to Pluto.
   Pluto is picked by Daisy to dance around the pig.
5. Active main clause; temporal adjunct
   Champion kisses Daisy before doing a somersault.
   Pluto hits Champion before hopping around the chicken.
   Daisy hugs Pluto before singing to Champion.
   Champion hugs Pluto before doing some reading.

6. Passive main clause; temporal adjunct
   Daisy is hit by Champion before dancing around Pluto.
   Pluto is hugged by Daisy before doing a somersault.
   Champion is kissed by Pluto before reading to the turtle.
   Daisy is kissed by Pluto before doing some reading.
7. Purpose clauses with object gap
   Daisy chooses Champion to run up to.
   Champion takes Daisy along to read to.
   Pluto picks Champion to sing to.
   Champion chooses Daisy to hop towards.

Test sentences – Part 2

Materials with lead sentences and transitive stress pattern[14]

Purpose clauses

Pluto loves running and dancing.
Pluto picks Daisy to rún around.

Daisy loves running and dancing.
Daisy takes Champion along to dánce around.

Champion loves hopping and skipping.
Champion chooses Pluto to hóp around.

Temporal adjuncts

Daisy loves singing and dancing.
Daisy hugs Pluto before dáncing around.

Champion loves running and hopping.
Champion hits Daisy before hópping around.

Pluto loves running and jumping.
Pluto kisses Champion before rúnning around.

Purpose clauses with intransitive stress pattern

Daisy takes Pluto along to run aróund.
Pluto chooses Champion to hop aróund.
Champion picks Daisy to dance aróund.

---

[14]The lead and test sentences were presented in two different combinations, equalizing across subjects and clause type the occurrence of the subordinate verb in the test sentence as first or second verb in the lead sentence.

8 Comments on Goodluck and Behne

Charles Jones
George Mason University

The primary finding of the research reported in Goodluck and Behne's chapter, that adult competence in certain control structures is acquired rather late, has significance beyond the simple empirical fact. A two-sided question arises about the nature of the differences between the structures that are learned early and those that are learned late. One side of the question concerns the nature of the adult grammar; the other side of the question concerns how the child grammar approximates the adult grammar. In these comments I want to discuss, somewhat speculatively, these differences.

My primary focus will be on the differences between temporal adjuncts and purpose clauses. I focus on these constructions for two reasons. First, Goodluck and Behne's research into the differences between purpose clauses and other adjuncts explores new territory. Second, their research raises interesting questions about the differences between the properties of S-adjuncts and VP-adjuncts.

These comments will be organized as follows. In Sec. 1, I discuss the nature of the adult grammar, and, within the framework of Williams's (1980) Predication theory of control, I propose a characterization of the adult grammar that differs from the characterization of it that Goodluck and Behne offer. In Sec. 2, I consider how the child grammar approximates the adult grammar in dealing with VP-adjuncts and S-adjuncts. In Sec. 3, I discuss the question of lexical grammar: How much of the syntax can be expected to be driven by the lexicon?

1. ADJUNCTS AND CONTROL

Goodluck and Behne find that, while children's performance on infinitive complements of a verb like *tell* and intransitive purpose complements of *choose* reflects adult competence, their performance on object-gap purpose clauses and temporal adjuncts does not. The nature of the adult grammar of these constructions, however, is not completely clear, especially in the case of temporals. In Sec. 1.1, I propose, and briefly justify, an alternative to Goodluck and Behne's characterization of the syntax of temporals. In Sec. 1.2, I contrast temporals with purpose clauses.

1.1 Temporals and Nonobligatory Control

Goodluck and Behne conclude that temporal adjuncts are free (arbitrary) control complements for children, and they contrast the children's grammar of control to the adult grammar of control, which they state involves obligatory control of the subject of the temporal adjunct by the main clause subject. Here I want to suggest an alternative analysis.

Williams (1980) proposes a theory of control in which there is a strict two-way distinction between structures of obligatory control (OC) and structures of nonobligatory control (NOC).[1] Williams proposes five criteria by which OC constructions can be distinguished from NOC constructions.

(1) OC1. Lexical NP cannot appear in the position of PRO
     OC2. The antecedent precedes the controlled PRO
     OC3. The antecedent c-commands the controlled PRO
     OC4. The antecedent is thematically . . . or grammatically . . . uniquely determined.
     OC5. There must be the antecedent. (from Williams, 1980, p. 209)

Williams suggests that there are no cases of control that have overlapping properties: "if any property of OC is lacking for a particular case of control, we would expect the other properties of OC to be lacking for that case as well" (p. 212).

Williams's fifth criterion for OC, OC5, entails that it should be impossible to find, in OC constructions, control from discourse or context. However, in a footnote, Goodluck and Behne acknowledge that such control is in fact possible for temporals: "In the adult grammar an arbitrary

---

[1]Williams (1980) proposes to reduce "control" to a more general phenomenon: "predication." I will not adopt Williams's proposed usage here, but will instead continue to use the more traditional term, "control," for the phenomena under discussion.

reading can be assigned to the subject of a temporal where there is no suitable controller in the main clause (as in "After skiing quickly, hot chocolate tastes good")" (footnote 10, Goodluck & Behne, This volume).

Such context control would, in Williams's theory, place temporals in the class of NOC constructions, and Williams would have us expect that the other criteria for OC to be absent as well. The criterion that will be of particular interest in these comments is the c-command requirement of OC3. If temporals are NOC structures, then their antecedents need not (strictly) c-command into them.[2] In what follows I will adopt a Williams-style analysis of temporals as S-level NOC adjuncts in the adult grammar, not strictly c-commanded by any element in the matrix sentence, keeping in mind that this conception is provisional.[3]

Control of NOC constituents, that is, finding some referent for the PRO other than the "arb" construal, is accomplished via coindexing the PRO of the construction with some NP that is not characterized by the properties in (1). The PRO of an NOC construction appears to be subject, more or less, to a principle like Recoverability of Deletion, insofar as finding an antecedent for it is more or less obligatory.[4] In cases where there are

---

[2]If temporals are actually S-level adjuncts, then this property of not being strictly c-commanded is anticipated by current thinking on adjunction structures. Cf. Chomsky (1986), where May's (1985) idea about *segments created by adjunction* is adopted. In adjunction structures of the form in (i), α is not dominated by β, because it is not dominated by every *segment* of β.

i. $[_\beta \, \alpha \, [_\beta \, \ldots \,]]$

α cannot strictly be c-commanded by any element in β, due to the characterization of c-command in terms of dominance. Elements in β are dominated by a categorial projection, namely β, that does not dominate α, hence nothing in β can c-command α. This revision of the notion of dominance has been developed largely within the theory of LF. I will not here attempt to work through the ramifications that these developments have for S-structure adjunctions, consequently throughout the rest of these comments I will continue with the more common assumption that c-command involves simple domination by some maximal projection. I will distinguish the common version of c-command from the newly developing "segmental" version by referring to the latter as "strict" c-command.

[3]It is not clear to me whether Williams's three other criteria, OC1, OC2, OC4, straightfor-wardly support (or not) the non-OC (i.e., NOC) status of temporals. That is, I can see various ways to view the facts that could support either position. This is not the place to sort these difficulties out in any detail, so I will assume with Williams (p. 213) that if "some of the cases seem to have some of the properties of OC . . . ;" then ". . . this is a mere appearance . . . ; usually there is an independent reason why a particular case of NOC appears to have a property of OC." The need for such a dodge on three of the criteria indicates just how unclear the syntactical status of temporals is for advocates of either the Goodluck and Behne OC hypothesis and the present NOC hypothesis.

[4]If Recoverability of Deletion works in addition to, rather than subsuming, or being subsumed by, the ordinary pronominal coreference strategies, then we may have the

(pragmatically) suitable NP antecedents "close enough" to PRO, then NOC indexing becomes possible. The nature of the closeness of the choices for antecedents in the examples in (2) indicates that there is a kind of "telescoping" set of locality preferences.

(2) a. John$_j$ kissed Mary$_m$ [before [PRO$_{j/*m/*arb}$ leaving]]
   b. [$_S$[PRO$_{i/arb?}$ to leave] would be fine with me$_i$]
   c. John$_j$ told Mary$_m$ that [$_S$[PRO$_{i/*j/*m/?arb}$ to leave] would be fine with me$_i$]
   d. John$_j$ told Mary$_m$ that [$_S$ it would be OK [PRO$_{j/m/j+m/arb}$ to leave]]
   e. John$_j$ gave Mary$_m$ the news. He$_j$ said that [$_S$ it would be OK [PRO$_{j/m/j+m/arb}$ to leave]]

Sentence (2a) shows that with two possible local NP antecedents, the NP that comes closest to c-commanding the NOC construction wins. (2b) shows that an antecedent need not c-command PRO, and (2c) shows that, where there are several possible antecedents, the closer antecedent, in terms of clause membership, wins. (2d) shows that NOC can work across embedded clause boundaries, and (2e) indicates that it can work across discourse boundaries. Also illustrated in the examples in (2) is that, as the antecedents get further away, the possibility of opting for the "arb" interpretation is enhanced.

I will assume the foregoing outline as a theory of the adult grammar. In a theory like this, the apparent OC by matrix subject that Goodluck and Behne claim for temporals is instead a consequence of (what I will refer to as) the NOC "telescope." In sections to follow, I present a characterization of the child grammar that differs from the adult grammar by not having the NOC telescope. That is, the adult grammar of NOC uses essentially pronominal coreference strategies within a telescoping set of locality preferences, while the child simply uses pronominal coreference.

1.2 Purpose Clauses and Obligatory Control

Goodluck and Behne's experimental material contains both kinds of VP-attached purpose clauses (PC), those with a single gap in subject position, which I refer to as "subject-gap purpose clauses" (SPC), and those with both a missing subject and a missing object, which I refer to as "object-gap purpose clauses" (OPC). The experimental materials do not deal with purposive S-adjoined *in order* clauses, which share with the

---

beginnings of an explanation for the kind of child grammar S-internal preferences for PRO found in research like Goodluck's (1987).

S-adjoined temporal adjuncts the possibility of having a context-controlled empty subject.

(3) The lights were turned off [(in order) PRO_{arb} to conserve electricity]

I will periodically refer to these constructions, however, because they have certain properties, such as S-adjunction, in which they differ from PC, and which they share with temporal adjuncts.[5]

I will assume here without argument that the control properties of SPC and OPC in the adult grammar are as in (4b, 5b), respectively.[6]

(4) SPC
    a. i. Daisy chooses $Pluto_i$ [PRO_i to do some reading]

                                           (= G&B (3))

      ii. $Daisy_i$ is chosen by Pluto [PRO_i to do some reading]

                                           (= G&B (4))

    b. Subject position is obligatorily controlled by matrix Theme argument.

(5) OPC
    a. i. $Daisy_i$ chooses $Pluto_j$ [PRO_i to read to e_j]   (= G&B (7))
      ii. $Daisy_i$ was chosen [PRO_{arb} to read to e_i]
    b. i. Object position is obligatorily controlled by matrix Theme argument.
      ii. Subject position is non-obligatorily controlled[7]

Goodluck and Behne's theoretical characterization of object-gap adjuncts as attached to VP in the child grammar is consistent with, but does not follow necessarily from, their results with the object-gap sentences. I will return to this matter in Sec. 2.2.1.2 to argue for an interpretation of the authors' results concerning their sentence (7 (= our (5ai)) and their Part 2 that does not necessitate a VP-attachment analysis for the child's (early)

---

[5]There is extensive discussion of S-level status for *in order* clauses vs. VP-level status for PC in Faraci (1974) and Jones (1985, in press). See Kirkpatrick (1982) for an opposing view. We return to this distinction in Sec. 2.2.1.2.

[6]Cf. Faraci (1974), Bach (1982), Jones (1985, in press) for discussion of these properties.

[7]NOC of the OPC subject can be seen by the possibility of the PRO_{arb} interpretation of the passivized subject of the OPC subject in (5aii). Removal of the subject argument by passivization is not necessary for such interpretation, however. Bach (1982) points out that in a sentence like (i) there is no necessary presupposition that I alone am going to drink the wine.

    i. I_i brought this $wine_j$ along [$PRO_{(i?)/arb}$ to drink e_j with dinner] grammar. For now let us assume, with Goodluck and Behne, the standard GB, "empty operator" analysis of (the adult) OPC, and follow their argument. In the standard analysis, the object gap within OPC is derived by what is essentially *wh*-movement of a phonetically empty operator, as in (6).

(6) $[_{S'} O_i [_S PRO \ldots e_i \ldots]]$

The standard assumption about the empty operator, from Chomsky (1982), is that it must be licensed by being coindexed by a strictly c-commanding matrix NP. Goodluck and Behne suggest that this principle will place the OPC within VP for a child grammar in which the c-command restriction is assumed to be operative. With the OPC in VP, the matrix object can control the operator, and the matrix subject can control the OPC subject, as in (7).

(7)

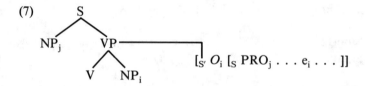

$[_{S'} O_i [_S PRO_j \ldots e_i \ldots]]$

However, there is another logically possible control pattern that is consistent with both the c-command restriction on binding and the (adult grammar) requirement that the empty operator be bound: that of Goodluck and Behne's Type 3 errors, in which the control pairs are switched, as in (8).

(8) $[NP_j [V NP_i [O_j [PRO_i \ldots e_j \ldots]]]]$ Type 3 errors

While 30% (51/168) of the OPC responses showed the correct control pattern in (7), another 29% (48/168) showed the switched-control pattern in (8). While there is no indication that the children who "get" the double-gap nature of OPC have any robust intuitions about any differences between the natures of the two gaps, the fact that 60% (99/168) of the responses have some form of interpretation of both gaps is consistent with the hypothesis that OPC attaches at VP, where there are two possible c-commanding antecedents available as controllers, is operative in the child grammar.[8]

---

[8]The adult grammar apparently has a more complex requirement on a binder than simple (i.e., branching node) c-command. Kirkpatrick (1982) points out that an OPC object gap within certain kinds of VPs can be controlled by an NP within a PP, as in (i, ii).

  i. They presented Mary $[_{PP}$ with [a copy of the charges against her]$_i]$ [to read e$_i$ while she waited to be fingerprinted].

What is not clear from Goodluck and Behne's grammatical interpretation of their results is why object-gap temporals never make it into the adult grammar. While the c-command restriction on binding and the requirement that the empty operator be bound are both consistent with a VP-adjoined OPC, they are not sufficient by themselves to rule out an S-level object-gap construction. Insofar as there is no evidence (in the adult grammar) that the PRO subject of an object-gap construction is subject to OC, there is no reason not to expect a construction like that in (9).

(9) a. *Daisy$_i$ hits Pluto [before [$_{S'}$ O_i [$_S$ PRO$_{arb}$ jumping around e$_i$]] (= G&B (10))

b.

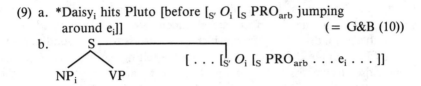

[. . . [$_{S'}$ O_i [$_S$ PRO$_{arb}$ . . . e$_i$ . . .]]

I will suggest in Sec. 2.2.3 that such a construction is impossible because S-level is a level of NOC. Subject NPs do not strictly c-command S-level adjuncts.

1.3 Summary

In this section I have tried to clarify certain aspects of the adult grammar with respect to two of the constructions that are included in Goodluck and Behne's experimental material: temporal adjuncts and purpose clauses. I have proposed that the PRO subjects of both temporal adjuncts and object-gap purpose clauses are not subject to strictly obligatory control in the adult grammar, and that object gaps are. The resultant picture of adult competence is quite complex. However, now that we can see it more or less clearly, we are in a better position to see how the child grammar approximates it.

2. VP-ADJUNCTION VS. S-ADJUNCTION

The authors under review assume throughout their chapter that there are two kinds of adjunction: adjunction to VP and adjunction to S. The two principal questions about these two kinds of adjunction would be (a) is there any syntactic reason to believe, or disbelieve, that such different adjunctions are in fact operative, at least in the adult grammar, and (b) if they are operative, are there characterizable differences between their

---

ii. Joan searched the skyline [$_{pp}$ for [the Empire State Building]$_i$] [to point e$_i$ out to Ralph].

properties? I take up these questions in turn, the first rather quickly and the second at some length.

2.1 Are There 2 Kinds of Adjunction?

The assumption of a general c-command requirement on binding and control makes the S-adjunction/VP-adjunction distinction attractive, insofar as it would preclude, as the authors suggest, object control mistakes for temporal adjuncts. Results like these don't often come for free, so it should take a strong set of counterarguments to make us abandon the simple structural distinction from which these results follow. Goodluck and Behne (this volume, footnote 9) acknowledge, citing Andrews (1982), that there exist arguments that temporal adjuncts are constituents of the projection of V. I will here briefly discuss how Andrews's argument bears on the work that the VP-adjunction/S-adjunction difference does in the theory of Goodluck and Behne.

Andrews's major claim about temporal adverbials is that they are allowed to "go along" with the VP in various transformations that appear to affect VP: VP Preposing (10a), *though*-movement (10b), and *wh*-clefting (10c).

(10) a. Daisy said she'd hug Pluto before singing to Champion, and [hug Pluto before singing to Champion] she did.
   b. [Hug Pluto before singing to Champion] though she may have, she still will go with him to the ball.
   c. What Daisy did was [hug Pluto before singing to Champion].

Let us sidestep the question of how strong a role such exotic constructions as VP Preposing and *though*-movement could play in the primary data available to the child learning the language. In what follows, I will deal only with the fairly quotidian *wh*-cleft. The force of Andrews's examples depends on how obligatory it is that the adjuncts accompany the clefted material. True VP elements such as subcategorized complements (11a) and purpose clauses (11b) cannot be separated from their VP in *wh*-clefts, while temporals (11c) and S-level *in order* clauses (11d) can.

(11) a. *What Daisy did [in the garage] was [put the car e].
   b. *What Daisy did [to read e] was [buy *Moby Dick* e].
   c. What Daisy did [before singing to Champion] was [hug Pluto].
   d. What Daisy did [(in order) to make Champion jealous] was [hug Pluto].

Andrews's examples do demonstrate that S-level adjuncts can participate with the VP in the constructions in question, and this fact of course calls for some kind of explanation. There are several possibilities. Perhaps these structures are derived by "stylistic rules" that operate on the ends of surface strings, either without regard to strict constituency, or with regard to some kind of reanalysis of the string-final structure. Another possibility would be that S-level adjuncts have no inherent level, but attach freely to either S or VP. Whatever the nature of the explanation for how temporals can "follow" VP in these rules, the fact that they are not obligated to, in contrast to true VP elements, is evidence that they are syntactically independent from VP. S-level is an appropriate level at which such independence can be established.

2.2 Differences

Does VP-adjunction contrast with S-adjunction? That is, are they two fundamentally different kinds of adjunction? The sets of properties in (12) appear to cluster around the two kinds of adjunction. The question arises whether these are true properties, or merely coincidences.

(12) VP-attachment   S-attachment
    a. obligatory control   a. (possible) "context" control
    b. object/Theme controller   b. subject/Agent orientation
    c. object gaps   c. no object gaps

2.2.1 OC vs. NOC

We have seen that *in order* clauses and temporal gerunds allow context control of their only gap: a subject gap. Is this a characteristic property of S-attached adjuncts?

The corresponding VP-attachment question, of course, is whether there are any demonstrably context-control adjuncts, or complements, at VP level. OPC, with its PRO_{arb} subject, cannot count as an instance, since the empty object calls for OC.[9]

---

[9]A candidate for a VP-level NOC construction is the infinitive complement of a verb like *want*. In Williams's (1980) theory, the fact that the subject position can hold lexical material, as in (ii), disqualifies such complements from OC status.

    i. Mary$_i$ wants [PRO$_i$ to leave].

    ii. Mary wants [John to leave].

The control of PRO in (i) must be accomplished by the NOC "telescope," not by OC. It is reasonable to attribute this unusual VP-level case of NOC to the lexical idiosyncrasy of the governing verb *want*.

2.2.1.1 S-adjunction.   Assume for the moment that the distinction between S-adjunction and VP-adjunction is a real one (abstracting away from lexically idiosyncratic cases like *want,* discussed in fn. 9). The beginning of a plausible story about the child grammar of S-adjoined structures, one for which there would be plenty of positive evidence around for a child to pick up, is that *before* and *after* complements both have finitely tensed counterparts.

(13) a. . . . before [I could get home]
     b. . . . after [I got home]

Further, there is a fully clausal purpose construction, the *so that* construction, that differs from the *in order* construction only by having finite tense.

(14) a. . . . so that [I could get home]
     b. . . . (in order) [(for me) to get home]

It would seem that there would be ample suggestive evidence to support a child grammar hypothesis that the complements of *before* and *after,* as well as the *so that* purposive construction, function more as clausal conjunctions, on a par, say, with *and S,* than as some kind of subordinated adjunct, and this conjunct analysis could be generalized to cover *before* and *after* phrases with subjectless *ing*-complements, *in order* complements, and extend to *with* and *without* phrases, which do not have finitely tensed complements.

The kind of picture outlined herein of the acquisition of S-level adjuncts suggests the following kind of story about the control properties of S-level constructions with empty subjects. If we assume that S-attached elements are effectively conjuncts in the early child grammar, that is, at a level of Discourse Grammar that is independent, and subsequent, to the level of Sentence Grammar (cf. Williams, 1977, for discussion of this distinction), then obligatory control, whose essential domain is S, is not possible.[10]

---

[10]In Manzini's (1983) theory of control, S-level adjuncts must be obligatorily controlled. Manzini is aware, however, of S-level *in order* sentences like (i), in which there is no lexically present controller.

i. Mary was fired [PRO to hire Bill].   (= Manzini's (54))

Manzini's theory requires control to be obligatory even in examples like these. Consequently, Manzini must assume that the arbitrary reference of the PRO is "the result of control by a phonologically null agent." I will continue to assume, *pace* Manzini, that the possibility of such PROs unbound by lexically present controllers is evidence that the position of the PRO is subject to NOC.

Rather, something like pronominal coreference strategies take over to find a referent for the empty subject NP. Alongside instances of sentences like (15a), with a freely referring pronominal, we have sentences like (15b)(= G&B (12)), with PRO. In the absence of any clues that might suggest other interpretations, both the pronoun and PRO gravitate to coreference to one of the NPs in the sentence. In the adult grammar, "the telescope" calls for NOC by the c-commanding subject NP.

(15) a. Before she jumped the fence, the princess kissed the woman.
    b. Before PRO jumping the fence, the princess kissed the woman.

It apparently takes a while for the child to learn that PRO construal is subject to the NOC "telescope," rather than to simple pronominal coreference. The child's control strategy appears to be a kind of "pronominal control." Goodluck and Behne, in their review of the experimental literature, report that the character of detected S-attached adjunct errors appears to vary from experiment to experiment. The kinds of errors they report: control by the matrix object, control from a *by* phrase, and control from context, are all characteristic of possible pronominal coreference.

(16) a. *The prince kissed the woman$_i$ before PRO$_i$ jumping the fence.
    b. The prince kissed the woman$_i$ before she$_i$ jumped the fence.

(17) a. *The prince was kissed by the woman$_i$ before PRO$_i$ jumping the fence.
    b. The prince was kissed by the woman$_i$ before she$_i$ jumped the fence.

(18) a. *The prince$_i$ kissed the woman$_j$ before PRO$_{i+j/k}$ jumping the fence.
    b. The prince$_i$ kissed the woman$_j$ before they$_{i+j/k}$ jumped the fence.

Goodluck and Behne note that "children's choice of a particular NP as subject of a temporal may be determined by particulars of the experimental situation." An essentially malleable pronominal strategy for control of S-attached adjuncts makes an attractive explanation.

The adult grammar distinguishes S-adjuncts, which are subject to the NOC telescope, from conjuncts, and this fact calls for some explanation. My best guess about the nature of the positive evidence that would distinguish these two kinds of constructions would be constructions in which S-level adjuncts are preposed, as in (19a). True conjuncts have preposing possibilities, illustrated in (19b), that differ from those of adjuncts, and these differences might indicate that adjuncts are more tightly attached to their S than are conjuncts.

(19) a. After he left, John felt sick. = John felt sick after he left.
     b. i. He left(,) and John felt sick. ≠ John felt sick and he left.
        ii. *And he left, John felt sick.

2.2.1.2 VP-adjunction. How the child assigns the VP-level constructions to VP may happen in a couple of different ways. For subcategorized complements of verbs like *tell,* I presume that the requirement of lexical government of V over its complements will effectively keep the complements in VP.

The general story for PC may be more complex. Goodluck and Behne use in their experimental material a verb, *choose,* which Bach (1982) convincingly argues actually subcategorizes for PC. Such subcategorization would place any PC complement to *choose* unambiguously inside VP. Jones (1985, in press), however, raises several questions about the argument/adjunct status of PC in general. Bach's characterization of the PC complement of *choose* as a subcategorized complement may be one of only a couple of special cases. If in fact PC are not in most cases subcategorized, but are in fact adjuncts to VP, then the child will have to use some strategy other than lexical government to put the PC inside VP.[11] I know of no simple kind of positive evidence available to the child that would determine this choice. (In fact it takes a considerable amount of argument to show that such a distinction actually exists, and makes a difference, in the general case; cf. fn. 5.)

Goodluck and Behne (p. 163, this volume) suggest that PC attachment to VP is simply universal.

> From the earliest stages, children assign approximately the correct phrase structure analysis to the complement types we have tested. That is, complements to *tell* and purpose clauses are treated as constituents at (levels of) the VP, and temporal adjunct clauses are attached at some higher level. We assume these constituent structures to be invariant for languages of the English configurational type, and to be essentially written into Universal Grammar . . .

If VP attachment of PC is simply a universal, as they suggest, then there is of course no problem posed by the fact that it is achieved in the adult

---

[11]Helen Goodluck (personal communication) suggests that the differences noted in Goodluck and Behne between responses involving *choose/pick* matrix verbs and *take along* may reflect this difference in the status of the PC between subcategorized complement and adjunct.

grammar. However, the child grammar pronominal control suggested above for S-attached adjuncts raises questions about how Goodluck and Behne's OPC data are to be interpreted. The 50/50 split between correct responses and Type 3 errors in the OPC examples that we have noted suggests that both the object gap and subject gap of OPC may be subject to the same kind of pronominal control in the child grammar that characterizes the (early) control of the subject of temporal adjuncts. If simple pronominal control is a general characteristic of conjuncts, then Goodluck and Behne's results do not necessarily argue against an early child grammar conjunct analysis of OPC like that in (20).

(20) $[_S$ S $[_{OPC}$ . . . pro . . . pro . . .]]

In addition to the 60% of the responses in which two gaps are apparently interpreted as pronominals, there is a very small 4% (7/168) of the responses that show simple subject control of a subject-gap only, and a more robust 22% (37/168) that show object control of a subject-gap only. Neither of these apparently subject-gap kinds of responses give any evidence that the child is not treating the PC as a conjunct, subject to simple pronominal control.

Because the adult grammar must end up having PC inside VP, it is a legitimate question whether the child must somehow learn this adjunction site, and, if it has to be learned, what kind of evidence could serve to trigger VP adjunction. A story along the lines developed here would be something like this: The child learns about conjunction first, and generalizes. As soon as the child figures out that certain purposive infinitives are primarily Theme controlled (rather than assuming, roughly speaking, the Agent orientation that characterizes S-level adjuncts), then the decision, or parameter, or whatever, that goes into effect is along the following lines: "That's not a conjunct. It's not Agent controlled either, so it's not an S-level adjunct. It must be attached elsewhere, and there's no place to attach but lower in the tree: Attach it to the next maximal projection down. Attach it to VP."

This account ties VP adjunction closely to the child's learning the obligatory Theme control of the OPC object. Such a development moves in the direction that a subset theory of acquisition would predict (cf., e.g., Wexler & Manzini, 1987). The initial set of adjunctions sites is (conjunction), the resultant (adult) set is (conjunction, S, VP). The initial set of control strategies is (pronominal control), the resultant (adult) set is (obligatory control, the NOC telescope, simple pronominal control (perhaps only as a last resort)). In the next two sections, I discuss further properties that seem to correlate with this kind of development.

2.2.2 Object/Theme Control vs. Subject/Agent Control

Goodluck and Behne's results show that, in the child grammar, c-command loses to thematic role: Agent is ascendent over Subject. When there is a decision between Subject, whose syntactic position c-commands everything (everything that is important to the argument structure, that is), and Agent; Agent wins, whether the Agent argument c-commands or not. When there is no Agent in the (passive) sentence, the child will go outside into the context, or into the prepositional *by*-phrase, in order to find an Agent to control the subject of the infinitive.

What this kind of error suggests is that the rules of control in the child grammar are articulated in a conceptual vocabulary that differs from the adults'. Not only does the child appear to handle control principally in terms of thematic relations (cf. Maratsos, 1974), the actual rule seems to involve some kind of thematic "matching": Empty subject positions, canonically the position of Agent (cf. Marantz, 1984), seek control by arguments that can qualify as Agents, no matter where they are. The adult rules of control are more complex.[12] We could imagine that the onset (or maturation; cf. Felix, 1984; Borer & Wexler, 1987) of a c-command requirement on control may cause the child to re-evaluate the thematic matching control rule in favor of whatever constitutes the adult rule.[13]

2.2.3 Object Gaps vs. No Object Gaps.

We find no readily available object-gap constructions at S-level in the adult grammar. That is, we find no constructions that have the properties hypothesized earlier in (9). Object-gap constructions are possible in the adult grammar only at VP.

It apparently takes a while before the child learns how to "build" an OPC correctly. That is, suppose that the standard analysis of OPC in (6) correctly characterizes the structure of OPC. It takes a while for the child to get from the structure in (20), which I have hypothesized for the child grammar, to (6). Suppose that knowledge of how to build an OPC includes knowledge of the conditions under which the OPC must be "licensed." There are various theoretical proposals about the nature of this licensing, all having in common a stricter licensing requirement on the hypothesized empty oper-

---

[12]I have suggested elsewhere (Jones, 1985, 1988) that the adult rule of obligatory control involves a kind of thematic matching, however nontraditional thematic roles do the work. See Ladusaw and Dowty (1988) for further discussion. See also Farkas (1988) for a theory that I think suggests a similar kind of nontraditional "thematic" matching.

[13]It could be that the c-command requirement on control differs somewhat from the c-command requirement on the binding relevant to the GB Principles A–C of Chomsky (1981). Cf. Kirkpatrick's (1982) examples in fn. 6. Any differences in the natures of the c-commands would provide for the possibility that the two kinds of c-command requirement might be learned at different times.

ator than NOC. Chomsky (1982), for example, suggests that the operator must be assigned a range, through being predicated of a c-commanding NP; Aoun and Clark (1985) suggest that, as an A-bar anaphor, the operator must be licensed either by A-bar-binding or predication. If S-level is characteristically a level of NOC, then there are no potential, that is, strictly c-commanding, controllers at that level. Were there a true empty operator construction at S-level, there would be nothing at that altitude to license it. The picture of the situation that emerges is this: Where there are no possible licensers, there are no licencees.

3. PROSPECTS FOR THE LEXICON

Goodluck and Behne's evidence that adult competence in an area of the grammar is established quite late begins to suggest the limits of what *lexical grammar* is capable of accounting for. Wasow (1985) insightfully notes that a common direction in at least three syntactic theories: GB, GPSG, and LFG; has been toward making increasingly richer syntactic phenomena follow from the lexical properties of the words involved. In a certain sense in all three theories, the words themselves generate much of the syntax. In a more or less parallel development in acquisition theory, the possibility that parametric choices are to be associated with lexical items is currently under serious discussion. Wexler and Manzini's (1987) *Lexical Parametrization Hypothesis* explicitly spells out this aim: "*Values of a parameter are associated not with particular languages, but with particular lexical items in a language.*"

Safir (1987), in his comments on Wexler and Manzini's paper, points out that lexicalization of parameters runs in a general direction toward undergeneralization. The question that arises for syntax, *qua* syntax, is whether there are (plausibly) syntactic phenomena for which there are no satisfying lexical generalizations. Control is an interesting case, insofar as the obligatory instances of it have frequently been held to be to a great extent lexically governed. I think that there can be reasonable interpretations of Goodluck and Behne's results that raise questions about the feasibility of a generally lexical account of control, including obligatory control.

In the case of S-adjuncts, if they are invariabley NOC constructions, then lexical grammar can say very little about them except for characterizing certain Principle B-type restrictions on the kind of pronominal coreference available to strategies of control.

Perhaps more surprisingly, however, the present considerations raise questions about how much lexical grammar can characterize S-internal VP-attached adjuncts. Consider the case of *choose*. Suppose that *choose* in fact subcategorizes for PC of both kinds: SPC and OPC. Does the child who does not know the adult construction of OPC "know" the lexical properties of *choose* only imperfectly? Or consider OPC with respect to verbs other than *choose;* that is, suppose that OPC is more generally an adjunct, one that can attach to a variety of semantically compatible VP, such as one headed by *buy.*

(22) I bought it$_i$ [to read e$_i$]

When one learns how to "build" an OPC, does one then learn something about the lexical properties of *buy?* It is not obvious that the answer to questions like these should be "Yes." The development of control of adjuncts and purpose clauses that I have outlined here is not as much concerned with the lexical properties of words as it is with a kind of structural experimentation on the part of the language learner.

Theoretical discussions of control often begin with a caveat, character-istically offered with a kind of deadpan understatement: "The theory of Control is not a homogenous one, in that it seems to involve information coming from syntax, semantics, and pragmatics. (Sells, 1985, p. 73). Research like that presented by Goodluck and Behne begins to sort out what the nature, or natures, of the components of control might be. Here is grist for the theoretical mill.

REFERENCES

Andrews, A. (1982). A note on the constituent structure of adverbials and auxiliaries. *Linguistic Inquiry, 13,* 313–317.

Aoun, J., & Clark, R. (1985). On non-overt operators. *Southern California Occasional Papers in Linguistics,* pp. 17–36. Los Angeles: University of Southern California.

Bach, E. (1982). Purpose clauses and control. In P. Jacobson & G. K. Pullum (Eds.), *The nature of syntactic representation.* Dordrecht, The Netherlands: Reidel.

Borer, H., & Wexler, K. (1987). The maturation of syntax. In T. Roeper & E. Williams (Eds.), *Parameter setting* (pp. 123–172). Dordrecht, The Netherlands: Reidel.

Chomsky, N. (1981). *Lectures on government and binding.* Dordrecht, The Netherlands: Foris.

Chomsky, N. (1982). *Some concepts and consequences of the theory of government and binding.* Cambridge, MA: MIT Press.

Chomsky, N. (1986). *Barriers.* Cambridge, MA: MIT Press.

Faraci, R. (1974). *Aspects of the grammar of infinitive and* for *phrases.* Unpublished doctoral dissertation, MIT, Cambridge, MA.

Farkas, D. (1988). On obligatory control. *Linguistics and Philosophy 11,* 27–58.

Felix, S. (1984). Maturational aspects of universal grammar. In A. Davies, C. Criper, & A. Howatt (Eds.), *Interlanguage,* pp. 133–161.

Goodluck, H. (1987). Children's interpretation of pronouns and null NPs: An alternative view. In B. Lust (Ed.), *Studies in the acquisition of anaphora* (Vol 2, pp. 247–269). Dordrecht, The Netherlands: Reidel.

Jones, C. (1985). *Syntax and thematics of infinitival adjuncts.* Unpublished doctoral dissertation, University of Massachusetts, Amherst.

Jones, C. (1988). Thematic relations in control. In W. Wilkins (Ed.), *Thematic relations, syntax, and semantics* (Vol. 21, pp. 75-89). New York: Academic Press.

Jones, C. (in press). *Purpose clauses.* Dordrecht, The Netherlands: Kluwer.

Kirkpatrick, C. (1982). The transitive purpose clause in English. *Texas Linguistic Forum, 19.*

Ladusaw, W., & Dowty, D. (1988). Toward a nongrammatical account of thematic roles. In W. Wilkins (Ed.), *Thematic relations, syntax, and semantics* (Vol. 21, pp. 61-73).

Manzini, M. R. (1983). On control and control theory. *Linguistic Inquiry, 14,* 421-446.

Marantz, A. (1984). *On the nature of grammatical relations.* MIT Press: Cambridge, MA.

Maratsos, M. (1974). How preschool children understand missing complement subjects. *Child Development, 45,* 700-706.

May, R. (1985). *Logical form.* Cambridge, MA: MIT Press.

Safir, K. (1987). Comments on Wexler and Manzini. In T. Roeper & E. Williams (Eds.), *Parameter setting* (pp. 77-89). Dordrecht, The Netherlands: Reidel.

Sells, P. (1985). Lectures on contemporary syntactic theories. *CSLI Lecture Notes,* No. 3, distributed by University of Chicago Press, Chicago.

Wasow, T. (1985). Postscript. In Sells, pp. 193-205.

Wexler, K., & Manzini, M. R. (1987). Parameters and learnability in binding theory. In T. Roeper & E. Williams (Eds.), *Parameter setting* (pp. 41-76). Dordrecht, The Netherlands: Reidel.

Williams, E. (1977). Discourse and logical form. *Linguistic Inquiry, 8,* 101-139.

Williams, E. (1980). Predication. *Linguistic Inquiry, 11,* 203-238.

9 Ordered Decisions in the Acquisition of Wh-questions

Thomas Roeper
University of Massachusetts

Jill de Villiers
Smith College

INTRODUCTION

Acquisition theory must respond to several domains of variation and theoretical uncertainty. It must critically examine linguistic theory, improve acquisition theory, and respect the diversity among languages. These perspectives interact although they are often isolated in acquisition work. Our discussion seeks to honor all of them while focusing narrowly on the question of how children acquire long-distance rules. These questions are paramount:

1. How do children navigate their way through an intricate set of constraints on long-distance movement? Our experimental evidence demonstrates that the theoretical vocabulary of parametric theory fits the ways in which children diverge from adult grammars.
2. How can alternatives in linguistic theory be resolved by examining the sequence in acquisition grammars? In particular we will argue that Exceptional Case-Marking structures do not involve a COMP node, although the literature is ambiguous on this point.
3. How should the acquisition mechanism be structured so as to avoid the misanalysis of primary data? We show that the misanalysis of a small number of structures can contaminate the whole system.
4. What forces the child's grammar to change when positive evidence is insufficient? We discuss how and why L-marking is a late

191

phenomenon which then permits long-distance extraction from small clauses.

1.1 Empirical Consequences of the Logic of Learnability

Our first focus will be one critical feature in the architecture of an acquisition device: How do decisions interact? In particular, can a small error in one domain contaminate an entire system?[1] The answer in linguistic theory must be affirmative. We will demonstrate it through a discussion of two issues: (1) how children receive and analyze primary linguistic data, and (2) how the analysis of primary data is relevant to more than one parameter.

We begin with a brief overview. The problem of contamination can be considered as a logical argument:

(1) a. Individual sentences pertain to many parameters.
     b. Misanalysis of one input datum can mis-set a parameter.
     c. One mis-set parameter can mis-set another parameter.
     d. There is no memory for sentences.
     e. Therefore correction of the original error will not lead to correction of the parametric decisions which that error caused.[2]

The solution to this incestuous nest of errors is to ensure that misanalysis of grammar does not occur in the first place. If a misanalysis of primary data occurs, then it must not be allowed to cause extensive revision of the grammar. We propose one constraint on an acquisition mechanism that guarantees this result: *ordered parameters.*[3]

---

[1]The original vision of acquisition in Chomsky's "Aspects"-model (1965) was that the process resembled a quadratic equation. The child had, simultaneously, to uncover the structure of phonology, syntax, and a mapping between sentences and the context. The problem seemed enormous, precisely because a decision in one domain could affect decisions in all others. The solution was to idealize the process to an "instantaneous model" and invoke an evaluation metric to choose among possible solutions. The effort to recast Universal Grammar as a system with a finite set of grammars offers the possibility of a simpler acquisition device. The primary data, which in principle is subject to infinite forms of misanalysis, keeps the problem alive. This essay tries to show how constraints on an acquisition device can constrain the negative effects of misanalyzed primary data.

[2]This logic can be repeated at several levels: reanalysis of a sentence may not lead to the reanalysis of structures, reanalysis of structures may not lead to the resetting of a parameter, and resetting of one parameter may not lead to the resetting of another parameter.

[3]Matthews (in press) and Manzini and Wexler (1987) assert that parameters must be independent. However, as current theory stands, they are not independent. Many parameters

(2) A decision in Parameter B is not executed until Parameter A is fixed.

In effect, this constitutes an input filter: A sentence that involves Parameter B will simply not receive a full grammatical analysis until the acquisition system is ready for revision (after Parameter A has been set).

If we assume no misanalysis of primary data, then the parameters are effectively *intrinsically* ordered. This is significant difference because it means that the ordering does not have to be explicitly stated in the grammar. The parametric decision that allows long-distance extraction cannot be made until other parametric decisions that eliminate certain barriers to extraction have been made.

If we assume that some primary data may be misanalyzed,[4] then the parameters must be *extrinsically* ordered to prevent the misanalysis in one parameter from influencing another module. We will illustrate how such a contamination could occur. Whether intrinsic or extrinsic ordering, the order of acquisition sheds light on the content of parameters, the nature of grammar, and the special assumptions of an acquisition device.

Our arguments in behalf of this claim are both logical and empirical. The domain of inquiry is Chomsky's Barriers framework (1986). We will demonstrate through the logic of learnability that long-distance (LD) wh-movement must be learned in several stages. The stages correspond to how parameters interact: (1) LD-movement connected to COMP requires that a feature of phrase structure (X-bar parameters) be present: a Complementizer Phrase. (2) LD-movement connected to Small Clauses requires that the possibility of Exceptional Case Marking (ECM) be fixed. The complementizer node is universal, and therefore, predictably, appears early, although language variation and stages exist here as well. The ECM effect depends on the existence of L-marking between a higher verb and the subject of a lower clause. It involves another module, the Case module, which is fundamentally different. This leads to a strikingly subtle prediction: children will learn the interpretation of (3a) before (3b):

(3) a. Complementizer: how$_i$ did John see that Bill ran t$_i$
    b. Small clause: how$_i$ did John see Bill run t$_i$

Our results, from experiments with more than 50 children, support precisely this prediction. These results are even more striking when a

---

refer to elements in different modules, which in turn are affected by different parameters. Our argument can be construed as a necessary device to guarantee independence.

[4]There is abundant evidence at the phonological and morphological level of children's misanalysis of primary data. The question is whether a parametrically relevant syntactic structure can be misanalyzed.

developmental fact is considered: Children use small clause forms such as *Bill run* long before they use forms such as *that Bill ran*. In addition, they learn adjunct questions (*how, when, where*) very early. In other words, although small clauses are present and *how* is present, extraction from small clauses must await the fixation of a different parameter. Long-distance extraction from sentences with COMP occurs much earlier. We will illustrate, in strictly logical terms, how failure to delay extraction from small clauses would lead to a superset[5] in English that cannot be unlearned. First, we will show how primary data can lead to subset problems.

2. CASE 1: SIMPLE WH-MOVEMENT

2.1 Language Variation

The parameter-setting model underestimates (by not addressing) the potential for misanalysis due to the piecemeal introduction of primary data. We illustrate here one of myriad missteps that could occur because the child does not bring the correct assumptions to the data he or she hears.

2.2 Echoes

Suppose the child hears:

(5) "You saw what"

This is acceptable in English as an echo-question. If the child hears such a sentence, however, she must know that it is an echo question, otherwise it will set the *in situ* parameter for wh-words. It follows immediately that the child must be aware of discourse. He or she must know that a previous statement is involved for which this is an echo (I saw him → "you saw what").[6] In fact echoes are enormously common in the adult speech; we have found hundreds of examples in child–adult dialogues at the earliest stages.[7] However, it does not seem, from a close examination of them, that

---

[5]A superset is a violation of the subset criterion for learnability that was formulated by Berwick (1985). We take the "subset concept" to be a heuristic pointing toward situations where an explanation for the restriction of grammar is needed, that is, wherever the child's grammar allows too many structures or interpretations. In most instances, successive grammars are not in a subset relation, but form interactive sets.

[6]This, of course, entails a further simplification, since echo-questions and echo-like questions sometimes occur with reference to a vague preceding discussion: "Now you are going where for vacation?" We ignore this (and many other) problems.

[7]See Brown corpus on CHILDES.

children understand that a particular constituent has been selected for repetition or further explanation. Other research on contrastive stress suggests that children are unable to interpret it correctly (Solan, 1983).

2.3 Ellipsis

Suppose a child hears from one speaker:

(6) Do you want to play this game?

and another says:

(7) I don't know how.

The child must know that (7) is elliptical or it should mis-set (or serve as mistaken confirmation) for the *in situ* parametric choice. Notice that the question interpretation is not contextually wrong: One might for (6) just as well say "How do you play."

Could the child learn discourse rules later and then reverse the decision? Not if we make the assumption common in acquisition work:

(8) A child has no memory for sentences. Only grammars are modified.

Once the parameter is set the child does not remember the data that set it and therefore cannot realize that the input data may have been misanalyzed that is, when the child learns, later, to comprehend ellipsis, then the child does not automatically have a reason to reanalyze the *in situ* decision, since the parameter has already been set allowing, *in situ, how.*

2.4 Knowledge of Discourse

The next question is: Do children understand discourse correctly? If discourse rules are universal, then children might understand ellipsis correctly at once. Little is known about language variation in discourse, but we can observe whether children understand discourse properly. No careful survey has been done, but there is abundant evidence that children do not initially compute ellipsis correctly. Consider this dialogue:

(9) Adult: "Can you finish your milk?"
   Child: "I don't."

In fact children make numerous elliptical remarks whose grammar does not connect to the discourse properly. Typically the sense but not the grammar of the missing material is presupposed in the child's response. Therefore it is reasonable to suppose that many features of discourse comprehension may not be immediately available.

2.5 Exceptions

In addition the child will also receive exceptional data that appear to confirm the *in situ* value of the parameter:[8]

(10) You know what?

This is not an echo-question, nor is it a response to a previous sentence in a discourse. In fact, (10) often initiates a conversation. Moreover, 3-year-old children use this expression often.[9] It is, however, exceptional. We do not find a sentence like:

(11) *You believe what?

But how does the child know that it is exceptional? And does she know it immediately? Do children overgeneralize such cases to say:

(12) *I played a game how?[10]

Does a child ever say "I played the game how"? In our search of the CHILDES[11] data base we have found no examples. Moreover, were such errors common, they would surely be noticed by parents and belong to the acquisition lore (like the overgeneralization of past tense). Nevertheless it is a clear possibility since acquisition data, though voluminous, is still only a sample. It may occur as a short-lived stage (say a week), which goes unnoticed. We need to search more data and see if attentive parents notice such examples.

---

[8]See Roeper and Weissenborn (1989) for further discussion with respect to French, where the *in situ* question is productive, but only in matrix clauses.

[9]Mervis found "know what" to be frequent among the first wh-expressions, produced at 22 months. Roeper (personal communication) has found the same result.

[10]Note that a further mis-analysis of an expression like "I sang somehow" into "I sang some (x's) how" could actually lead the child to think that the conclusion reached from having heard (f) does generalize.

[11]The CHILDES computer data base (MacWhinney & Snow, 1985) contains transcripts of child language from English and several other languages.

2.6 Fronted Wh-

Now, of course, we must consider the impact of normal wh-movement that occurs in the child's environment every day.

(13) What did you hear?

Intuitively one might think that the presence of explicit movement in the data settles the issue for the child. This may be true, but it does not follow from parametric theory as currently postulated. As it stands the child must deal with data that have *contradictory* implications. The child hears both: "you know what," which would set his or her grammar against wh-movement, and (13), which sets the grammar toward movement. Is the acquisition mechanism paralyzed? If it were, how would the issue be settled? We can resolve the problem by adding a stipulation to parameter theory:

(14) Unique Trigger: Each parameter has a unique trigger.

The natural proposal here is:

(15) If wh-movement occurs, all other counterevidence is exceptional.

Now since wh-movement occurs constantly, then "you know what" should be automatically an exception. This may seem obvious to an English speaker, but far from obvious to a speaker of an Asian language, who might have assumed the opposite: if wh-*in-situ* occurs, then all wh-'s are *in situ*.

The unique trigger we have just proposed does not sail through as easily as one might think. The Chinese language allows a form of *topicalization* that may include a wh-word. We could paraphrase it in a manner close to an English exclamatory sentence (often found in children's books):

(16) What beautiful clothes he is wearing!

Such sentences suggest opposite options for Chinese and American children: (a) The Chinese children could regard such a sentence as an instance of wh-movement, while (b) The English child could regard true wh-moved sentences as instances of topicalization. Unless the Chinese children can recognize that these moved wh-words are marked occurrences occurring in certain discourse conditions (like the English child's echoes), then the parameter would be mis-set by those examples.

One might take the next step and argue that inversion is the clue to distinguish such sentences:

(17) What beautiful clothes could he wear.

Once again the same problem arises: Inversion can occur with topicalization:

(18) No hat could he wear.

Therefore inversion is not a unique clue to wh-movement. Each step reveals a further problem.[12]

What does the evidence say? First, wh-movement occurs early for English-speaking children, which favors the Unique Trigger Hypothesis. However, many children produce forms such as:

(19) "What he can do"

However, (19) could be considered an instance of topicalization, which exists in Asian languages, rather than true wh-movement. Therefore, the fact that children appear to use wh-movement at an early age does not immediately settle this question.

We do not believe that the child's analysis of early input can receive a fully satisfactory analysis at this stage in acquisition research. There are too many alternative paths that the child could follow through the input data. Our analysis has been designed primarily to illustrate the nature of a problem that has been implicit in many acquisition discussions.

Our approach to the problem is to work backwards from the adult grammar: What evidence for parametric ordering can we find in later stages of acquisition? In the later stages, the range of decisions is considerably narrowed. Therefore, the process may be seen more clearly, although the grammatical decisions are more complex. We will examine the decisions involved in long-distance movement.

To recapitulate, we have thus far arrived at several conclusions about a more elaborate theory of parameter setting:

---

[12]Nevertheless our proposal could be strengthened to serve as a unique trigger as follows:

(i) If wh-fronting occurs, with a discourse indication of question formation, then the parameter is set.

In what follows we will pursue a more complex definition of wh-movement.

(20) If both semantic interpretations and discourse ellipsis are un-
known, then primary data may be misanalyzed.

(21) If primary data is misanalyzed, then input data is contradictory.

(22) The solution to this problem is to assign a *unique trigger* within
the parameter.[13]

These examples each reveal how misanalysis of discourse (or lexical
exceptions) could mis-set syntactic parameters. Consequently acquisition
decisions must be arranged so that discourse prerequisites are met before
syntactic parameters are set.

3.0 CASE 2: LONG-DISTANCE MOVEMENT

3.1 Language Variation

The movement module allows three basic alternatives (with again dialect
variants of interest):[14]

(23) a. no movement
b. local movement
c. long-distance movement

We have argued that there is reason to believe that the child begins with the
assumption of no movement (as in Asian languages) before long-distance
movement appears. We have not addressed that possibility experimentally,
but we will return to the question.

The possibility of *local* movement results, in some dialects, in a form of
copying. In German, it is possible to say:

(24) *Was₁ hast du gesagt wie₁ man Kuchen machen kann t₁?*
(What₁ did you say how₁ one can bake cake?)

In adult English, the *how* can exhibit LD movement:

---

[13]Elsewhere we have pursued the same logic with respect to binding theory and prodrop (see
Roeper (1988). It is argued there that parameters must be ordered with *pro*-drop preceding
binding in order to prevent an interaction that makes acquisition impossible.

[14]We refer the reader to McDaniel (1989) for a particularly interesting discussion of
alternatives in this domain.

(25) how$_i$ did you say t$_i$ one can bake a cake t$_i$[15]

Is there an intermediate stage in English acquisition that matches the local movement option? This is a logical possibility.

3.2 Constraints on LD-movement: Factivity

There are three constraints on long-distance movement that our experiments also explore: factivity, barriers, and the argument/adjunct distinction. Each of them is a part of universal grammar and therefore should allow no exceptions during acquisition. Our work is also consistent with Otsu's (1981) research on subjacency effects for NP's, and builds on his initial evidence that children are sensitive to constraints on LD extraction.

Long-distance movement is lexically sensitive to the factivity of the matrix verb, producing this contrast:

(26) a. factive (say): when$_i$ did the boy (t$_i$) say he hurt himself (t$_i$)?
    b. nonfactive (know): when$_i$ did the boy know t$_i$ he hurt himself?

Many adult speakers detect an ambiguity in (26a): does it mean when-say or when-hurt? In (26b), however, the second option is not present: It only means when-know. The factive nature of *know* (it presupposes that the complement sentence is a fact) blocks extraction.

3.3 Barriers

The presence of a wh-word in a lower COMP blocks extraction:[16]

(27) a. when did the boy say [(t$_i$) he hurt himself (t$_i$)]
    b. when did the boy say t$_i$ [how he hurt himself *t$_i$]

Only the upper-clause (local) interpretation is possible in (27b) when *how* is present. This demonstrates how successive-cyclicity works. The lower clause adjunct-when should move through its COMP position, but it cannot do so if the position is filled. Therefore only the upper clause interpretation is left.

---

[15]First discussed in van Riemsdijk (1983), also in Bayer (1984), and in great detail in McDaniel (1986). She also discusses a variety of other languages and dialects in which the phenomenon occurs.

[16]This is again a simplification of barriers theory. See Chomsky (1986) for extensive discussion and ramifications.

3.4 Lexical Government (The Empty Category Principle)

There is a second method whereby long-distance movement can be licensed: lexical government licenses the trace in embedded object position (bake → object). The fact that *bake* subcategorizes for an object allows the sentence to be grammatical even if successive-cyclicity does not go through because of the presence of an adjunct in the medial COMP:[17]

(28) a. what$_i$ did you know how to bake t$_i$

This is known as the Empty Category Principle. It is a universal principle and therefore should license long-distance extraction at every stage. Thus there is a sharp contrast in the movement of adjuncts and arguments: Adjuncts may not pass over a medial wh-word, while arguments can pass over a medial wh-word.

If children prove sensitive to these restrictions on long-distance movement, then we have direct evidence that they are in fact performing long-distance movement and do not use inference to connect a wh-word to a lower clause. Were sheer inference involved, we would expect that a question word could connect to any element in a sentence. For instance, one might have an inferential connection between a wh-word and a noun:

(29) a. question: how did you like his performance
      answer: *without assistance (=his performance without assistance)

The inference is possible, but the syntactic extraction is not. The sentence therefore can test which method children use. We will return to this question when we discuss how children treat nominalizations.

3.5 Pilot Studies

3.5.1. Bridge Verbs and Movement

Our initial pilot work on LD movement was divided into two studies: (1) a direct approach to whether children allow LD movement, and (2) a test of bridge verbs (say) and nonbridge verbs (know). Do children allow LD movement only over bridge verbs?

For each study we used four stories and four questions. A story (with

---

[17]See deVilliers et al (1990) for extensive discussion of how this works technically. See also Lasnik and Uriagereka (1988) for discussion of the internal structure of the COMP node.

accompanying pictures) was presented in which two kinds of "manner adverbial" were highlighted. Then the child was asked a question with two verbs and "how" or "when," for which there was a possible adverbial answer for the upper or lower clause. Sixteen children from 3.5 to 6.6 years old were tested. Here is a sample story, with two questions, only one of which was given to a particular child (see Fig. 9.1). We encourage the reader to try the experiment on himself, using the pictures:

"The boy loved climbing trees in the forest. One afternoon he slipped and fell to the ground. He picked himself up and went home. When he had a bath that night, he found a big bruise on his arm. He said to his dad, 'I must have hurt my arm when I fell this afternoon'."

(30) When did the boy say he got a bruise?

(31) When did the boy know he got a bruise?

Table 9.1 summarizes the data from the two pilot studies of long-distance movement. Note that in the pilot study with factive and nonfactive verbs, each child made a total of four responses.

The children readily chose either first or last clause as the origin of the wh-adjunct:

(32) 37/64 → First clause
     23/64 → Last clause[18]

Fifteen children gave both first- and last-clause responses, while only one child (not the youngest) gave only first-clause responses. The major conclusion is this:

(33) Children readily extract from lower clauses.

If we examine the children's responses to the specific verbs *say* versus *know,* no distinction is evident in the data. (First clause = exclusively first clause, while Last clause = at least one last clause.)

(34) *say* (nonfactive)
     6 children → First clause
     10 children → Last clause (= some long-distance)
    know (factive)
     3 → First clause
     11 children → Last clause

---

[18]There were three "wrong" responses, referring to neither clause appropriately.

FIG. 1 A typical pictured story in the pilot study to accompany questions (30) or (31).

TABLE 9.1
Clause Chosen as Site of Origin of Wh-word: Long Distance Movement

Subjects		Two clause, no medial Wh		Two clause, medial Wh		
		Factive[a]	Nonfactive[b]	Nonfactive Adjunct[c]	Factive Adjunct[d]	Nonfactive Argument[e]
Age	Sex					
6.6	F	first/last	first/last	first	first	last
5.9	F	first/first	first/last	first	first	last
5.9	M	last/first	first/last	first	wrong Q	last
5.5	M	last/last	first/first	first	first	last
5.5	F	first/last	first/first	first	first	wrong Q
5.5	M	first/wrong	last/first	first	first	last
5.5	F	last/first	last/first	wrong Q	–	wrong Q
5.5	M	first/last	last/first	first	wrong Q	last
5.4	F	first/both	first/first	first	wrong Q	last
5.4	M	first/first	first/first	first	first	last
5.3	F	first/first	first/last	first	first	last
4.7	F	wrong/last	first/first	wrong Q	wrong Q	last
4.5	F	last/first	first/first	wrong Q	wrong Q	last
4.5	M	wrong/last	last/last	wrong Q	wrong Q	last
4.3	M	first/last	last/first	wrong Q	–	last
3.5	F	last/first	last/first	wrong Q	wrong Q	last,wrong Q

[a]When did the boy know he hurt himself?
[b]When did the boy say he hurt himself?
[c]How did the mother learn what to bake?
[d]When did the kitten know how to swim?
[e]What did the mother learn how to bake?

The pattern is virtually identical. We find that the profile for bridge verbs and nonbridge verbs is the same. Comparison with the second pilot experiment (described later), where extraction is sharply blocked, shows that the result is not random but reflects principles of grammar. In conclusion, from this first study it appears that children 3.5 and older allow long-distance movement. But we find no evidence that children at this stage have distinguished bridge verbs from other kinds.

3.5.2 Wh-argument as Barrier

The second pilot experiment involved sentences with two wh-words, one in a medial position, varying between adjuncts *how, when,* and an argument *what.* Each child had one *what* question, and three adjunct questions: two with another adjunct, and one with an internal *what.* The four stories were constructed to provide adverbial information for each verb. Each of the 16 children aged 3.5–6.6 received only one of the two questions (36) or (37) about a given story.

One story was:

(35) "The mother didn't know how to bake a cake. She watched a TV program about cooking. She learned to make a lovely cake with chocolate pudding mix" (see Fig. 9.2).

(36) What did the mother learn how to bake?

(37) How did the mother learn what to bake?

Table 9.1 provides the summary of these data also. For sentence type (36), 13 children gave a long-distance response ("a cake"), 2 children answered the second clause "how" instead ("wrong Q").[19] Conclusion:

(38) *No* children gave a *short-distance* answer with a medial adjunct.

That is, they never linked *what* to "learn" rather than "bake."
For sentence type (37), 10 children gave a short-movement answer ("from TV"), 6 children answered the second clause "what" instead (wrong question). Conclusion:

(39) *No* children gave a *long-distance* answer with a medial argument.

The results are exactly opposite for the two questions (36) and (37). Had they answered "with a chocolate pudding mix" to (37), they would have construed the *how* with *to bake* and not with *to know*.
We can compare the children's interpretations on this task with evidence from spontaneous speech and diary data. An example such as Adam's:

(40) Adam (55): "What else you know how to make."

This utterance reveals a command over the syntax of wh-arguments that complements the data from interpretations, as it contains an argument question apparently connected to a lower verb. It is equally important to note the following: there were *no* instances in the Adam corpus of *how* moving over a medial wh-word and 25 (roughly speaking, since there were ambiguities) like (40).

---

[19]Note also that five out of seven children who answered with the second clause instead (for both medial argument *what* and adjunct *when*), were under 5. Although none of the less-than-5-year-old children allowed long-distance movement over a wh-word, they follow a different strategy: answer the second wh-word. Recall that with bridge verbs, long-distance and short-movement are both possible for these children. Why did they use this strategy? We provide extensive discussion of the implication of these results in deVilliers et al (1990).

FIG. 9.2 Pictures to accompany story (35).

Tentative conclusions from this second pilot study suggest:

(41) Children block long-distance movement with *adjuncts* if another wh-word intervenes (either an argument or an adjunct).

(42) Children do not block long-distance movement with *arguments* if another wh-word intervenes.

(43) Children therefore distinguish arguments from adjuncts.

STUDY 1: LONG-DISTANCE MOVEMENT WITH MEDIAL COMP

One defect in our pilot experiment lies in the fact that the alternative answer to the *what* question is somewhat less pragmatically obvious. Sentence (36) did not easily allow a short-movement answer to "what." The only possible answer was an entire clause: "What did the mother learn how to bake" = > "how to bake a cake." Perhaps the child is answering (correctly) "cake," not because he or she knows a distinction between adjunct and argument, but because it is easier than answering with a clause.

We remedied this asymmetry in the next study by using the verb "ask," which has an indirect object position from which a wh-word can be extracted:

(44) who$_i$ did you ask t$_i$ how to paint t$_i$?

Note that the subordinate verb also has both a transitive and an intransitive reading, so either long or short movement is grammatical.

4.1 Pragmatic Bias

In addition we decided to take an experimental risk: We created a pragmatic bias toward the lower-clause answer, which is ungrammatical. If children follow the bias, then we know nothing. If they resist the bias because a grammatical barrier is present, then we have genuinely revealed the power of the barrier.

Here's how it worked: The children are told a story which, once again, involved manner information about two clauses. At the end of the story the child is shown a picture by a second experimenter, shielded from the interlocutor, with information about the lower clause. Thus, the child's attention is diverted to that information. Here is one story (the reader should follow the story with Fig. 9.3 in order to get the feel of the experiment):

FIG. 9.3   a,b,c,d: Pictures to accompany story (45).

(45) Kermit and Cookie Monster were baking (a)
Big Bird came in and wanted to help someone. He wanted to do his favorite kind of baking, but he didn't know who he should help. (b)

So he asked Bert with a big shout: "Who should I help with my favorite kind of baking?" (c)

Here's a picture of Big Bird.(d)

Now listen carefully to my questions: "What is Cookie Monster wearing?"

(The last question guarantees that the child is looking at the new picture.) Then the crucial question comes:

(46) "How did Big Bird ask who to help."

In order to answer such a question, where extraction is blocked (for adults), the child must look away from the picture that has been revealed to his eyes alone, in which Big Bird is helping *by cutting out cookies,* and give an answer that the questioner can also see and therefore presumably knows: *by shouting.*[20] The situational pragmatics could easily overwhelm grammatical preferences. Once again, if the children block extraction in spite of the pragmatic bias, then they reveal the strength of the grammatical principle.

4.2 Design

The experiment used the following, more complete, set of sentence types:

Argument -wh sentences:
(47) *O-medial:*
Who$_i$ did the girl ask t_i to help t_i?

(48) *Argument-wh medial:*
Who$_i$ did the girl ask t_i what to throw *t_i?

(49) *Adjunct-wh medial:*
Who$_i$ did Big Bird ask t_i how to paint t_i?
Adjunct wh-sentences:

---

[20]Often the answer is rephrased (e.g., "by yelling") but the interpretive location is clearly the upper clause.

(50) *O medial:*
    When$_i$ did the boy say t_i he hurt himself t_i?

(51) *Argument-wh medial:*
    How$_i$ did Kermit ask t_i who to help *t_i?

(52) *Adjunct -wh medial:*
    When$_i$ did the boy know t_i how he hurt himself *t_i?

Subjects were 25 preschool children tested in a small room in their nursery school. There were 12 boys and 13 girls aged 3:7 to 6:11 years. All spoke English as a first language.

We argued that if the children show an adult pattern of response, they should allow long-distance movement for the following:

(47) Argument with O-medial

(49) Argument with adjunct medial

(50) Adjunct with O-medial

and should prohibit it for the following:

(51) Adjunct with argument medial

(52) Adjunct with adjunct medial.

The sixth logical member of the set involves special factors:

(48) Argument with argument medial
    (Who$_1$ did the girl ask what$_2$ to throw t_1 t_2)

The sentence (48) is not always seen as grammatical by adults, particularly with a long-distance interpretation (throw the girl the ball). If children use the ECP to move directly forward, then long-distance movement should be possible.

If they move successive-cyclically, then the internal properties of the COMP node (which may be parameterized) play a role. We provide extensive discussion of this case and our results in terms of index percolation in COMP in de Villiers, Roeper, and Vainikka (1990; see Lasnik & Uriagereka, 1988, for discussion).

Four stories were designed for each of the types (49) and (51), and two for the remaining types, for a total of 16 stories. The dependent variable in the study was the child's answer to the question. The answers fell into four major categories: the child could answer the first question (correct) with an upstairs reading or downstairs reading, or could answer the medial wh-word (wrong) with either the upstairs verb or the downstairs verb.

4.3 Results

Our first experiment was replicated under these more demanding conditions:

(53) (a) Children allowed long-distance extraction.
    (b) Children distinguished arguments from adjuncts.

Finally, they were sensitive to the nature of the medial COMP in extraction from the lower clause.

The results were analyzed in several ways, and comprehensive analysis is provided in de Villiers et al. (1990). Here we will provide only the major results. A useful summary is in Table 9.2, in which +LD refers to a long-distance or lower-clause response; −LD to a short distance or upper clause response. Table 9.3 provides the details of a prevalent response pattern of answering the medial question.

An ANOVA[21] was run with the type of question (argument versus adjunct), the type of medial (argument versus adjunct) and the clause of origin (upper versus lower) as between-subject variables, and age (3½–5 versus 5–6 years) as a within-subject variable. Results revealed that children allow more downstairs responses (long-distance) to:

(47) the argument question with 0 medial (32%);

(50) the adjunct question with 0 medial (44%);

(49) the argument question with adjunct medial (30%).

than they allow downstairs responses to:

(51) the adjunct question with argument medial (8%);

(52) the adjunct question with adjunct medial (6%); and

---

[21]An analysis of variance, a statistical procedure that provides an estimate of how robust any differences in responses to different stimuli are across a group of subjects. Any result in which the value of p is less than .05 is taken as statistically significant.

TABLE 9.2
Site of Interpretation for wh-question

	Argument		Adjunct	
Medial:	−Ld	+LD	−LD	+LD
0	68% (34)	32% (16)	50% (25)	44% (22)
Arg	70% (35)	2% (1)	23% (23)	8% (8)
Adj	63% (63)	30% (30)	48% (24)	6% (3)

TABLE 9.3
Incidence of Answering the Medial Question

	Initial wh:	
Medial:	Argument	Adjunct
Argument	28% (14)	68% (68)
Adjunct	4% (4)	40% (20)

(48) the argument question with argument medial (2%).

There is clearly a stunning difference in LD-extraction that corresponds precisely to the predictions derived from Barrier theory.[22]

If we look at the crucial contrast: *adj* + *arg* and *arg* + *adj*, we have the following results: There were 30 +LD answers to arg + adj and only eight such answers to adj + arg (see Table 9.2). Of those eight, six were in answer to a single story involving a Mickey Mouse phone as the "how" to call:

(54) How did Kermit ask who to call?

to which six children answered "Mickey Mouse." This answer was an apparent violation of the constraint, which could have been interpreted as a (false) answer to the medial "who." Note that they did not say "with a Mickey Mouse phone," which would have been corresponded to a true extraction of an adjunct over a medial argument. Therefore the central contrast is very clearly confirmed in this data.

In general, the patterns of responses seem to be a function of the interaction of at least two variables:[23]

---

[22]In addition, the results reveal virtually no LD-movement with arg-over-arg structures as well. Whether this is a robust finding we are not yet sure, for the sentences in question could only use a limited set of verbs that are ambiguous between two and three-argument readings. It might be argued that children are not in control of the double object construction needed for these interpretations.

[23]In deVilliers et al. (1990) we discuss the question of whether there is a general preference for answering arguments rather than adjuncts.

(55) Argument-wh as a barrier to movement

(56) A difference between argument and adjuncts in their movement over adjunct wh

Thus despite the introduction of the pragmatic bias, +LD readings were still quite rare for both sentence types.

However, another angle on these results emerged: It was also found that adj + arg and arg + adj sentences differed significantly in the likelihood of an "appropriate" response (93% versus 31%) ($F = 31.23$, $p < .0000$, df = 23). Many "wrong question" responses were given to the adj + arg sentence. A few such responses for the adj + adj sentences also occurred.

4.3.1 Digression: The "Wrong Question" Phenomenon

We digress briefly here to discuss the "wrong Q" response, which we address in depth elsewhere. We have in fact received supporting evidence from other experiments and from naturalistic interactions that suggests an important phenomenon is present. The response we obtained is clearly not a function of experimental circumstances. If we ask 3-year-old children a question about a story like:

(57) "How does the boy know where to go?"

They will often answer, for instance "to school." How should such a response be interpreted?

We considered the possibility that the children treat the two wh-words as linked in the manner of German and other languages in which the wh-word is "copied" into each COMP of a complex sentence, as in (18), namely:

(58) one wh-word is a scope marker for the other wh-word.

Thus there is a variant of grammars without long-distance movement: The question is indexed by a wh-word in each clause. The results we obtained suggest that children may begin with the assumption that grammars allow coindexation rather than long-distance movement—a natural assumption if long-distance movement is a marked phenomenon in language. The logical possibility that follows from this claim is:

(59) Initially children have no long-distance movement.

This is equivalent to the assertion that children lack successive-cyclical movement. In partial support for this argument, Steven Crain and his associates (University of Massachusetts lecture) found similar data in spontaneous production:

(60) What do you think what's in the box?

(61) Who do you think what's in there?

Initial results from experiments aimed at this issue show that English children allow copying of identical wh-words as well, giving frequent LD-interpretations of *how* in *how did he say how he hurt himself,* but none in *how did he say when he hurt himself* (see deVilliers et al., 1990).

4.4 Conclusion

We have now assembled abundant evidence that 3–4-year-old children can carry out long-distance interpretations in sentences that have a complementizer. They exhibit sensitivity to a movement constraint:

(62) A wh-word is a barrier in the complementizer system.

The constraint in (62) is just a part of a larger system. One fundamental concept in Barrier theory controls the entire system:

(63) Maximal Projections are barriers.[24]

Extraction via the "escape hatch," Spec of CP, constitutes a systematic exception to a general prohibition on extraction from Maximal Projections.

The next logical step is to see how children learn to command a larger range of extraction phenomena. We can then both scrutinize linguistic theory and project the architecture of an acquisition device. We focus upon less-resolved domains in linguistic theory, which, we believe, can be illuminated by acquisition data. Consider this example:

(64) How did you like his singing?

The answer cannot be "strangely" (while it can be "very much"), although it is possible to say *I liked his singing strangely.* The NP nominalization *his singing* permits an adjunct, but the adjunct cannot be extracted. We can capture this fact by the claim that the NP node functions as a barrier because it is a Maximal Projection.

---

[24]We do not present here some of the technical formulations in *Barriers* in favor of an intuitive notion of a barrier.

The barrier for adjuncts does not always hold for arguments, just as we found with wh-islands. Consider (65) compared to (64):

(65) what$_i$ did you enjoy his singing t$_i$

In (65) we find an extraction which is possible (or at least marginally possible). This follows, once again, from the fact that lexical domination allows extraction (the ECP). Our next experiment seeks to investigate the presence of the Maximal Projection constraint in children's grammars.

5. THE SPECIAL STATUS OF SMALL CLAUSES

5.1 Introduction

We chose to examine a structure with a minimal contrast: verbal small clauses. The contrast is:

(66) Nominalizations: How did you show his singing *t?

(67) Small clauses: How did you show him singing t?

How does (67) permit LD extraction? Thus far the available analyses have been somewhat unresolved (see Chomsky, 1986; Clark, 1988; Stowell, 1988). We present one analysis, which fits our data. The fact that it fits our data we take to be significant evidence in its behalf. Consider again the following pair, each of which allows extraction:

(68) how$_i$ did you see him run t$_i$

(69) how$_i$ did you see (that) he ran t$_i$

Each example allows adjunct extraction (answer: quickly). An adult hardly notices a difference between them. Yet does the extraction occur in the same way? One of them allows no CP node:

(70) *did you see how him run

(71) did you see how he ran.[25]

---

[25]This observation is due to Stowell (1981), whose analysis we essentially follow.

If extraction occurs in (68), then it has not occurred via an explicit CP node because none seems to be present.[26] Therefore it must require a different analysis. Intuitively, the fact that the subject appears to receive accusative case from a higher verb, seems to "open" the lower clause and make extraction possible. It is necessary to consider Exceptional Case-marking structures and to distinguish them from very similar cases in order to see how this is done. The presence of ECM is a result of a more general relation of L-marking, which involves the lexical domination of a clause by a higher verb with the result that a Maximal Projection is eliminated, or put differently, that V-2 is reduced to V-1 (bar reduction). This allows case-marking.

In general, we argue that the appearance of L-marking is delayed. When the MP is eliminated by L-marking, the small clause (which is now V-1) allows the extraction of an adjunct because the barrier is gone. L-marking and bar reduction seem to be the crucial ingredients for extraction. We will explore one approach that explains the use of bar reduction in terms of assigning thematic roles from the higher verb to the small clause.

5.2 DS and LF Small Clauses

The special status of small clauses is revealed overtly in children's speech. This is argued independently by Lebeaux (1988), Radford (1988), and Bloom (1990). It is well known that children initially say things like:

(72) it big
     me here
     him gone

These pronouns, which occur in the accusative, are clearly appearing without any overt case assigner in children's grammar.

In addition, Bloom (1990) has made a careful study of such structures and he has found that there are no cases of the form *big it. Just such structures are not possible as small clauses. If the two-word combinations were grammar-free collocations, then there is no explanation for why *it big* is possible but not *big it*.

---

[26]Chomsky (1986) discusses this particular problem, suggesting that the analysis is not yet clear. One possibility that he outlines is that there is an Operator associated with the small clause in any case. The analysis to be presented might be shifted into an argument that children lack an Operator at a certain stage. Such a claim, however, presents its own problems (See Goodluck & Behne (this volume) for interesting discussion. Lebeaux (1988) makes the contrary argument that the Operator is a default operation, for which he presents evidence from very early stages. The fact that children at two can use tough-like constructions such as "this is to eat" supports this view.

Lebeaux (1988) argues that there are two levels of representation for small clauses: D-structure and LF. Those that have lexical selection at D-structure undergo reanalysis into small clauses at LF (73):

(73) John picked it up = DS: [picked [it] [up]]$_{vp}$ = > LF: [it up]$_{sc}$

Others have SC structure at both DS and LF (79):

(74) John wants him off the ship = want [him off the ship]$_{sc}$

The difference appears in cleft structures:

(75) *what John picked was it up

(76) What John wanted was him off the ship.[27]

We find that although the resultant states are similar ("it is up" and "he is off the ship"), in the first case there is clear lexical selection, since *pick up* is a complex verb while *want off the ship* is not.[28]

Before we turn to a discussion of case-marking, we can elucidate the two kinds of small clauses more carefully with some subtle data from acquisition.

5.3 Acquisition Evidence

Among causatives another phenomenon persistently recurs in the samples of Bowerman (1982):

(77) a. Put it be over.
   b. I combed him baldheaded.
   c. I pulled it unstapled.

---

[27]Note the following contrast, where no case-marking verb is present:

(i) him off the ship would be great

(ii) *it up would be great

[28]That is, *it* is the object of the verb *pick* and then it is further modified by *up*. However, *him* is never the object of the verb *want* (he doesn't want him), but rather the whole clause (*him off the ship*) is the object of the verb *want*. The noun *him* is modified only by *off the ship*. The lexical selection of *it* as an object in (78) blocks cleft formation in (80) where *what* must equal the whole small clause *it up*, but cleft formation is possible for (81) because *him off the ship* is a small clause at every level of analysis.

Such sentences are frequently observed in children's speech but they are unacceptable to adults. Lebeaux explains these examples by arguing that children initially have a small-clause structure that is not correctly analyzed at D-structure. The fact is that we can say *I pulled it apart* but not **I pulled it unstapled*. On the other hand, we can say *I found it unstapled*. Lebeaux argues, as seen here, that with *pull* each phrase in the causative interpretation is thematically controlled by the verb and therefore directly dominates (or bears a sister relation) to the verb:

(78)

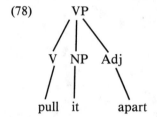

However in the case of *I found it unstapled* we have a verb that in effect takes a D-structure small clause, *found [NP AP]:*

(79)

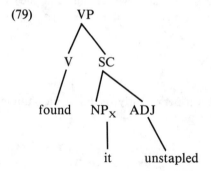

The verb in (79) does not select beyond the SC node itself, and so it has no control over the adjectival phrase (ADJ). The ADJ then projects a thematic role to the subject NP_x without any influence from the higher verb. Therefore the choice of adjective is free. Every adjective can appear in a small clause, but every adjective is not selected by a higher verb. Consequently *unstapled* is a possibility. It is precisely this kind of result adjective which typically occurs in small clauses.

Note that in the lexical analysis (78), there is no Maximal Projection: The verb directly dominates the object and the adjective or verb. In the small-clause structure (79), there is always an MP present (VP, AP, or some other SC node). If there is direct lexical government, then there is no MP to block extraction of an adjunct. Therefore Lebeaux's account provides a formal explanation for why adjunct extraction should be possible.

What we see in the children's utterances, then, is that they have overgeneralized the potential for small clauses to verbs which in adult grammar require selection. They have (80), where they should only have (81):

(80) comb [him baldheaded]$_{sc}$

(81) comb [him] [bald]

Once again, in (80) the verb has no selectional power over the adjective, while in (81) the adjective must be selected. There is, in fact, substantial independent evidence that children's small clauses are initially generated without any subcategorization from a higher verb.

Lebeaux's approach is not the only approach. Any method that would cause bar reduction would also permit extraction. We leave open the question of whether there are other procedures in acquisition that would bring about bar reduction.[29]

5.4 Default Case-marking

A basic principle of UG is:

(82) Every NP must be case-marked.

Therefore we must articulate a principle that will account for case-marking in children's small clauses. Vainikka (1986) and Lebeaux (1988) argue that children initially have a "default" case-marking system[30] or a "structural" case-marking system before they absorb the language-particular evidence.[31] These work for constructions where neither a sister verb nor an INFL conveys case to an NP. The primitive rule is:

---

[29]For instance, suppose both of these types involve an intermediary node, say an AP. Then L-marking has caused it to be a non-MP and therefore transparent. We are indebted to N. Chomsky for making this point clear to us.

[30]Vainikka (1986) provides extensive cross-linguistic evidence that genitive is the unmarked case. This is revealed in English by the fact that nominalizations put the subject into the genitive: *my selection of the desert.*

[31]The concept of "structural case" is also justified by numerous other theoretical arguments. See Larson (1988) for recent arguments to the effect that the two case-markings in *John gave Bill a dollar* result from the fact that there is both structurally-assigned case (indirect object) and lexically assigned case (direct object).

(83) Assign case to elements dominated by a higher (MP) node.

This is a default rule: Rule (83) applies where no verbal sister element assigns case (V or INFL). If there is no lexical case-assignment, then higher structure (S, VP, or small clause) can confer case on the small-clause subject.[32] The claim that a real form of case-assignment exists in early stages is important for our argument, because we argue it remains an "elsewhere" option in later stages.

It is notable that the adult language also allows accusative subjects in a marginal construction, originally noted by Klima.[33]

(84) a. me give you money, no sir!
     b. (in isolation) him/*he

A natural view of such constructions is that they are the residue of the acquisition process. Thus, as Lebeaux argues, a very general default assignment may be present in the adult language as well.

As noted earlier, in the early stages of acquisition children produce sentences such as:

(85) Me dress.

The next stage of acquisition provides the central puzzle. Two-year-old children, who rarely use more than three-word utterances, freely use sentences like:

(86) "help me dress."
     "want you eat."
     "make me up." (=make me go up on a swing)

Which analysis should such sentences have? If a child uses such a "default" method of case-assignment, then early embeddings of the form in (86) should continue to have the same default system of case-marking underlying them. The similarity (and frequency) of these forms *me dress* and *help me dress* would bring them to the attention of the child. Slobin (1973) has

---

[32]The particular version of "higher structure" we have in mind is a VP that has a subject position, as Vainikka and Lebeaux (and many others) have argued. Lebeaux (1988) argues that it is the VP node that gives case to the subject of the VP following current arguments that VP's have subjects. When the child learns that the agent must move to subject position, then he or she can no longer get case from the VP. Alternatively the child may shift from a definition of the small clause as a VP to one as an AP. There are several possibilities here that do not change the basic claim that the small clause subject must get case from above and not from within the small clause.

[33]Pointed out to us by B. Partee (personal communication).

composed a broad generalization: "New meanings are in old forms." For instance, accusative is learned first, so we have "we want" before "I want." If true, we would expect the child first to have the "old forms" analysis (87a), and later acquire the "new forms" analysis (87b):

(87) a. help [*me dress*]
      b. *[₁help [₂me ₁] dress ₂]*

which is implied by ECM.[34] Such a shift would be subtle, and not evident to the naked eye.[35]

In fact there is some explicit evidence that, at least for very young children, the ECM verbs do not require a case-marked object. Vainikka has argued that the genitive is also a default case-marker to explain the presence of forms like "my did it" in the data of numerous naturalistic corpora. We find that the same forms also occur with ECM verbs:

(88) "Help my eat it."
      "See my ride it."
      "See my do it backwards."
      "Want Ria's get it."[36]

In contrast, there are no cases where a simple object gets "my" ("*see my" for *see me*). This shows explicitly that the object is not getting case from the verb when the verb is first learned.

If the child were shifting to a new kind of lexical case-marking, namely ECM, then one might expect that an expression like (87b) would appear late. Instead it is early, suggesting default Accusative case and an analysis like (87a), parallel to (88).

5.5 Problems of Identifying the ECM Verbs

Why shouldn't the child get the correct analysis immediately? Alternatively, why would the child ever give up the non-ECM analysis of small clauses? Why not stick with: Help [me dress]? The answer to this question depends on understanding what information triggers the correct analysis. We have no definitive answer to this question, but we can point in some promising directions.

The child's task in identifying the class of ECM verbs is not an easy one. There are several kinds of ambiguity that he or she must sweep away. Consider the following cases:

---

[34]See subsequent sections for a discussion of the theta-criterion with respect to this double analysis.

[35]The evidence cited earlier with "put it be over" suggests that just such an analysis is correct.

[36]See Vainikka (1986).

(89) John saw me run.

(90) John saw me running.

(91) John enjoys me running.

(92) *John enjoys me run.

What difference between (89) and (92) is absent in the comparison of (90) and (91)? Are both *saw* and *enjoy* ECM verbs? We argue that the construction in (91) with *enjoy,* although resembling that of (90), in fact has a different origin. There is a construction in English known as ACC-ing, identified in such contexts as:

(93) Him playing the piano is always fun.

The subject receives ACC from the presence of the *-ing* inflection (see Reuland, 1981, for discussion). It stands in contrast to a case like:

(94) *Him play the piano is fun.

Hence in (91) the case assignment comes from the *-ing* inflection. However, in (90) the adult apparently assigns accusative case from the verb. Note that there is an extraction difference:

(95) a. how did he see me running t
     b. *how did he enjoy me running t

In other words, there is a complete overlap in the surface of the ECM and the ACC-ing construction. The child could easily have the mistaken belief that *enjoy* belongs to the ECM class. In a word, the child must discriminate the ACC-ing construction in order to prevent an overgeneralization from *see* to *enjoy.*

What could serve to identify true ECM verbs? The child could look for reflexivization evidence to postulate the presence of ECM:

(96) John saw himself run.

In (96) the reflexive must be linked to the upper verb and could trigger direct domination.[37] However, this piece of evidence must in turn depend on the

---

[37]See Lebeaux (1988) for extensive discussion. See also Roeper and Keyser (in press) (and references) for discussion of the possibility that a VP–NP government relation may not be

correct analysis of reflexives. It it not entirely clear that children at early stages know that reflexives are clause-bound. This then points to the possibility that another form of parametric ordering is required: that a binding module must be present before ECM can be fixed. We will return to this question.

5.6 Predictions for Acquisition

What predictions follow for acquisition? If extraction from small clauses is equal to extraction from a simple clause, then one prediction follows:

(97) Extraction from small clauses should occur very early and earlier than over CP.

If, however, extraction from a small clause occurs only when ECM is correctly analyzed, then another prediction follows:

(98) Extraction may be significantly later from small clauses than over CP.[38]

Both predictions suggest that extraction from small clauses should differ from extraction through CP, but the order is different on the two accounts. We turn now to the experimental evidence.

6. STUDY 2: EXTRACTION FROM SMALL CLAUSES

We focus here on the contrast between a nominalization:

(99) How did you show his copying (*t)?

and a small clause:

(100) How did you show him copying (t)?

---

universal. In particular some languages seem to involve a Verb-clitic construction with the object NP in an extraposed position.

[38]Note that we are arguing as if there must be successive cyclical movement. In fact, in an earlier paper we have argued that *how* may originate in CP. Thus one might substitute "from CP" for "through CP" to obtain compatibility with our earlier claims.

In (100) it seems possible to get the adjunct from the lower clause, but not in (99). However, the argument seems to extract from both structures (although marginally for some speakers), as it is lexically governed:

(101) Who did the mother see his hugging?

(102) Who did the mother see him hugging?

The experiment was designed to investigate when children get

(103) the argument/adjunct contrast in extraction.

(104) the MP barrier for nominalizations

and

(105) the possibility of adjunct extraction in structures with no COMP

6.1 Subjects and Procedure

We tested 12 adults, all of them female students aged 18 to 22, to check on the various interpretations of the questions. In addition, 16 children aged 4 to 6.5, were tested (6 girls and 10 boys). Each child was seen individually for two short sessions in which the crucial sentences were among a varied set of sentences they were presented. There were eight scenarios constructed to allow two questions of each of the four types for each child. Each scenario was associated with two versions of a question, nominalization versus small clause, by varying the form of the pronoun from genitive to accusative. Thus there were two sets of questions and a given child received only one such question about each picture set. A typical picture set is shown in Fig. 9.4. The child answered the question and that answer was coded for its origin in either the upper or lower clause.

6.2 Results

First consider the data from the adult subjects, shown in Table 9.4. +LD refers to a long distance or lower clause response; −LD to a short distance or upper clause response. A three-way ANOVA was run with type of question (argument versus adjunct), type of clause (nominalization versus small clause) and site of extraction (upper or lower clause) as within-subject variables. The results showed that arguments were provided LD interpre

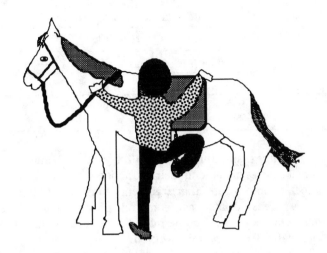

The little boy went for his first ride on a horse.

His mother saw him in the distance and looked through a telescope.
What a surprise she got— he was on the horse backwards!

How did the mother see his riding?
or: How did the mother see him riding?

FIG. 9.4 A typical pictured story in the experiment on small clauses.

TABLE 9.4
Adult S's: Site of Interpretation of wh-question

	Initial wh:			
	Argument		Adjunct	
	−LD	+LD	−LD	+LD
Small clause:	12.5%	83.3%	54.2%	45.8%
Nominalization:	54.5%	37.5%	91.7%	1%

tations more frequently than adjuncts ($F = 19.8$, $p < .001$), and nominalizations and small clauses differed in their extraction ($F = 16.2$, $p < .002$). However, Table 9.4 demonstrates that arguments come readily out of both types of clause, whereas adjuncts can come out of small clauses but not nominalizations. Only one subject permitted one reading in which an adjunct question came from a nominalization.

An identical ANOVA was run for the child data, shown in Table 9.5. That analysis showed that children were more likely to give a +LD interpretation to argument questions than to adjunct questions ($F = 15.8$, $p < .0015$). Older children in this age range did not differ significantly from younger children in any regard. All the children were more likely to attribute a lower-clause origin to an argument question than an adjunct question: that is, more LD movement for arguments than adjuncts. However, they did so preferentially for small clauses rather than nominalizations: as Table 9.5 shows, they *preferred* long-distance interpretation (+LD) for arguments in small-clause sentences (62.5%), and short-distance interpretation (−LD) for all the other forms ($F = 6.32$, $p < .025$). Arguments and adjuncts were significantly different in their movement out of small clauses (62.5% versus 18.75%, t-test, $p < .01$). In particular, unlike the adult subjects (see Table 9.4), children in this age range block adjunct extraction (+LD) out of small clauses (18.75%) as well as out of nominalizations (12.5%).

TABLE 9.5
Child S's: Site of Interpretation of wh-question

	Initial wh:			
	Argument		Adjunct	
	−LD	+LD	−LD	+LD
Small clause:	25%	62.5%	81.25%	18.75%
Nominalization:	53.1%	25.0%	87.5%	12.5%

6.3 Result Summary

We can lay out the results as follows (A = adult, C = Child) with the percentages under the potential gaps in the sentences:

(106) *Argument*
    (a) small clause: who did the boy show ___ him copying ___
                      (12%A,25%C)   (83%A,62%C)
    (b) nominalization: who did the boy show ___ his copying ___
                      (54%A,53%C)   (37%A,25%C)

    Adjunct
    (c) small clause: how did the boy show ___ him copying ___
                      (54%A,*81%C*)   (45%A,*18%C*)
    (d) nominalization: how did the boy show ___ his copying ___
                      (91%A, 88%C)   (1%A, 12%C)

What do these results mean? First, note that once again there is a robust difference between adjuncts (106c = 18%) and arguments (106a = 62%) in children's long-distance extraction from small clauses. This supports the claims of the previous experiment that children in this age range recognize this difference. Second, note that despite the fragile cue (*his* versus *him*), children clearly distinguish between small clauses and nominalizations, as the contrast between (a,c) and (b,d) reveals. However, children differ from the adults in one crucial respect:

(107) a. Adults freely extract adjuncts from small clauses (45%).
      b. Children block extraction of adjuncts from small clauses.

When we compare these results to extraction from subordinate clauses with a CP, a clear contrast in a subtle domain is evident. Recall that children of all ages (and adults) allow extraction of an adjunct from a subordinate clause with CP clause roughly half of the time:

(108) When did the boy say ___ he hurt himself ___ (44%).

The 18% extraction from small clauses is just slightly greater than the 12% extraction from nominalizations, which we count as random error. The contrast of this 18% with 44% extraction from CP subordinate clauses is stark.

6.4 Discussion of Study 2

The results suggest clearly:

> (109) 1. children discriminate between:
>   (a) adjuncts and arguments in extraction,
>   and (b) nominalizations and small clauses.
>   2. Nominalization constitutes a barrier to the movement of
>   adjuncts for children as well as adults,
>   3. Therefore, the Maximal Projection Constraint is operative in
>   young children's grammar.
>   4. Adjunct extraction from small clauses is delayed.
>   5. The argument that adjunct extraction follows the acquisition
>   of ECM is supported.

These results suggest that Universal Grammar must in effect "know" where some pitfalls lie and order the process to avoid them.[39]

The suggestion that adjunct-extraction follows mastery of ECM does not mean that all of the Case module precedes the movement module. We assume that the child of four or five has progressed in the acquisition of case through several steps, but not through all of them by the time that they deal with LD-extraction:

> (110) a. Lexical case is present ($verb_{trans}$-object).
>   b. INFL case is present (Tense-Subject).
>   c. Cross-clausal case is *not* present.

The child has realized that nominative case arises with the appearance of INFL and that accusative case requires a transitive verb.[40] However, the analysis does not extend to *cross-clausal* case-assignment.

We have argued that children use instead a default assumption about case-assignment:

> (111) Structural case: Assign case to a noun dominated by a Maximal
>   Projection.

---

[39]Another possibility has been proposed by Lebeaux. He argues that children may have provisional rules that are not fixed in the grammar until they are confirmed. Thus the child might allow all subordinate clauses to extract adjuncts, but regard it as unconfirmed until argument extraction confirms that exceptional case-marking has occurred.

[40]Lebeaux argues that a more general notion of "any verb gives case" allows children to overgeneralize the causative ("Don't giggle me") and then retreat from that generalization later.

What is the nature of just such assumptions? The notion of Default functions like an *elsewhere* condition. There is evidence that a wide variety of default assumptions play a role in acquisition, including residual pronouns (small pro), conjoined structural attachment, as well as case.

6.5 Inferences

We have alluded to the role of inferences but we have not discussed them directly. One possible use of inferences is that a child may seem to understand structures that he or she does not properly compute. What does the child do when confronted with a sentence of this form at an early stage in acquisition:

(112) Now how did you see me tie my shoes?

Situational pragmatics are powerful. Contextual inference can inform him or her that the "how" relates to the lower verb (it is how you tie a knot, not how you see through your eyes). The question then, is, does the child revise his or her grammar in terms of this inference? Let us assume that the child does revise his or her grammar before the class of ECM verbs is identified. What conclusion is reached?

(113) Extraction of *adjuncts* from subordinate clauses is permissible in all clauses.

What representation arises? The child could use the inference of extraction to posit a COMP node in the small clause.[41] The current grammar makes no distinction between ACC-ING constructions and the set of verbs which govern into small clauses. The child would therefore, throughout life, mistakenly think that a sentence such as:

(114) When did you appreciate (t) John winning the race (t)

would allow extraction from both the upper and the lower clause. They would allow both *when he won* and *when you appreciated it,* while adults allow only the latter (although of course adults allow *when* to go long distance in *when did you say that John won the race*).

What happens when the child correctly learns cross-clausal case-assignment and the verb class for which it applies? Would a change in the

---

[41]In fact Lebeaux (1988) has independently suggested a default operator structure which the child can use for small clauses, much like Chomsky's proposal for these verbal small clauses (1986). The early appearance of sentences like "this is to eat" supports this idea.

case module automatically filter into the movement module? One major assumption of learnability theory states that the child has no memory for particular sentences. This fact has an impact on a modular system. Let us make these two assumptions, implicit in modularity theory:

(115) A. The case module refers to lexical items.
      B. The movement module refers to syntactic structures.

It follows that the child could modify the case-marking properties of verbs, like *see* because the case module refers to the lexicon. However, if the movement module refers to structures, then a lexical change cannot translate into a modification of the movement module. In other words, the child would not remember whether *see* or *enjoy* was involved in the sentence that allowed adjunct extraction. He or she would not know that a change in lexical entries, allowing a few verbs to case-mark across a sentence boundary, would call for revision in the movement module. Therefore, there is no method to make the case-change affect the movement module.[42, 43]

Now let us see if we can rescue the child by making the opposite assumption. Assume that the parameters are extrinsically ordered:

(116) All case parameters are fixed, then,

(117) All movement parameters are fixed.

It follows automatically that the set of subordinating verbs will be crucially differentiated into two classes: those with exceptional case-marking and those without. Therefore when extraction occurs, the child will automatically register the fact that it is the ECM cases that permit extraction:

(118) Extraction of adjuncts is permitted where ECM can occur.

Now we have no errors, but we have a prediction, namely that the extraction of adjuncts in these constructions must be delayed until all features of the case-system are understood. In the language-acquisition

---

[42]In fact, Nishigauchi and Roeper (1987) have proposed that there is an acquisition limit on change that requires a change to occur in each module separately.

[43]There is one way out: The movement module could list the contents of the case-module as a subpart. This would nullify the central tenet of modularity theory, which seeks to simplify acquisition, namely that each module should represent information at its own level of abstraction. Similar logical complications would arise if we dissolved the boundary between modules.

device, then there is a parameter that is marked + or − ECM. Once that is set to +ECM, then, in gross terms, the movement module is opened.

We can express the advantages of extrinsic ordering in terms of subset theory. Were the child to infer long-distance interpretation for:

(119) How did you see him running?

and extend it to the case of:

(120) How did you enjoy him running?

then the child would have an extra interpretation unavailable in the adult grammar and no way to retreat.

Our argument deserves a caveat, as we have remarked (thanks to N. Chomsky). Assume that children do not misanalyze the primary data. Then we must assume that they immediately know the difference between ACC-ing constructions and ECM constructions. It follows immediately that no overgeneralization will result from ACC-ing constructions. Now the order of acquisition follows the *intrinsic* order of parameters: Extraction from small clauses will not occur until ECM, which follows from L-marking, causes the elimination of the MP. When the barrier is down, then extraction can occur. The order of parameters would not need to be explicitly stated. In either case the acquisition order reflects the structure of the grammar and gives special credence to the theory that small clauses do not involve extraction via a CP node.

6.6 The Concept of "Exception" and Thematic Roles

Our account has met the logical requirements of explanation. But questions still remain. We have argued that children do not learn Exceptional Case-marking initially. The word "exceptional" seems to bear the weight of the explanation in this formulation. The implicit assumption is that "children learn exceptions after regular rules." This is, however, not really an explanation. Moreover, children sometimes learn exceptional forms very early. What deeper explanation might one give?

The first observation to be made is that ECM involves not simply a lexical exception but an exception to case theory, which requires local case-assignment under adjacency. The word "local" means within the same clause. Extension of case-assignment beyond the clause violates that constraint.

There is, however, a second factor which favors the small-clause analysis. It is traditionally argued that case-assignment does not necessarily carry thematic information. ECM is exceptional because case is assigned to a lower-clause subject without assigning a thematic role to that subject. We have followed the view that complex verbs may also involve small-clause structure.[44] Such structures, like *pick it up* or *consider him smart,* may very plausibly involve both case-assignment and theta-assignment. The result is that one noun receives two thematic roles, much as in the theory of "secondary thematic roles."[45]

If, for the adult, the object in ECM structures may receive a theta-role from the higher verb and a secondary theta-role from the lower verb or adjective, then we have the systematic violation of a basic principle of Universal Grammar, the theta-criterion.

(121) Every argument has only one thematic role.

If the child seeks to obey the theta-criterion, then it would resist analyses which violate it. We have therefore a subregularity that is an exception to a *principle,* not an exception to a language-particular *parameter.* We can express this as an acquisition principle:

(122) The child does not assign two thematic roles to one argument.

The child's small clauses and the adult LF representation meet this criterion. But small clause sentences which undergo reanalysis disobey the theta-criterion in a structured way. Thus we argue that some small clauses are an exception both with respect to case theory and to the Theta-criterion: The verb assigns both case and a thematic role to an element that receives a thematic role from elsewhere. This corresponds to a simple intuition: In "help me dress" the *me* is simultaneously a subject and an object for the adult. For the child, we argue, the sentence "help me dress" still has a small clause "me dress" within it. It receives an analysis like *I kept John singing,* which need not entail that *I kept John.*

Borer and Wexler (1988) have introduced a related notion that they call the Unique External Argument Principle. They argue with respect to overgeneralized small-clause phenomena in Italian that children require a single external argument for each verb. Our claim, in effect, extends that view to include all cases where two thematic roles are projected onto one NP. This view does not entail an independent acquisition principle, but rather the unexceptional application of an existing principle.

By what means does the child admit the subregularity into his grammar? Borer and Wexler (1988) suggest that maturation may be involved: the

---

[44]See Lebeaux (1988) and references therein.
[45]See Zubizaretta (1982).

Unique External Argument Principle disappears. We think that maturation may be involved in allowing a second thematic projection onto an NP, but it is not clear that a separate acquisition principle is needed. In addition, the lexical problems in differentiating the primary data, when coupled with the fact that an exceptional subregularity is involved, may provide an explanation for the temporal delay. Many interesting claims and issues arise when one considers these questions in depth, but they go beyond the scope of this chapter.[46]

7. GENERAL CONCLUSION

Our argument proceeds at three levels: linguistic theory, learnability theory, and naturalistic data. We approached a set of questions that involved uncertainties in each domain. We resolved them by arguments that crossed domains.

In linguistic theory we pursued an hypothesis that verbal small clauses (*help me run*) involve no CP node, although the hypothesis has been controversial. In learnability theory, we demonstrated that a misanalysis of primary data could lead to parametric mistriggering and the creation of supersets which violate the subset criterion. We suggested that there was a potential point of confusion in the input data if the child learned extraction before he or she had a three-way distinction among small-clause ECM structures, ACC-ing structures, and tensed Ss with a CP node. If the child did not identify a class of exceptional case-marking verbs, which also take ACC-ing, then he or she would mistakenly conclude on the basis of (123) that (124) was possible. Consider the phrase *him running with spiked shoes:*

(123) how did you see him running t?
(answer: with binoculars/with spiked shoes)

---

[46]If (122) is true, we would expect it to manifest itself elsewhere. Note that adverbs constitute another violation of the theta-criterion. It is also not honored with adverbial phrases. Consider (i):

(i) The man was arrested voluntarily

Here the word *man* is the object of arrest but the *agent* of the adverb voluntarily. In principle all unsubcategorized adverbs add another theta role, although it may be identical to the first. Consider a phrase like:

(ii) John played the game angrily.

where John is both the player and the angry one. The rough evidence available is that all adverbs which are not subcategorized occur significantly later in the acquisition process.

(124) *how did you enjoy him running t?
(answer: very much/*with spiked shoes)

We resolved the problem theoretically by asserting that parameters must be at least intrinsically ordered. In particular, the following ordering is necessary:

(125) Exceptional case assignment must precede adjunct movement from the lower clause of a sentence containing a small clause.

If parameters are ordered in this fashion, then a surprising empirical prediction is made: Sentences with small clauses will allow extraction later than sentences that involve a CP node. This follows because the CP node, when it appears, has no constraints that depend on a different module. Therefore, on logical grounds, it is not surprising if extraction through CP occurs earlier than small-clause extraction.

From a naturalistic perspective, the opposite prediction would seem likely. Children use small clauses ("me big") at the earliest stage; therefore, one might predict that it would be easy for them to extract an adjunct from a small clause:

(126) how did you see me tie my shoes t?

In particular, it should be easier than the extraction of an adjunct from sentences which contain a complementizer:

(127) how did you see that I tied my shoes t?

Children do not use complementizer sentences (that I run) until long after they have both small clauses and embedded small clauses (like "help me dress"). From this perspective, one would predict that extraction through CP would be late.

Our experiments revealed exactly the opposite result which, however, fits both the learnability argument and our chosen version of small-clause structure. The children resist adjunct extraction from small clauses, but allow them from tensed clauses which have a CP.

The presence of a CP node was independently demonstrated by showing the barrier effect of a filled CP:

(128) a. how did he learn to bake a cake t?
b. *how did she learn what to bake t?

Where a medial CP was filled, extraction was uniformly blocked at every stage of acquisition. These results in turn confirm the particular theory of successive-cyclical movement proposed in *Barriers*.

Our general view is that linguistic theory can reach its explanatory goal of providing a logic for acquisition only by careful arguments that explain robust data about the stages of acquisition.

The work reported here was supported by NSF grant BNS-8820314 held jointly by the authors. We thank N. Chomsky and H. Goodluck for a number of helpful remarks, and the audience at Glow, Utrecht (1989).

REFERENCES

Bayer, J. (1984). COMP in Bavarian syntax, *Linguistic Review, 3.*

Berwick, R. (1985). *The acquisition of syntactic knowledge.* Cambridge, MA: MIT Press.

Bloom, P. (1990). Syntactic distinctions in child language. *Journal of Child Language, 17,* 343–355.

Borer, H., & Wexler, K. (1988). *The acquisition of particle agreement: A maturational account,* University of California, Irvine.

Bowerman, M. (1982). Reorganizational processes in lexical and syntactic development. In E. Wanner & L. Gleitman (Eds.), *Language acquisition: The state of the Art.* New York: Cambridge University Press.

Chomsky, N. (1965). *Aspects of the theory of syntax.* Cambridge, MA: MIT Press.

Chomsky, N. (1986). *Barriers.* Cambridge, MA: MIT Press.

Clark, R. (1988). *Minimality and verbal small clauses,* Carnegie-Mellon, Pittsburgh.

de Villiers, J., Roeper, T., & Vainikka, A. (1990). The acquisition of long-distance rules. In L. Frazier, & J. deVilliers (Eds.), *Language processing and acquisition.* Dordrecht, The Netherlands: Kluwer.

Goodluck, H., & D. Behne (1990). Development in control and extraction (this volume).

Larson, R. (1988). On the double object construction. *Linguistic Inquiry, 19.8,* 335–393.

Lasnik, H., & Uriagereka, J. (1988). *A course in GB syntax.* Cambridge, MA: MIT Press.

Lebeaux, D. (1988). Language acquisition and the form of the grammar. Unpublished doctoral dissertation, University of Massachusetts, Amherst.

Manzini, R., & Wexler, K. (1987). Parameters, binding theory, and learnability. *Linguistic Inquiry, 18,*[3].

Matthews, R. (in press). Introduction to R. Matthews & W. Demopoulous (Eds.), *Proceedings of the Ontario Conference on Learnability.* Dordrecht, The Netherlands: Reidel.

McDaniel, D. (1989). Partial and multiple Wh-movement. *NLLT, 7,4,* 565–605.

Nishigauchi, T., & Roeper, T. (1987). Deductive parameters and the growth of empty categories. In T. Roeper & E. Williams (Eds.), Parameter setting. Dordrecht, The Netherlands: Reidel.

Otsu, Y. (1981). Universal grammar and syntactic development of children. Unpublished doctoral dissertation, MIT, Cambridge, MA.

Radford, A. (1988). Small children's small clauses. *Transactions of the Philological Society,* pp. 1–46.

Reuland, E. (1983). Governing -ing. *Linguistic Inquiry, 14,* 621–624.

Roeper, T. (1988). Formal and substantive features of language acquisition. in S. Steele & S. Schiffer (Eds.), *Cognition and representation.* Boulder, Co: Westview.

Roeper, T., & Keyser, S. J. (in press). Re: The abstract clitic hypothesis. *Linguistic Inquiry.*

Roeper, T., & Weissenborn, J. (1989). How to make parameters work. In L. Frazier & J. de Villiers (Eds.) *Language processing and acquisition.* Dordrecht: Kluwer.

Slobin, D. (1973). Cognitive prerequisites for the development of grammar. In C. A. Ferguson & D. Slobin (Eds.), *Studies of child language development.* New York: Holt, Rinehart and Winston.

Solan, L. (1983). *Pronominal reference.* Dordrecht, The Netherlands: Reidel.

Stowell, T. (1981). *Origins of phrase structure.* Unpublished doctoral dissertation, MIT, Cambridge, MA.

Stowell, T. (1988). *Small clause restructuring,* UCLA.

Vainikka, A. (1986). *A theory of default rules,* University of Massachusetts, Amherst.

van Riemsdijk, H. (1983). Correspondence effects and the empty category principle. in Y. Otsu, H. van Riemsdijk, K. Inoue, A. Kamio, & N. Kawasaki (Eds.), *Studies in generative grammar and language acquisition.* (Published by Monbusho grant).

Zubizaretta, M. L. (1982). On the relationship of the lexicon to the syntax. Unpublished doctoral dissertation, MIT, Cambridge, MA.

10 Comments on Roeper and de Villiers

Andrew Radford
University of Essex, England

The primary empirical finding of the intriguing research by Roeper and de Villiers (= RDV) is that children 3–6 years old can interpret an initial wh-adjunct in a matrix clause as having been extracted out of a CP complement with an empty specifier, but not out of a CP complement with a filled specifier, nor out of a C-less complement with a genitive or objective subject. From this, they conclude that child grammars of English resemble their adult counterparts in that complements with a filled C-specifier or with a genitive subject are barriers to the extraction of wh-adjuncts. However, the two differ in that whereas adult C-less complements with objective subjects are barriers to adjunct extraction only if the subject receives case internally (but not if it receives case externally), both types of objective–subject complement are barriers in child grammars.

The most significant adult–child contrast revealed by RDV's research is that "exceptional clauses" (i.e., complement clauses whose subjects are exceptionally assigned objective case across the clause boundary by a preceding transitive matrix predicate) are barriers to extraction of wh-adjuncts in child grammars, even though they are not in adult grammars. The obvious question to ask is why this should be. If we take cross-clausal exceptional case-marking (= ECM) in adult grammars to be indicative of the voiding of the barrierhood of exceptional clauses, then we might follow RDV in hypothesizing that 3–6-year-olds have no ECM mechanism in their grammars (hence no barrierhood-voiding mechanism for C-less complements).

However, the problem posed by this assumption is how we account for the fact that what might seem to be ECM structures are typically acquired by the age of 2, as examples such as the following (taken from a naturalistic corpus of my own) illustrate:

(1) (a) Keep *her warm* (Holly, 2.0).
   (b) Let *me walk up* (*to*) *the shops* (Penny, 2.0).
   (c) Put *me down* (Michael, 2.0).
   (d) Take *them off* (Lucy, 2.0).
   (e) Let *me see that* (Angela, 2.1).
   (f) Pick *me up*. Help *me up*. Get *me up* (Robert, 2.2).
   (g) Want *us turn over*. Let *me cry*. Put *him in* (Jem, 2.3).
   (h) Make *him go* (Laura, 2.4).
   (i) I don't want *them in*. But I can't pull *them up* (Christine, 2.7).
   (j) Didn't get *them on*. Do you want to hear *me counting up to 7?* (Robert, 2.9).
   (k) I don't like *them in my garden*. It makes *me fall* (Kirsty, 2.9).
   (l) Put *them on*. I'm gonna roll *him in* again (Anna, 2.10).
   (m) We don't want *them on*. Get *them off her*. Just put *them on her*. Gotta throw *them in the bin* (Lisa, 2.10).

Given the assumptions that RDV make about early child grammars, it seems clear that they would regard the italicized sequences as small clauses with verbal/prepositional predicates. If ECM is not acquired until some time after 6, the obvious question to ask is how we can account for the fact that the 2-year-olds are producing small clauses with objective subjects as the complements of transitive matrix verbs?

RDV's answer to this question is to suggest that the case module in early child grammars may contain a structural default rule whereby a specifier NP (i.e., an NP immediately dominated by a maximal projection) can be assigned objective case from internally within its containing maximal projection, provided that it cannot receive case from elsewhere. This (they suggest) would account for the fact that 2-year-olds produce small clauses such as "Me dress," "Him gone," as independent sentences. Now, if children misanalyze ECM structures as clauses with internally case-marked subjects, and if C-less complements with internally case-marked subjects are barriers to adjunct extraction, then we have a very elegant account of why children do not permit adjunct extraction out of (what for adults would be) exceptional clauses.

The question that remains to be answered under this account is why ECM is late-acquired. RDV argue that ECM is a heavily marked phenomenon in that it is an exception to UG principles of Case theory and Theta theory. Case-marking (they claim) is generally a local operation (in that the assigner and assignee are contained within the same maximal projections); however,

ECM is nonlocal, and is thus an "exception" to the locality principle which constrains other types of case-marking. ECM is also (RDV suggest) an exception to the Theta-criterion requirement that each argument carries only a single theta-role; they maintain that the subject of an exceptional clause is theta-marked by both the matrix predicate and the complement predicate (so that in "Let [*him* go]", *him* receives one theta-role from *let* and another from *go*). RDV argue that the earliest grammars developed by children adhere strictly to Universal Grammar principles (with no exceptions to these principles being admitted until a subsequent point of maturation), so that early grammars do not license the exceptional case and theta-marking involved in ECM structures. Since such complements cannot be assigned case externally, children are "forced" (in order to avoid violating the case filter) to develop a rule assigning the complement subject case internally; given that C-less complements with internally case-marked subjects do not permit adjunct extraction, it follows that the relevant complements will automatically be barriers to adjunct extraction in child grammars.

In my discussion here, I shall take for granted the undoubted merits and importance of the kind of experimental research conducted by RDV. I shall leave to others the task of evaluating the experimental design, and confine myself instead to commenting on RDV's conclusions about the nature of early child grammars. It seems to me that the most interesting (and radical) proposal that they make relates to the nature of the case module in early child grammars. There are two important respects in which they see the child's case module as differing from its adult counterpart: (1) Child grammars have a "spurious" structural case rule assigning objective case to the subject of nonfinite complements (the rule is spurious in the sense that it has no exact counterpart in adult English), and (2) (objective) case-marking is subject to a strict locality condition in child grammars which does not operate (without exception) in adult English. I shall argue here that both of these conclusions are questionable on theoretical and empirical grounds alike.

Consider first the possibility of the child developing a spurious structural case assignment rule. It is not entirely clear to me how such a rule would operate (given the rather vague formulation suggested by RDV), but I infer that one of the things it would do is assign objective case to a caseless subject NP (i.e., to an NP immediately dominated by a Maximal Projection, provided that the NP occupies a position in which it cannot receive case from elsewhere). Thus, if the italicized sequences in early child utterances such as "*Me have one*" and "Let [*me have one*]" are analyzed as VPs in which *me* is the specifier (i.e., subject) of the VP, and if case-marking is strictly local in early child grammars, then it follows that the subject *me* will be assigned default objective case by virtue of the structural (i.e., specifier) position that it occupies within its containing clause.

It seems to me, however, that the proposed structural case-marking rule would pose a myriad of problems. For one thing, such a rule offers no obvious account of why the subject always precedes the predicate in nonfinite clauses (so, children say "[*Her* crying]" but not *"[Crying *her*]", and "Let [*me* see]," not *"Let [see *me*]"): if the bracketed structures are VPs in which the italicized NP is a specifier, then a purely structural case-rule would assign objective case to the italicized specifier irrespective of its linear position in the VP, so predicting (counterfactually) that the subject can freely occur before or after its predicate. I do not feel that it would be plausible to attempt to account for the consistent subject–predicate word order in terms of directionality of theta-marking (e.g., by arguing that predicates theta-mark their external arguments leftwards), since nonthematic subjects also precede their predicates in child speech, for example, in structures such as "I don't like [*it* snowing]" (produced by Tony at age 2.3).

A second problem with a structural case rule is that it arguably violates case principles of UG: Recent research has suggested that Case theory incorporates the principle that all "core" case-marking takes place under directional government by an appropriate head, so that nominative case in adult English is assigned under leftward government by a finite head (whether I, T, or AGR), objective case under rightward government by a strictly adjacent transitive head (V, P, or C), and genitive case under leftward government by a genitive head (D in some analyses, K in others). Moreover, as RDV themselves note, the conventional treatment of complements with internally case-marked objective subjects in adult English is in terms of government: for example, in a structure such as that bracketed in (2):

(2) [*Him* playing the piano] is always fun.

it is generally assumed that the italicized subject pronoun *him* is assigned objective case under leftward government by a particular type of gerundive head (which might be taken to be the V *playing,* or an abstract gerundive I containing +*ing*). We might see objective marking of subjects in child grammars as essentially an overgeneralization of this mechanism, so that child grammars incorporate a spurious case rule whereby a nonfinite head of any kind (not just a gerundive head) assigns objective case to a (specifier) NP to its left under government.

This "objective subject" rule would then operate in a way essentially parallel to the "nominative subject" rule (under which a finite head assigns nominative case to a subject NP under leftward government). Since the two rules operate in complementary environments (one in finite structures, the other in nonfinite structures), there would no longer be any necessity to think of the objective subject rule as a default rule (thereby offering a potential theoretical advantage, since we might argue that a maximally constrained Case theory should exclude in principle the possibility of default case rules). Indeed, the very fact that the nominative subject and objective subject rules are complementary means that the two rules could be collapsed into a single "generalized subject rule," whose operation we might outline informally as:

(3) (Subject) NP is assigned nominative/objective case under leftward government by a finite/nonfinite head (respectively)

Such a generalized subject rule might seem to provide one way of accounting for alternations such as the following in the speech output of 2-year-olds (examples from my own corpus):

(4) (a) *I'm* pulling this. *Me* going make a castle (Holly, 2.0).
    (b) *She's* gone. *Her* gone school (Domenico, 2.0).
    (c) *I* can't do it. *Me* want to get down (Michael, 2.0).
    (d) *He's* kicking a beach ball. *Her* climbing up the ladder there (Jem, 2.0).
    (e) *I* can mend it. *Me* finding something (Adam, 2.2).
    (f) *I'm* having this. *Me* driving (Rebecca, 2.2).

We might suppose that the first clause in each pair is finite, and the second nonfinite, and that the *I/she/he* subjects are assigned nominative case under leftward government by a finite head (*'m/'s/can't/can*), whereas the *me/her* subjects are assigned objective case under leftward government by a nonfinite head (which we might either take to be the nonfinite Verbs *going/gone/want/climbing/finding/driving,* or an abstract nonfinite I).

The government account of objective subjects offered here seems to me to be superior to the structural account offered by RDV in another respect—namely that it avoids developmental discontinuity. Under RDV's account, the child at some later stage of development (after the age of 6) has to "unlearn" (i.e., discard) the structural objective subject rule, and in addition has to acquire an entirely new (and seemingly unrelated) government-based objective subject rule to handle gerund structures such as that bracketed in (2). By contrast, under a government account of objective subjects such as that in (3), all the child has to "learn" after the age of 6 is to subdivide nonfinite heads into two classes, namely gerundive heads (which have the power to assign objective case to their subjects), and nongerundive heads (which do not). Under the government analysis, the child does not have to abandon the objective subject rule, but simply has to narrow down the class of nonfinite heads that fall within the domain of the rule to (a specific type of) gerundive heads. Thus, from a developmental point of view, objective subjects in child grammars can be handled more naturally by a government rule than by a structural rule.

One final advantage that the government account of objective subjects appears to offer is that it avoids the need to stipulate (as RDV do) that case-marking in early child grammars is subject to a strict locality principle (to the effect that a case-assignee must be contained within the same maximal projections as its case-assigner), which only admits exceptions at a later stage of development (at some unspecified point beyond the age of 6). There seem to me to be several problems posed by this stipulation. For one thing, it presupposes an essential discontinuity between adult and child case modules, since a specific locality principle that operates without exception in early child grammars has to be "relaxed" (and hence in effect abandoned) by the child at some point. What makes this assumption even less plausible is that recent versions of Case theory have sought to establish as a principle of UG that all "core" case-marking takes place under government by an appropriate kind of head; and yet government is given a putatively universal definition as a potentially nonlocal relation (potentially so, since the presence of intervening barriers will block nonlocal government). Indeed, the assumption that government can "reach across" certain types of constituent boundary plays a crucial role in accounting for contrasts such as "I am anxious for [*him/*PRO* to be there]," where it is crucial to a principled account of the distribution of objective pronouns and PRO to posit that the italicized subject position be governed by the Complementizer *for* across the bracketed IP boundary (cf. Kayne, 1984, for a parallel argument that government can also reach across a CP boundary). Since Complementizers may similarly govern complement specifiers in other languages (e.g., Arabic; cf. Fassi-Fehri, 1989), it is likely that government is universally a potentially nonlocal relation. But if this is so, it seems implausible that government could be taken to be an intrinsically local relation in child grammars.

Given RDV's structural case rule, it is necessary to stipulate that all case-marking is inherently local in child grammars, in order to block ECM (and associated voiding of the barrierhood of the complement). However, under the alternative government account of objective subjects outlined here, we can preserve the universal principle that case-marking takes place under (potentially) nonlocal government, since the apparent locality of case-marking will follow from an independent principle of UG, namely the minimality condition (which will prevent the subject of a nonfinite comple-ment from being externally governed and case-marked because it is already internally governed and case-marked). Thus, the government analysis of objective subjects would provide a more principled account of the barrier-hood properties of complements with objective subjects. It would predict that ECM will appear as soon as the child becomes (tacitly) "aware" that not all nonfinite heads govern and case-mark their specifiers: for example, as soon as the child "realizes" that infinitives do not govern and case-mark their subjects, the minimality condition will license ECM of infinitive subjects.

Thus far, I have assumed (along with RDV) that it is plausible to posit that 2-year-old children develop a "nonfinite objective subject" rule (what-ever its precise form) whereby the subject of a nonfinite clause is assigned objective case internally. (Of course, it is a crucial additional assumption of RDV's chapter that this rule is still operative in the grammars of 6-year-olds.) If this is so, we might expect to find that naturalistic samples of children's spontaneous speech production will provide empirical evidence in support of the postulated nonfinite objective subject rule. To check this possibility, I analyzed transcripts of the spontaneous speech production of 100 children, age 24–42 months (from my own corpus); each transcript contained several hundred utterances produced by the child in question. All of the children in the study had a stable case system, with clear evidence of a systematic nominative/objective/genitive contrast. I looked at the case which children assigned to the subjects of independent sentences (in examples involving pronoun subjects such as *I/me/my* whose case is unambiguously identifiable). All of the children made productive use of nominative subjects (there were abundant examples in each transcript); half of the 2-year-olds (30 out of 60), and a fifth of the 3-year-olds (8 out of 40) also made some use of objective subjects (though this was very limited in the 3-year-old group); in addition, a couple of 2-year-olds made very sporadic use of what seemed to be genitive *my* as a subject, producing a handful of examples like "My want a wee" but otherwise using only nominative subjects; cf. "I want my car back" (both examples from Matthew, aged 2.6). If these figures are representative, they suggest that 50% of 2-year-olds and 80% of 3-year-olds show no evidence whatever of having a nonfinite objective subject rule: and this clearly casts doubt on RDV's assumption that all 6-year-olds have such a rule operating in their grammars.

Moreover, careful analysis of the relevant transcripts shows that even those sentences with objective subjects are not the result of a rule assigning objective case internally to the subject of a nonfinite clause. What makes any such suggestion somewhat less than plausible is that Aldridge (1989) has argued at great length that children typically acquire an I-system at around 24 months of age (at which point, we start to see evidence of productive use of finite verbs and auxiliaries, infinitival *to,* etc.). She also argues that once the I-system has been acquired, all independent sentences produced by 2-year-olds have the status of finite IPs, headed by an overt or covert I constituent (hence, e.g., the absence of *to* infinitives used as independent sentences). The main surface difference between adult and child finite clauses in 2-year-olds is that children sometimes use covert finite inflections where adults use overt inflections, and sometimes use null allomorphs of Auxiliaries like *be/have/do* where adults use clitic allomorphs (so that in this latter respect, Early Child English resembles Nonstandard Negro adult English somewhat).

Part of the evidence that Aldridge adduces in support of her claim that sentences which appear to be nonfinite are best analyzed as finite clauses headed by a covert I constituent comes from the fact that the relevant sentences may have nominative subjects, and finite tags—as we see from examples such as the following:

(5) (a) I singing. I done it (Angela, 2.1).
    (b) I on it, aren't I? (Sarah, 2.2).
    (c) I on this one, aren't I? (Elizabeth, 2.2).
    (d) I see Granny, I do. I see Timmy, I do (Robert, 2.2).
    (e) I been in pub. He gone (Alexander, 2.2).
    (f) He hiding (Katy, 2.4).
    (g) He play with me, he did. He play with Laura, he does (Laura, 2.8).

Now, if all independent sentences produced by children from 2 years of age on are finite clauses headed by an (overt or covert) finite I constituent, then it follows that the objective case which children like those exemplified in (4) assign to subjects of independent sentences cannot be assigned under government by a nonfinite head, but rather must be assigned under government by a finite head.

If objective sentence subjects receive case under government by a finite head, then we should expect to find empirical evidence that 2-year-old children assign objective case to the subjects of what are clearly finite verbs and auxiliaries. Relevant evidence comes from examples such as:

(6) (a) *Me* falled in a grave. *Me*'s painted that this afternoon. *Me* didn't paint that. *Him* don't stroke me (Adam, 2.2).
    (b) *Me* haven't seen Spider. *Him* came down and had porridge. *Me* can have apple? (Jem, 2.2, 2.3, 2.4).
    (c) *Me* can make a hen. Can *me* put lots and lots? *Him* can see fire. *Him* does go there. *Her* does go there. Because *him* is tired (Hannah, 2.4, 2.6).

Indeed, the children concerned seem to alternate between using objective and nominative subjects for finite clauses, as we see from examples like the following:

(7) (a) *I* need this one, *me* does (Adam, 2.2).
   (b) No! *Me* can't, *I* can't (Hannah, 2.4).
   (c) *Me* can get this off. *I* can open it (Michelle, 2.5).

What all of this suggests is that objective case is assigned to the subjects of such sentences under government by an (overt or covert) finite I, not by a nonfinite I. It would seem that objective subject children (who all use nominative subjects for finite clauses alongside objective subjects) have incorporated into their grammars a case-rule such as the following:

(8) A finite head assigns nominative (*or objective*) case to an NP to its left under government.

Those children who use only nominative subjects for finite clauses have developed a parallel rule that lacks only the italicized condition.

The significant conclusion to be drawn from our discussion here is that there is simply no empirical evidence whatever that even children as young as 2 have in their grammars any nonfinite objective subject rule that assigns objective case to the specifier of a nonfinite head. This in itself makes it implausible that such a rule should operate in the grammars of all RDV's 4–6-year-old subjects. There are several other factors that lead us to the same conclusion. For example, as we noted earlier, objective subject structures like those in (4) are simply not attested in the speech output of the vast majority of 3-year-olds. Moreover, any internal nonfinite objective subject rule would massively overgenerate, and, for example, predict that children would make productive use of structures such as:

(9) (a) *I don't know what [$_{IP}$ *him* to do]
   (b) *I don't know what to [$_{VP}$ *him* do]

The reason why we would expect such utterances to occur is that the italicized subject would receive objective case from internally within the bracketed structure, so that the resultant sentences would involve no violation of the case filter, and thus would be predicted to occur. However, this prediction is entirely false: I have never encountered any such structure produced by young children at any age. Indeed, in my own corpus, the only wh-infinitive clauses we find are those with PRO subjects:

(10) (a) He don't know where [PRO to put them] (Laura, 2.8).
    (b) It tells you how [PRO to make a helicopter] (Per, 3.5).
    (c) I know how [PRO to get it on] and how [PRO to get it off] (Scott, 3.5).

Since PRO occurs only in positions that are caseless (and ungoverned), it seems clear that subject position in a *to* infinitive complement is not internally case-marked. But this in turn means that in sentences such as:

(11) (a) We want [*the pig* to go in and out] (Helen, 2.7).
   (b) I want [*you* to read me that story to me] (Anna, 2.10).
   (c) I want [*you* to help me] (Geoffrey, 3.0).

the italicized NP cannot receive case from internally within the bracketed complement, and so must receive case externally (from the matrix verb *want*). This leads us to the conclusion that even 2- and 3-year-old children must have an ECM mechanism operating in their grammars (thereby falsifying RDV's conclusion that ECM is acquired some time after the age of 6). Indeed, the very fact that among the many hundreds of examples of the relevant complement constructions in my corpus every single example (without exception) involves the putative "subject" NP being immediately positioned after a transitive verb or after the transitive prepositions *with/without* (so satisfying the case adjacency requirement) suggests that ECM is involved.

Of course, we might retort that the experiment conducted by RDV involved attempted adjunct extraction out of a gerund complement (namely, "How$_i$ did the boy show [him/his copying t_i?"), and that it might be plausible to suggest that 4–6-year-old children develop an internal objective subject rule that is restricted to being triggered specifically by gerund heads (rather than by nonfinite heads in general). However, I am skeptical about any such suggestion. On the assumption that genitive subjects in gerunds have internally assigned case, we might expect to find that if young children have developed an internal case assignment rule for gerund subjects, they will make productive use of gerund complements with genitive subjects. However, my own corpus contains not a single example of a gerund complement with a genitive subject (in spite of the fact that we find nominal structures with genitive possessors being used productively from age 24 months onwards). This fact calls into question the assumption that children have developed an internal case-assignment rule for gerundive subjects (and more generally, leads us to wonder whether genitive gerund structures are within the productive competence of preschool children at all).

Although my corpus contains no examples of gerunds with genitive subjects, it does contain examples of (what might be analyzed as) gerunds with objective subjects:

(12) (a) Do you want to hear [*me* counting up to 7]? (Robert, 2.9).
   (b) That's a bit which keeps [*the rain* coming down] (= "which

keeps the rain from coming down"). They're for [*them* killing people] (= "Caterpillars have horns so that they can kill people") (Brett, 3.1).

(c) I don't like [*this spot* being like this] (Matthew, 3.5).

(d) Look at [*this doggy* digging] (Peter, 3.9).

The fact that the italicized (putative) subject is immediately adjacent to a transitive case-assigner in each example suggests to me that ECM is likely to be involved here. Indeed, I would venture to suggest (in diametrical opposition to the analysis proposed by RDV) that ECM is the only mechanism by which nonfinite subjects can receive case in early child grammars (so that gerund structures with internally case-marked subjects like "[*Him/His* doing that] annoyed me" are peripheral, i.e., esoteric, structures that are late-acquired, and may well be inculcated at school).

If our overall conclusion is correct that subjects of nonfinite clauses in preschool children's grammars can only receive case externally (not internally), then the theoretical underpinnings of RDV's account of why adjunct extraction is resisted out of exceptional clauses are fatally undermined. This in turn would lead us to look for alternative interpretations of the adjunct extraction data, and question the extent to which the nonextractability of adjuncts out of gerund complements is (or is not) mirrored with other types of "exceptional clause" complement that more clearly fall within the productive competence of the preschool child. For example, we might ask whether preschool children always interpret *how* in exceptional clause structures such as the following as an adjunct to the matrix clause, or whether they can also interpret it as an adjunct to the complement clause:

(13) (a) How did Kermit get [him to bake the cake]?

(b) How did Kermit make [him bake the cake]?

(That *get/make* can function as two-place predicates taking an exceptional clause complement is clear from the fact that the complement can have a nonthematic subject like "weather *it*," as in examples such as "Do you think scientists will ever be able to make *it* rain/get *it* to rain at the touch of a button?"). I await the results of further experimentation with eager anticipation!

I should like to end on a positive note. While I am skeptical about the validity of the theoretical explanation that RDV propose for their extraction data, I applaud wholeheartedly their application of experimental techniques to investigate the operation of principles and parameters in child grammars. What needs to be underlined, however, is that (wherever possible) we should seek to monitor conclusions drawn on the basis of experimental data in the light of data from naturalistic studies (and vice versa).

REFERENCES

Aldridge, M. (1989). *The acquisition of INFL.* Mimeograph, Indiana University Linguistics Club, Bloomington, IN.

Fassi Fehri, A. (1989). Generalized IP structure, case, and VS order. *MIT Working Papers in Linguistics, 10,* 75–112.

Kayne, R. S. (1984). *Connectedness and binary branching.* Foris: Dordrecht, the Netherlands.

11 A Reanalysis of Null Subjects in Child Language

Nina Hyams
University of California, Los Angeles

INTRODUCTION

In this chapter I will provide a new analysis of the null-subject phenomenon in early child language that departs in crucial respects from previous analyses, in particular, that of Hyams (1983, 1986). We adopt the principles and parameters framework (Chomsky, 1981) and show that this formulation of Universal Grammar (UG) provides an explanatory framework within which to address both the logical and developmental problems of language acquisition. We take the logical problem of language acquisition to be the problem of explaining how the child can in principle arrive at an adult grammatical system, given the various boundary conditions under which acquisition takes place, for example, the lack of negative evidence and the inaccessibility of certain crucial data in the input. The developmental problem of language acquisition, on the other hand, involves elucidating the mechanisms by which the child passes through the intermediate stages of language development and arrives ultimately at a steady state grammar.

With respect to the logical problem, the principles and parameters of UG provide the child with a narrowly defined set of grammatical options where, ideally, the choice between them can be made on the basis of positive evidence. Thus, the leap from an impoverished input to a highly structured output is mediated by a rich innate schema. In addition, however, a parameterized UG can explicate the developmental sequence. During the course of development, child language varies from adult language in systematic ways. It is often the case that such deviations from a particular target language can be understood as variation within the limits defined by UG, or more to the point, as "mis-settings" along a particular parameter or parameters. The parametrized approach thus allows for a principled description of what often appear to be several unrelated properties of child language. It also provides an explanation for the child's transition from one developmental stage to another, where this is the result of the resetting of certain parameters.

Notice that it is neither necessary nor obvious that the principles and parameters approach should provide answers to the developmental question. It is entirely possible, a priori, that for the first years child language is governed by mechanisms that are distinct from those which characterize adult languages. (This is in fact the position of many developmental psychologists and psycholinguists). It is possible that at some later point, for example, age 3 or 4, UG or parts thereof mature and the parameters are set (correctly) at that time. Such maturational accounts have been proposed by Borer and Wexler (1987) and Felix (1987). If something along these lines is true, we would still have an account of the leap from data to grammar, but the principles and parameters of UG would be irrelevant to the developmental issue — at least at the earliest stages of acquisition. In effect, we would have a situation very close to the idealized "instantaneous acquisition" (Chomsky, 1965). It is therefore of some interest that even at the earliest stages of development, child grammars appear to be constrained by the principles and parameters of UG. In particular, it seems that successive stages of development can be explained as an initial mis-setting with a subsequent resetting along some parameter.

Hyams (1983, 1986) proposes an account of the null-subject phenomenon in early child language. I note there that thematic (referential) lexical subjects are optional in early child language and that expletive subjects are entirely lacking and that this phenomenon appears to be a universal property of child language. Examples from English are provided in (1); the sentences in (1a) have null thematic subjects, those in (1b) null expletive subjects.

(1) a. Want more apple.
See under there.
No play matches.
Show Mommy that.
b. Outside cold.
Is toys in there.

(Bloom, Lightbown, & Hood, 1975)

In Hyams (1983, 1986) I argued that null subjects in early language could be explained much in the manner of adult null-subject languages such as

Italian and Spanish. Specifically, I proposed that the Null-subject Parameter, a parameter of UG that accounts for the difference between languages, such as Italian and English with respect to the possibility for unexpressed subjects, comes fixed at an initial setting, one which permits phonologically null subjects. The central claim of that analysis was that all children start out speaking an Italian-like language. The child acquiring a non-null-subject language, such as English, eventually changes the initial parameter setting based on certain information in the input data.

Although we believe that the acquisition facts still support a parametrized account of the null-subject phenomenon, a number of empirical problems have surfaced that cast doubt on the original analysis. Thus in this chapter we would like to propose a reanalysis of null subjects in child language, one which we think overcomes these problems and which also sheds light on a number of other properties of child language that were not explained under the original analysis. The new null-subject analysis is based on the notion of "morphological uniformity," proposed by Jaeggli and Safir (1989), and on the analysis of morphological development proposed in Hyams (1988). The chapter is organized as follows: In the next section we discuss some of the inadequacies of the original analysis. In Sec. 3 we shall briefly outline the theory of null subjects that we adopt. We then turn to the developmental issues. Secs. 4–8 provide an account of a number of properties of early language in several typologically distinct languages, including English and German, American Sign Language (ASL), and Japanese. Finally, in Sec. 9 we briefly discuss an alternative analysis of the null subjects in child language proposed in Mazuka, Lust, Wakayama, and Snyder (1986) based in part on the null-subject phenomenon in Japanese child language.

2. INADEQUACIES OF HYAMS (1983, 1986)

First, Guilfoyle (1984) has noted that English-speaking children begin using verbal inflection at around the time they shift from null-subject to a non-null-subject grammar. Intuitively, these two events would seem to be related, particularly in light of the fact that on most analyses the possibility for null subjects is closely related to properties of the INFL node.[1] As Guilfoyle points out, my analysis did not explain the close association of these two properties.

A second problem concerns my treatment of the acquisition of modals and auxiliary *be*. The original analysis predicted that English-speaking children would acquire these elements at roughly the same point at which

---

[1]See, for example, Rizzi (1982), Jaeggli (1982), Chomsky (1981), Borer (1983), among others.

they abandoned null subjects. This claim proves problematical in two respects. First, it turns out that that the infinitive marker *to* also emerges alongside the modals (Bloom, Tackeff, & Lahey, 1984; Hyams, 1984), a fact that I take not to be coincidental and one which, for principled reasons cannot be explained within the original analysis.[2] In addition, Maratsos (personal communication) has noted (and our own investigation confirms; see Sec. 4) that while the modals begin to appear at the point of shift to a non-null-subject grammar, they are used infrequently at this time. For some children there may be a delay of several weeks to several months before the modals become fully productive. This delay may simply be the result of lexical learning, which would mean that while the early grammar licenses lexical elements in INFL at this point, it takes the child time to learn the individual members of the category. On the other hand, the delay coupled with the *to* fact noted herein seems to show that the generalization concerning the relationship between null subjects and modals is not as direct as my original analysis suggests.

Finally, there is a problem of a less empirical and more theory-internal nature. In the original analysis I argued, following in the spirit of Rizzi (1982), that null subjects are possible in languages in which agreement features are pronominal in some sense. This is the case for adult languages such as Italian and Spanish and, I argued, child language as well. Although the notion of pronominal agreement features is an abstract one, it is usually the case in adult languages that these features get morphologically realized in the form of "rich" overt inflection, wherein the latter serves to "recover" or "identify" the content of the null category. However, this is not necessarily the case in child language. Children acquiring richly inflected languages such as Italian (cf. Hyams, 1986) and Polish (cf. Weist & Witkowska-Stadnik, 1985) do acquire the inflectional system at a very early age, and thus the null subjects in their grammar are "identified." However, English-speaking children use null subjects despite the fact that verbal morphology, such as it is in English, is not yet acquired at this point. A similar situation exists in French (Pierce, personal communication) and in American Sign Language, as discussed by Lillo-Martin (1986), languages in which inflectional paradigms are acquired after children are productive in their use of null subjects. Thus, if young English-speaking children are speaking "Italian," as I proposed originally, they are speaking an Italian that shares only the abstract properties of this language, that is, the

---

[2]In Hyams (1983, 1986) the absence of auxiliaries during the null-subject stage was explained (in part) as an effect of the presence of a pronominal AGR(eement) node in INFL that blocks lexical material from appearing in AUX. Under standard assumptions infinitivals do not contain AGR features and hence this analysis fails to explain why the infinitive marker *to* should also be lacking during the null-subject stage.

pronominal agreement features, but lacks the overt manifestation of these features in the form of rich agreement. It seems fair to ask, then, if this does not violate the spirit of a recoverability condition, or in more recent terms, an identification requirement on null elements.

These various problems are summarized:

(2) a. The development of tense accompanying the transition to a non-null-subject grammar is unaccounted for.
   b. The emergence of infinitive marker *to* alongside modals is not predicted.
   c. Modals infrequent initially.
   d. Null subjects are "unidentified."

In what follows we would like to propose an alternative to my original null-subject analysis, one which we believe overcomes these problems. Before turning to the acquisition facts, however, we will need to outline the theory of null subjects that we am adopting, which, as noted earlier, is based on the work of Jaeggli and Safir (1989) and the analysis of morphological development proposed in Hyams (1988).

3. MORPHOLOGICAL UNIFORMITY AND NULL SUBJECTS

As a point of departure we should note that the notion of "rich agreement" mentioned above is problematical even for the analysis of adult null-subject languages. As is often observed, not all adult null-subject languages have rich inflectional paradigms and many languages that do have rich inflectional systems are not null-subject languages. German and Icelandic are examples of the latter. These two languages do not allow null thematic subjects, although they do have null expletives, a point that we will return to. On the other hand, there are languages like Chinese that have no verbal inflection whatsoever, but which are nevertheless null-subject languages. This suggests that "rich agreement" is neither a necessary nor sufficient condition for null subjects.

Given this state of affairs, Jaeggli and Safir propose a different approach to the null-subject phenomenon. On their analysis the essential property that accounts for the possibility of null subjects is "morphological uniformity." They propose that null-subject effects can be accounted for by the Morphological Uniformity Principle:

(3) Null subjects are permitted in all and only those language which have morphologically uniform inflectional paradigms.

A morphological paradigm is uniform if all its forms are morphologically complex or none of them are. To illustrate the principle briefly, consider the cases of Italian, English, and Chinese. The Italian inflectional paradigm consists entirely of morphologically complex forms; hence null subjects are allowed. As an example, the present tense paradigm for the verb *to speak* is:

(4) *parlare* — to speak
    parl*o* parl*iamo*
    parl*i* parl*ate*
    parl*a* parl*ono*

In Chinese, no forms are morphologically complex; for example, the form of the verb *to like* is *xihuan* with all subjects; hence the same result. In English, on the other hand, morphologically complex forms such as *talks, talked, talking,* coexist with morphologically simple forms, such as *talk.* Thus, English is a "mixed" system and null subjects are prohibited.

As noted, some languages have morphologically uniform paradigms but do not have thematic null subjects. This is the case of German, Icelandic, and other verb second (V2) languages. To explain these cases, Jaeggli and Safir distinguish the *licensing* of null subjects from their *identification.*[3] Morphological uniformity constitutes the licensing condition; it describes when a null subject is possible. However, any token thematic null subject must also be identified, that is, its referential value must be recovered. The null subject can be identified by one of three elements; local AGR(eement), which must include a tense feature; a c-commanding nominal; or a Topic. In languages such as Italian and Spanish, the null subject is identified by AGR containing tense. In languages that uniformly lack agreement, such as Chinese, the subject is identified either by a c-commanding nominal — this will be the case for embedded subjects — or a Topic. We return to the issue of identification by topic in Sec. 7.1. Thus, languages like Italian and Chinese satisfy both morphological uniformity and the identification requirement and hence null thematic subjects are permitted.

But what about the case of German and Icelandic? These languages are morphologically uniform but do not have null thematic subjects. Following Platzack (1985), Jaeggli and Safir assume that in these languages the tense features are located in head of COMP, that is, second position, the position to which the verb moves. Because the tense features are separate from the agreement features, which are in INFL, the identification requirement is not satisfied. The V2 configuration is given in (5) (irrelevant details omitted).

---

[3]Rizzi (1986) and Lillo-Martin (1986) also propose separating the licensing and identification requirements.

(5) [$_{COMP}$ [+/−Tense] [$_S$ NP VP [$_{INFL}$ AGR]]]

Thus, in these language null thematic subjects are not identified and hence impossible. Null expletives, in contrast, are allowed since they have no referential content to be recovered; they need only be licensed.

Although we have omitted many details, the analysis of null subjects just outlined provides a unified account of the null-subject phenomenon across a wide range of adult languages (see Jaeggli & Safir, 1989, for detailed discussion). Moreover, the analysis has rather direct implications for grammatical development in children, particularly as regards the use of null subjects and the acquisition of verbal inflection. So let us now turn to the acquisition facts. We begin with a discussion of the acquisition of "mixed" languages, such as English.

4. THE ACQUISITION OF "MIXED" LANGUAGES

As noted at the beginning of this chapter, the optionality of lexical subjects appears to be a universal property of child language, whether or not the adult language is a null-subject language. According to the analysis proposed here, the possibility for null subjects presupposes morphological uniformity. Thus, the child who allows null subjects must also be analyzing his or her language as morphologically uniform. With regard to the development of "mixed" (nonuniform) languages, like English, two predictions follow. First, we expect that these children will omit inflection during their null-subject stage thereby rendering their morphological system uniform. As is well known, young English-speaking children omit inflectional morphology; this being one of the characteristics that lends their speech its "telegraphic" quality (Brown, 1983). Adult English is not uniform, however, and thus our second prediction is that once the English-speaking child learns the properties of the inflectional system and realizes that it is not uniform, he or she will abandon the null-subject grammar.

Bellugi (1967) and Guilfoyle (1984) describe the emergence of tense inflection as coinciding with the end of the null-subject stage and our own analysis of the longitundinal records of Adam from Brown's Harvard study, provided by the CHILDES Data Exchange System, confirms this description. Fig. 11.1 gives the percentage of null subjects and inflectional morphemes, including third-person singular -s, and regular and irregular past tense, used by Adam between the ages of 2;7 and 3;0. We see a sharp decrease (from 70% to 10%) in the use of null subjects during this 5-month period. At the same time the use of inflectional morphology increases from 30% to 75%. This inverse relationship is exactly what we would expect given the uniformity principle. Once the child realizes that English is a

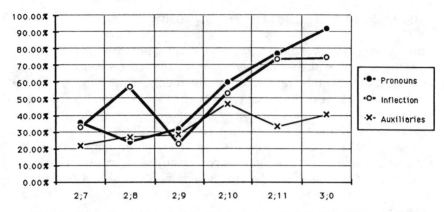

FIG. 1   Percentage of lexical subject pronouns, inflectional morphology and auxiliaries for Adam.

"mixed" morphological system, evidenced by the fact that his verbs are surfacing with inflectional morphemes, null subjects are no longer licensed.[4]

Notice that it is not necessary for the child to be fully productive in the use of English inflection for the latter to mark a shift away from the null-subject option. All that the analysis requires is that the child "realize" that English has a nonuniform system. It is thus sufficient that he or she be using inflection in a manner that is "appropriate" for a mixed system. So, for example, third-person -s should appear on the verb—when it does appear—only with third-person subjects and should not occur with first- and second-person subjects. If the child were overregularizing the use of the third-person morpheme to other grammatical persons, he or she would in effect be making the system uniform, and hence null subjects would continue to be licensed. Thus, the uniformity hypothesis leads us to expect particular patterns of overregularization; the child who knows his or her system is mixed may incorrectly inflect an irregular form with a regular affix, for example, *bes, dos, haves, goed,* and so on. He should not, however, systematically extend the use of an affix to forms that are "bare" in the adult language, for example, *I goes, you eats.* To our knowledge the latter pattern of overregularization does not typically occur with English-speaking children. In contrast, children acquiring richly inflected morphologically uniform languages often do overextend an affix within a particular paradigm, a phenomenon that Slobin (1973) refers to as "inflectional imperialism." I will return to this phenomenon in Sec. 6.

---

[4]We are currently analyzing the computerized CHILDES transcripts of the two other Harvard children, Eve and Sarah.

4.1 The Development of Auxiliaries

Turning now to the development of lexical auxiliaries, we see in Fig. 11.1 that although they appear in spontaneous speech during this period, their frequency of occurrence does not change substantially.[5] Their frequency increases only later, after the child is fully productive in his use of verbal inflection. It thus appears, as proposed in Guilfoyle (1984), that the emergence of the English auxiliaries, including modals, *be* and *to,* depends on the development of a $+/-$ tense distinction. In what follows we shall show why this is so.

As is well known, English modals require a [+tense] feature, as illustrated in (6a,b) and *to* requires a [−tense] feature]. Thus the latter may appear in infinitives, as in (6c), but not in small-clause complements such as (6d), which have no INFL node (Stowell, 1983) and hence are unspecified for tense.

> (6) a.   John hopes that Mary can come.
>   b.   *John wants Mary to can come.
>   (cf. John wants Mary to be able to come.)
>   c.   John wants Mary to come.
>   d.   *John sees Mary to come.

Similarly, though the auxiliary *be* appears in tensed and infinitival sentences, it may not occur in small clauses with an existential interpretation. Thus, in the sentence in (7a) *be* does not mean what it does in (7b). Rather it has the meaning of *become* or *behave.*

> (7) a.   ??I let (made, saw, heard, watched) John be crazy.
>   b.   John is crazy.

We will assume that the *be* that occurs in copula and progressive constructions is an expletive verb, that is, semantically empty, but necessary to carry the tense specification of the sentence.[6] Given these facts, the development of tense is logically prior to the acquisition of *be,* as well as the modals and *to.* In contrast to the analysis of Hyams (1983, 1986), then, the emergence

---

[5]Auxiliary use was calculated on the basis of their frequency of occurrence in obligatory contexts. Thus the count includes only those elements for which obligatory contexts can be determined, for example, copula and progressive *be, do,* perfective *have* and *will.* The obligatory context for the modal *will* was determined on the basis of linguistic and nonlinguistic context, for example, a situation in which the child was clearly talking about some future event. Because obligatory contexts for the other English modals cannot be determined, this count is conservative.

[6]A similar position is developed in more detail in Scholten (1988).

of lexical auxiliaries is not a direct effect of the null-subject parameter. Rather, the two phenomena, null subjects and auxiliaries, are indirectly related through their interaction with the development of tense. The current analysis thus avoids the problems noted in (2a,b,c).

We can now outline two developmental stages (read grammars). During the first stage, which we may refer to as the "uniformity stage," the child's grammar requires uniform inflectional paradigms and thus is unspecified with respect to tense. As a result, modals, *to* and *be* are unexpressed during this stage. At the same time, the morphologically uniform system permits null subjects. At a later point, when the child develops the ability to analyze the weak inflectional system of English, he or she "realizes" that it is nonuniform and hence that null subjects are not licensed. This is the "mixed" stage, which corresponds to the adult grammar.

Finally, we should note that the pattern of development that Adam exhibits with respect to subjects, inflection and auxiliaries shows the relationship between subject use and inflection is not simply an effect of overall development or general language learning. It is not the case that all aspects of grammar are undergoing steady development toward the target grammar during this period. Auxiliary use remains relatively constant during this period, staying at around 30%. Thus, we find development along two specific dimensions—obligatory use of subjects and inflectional morphology—those that are singled out by the uniformity hypothesis.

5. THE ACQUISITION OF V2 LANGUAGES

Let us now consider the morphologically uniform V2 languages, taking German as a paradigm case. Recall that German has a uniform inflectional paradigm and hence null subjects are *licensed* in this language. However, the agreement features fail to satisfy the identification condition because of the verb second requirement (see (5)). Thus, adult German does not have thematic null subjects, though it does have null expletives.

In contrast to the adult language, however, early German is a null-subject language. Clahsen (1986) observes that German children use lexical subjects only about 45% of the time during his stages II and III. Interestingly, during this same period, German children fail to respect systematically the V2 requirement. The predominant word order at this point is SOV, although the correct adult order in simple clauses in SVO. Clahsen's Stage IV is marked by three important changes. First, the use of null subjects falls to 10%. At the same time, the use of verb second jumps to 90%. Both of these changes are dramatic by acquisition standards.[7]

---

[7]Clahsen (1986) also shows that German children achieve productive control of agreement morphology during Stage IV, whereas in the earlier stages only some of the agreement markers

The co-occurrence of these two grammatical developments follows from the analysis of null subjects being proposed. In the early grammar of German, null subjects are both licensed and identified; at this point we may assume that the tense features are in INFL with the agreement features and thus the identification requirement is satisfied. Recall that a null subject can be identified by AGR only if it includes a tense feature (cf. Sec. 3). However, when the early grammar of German restructures such that tense is situated in COMP, evidenced by the onset of the V2 rule, identification is blocked and null subjects are no longer licit.[8]

6. THE ACQUISITION OF INFLECTION

To this point we have discussed the use of null subjects and its real-time relation to other grammatical phenomena such as the V2 rule in German and the acquisition of tense morphology in English. There are, in addition, other more general properties of child language that are explicated by this analysis.

A number of people have observed that morphological development is a lot quicker and less errorful for children acquiring languages that are morphologically rich, such as Italian (Hyams, 1983) and Polish (Weist, Witkowska-Stadnik, 1985) than for children acquiring English, in which acquisition of verbal inflection is very late (Brown, 1973). This result follows if, as we are proposing, the child's initial hypothesis (in advance of any linguistic experience) is that his or her language is morphologically uniform. Those languages that meet this expectation will be "easier" to acquire than those that do not. Moreover, it has been noted, particularly by D. Slobin and colleagues, that children tend to make uniform those paradigms which are not. The omission of inflection, as in English, is one example of how they do this. Another is the tendency that children have to "avoid 0 affixation," in morphologically rich languages, for example, Russian and Serbo-Croatian (Slobin, 1973). This phenomenon can be explained, if we assume, that zero affixes do not count as affixes for the child. He or she would then tend to replace zero forms with overt ones in order to ensure a uniform paradigm.

7. THE INITIAL STATE

Taking the MUP given in (3) to be the correct statement of the null-subject parameter, we are proposing that uniformity represents the child's initial

---

are used and may in fact be encoding something other than agreement with the subject. The development of German morphology as it relates to the uniformity hypothesis is discussed in Hyams and Jaeggli (1989).

[8]This analysis predicts that children may still use null expletives beyond this point. However, this prediction proves difficult to test empirically since null expletives in German occur only in embedded contexts and children at this stage do not control such structures.

assumption concerning his or her morphological system; it follows that null subjects are *licensed* in the child's grammar. The first question that arises is why should this be the case. A second issue concerns the status of *identification* at the initial state. Let us address these issues in turn.

With regard to the first point it should be noted that from the viewpoint of linguistic theory, or UG, there is no reason that "uniformity" should represent an initial "unmarked" hypothesis. In fact, we assume in the general case that linguistic theory is neutral with respect to the question of initial parameter settings or hypotheses. However, viewed from the perspective of learnability, it becomes obvious that uniformity is a more restrictive hypothesis than nonuniformity. That is to say that if the child assumes that no forms are inflected or that all forms are, positive evidence will tell him or her otherwise. If, on the other hand, one assumes that one's language is "mixed," when in fact it is not, no number of inflected or uninflected tokens will suffice to induce a reanalysis. In short, the fact that the child adopts uniformity as an initial assumption follows from some version of the Subset Principle (Berwick, 1985).

Let us turn now to the question of identification in the early grammar. As noted earlier, children acquiring richly inflected languages such as Italian and Polish learn the inflectional system fairly early and thus it seems reasonable to assume that in these cases the null subject is identified by AGR(eement), as is the case in the adult grammar of these languages. On the other hand, in the early grammar of languages like English, and ASL, (which we turn to shortly) something other than agreement features must be satisfying the identification requirement. We propose that in these cases the null subject is identified by a Topic, as has been proposed for Chinese and other adult null-subject languages which uniformly lack morphology.

This idea follows in the spirit of Huang's (1984) analysis of Chinese. Huang distinguishes "discourse-oriented" languages from "sentence-oriented" languages. The discourse-oriented languages, such as Chinese, have a rule of "topic-chaining" by which the discourse topic is grammatically linked to a nullsentence topic which in turn identifies a null argument (specifically, a variable in GB terms). Modifying Huang's analysis somewhat, we propose that in the early grammar the null subject is a pronominal (pro), which is identified by a null topic. Thus, the difference between the early grammar of Italian, on the one hand, and English and Chinese, on the other, is not the content of the empty subject position but rather the method of identification, as schematized in (8) (irrelevant structure is omitted). I will discuss these structures further:

(8) a. $[_S \text{pro}_i \ [_{INFL} \text{AG}_i/\text{Tense}] \ . \ . \ . \ . \ . \ ]$ Italian
    b. DISCOURSE
        $\text{TOPIC}_i \ [\text{topic}_i \ [_S \text{pro}_i \ [\text{INFL}] \ . \ . \ . \ . \ ]$ Chinese/English

Thus, in contrast to the analysis in Hyams (1983, 1986), the current proposal is that some children start out speaking Italian while others start out speaking Chinese; English-speaking children fall into this latter category. They will ultimately abandon this grammar when they realize that English is not morphologically uniform and hence fails to satisfy the licensing condition.

This proposal raises a number of issues — one of which is that adult discourse-oriented languages such as Chinese typically allow null objects in addition to null subjects and this has obvious implications for the acquisition analysis we are proposing. So we will discuss this issue in some detail. In this context we will also describe the development of null subjects in American Sign Language, a language that represents an interesting test case for the analysis presented here. Finally, in Sec. 9 we will address a proposal by Mazuka, et al. (1986) to the effect that the null-subject phenomenon in early language is not an effect of a specific null-subject parameter (however stated), but rather due to the interaction of performance constraints and Lust's Principle Branching Direction Parameter.

7.1 Null Objects

Let us turn first to the null-object phenomenon. As noted earlier, on Huang's analysis a topic may bind a variable in either subject or object position, as illustrated in (9), (TOPIC = discourse topic; topic = sentence topic):

(9) a. $TOPIC_i$ [$Topic_i$ [$_S$[e_i] INFL VP]]
    b. $TOPIC_i$ [$Topic_i$ [$_S$ NP INFL [V [e_i]]]]

Since the null-subject and null-object phenomena are grammatically equivalent, all else being equal this analysis predicts that a discourse-oriented child language will have both null subjects *and* null objects.

Modifying Huant's analysis somewhat, we will propose that in the adult language in addition to the topic-variable structures, a topic may also bind a null pronominal in subject position, as illustrated in (10a) (= 8b). However, as Huang shows, a topic cannot identify a null pronoun in object position.[9] Thus, (10b) is an impossible structure in Chinese.

---

[9]Huang (1984) proposes that an empty argument must be identified by the closest possible identifier (Generalized Control Rule). For a null object, the subject is the closest identifier. However, if the null object is pronominal, coindexation with the subject would result in a violation of Condition B of the Binding Theory (Chomsky, 1981), which requires that a pronominal be free in its governing category.

(10) a.   TOPIC$_i$ [topic$_i$ [pro$_i$ INFL VP]]
      b. *TOPIC$_i$ [topic$_i$ [NP INFL [V pro$_i$]]

This analysis predicts that there could be a discourse-oriented grammar (in Huang's sense) with a subject/object asymmetry, that is, one in which null subjects are possible, but which disallows null objects. This would be true just in case the grammar had null pronominals, but not variables. Such a grammar would rule out the representations in (9a,b) and, for independent reasons (see footnote 9) the representation in (10b), allowing only (10a). We claim that this is in fact the case. Specifically, we propose that in the early grammar (the null-subject stage) the inventory of null elements includes little *pro,* but not variables. We will assume for the present that the latter are maturationally determined to emerge at a later point.[10]

Returning to the acquisition data, our prediction of a null-subject/null-object asymmetry is certainly confirmed in the case of English, in which children systematically omit subjects, but rarely objects (Hyams and Wexler, 1991). More interestingly, however, this asymmetry seems to exist for Japanese-speaking children as well, despite the fact that Japanese, like Chinese, is a discourse-oriented language with null objects. In a study of the acquisition of Japanese, Mazuka, et al. (1986) calculate the frequency of various null constituents in the two-word utterances of several Japanese children. Their results show that null subjects occur in approximately 56% of the subject–predicate constructions, while null objects appeared in only 17% of the transitive verb constructions. Thus, both English- and Japanese-speaking children exhibit a strong asymmetry in their use of null subjects and objects supporting our proposal for topic-identified *pro.*

To sum up, we are proposing that the early grammar is a null-subject grammar in which a null pronominal subject (*pro*) is licensed by morphological uniformity; this property is invariant across children. However, the early grammar can vary in the manner of identification; the null subject may be identified by agreement in some languages and by topic in others. We assume that this is largely, though perhaps not completely, determined by properties of the input language. Moreover, in those languages with topic-identification, null subjects do not necessarily imply null objects for the reasons noted. This accounts for the subject/object asymmetry that we find in the child's use of null arguments, even in those languages that allow null arguments in both positions. Our analysis further predicts that children

---

[10]The claim that *pro* emerges prior to variables in the early grammar was first proposed by Roeper, Rooth, Mallis, and Akiyama (1984), who argue for this on the basis of entirely independent experimental evidence. We would not want to claim, however, that this no variable stage persists beyond ages 2.5 or 3 since there is good evidence that children do have operator-variable structures at a fairly early age. See, for example, Goodluck & Behne (this volume).

acquiring real discourse-oriented languages will produce null-object structures at the point at which they develop variables, as evidenced, for
example, by emergence of quantification and so on. We do not at present
know what the acquisition data show in this regard.

8. NULL SUBJECTS IN ASL

As noted earlier, ASL is an interesting case to consider given the details of
this analysis. According to Lillo-Martin (1986), ASL represents a cross
between a discourse-oriented and sentence-oriented language. There are two
classes of verbs, the inflecting verbs and the uninflecting verbs, both of
which take null subjects. In Lillo-Martin's analysis the null subject of an
inflecting verb is identified by AGR(reement), while the null subject (or
object) of an uninflecting verb is identified by a null topic in the manner
suggested by Huang for Chinese. Within the framework we are proposing,
adult ASL is a morphologically uniform language since each verbal
paradigm is either uniformly inflected or uninflected, and thus null subjects
are licensed. We follow Lillo-Martin's analysis of identification, which will
be outlined.

In her very interesting analysis of development of null subjects in ASL,
Lillo-Martin (1986) identifies three major developmental stages. During the
initial stage ASL-signing-children assume that ASL is a null-subject language; however, they do not use agreement on the inflecting verbs.
According to Lillo-Martin, null subjects are unidentified at this stage. In the
next stage, around 3;6 years old, the children develop a restricted use of
agreement morphology; they use agreement for present referents. Lillo-
Martin proposes that at this point the child understands the identification
requirement. This is supported by the observation that at this point they
cease using null subjects with nonpresent referents, the latter being the case
in which they fail to use morphology. Finally, agreement morphology is
extended to situations in which the referent is not present, and null subjects
are again used in this circumstance as well.

Our analysis of the development of null subjects in ASL differs only
minimally from Lillo-Martin's. Recasting the preceding description into our
framework, we have the following developmental sequence. The ASL-
signing child initially assumes his language is morphologically uniform, as
do all children, and hence null subjects are *licensed*. Moreover, we will
assume that at this stage the null element is topic-identified, as is the case
for English-speaking children. At Stage 2, having developed a rich inflectional system, the child switches to agreement-identification. We may
assume for the purposes of this discussion that there is a Unique Identifier
Principle, which specifies that given a choice between two possible identi-

fiers, you choose the "closest" or most local one. (This is similar in spirit to Huang's [1984] Generalized Control Rule, discussed in footnote 9.) Thus, agreement will win out over topic. As in Lillo-Martin's account, it follows that at this stage, once the child has determined an identifier, null subjects are blocked when the identification requirement is not satisfied as, for example, with nonpresent referents. Finally, the use of agreement extends to nonpresent referents and thus null subjects are once again identified in this case as well.

In this section we have seen that the Morphological Uniformity Principle, independently motivated on linguistic grounds (see Jaeggli & Safir, 1989), provides an explanatory account of a number of properties of several typologically distinct child languages. In the section that follows we briefly discuss a proposal in Mazuka et al. (1986) since they offer a rather different account of the null-subject facts in child language.

9. PRINCIPLE BRANCHING DIRECTION AND NULL SUBJECTS

Mazuka et al. claim that the null-subject phenomenon is more pronounced in English than in Japanese, although they report statistics only for the Japanese children. They argue on this basis that what they call "preferential subject omission (PSO)" is not universal in child language and hence cannot be due to an initial setting along some specific Null-subject Parameter. Rather, in their analysis, null subjects in English result from the interaction of performance constraints (an upper limit on the length of utterance a child can produce) and the rightward branching direction of English; complexity builds in a rightward direction resulting in reduction or omission of elements to the left, that is, subjects.

The first question we might ask is of a conceptual nature, namely: Why should branching direction determine the locus of deletion in this way? That is, assuming, as seems reasonable, that there is a performance limit on what the child can produce, why should he or she drop elements that occur in the nonbranching direction. It seems much more plausible, a priori, that the child would eliminate elements at the point at which the complexity builds, namely, in the branching direction. So for English, we would expect child to reduce complexity by eliminating material in the VP, rather than the subject. But, let us assume for the sake of argument that the Principle Branching Direction Parameter plus performance constraints can account for the null-subject facts in English, what does this analysis predict concerning the acquisition of Japanese, which is an SOV language, that is, left-branching.

Although Mazuka et al. do not address this question in detail, as I understand their proposal, there are at least two predictions that follow. First, the analysis leads us to expect that performance constraints in Japanese children will result in the omission of constituents on the right, namely verbs. Their data show that Japanese children omit the copula, but since this is also the case for English-speaking children, it must be independent of branching direction. Japanese children also omit other verbs, but no more frequently than English children do.

Second, there should be no null subject effects in a language like German since the language is left-branching and subjects are on the left. Thus, following the logic of the their proposal, left is the direction where complexity builds, and so should not be the direction in which you find reduction or omission of constituents. Thus, the German acquisition data, discussed in Sec. 5, are also problematical for this analysis. German is underlyingly SOV (left-branching), like Japanese, and as we noted earlier, young German children initially prefer SOV order in their monoclausal utterances (though this is incorrect in the adult language). We must conclude, then, that German children know the SOV branching direction of their language and thus we would expect no null-subject effects in this case as well. As noted earlier, however, German children do omit lexical subjects and they do so precisely during the period in which they use predominately SOV word order.

Let me conclude by noting that the argument for an early null-subject grammar has always been based on the *optionality* of lexical subjects and not on their *frequency*—beyond the obvious need to establish that the phenomenon is indeed systematic. Thus, I question Mazuka et al.'s basic premise that a Null-subject Parameter account (however formulated) of null subjects in child language is weakened or falsified by the fact that children vary in the frequency with which they use null subjects. (It should be noted in this regard that even within a single language, e.g., English, children vary in the frequency with which they use null subjects). Finally, the fact that Japanese children exhibit the same null-subject/null-object asymmetry as English-speaking children, despite dramatic differences in the input they receive provides rather compelling evidence for certain a priori, language-independent properties of early grammar.[11]

10. CONCLUSION

In this chapter we have noted a number of empirical and conceptual problems in Hyams' (1983, 1986) account of the null-subject phenomenon

---

[11]See Hyams and Wexler (1991) for a detailed discussion of a number of other recent nongrammatical accounts of the null-subject phenomenon in child language.

in child language. We have proposed instead that the early grammar (like adult grammars) is constrained by the Morphological Uniformity Principle (Jaeggli & Safir, 1989) which licenses null subjects in languages with morphologically uniform inflectional paradigms. This account captures a number of properties of child (and adult) language in such typologically distinct cases as English, German, Japanese, and ASL. This analysis claims that the child's use of null subjects represents a grammatical option. This is in contrast to the proposal in Mazuka et al., which proposes that the null-subject phenomenon is a performance effect, albeit modulated by certain grammatical properties of the target language. We saw that there are a number of empirical problems with this particular proposal (see Note 11). Finally, we hope to have shown that the conception of UG as a system of principles and parameters that constrain the intermediate as well as final state grammars offers an explanatory approach to both the logical and developmental problems of language acquisition.

ACKNOWLEDGMENTS

A shorter version of this paper was presented at the 1987 Boston University Conference on Child Language Development. Some of the material in Secs. 3–7 was also presented at the 1987 NELS meeting and appears in the Proceedings of NELS 17 (Jaeggli & Hyams, 1988). I would like to thank the participants of those conferences for their valuable comments and criticisms. I would also like to express my deep appreciation to Osvaldo Jaeggli and Tom Cornell for their many ideas and insights and more thanks to Tom for compiling the data on Adam presented in Sec. 4. Thanks finally to the editors of this volume for suggestions on earlier drafts.

The transcripts of the Brown corpora were made available to me through the Child Language Data Exchange System (CHILDES), Department of Psychology, Carnegie Mellon University.

REFERENCES

Bellugi, U. (1967). *The acquisition of negation.* Unpublished doctoral dissertation. Harvard University, Cambridge, MA.
Berwick, R. (1985). *The acquisition of syntactic knowledge.* Cambridge, MA: MIT Press.
Bloom, L., Lightbown, P., & Hood, L. (1975). *Structure and variation in child language.* Monograph of the Society for Research in Child Development, *40* (2).
Bloom, L., Tackeff, J., & Lahey, M. (1984). Learning *to* in complement constructions. *Journal of Child Language, 11.*
Borer, H. (1983). *Parametric syntax.* Dordrecht, the Netherlands: Foris.
Borer, H., & Wexler, K. (1987). The Maturation of Syntax. In T. Roeper & E. Williams (Eds.), *Parameter setting.* Dordrecht, the Netherlands: Reidel.
Brown, R. (1973). *A first language: The early stages.* Cambridge, MA: Harvard University Press.
Chomsky, N. (1965). *Aspects of the theory of syntax.* Cambridge, MA: MIT Press.

Chomsky, N. (1981). *Lectures on government and binding*. Dordrecht, The Netherlands: Foris.

Clahsen, H. (1986). Verb inflection in German child language: Acquisition of agreement marking and the functions they encode. *Linguistics, 24.*

Felix, S. (1987). *Cognition and language growth*. Dordrecht, The Netherlands: Foris.

Guilfoyle, E. (1984). The acquisition of tense and the emergence of lexical subjects. *McGill working papers in linguistics*. McGill University.

Huang, J. (1984). On the distribution and reference of empty pronouns. *Linguistic inquiry, 15.*

Hyams, N. (1988). The acquisition of inflection: A parameter-setting approach. UCLA.

Hyams, N. (1986). *Language acquisition and the theory of parameters*. Dordrecht, The Netherlands: Reidel.

Hyams, N. (1984). The acquisition of *to:* A reply to Bloom, Tackeff & Lahey. *Journal of Child Language, 11.*

Hyams, N. (1983). *The acquisition of parameterized grammars*. Unpublished doctoral dissertation, City University of New York.

Hyams, N. & Jaeggli, O. (1989). *Null subjects and morphological development in children*. UCLA & USC.

Hyams, N. & Wexler, K. (1991). *On the grammatical basis of null subjects in child language*. UCLA and MIT.

Jaeggli, O. (1982). *Topics in romance syntax*. Dordrecht, The Netherlands: Foris.

Jaeggli, O., & Hyams, N. (1988). Morphological uniformity and the setting of the null subject parameter. *Proceedings of NELS, 17.*

Jaeggli, O., & Safir, K. (1989). The null subject parameter and parametric theory. In O. Jaeggli & K. Safir (Eds.), *The null subject parameter*. Dordrecht, The Netherlands: Reidel.

Lillo-Martin, D. (1986). *Parameter setting: Evidence from use, acquisition and breakdown in American Sign Language*. Unpublished doctoral dissertation, University of California, San Diego.

Mazuka, R., Lust, B., Wakayama, T., & Snyder, W. (1986). Distinguishing effects of parameters in early syntax acquisition: A cross-linguistic study of Japanese and English. *Papers and Reports in Child Language Development, 25,* 73–82.

Platzack, C. (1985). The Scandinavian languages and the null-subject parameter. *Working Papers in Scadinavian Syntax, 20.*

Rizzi, L. (1982). *Issues in Italian syntax*. Dordrecht, The Netherlands: Foris.

Rizzi, L. (1986). Null objects in Italian and the theory of *pro. Linguistic Inquiry, 17,* 3.

Roeper, T., Rooth, M., Mallis, L., & Akiyama, A. (1984). The problem of empty categories and bound variables in language acquisition. University of Massachusetts, Amherst.

Scholten, C. (1988). *Principles of universal grammar and the auxiliary verb phenomenon*. Unpublished doctoral dissertation, University of Maryland, College Park.

Slobin, D. (1973). Cognitive prerequisites for the development of grammar. In C. Ferguson & D. Slobin (Eds.), *Studies in child language development*. New York: Holt, Rinehart, & Winston.

Stowell, T. (1983). Subjects across categories. *Linguistic Review, 2,* 285–312.

Weist, R., & Witkowska-Stadnik, K. (1985). Basic relations in child language and the word order myth. Unpublished manuscript, State University of New York, Fredonia, and Adam Mickiewicz University.

12 Null Subjects in Early Grammars: Implications for Parameter-setting Theories

Jürgen Weissenborn
Max Planck Institut für Psycholinguistik,
Nijmegen, The Netherlands

INTRODUCTION

The importance of the notion of parameter setting in recent linguistic theory conceived as a cognitive science resides in the fact that it combines a model of language variation with a model of how a given language can be acquired under normal circumstances of language development. The aim of the present study is to show, on the basis of longitudinal data from French and German, that the parameter-setting approach to language acquisition encounters a number of problems, and further, to suggest what modifications might be made to alleviate them.

My discussion will be based on an apparently exceptionless property of early child language: During a certain period in development, children omit lexical subjects, even in languages that normally require them, such as English, French, or German. Recently, acquisition studies in a Universal Grammar framework have related the omission of lexical subjects in languages of this type to versions of the Null-subject Parameter,[1] assuming that the child begins by analyzing the input language as a null-subject language (i.e., a language in which lexical subjects are optional, such as Italian or Chinese) and then resets the parameter when disconfirming input data become available.

Under the assumption that the missing subjects in early child language are

---

[1]There is an extensive literature about the pro-drop, and more specifically the null-subject parameter. Recent discussions are Huang (1984), Rizzi (1986), and the contributions in Jaeggli and Safir (1989b).

cases of *pro*-drop, they must be both licensed and identified by UG principles.[2] This is the approach taken by authors like Hyams (1986, 1989, this volume); Borer and Wexler (1988); and Clahsen (1988, 1991), who all assume that children's initial null-subjects in non-null-subject languages are made possible by the fact that the language of the child differs from the target in some property of INFL.[3, 4] The subsequent development of the INFL-component is assumed to be crucial for the child's finding out

---

[2]Licensing and identification are subject to parametric variation. Terms like pro-drop or null subject parameter are thus just short-hand labels for these different parametric dimensions. In Rizzi (1986) these parameters take the following form: (1) Licensing parameter: "pro" is case-marked by X, where X is a case-assigning head. (2) Interpretation parameter: Let X be the licensing head of an occurrence of "pro": then "pro" has the grammatical specification of the features on X coindexed with it.

According to Jaeggli and Safir (1989a, pp. 32–37), null subjects are licensed by "Morphological Uniformity." Only morphologically uniform languages allow null subjects. There are two types of morphologically uniform languages: those that are morphologically complex, like Italian, and those that have no inflection at all, like Chinese. Morphologically mixed languages, like English or French, always require subjects. The identification of null subjects can be done in one of the following ways: (a) Locally if AGR-TENSE governs, respectively if AGR case-governs the empty category. (b) Nonlocally, following Huang, by (i) a null topic, itself related to a Discourse Topic, that binds a variable in subject position, and (ii) by control of *pro,* by a c-commanding NP. (i) applies mainly to null subjects in main clauses, (ii) to null subjects in embedded clauses.

Huang (1984, p. 549) originally suggested that the cross-linguistic distribution of lexical and null subjects can be accounted for by distinguishing two parameters: (1) one that distinguishes zero-topic languages (Chinese) from non-zero-topic languages (English, Italian), and (2) one that distinguishes languages that allow null subjects (*pro*-drop) in tensed clauses (Spanish, Italian) from those that do not (English, French). The first type of language is *discourse-oriented* insofar as the zero topic that binds the null subject, a variable, is coindexed with a preceding Discourse Topic. The second type of language is *sentence-oriented*. Here, the null subject is *pronominal,* and its content is determined through rich agreement on the verb. The combination of (1) and (2) allows for four different types of languages: (1) non-zero-topic, non-*pro*-drop: English, French; (2) zero-topic, pro-drop: Chinese, Portuguese; (3) non-zero-topic, *pro*-drop: Italian, Spanish; (4) zero-topic, non-*pro*-drop: German.

[3]Borer and Wexler (1988) assume that the child's initial grammar is additionally constrained by a learning principle, the Unique External Argument Principle (UEAP), which requires that every predicate be associated with a unique external argument and that every external argument be associated with a unique predicate. This constraint would force the English-learning child to analyze the input as if it were Italian.

[4]An alternative account assumes that there is an initial stage in the child's grammar where INFL (and its recent offsprings TP, AP, AGRP) and other functional categories, e.g., COMP and DET, are absent. Under this view, missing subjects are not cases of *pro*-drop. Rather, they are explained by assuming that at the earliest developmental stages arguments are not obligatorily projected in the syntax (Guilfoyle & Noonan, 1988; Lebeaux, 1988; Radford, 1990).

whether or not null subjects are possible in the target language: learning the adult properties of the verbal inflectional system (e.g., finiteness, tense, agreement) should lead the child acquiring a non-null-subject language such as German, English, or French to move from the initial null-subject stage to the adult version of the parameter, so that null subjects are no longer possible.[5] This theory makes a prediction:

> PREDICTION 1: The acquisition of the properties of the INFL component of the target language should lead the null-subject parameter to be set to its correct value. Once this happens null subjects should no longer occur.

We will show that there is evidence from French and German that this prediction is not borne out. We conclude that in these languages the acquisition of properties of the INFL-component is not sufficient for the child to determine whether or not he or she is acquiring a null-subject language.

We will propose an alternative account based on data that indicate that the setting of the null-subject parameter must be related to the presence in the child's language of structures with a lexically filled COMP position. This suggests that the setting of another parameter, the wh-parameter, which determines whether or not a language has wh-movement at s-structure, is also involved.

The present study is based on data from three German and three French children. Only utterances containing at least one verb have been taken into account. The size and the age range of the data base for the different children is as follows:

German
S: 22;20 to 32;15 (months;days); 1476 utterances
B: 21;07 to 32;00 (months;days); 954 utterances
H: 22;20 to 30;00 (months;days); occasional diary data
French
P: 25;19 to 32;22 (months;days); 2527 utterances
B: 21;19 to 33;06 (months;days); 1867 utterances
F: 22;26 to 32;25 (months;days); 757 utterances

---

[5]This dependency on properties of INFL as a trigger to further development does not hold in this direct way of Borer and Wexler's (1988) approach. Under their approach, the maturationally determined disappearance of UEAP makes a reanalysis of properties of the verbal inflectional system possible that then leads to changes in the child's grammar.

1. IS INFLECTION A TRIGGER FOR THE SETTING OF THE NULL-SUBJECT PARAMETER?

Is the acquisition of inflection the trigger for the setting of the null-subject parameter? In this section we will show that during the acquisition of German and French we find a stage where the child has acquired the properties of the inflectional system but still does not show the adult use of subjects. The data for the distribution of lexical subjects and null subjects in finite sentences for S and P, the French and German children for whom the data is the most extensive, is shown in Tables 12.1 and 12.2.[6] After discussing the languages separately, the two will be compared.

1.1 German

Two accounts will be the focus of the discussion of German, Clahsen (1991) and Hyams (this volume).

1.1.1 Clahsen

Clahsen's (1991) account of null subjects is based on Rizzi's (1986) theory of when null subjects can occur. Two parameters are involved, a licensing parameter and an identification parameter. For null subjects to be allowed in a language, they must be (a) licensed and (b) identified. They are licensed by the presence of a case-assigning INFL. They are identified by receiving person–number agreement features from INFL. More specifically, Clahsen assumes that in early German (developmental stage II/III in Clahsen, 1988), missing subjects are all cases of *pro*. They are licensed by a finiteness feature [+F], corresponding to Rizzi's INFL. They are identified vacuously, because at this stage children have no subject–verb agreement. Essentially, this amounts to saying that at this stage, the identification parameter is not yet set. Null subjects are no longer permitted in Clahsen's subsequent stage IV when the child acquires subject–verb agreement, which allows him or her to set the identification parameter correctly to the value [AGR =- pronominal], the setting that excludes thematic null subjects.

In the following, I will argue that early German is not a null-subject language with INFL licensing *pro*. Rather, nearly all cases of actual missing subjects can be accounted for by the same mechanisms as missing subjects in the adult language. Further, there is evidence that subject–verb agreement may be already present at this stage.

---

[6]For French, only lexical subjects in the canonical preverbal position were taken into account. Thus, an utterance like *mange moi* with a postverbal lexical subject was counted as containing a null subject. For German, only preverbal null subjects are taken into account. The number of postverbal null subjects does not exceed 5% and seems not to vary much over time.

TABLE 12.1
FRENCH (P): Null Subjects vs. Lexical Subjects in Declarative Matrix Clauses

Age (months; days)	Null subjects (%)	Lexical subjects (%)
25;19–25;26	30.3	69.7
26;03–26;26	36.4	63.5
27;00–27;21	29.7	70.3
30;13–30;27	8.8	91.2
31;11–31;25	12.9	87.1
32;01–32;29	4.3	95.7
33;15	6.3	93.7

TABLE 12.2
GERMAN (S): Null Subjects vs. Lexical Subjects in Declarative Matrix Clauses

Age (months; days)	Null subjects (%)	Lexical subjects (%)
22;20–22;28	81.6	18.4
23;13–23;23	82.6	17.4
25;12–25;21	55.9	44.1
26;03–26;21	39.4	60.6
28;17–28;21	16.1	85.9
32;09–32;15	23.4	76.6

Moreover, the arguments for how a *pro* would be licensed and identified are problematical. The problems can be grouped into problems related to INFL licensing *pro* and problems related to INFL identifying *pro*. We will begin with the *licensing* problems and then turn to the *identification* problems.

The first two licensing problems come from facts about subjects in adult German unnoticed by Clahsen. Contrary to French or English, adult German has the possibility to omit thematic lexical subjects. They can be omitted in the preverbal position of tensed matrix clauses, given an appropriate context, such as the following question–answer pair:

(1) A: *Was machte Hans, als du ihn sahst?* B: *(Er) sah fern.*
    What was Hans doing when you saw him? (He) was watching TV.

They can also be omitted in contexts such as the following, where a bare VP infinitive is supplied as an answer to a question:

(2) A: *Was willst du jetzt machen?* B: *(Ich will) Kuchen essen.*
    What do you want to do now? B: (I want) cake to-eat.

In order to evaluate the child's omission of subjects, one has to distinguish between permissible subjectless structures as in examples (1) and (2), which are grammatical (if pragmatically conditioned) and omissions of subjects that are clearly ungrammatical, such as the one in the postverbal position in (3):

(3) *Kuchen isst *(er).*
     Cake eats (he).

Most of the subjectless constructions of the child are of type (1) or (2), just like the ones that are also grammatical in the adult. The following examples illustrate this:

(4) *Glaub nich.*   B 25;07
     Believe(1sg) not.

(5) *Brauche nich lala.*   S 24;02
     Need not pacifier.

(6) *Male eier.*   S 22;20
     Paint eggs.

(7) *Backe kuchen.*   S 22;20
     Bake cake.

(8) *Baue haus.*   S 22;28
     Built house.

(9) *Esse pudding.*   S 22;28
     Eats pudding.

(10) *Geht nich.*   S 23;13
     (This) works not.

(11) *Brauche lala.*   S 23;13
     Need pacifier.

(12) *Will lala habe.*   S 23;13
     Want pacifier to have.

(13) *Schmeckt auch nich.*   S 25;12
     Tastes also not.

(14) *Brauche seife.*   S 25;12
     Need soap.

(15) *Machen knödel.*   S 25;12
     Make dumplings.

(16) *Macht das.*   B 26;09
     Does it.

(17) *Macht tange (=Zange).*   B 26;15
     Does (it with) snippers.

(18) *Zähne putzen.*   S 22;22
     Teeth to brush.

(19) *Apfel habe.*   S 23;13
     Apple to have.

(20) *Schuh ausziehn.*   S 23;13
     Shoe to take off.

(21) *Schwamm holn.*   S 23;14
     Sponge to get.

(22) *Blumen giesse.*   S 25;12
     Flowers to water.

(23) *Flasche trinken.*   S 25;12
     Bottle to drink.

(24) *Haare waschen.*   S 25;16
     Hair to wash.

The first licensing problem concerns empty preverbal subjects. Examples (1)–(17) illustrate cases of preverbal missing subjects in matrix clauses. We would claim that these are not cases of INFL-licensed *pro;* rather, as in adult German, they are allowable cases of empty topics. And we claim that they are identified, as in adult German, through a topic chain, following Huang (1984).

The second licensing problem concerns examples (18)–(24), cases of bare VPs. How is *pro* licensed here? It cannot be by INFL which is empty in infinitives, and thus cannot license *pro*. Again, we would claim, these cases are accounted for as they are in the adult.

We conclude that, so far, there is no need to claim that missing preverbal subjects in matrix clauses in the child's grammar are licensed by finite INFL.

The next set of problems concerns the identification of *pro* by INFL. The first problem is related to the claim that INFL can only initially license subject *pro* in German as long as the child cannot set the identification parameter [AGR = +/− pronominal]. Clahsen suggests that the subsequent acquisition of subject–verb agreement tells the child that AGR is [− *pro*] and thus does not identify thematic null subjects in German. The question remains how the child finds out that [AGR = − *pro*]. The development of subject–verb agreement by itself is not enough. Italian, for example, a null-subject language, thus with [AGR = +*pro*], has subject–verb agreement too. Thus, without independent evidence that [AGR = − *pro*] the identification parameter cannot be set.

The second problem concerns the fact that the absence of subject–verb agreement is a prerequisite for Clahsen's claim that finite INFL is the licenser of subject *pro*. The difficulty is that there is evidence that children already have subject–verb agreement at the supposed null-subject stage. The evidence comes from morphological marking.

We want to argue that at the time when inflections first appear on children's verb forms, they agree with their subjects in person, and number. If inflectional morphemes were not sensitive to the features of the subject, then we should find a random distribution of inflectional morphological endings across subjects; this is not the case. (The reader is referred to Tables 1 and 2 in Clahsen, 1986; for further details see Mills, 1985; Verrips & Weissenborn, in preparation; Weissenborn, 1990.)[7]

The third identification problem is related to the following prediction:

PREDICTION 2: If INFL licenses subject *pro* then *pro* should occur in all finite contexts.

This prediction is not borne out, however. In some finite contexts *pro* subjects occur only rarely: (1) in matrix clauses when a constituent other than the subject occupies the preverbal position, (2) in wh-questions, and (3) in embedded clauses.[8] This is not accidental. We will discuss this in

---

[7]Mills (1985, p. 215), analyzing the data of the two children studied in Miller (1979), also comes to the conclusion that the children have subject–verb agreement. Her analysis includes data from S, studied in the present chapter.

[8]See Valian (1990c) with respect to wh-questions. Until recently, it has been assumed that embedded clauses with overt complementizers emerge relatively late, that is, around the second half of the third year (Clahsen 1982; Rothweiler, 1989). Our own data, and work by Tracy, Fritzenschaft, Gawlitzek-Maiwald, and Winkler (1990), suggest that there must be considerable individual variation, because subordinate clauses can be observed already at around age 2. As first pointed out by Stern and Stern (1928), there may be a stage where the grammar of the child, contrary to the adult language, allows for complementizerless verb-final embedded clauses, as shown in the following examples:

greater detail in Sec. 3.

1.1.2 Hyams

Hyams (this volume) offers an account of German, which, like Clahsen's, assumes that early German contains *pro* but differs in two respects. First, according to her analysis, only verb-final structures should allow null subjects. Second, although *pro* must be licensed and identified, the mechanisms are different. Hyams uses the conditions proposed in Jaeggli and Safir (1989b),[9] in which *pro* is identified not by person–number agreement features alone, but also by tense features. *Pro* is licensed by a Morphological Uniformity Condition, which is not relevant here, but will be discussed when we consider French in Sec. 2. There are two problems with this account. First, the prediction that null subjects should only occur in verb-final structures is not borne out; there are many cases of null subjects in V-second structures, as shown by some of the examples given herein and which are repeated here:

(25) *Glaub nich.*   B 25;07
     Believe not.

(26) *Brauche nich lala.*   S 24;02
     Need not pacifier.

(27) *Male eier.*   S 22;20
     Paint eggs.

(28) *Backe kuchen.*   S 22;20
     Bake cake.

(i) (..) *pappi aufewacht is, morgen omi* H 25;04
   (when) p. woken up is, tomorrow, grandma (comes)

(ii) (..) *mami flugzeug wegfahrt, angst* H 25;04
   (when) m. (with) airplane leaves, (I am) afraid

(iii) *papi sagt* (..) *schöne hose anzieht hat* H 25;18
   p. says (that) nice pants put-on has

(iv) *rutschsocken* (..) *mami wasch hat* H 25;18
   socks (that) m. washed has)

Adjunct clauses (*weil*, "because," *wenn*, "when") are acquired before argument clauses (*dass*, "that"). There is no systematic study of the acquisition of embedded clauses in French, but here too, adjunct clauses seem to precede argument clauses (see Clark, 1985).

[9]For details see footnote 2.

(29) *Baue haus.*   S 22;28
     Built house.

(30) *Esse pudding.*   S 22;28
     Eats pudding.

(31) *Brauche seife.*   S 25;12
     Need soap.

(32) *Machen knödel.*   S 25;12
     Make dumplings.

(33) *Macht das.*   B 26;09
     Does it.

(34) *Macht tange* (= Zange).   B 26;15
     Does (it with) snippers.

Second, as shown in examples (18)–(24), the verb-final structures that occur are infinitival VPs. Thus, they do not contain the tense and agreement features necessary to identify a subject *pro*. Moreover, on the basis of Hyams' account for null subjects in children, one would also predict null subjects to occur in adult German in embedded clauses which do not have V-to-C movement.

Summarizing the preceding discussion, we conclude that the German data do not support the claim that the acquisition of verbal inflection and the distribution of missing subjects across time are related in the sense that the former leads to the disappearance of the latter, acting as a trigger for the setting of the null-subject parameter. Rather, we claim that the omission of lexical subjects in children does not differ in nature from the one in adults.

1.2 French

French provides a second test for the theory that learning properties of INFL is the trigger that tells the child that his or her language is not a null-subject language. And, as in German, the data run counter to the predictions.

Although Hyams (this volume) does not focus on French, she suggests that *pro* can initially be licensed if French, like English, is analyzed by the child as having no verbal inflection at all, that is, as being morphologically uniform (thus satisfying Jaeggli and Safir's [1989b] Morphological Uniformity Condition[10] for null subjects). Following Huang (1984), she assumes identification of the null subject by a topic chain; but contrary to Huang, she proposes that the null subject is *pro,* and not a variable:

(35) Discourse Topic$_i$ [topic$_i$ [S pro$_i$ [INFL] . . .]]

As illustrated by the examples in (36–65), French children continue to use null subjects, along with lexical subjects, although there is clear evidence that they have analyzed verbal morphology, (i.e., that they have both agreement and tense correct). This finding is at variance with Hyams's account, since correctly learning agreement and tense means that the children know that French is a morphologically mixed language. It, therefore, should no longer allow null subjects (see also Hulk, 1987).

Explicit Subjects

(36) *Ze boi (= je bois).*   B 24;01
     I drink.

(37) *Il pleut.*   B 24;22
     It rains.

(38) *Il est cassé papa?*   B 24;22
     It is broken daddy?

(39) *Attention, je monte.*   B 24;22
     "Attention, I come up.

(40) *Elle veut l'assiette.*   F 22;16
     She wants the plate.

(41) *Il pleut.*   F 22;16
     It is raining.

(42) *Le chat est parti.*   F 22;16
     The cat left.

(43) *Ca on va l'enlever.*   F 24;13
     This we will it-take off.

(44) *Je vais te chercher un mouchoir.*   F 26;11
     I will you-get a handkerchief.

(45) *Il pleure le bébé.*   P 25;26
     It is crying the baby.

---

[10]See footnote 2 for details about the notion of Morphological Uniformity.

(46) *Je veux ça.*   P 25;26
     I want this.

(47) *Papa répare le tracteur.*   P 25;26
     Daddy repairs the tractor.

(48) *Il pleut dehors.*   P 25;26
     It is raining outside.

(49) *Elle réveille la dame et le monsieur.*   P 25;26
     She wakes up the lady and the gentleman.

(50) *Elle est lourde la raquette.*   P 25;26
     It is heavy the (tennis) racket.

(51) *Voilà je vais la fermer moi.*   P 27;14
     Ok, I will it-close, me.

Null Subjects

(52) *Peux le faire.*   B 24;01
     Can it-do.

(53) *Ai mangé des quettes* (=crêpes)   B 26;02
     Have eaten pancakes.

(54) *Sont pas là les gâteaux.*   B 26;18
     Are not there the cookies.

(55) *Est sale.*   F 22;26
     Is dirty.

(56) *Veux pas.*   F 22;26
     Want not.

(57) *Veux manger.*   F 22;26
     Want to eat.

(58) *Est sale la poupée.*   F 22;26
     Is dirty the doll.

(59) *A fait.*   P 25;19
     Has made.

(60) *Est tombé.*   P 25;19
     Has fallen.

(61) *Va chercher un avion.*   P 25;19
     Going to look for a plane.

(62) *Faut les mettre dans le garage.*   P 25;26
     Must put them in the garage.

(63) *Ai tout bu le verre moi.*   P 25;26
     Have drunk the whole glass me.

(64) *Est dur celui-là.*   P 25;26
     Is hard that.

(65) *Me souviens pas.*   P 30;13
     Me remember not.

(66) *Mangeaient les enfants.*   P 30;13
     Ate the children.

The foregoing cases show correct verb endings. But one does not know from this fact alone that these are actually analyzed by the child. However, that verbal inflectional morphology has in fact been analyzed by the child is shown by the following findings. First, subject–verb agreement is clearly evident. Although verbal inflection in French is relatively reduced, especially in the present tense singular, there are a several verbs, *avoir, être,* and *aller,* which distinguish between first-person singular on the one hand and second- and third-person singular on the other hand. Thus examples (38, 43, 44) show that the child combines a given verb form with the appropriate form of the subject clitic pronoun.[11] As observed by Pierce (1989), the fact that subject clitic pronouns, as in the adult language, occur exclusively with finite verbs, is additional evidence for subject–verb agreement.[12]

Independent evidence for the child's mastering of subject–verb agreement comes from other forms of agreement that occur at the same time, such as agreement between a subject clitic and an extraposed coreferential NP or an object clitic and an extraposed coreferential NP as shown in (67) and (68), respectively:

(67) *Elle est lourde la raquette.* P 25;26
     It is heavy the racket.

---

[11]There are a few examples of *je va* in this early stage. Notice that this particular combination may also occur in adults. There is a "late" example of *j'a:* (i) *j'a fa* (=*froid*) B 26;02 but no examples of *j'est, tu vais,* or *tu suis.*

[12]We don't share Pierce's assumption that subject clitics have the status of inflectional morphemes in the language of the child. Inflectional morphemes are obligatory; thus utterances with a null subject, or a nonclitic subject, that is, (i) *Jean mange* ("Jean eats") should not be generated by the grammar of the child after the first subject clitics have been acquired. The prediction is that if there is a lexical subject, there should also be a subject clitic. That is, instead of (i) we should only find: (ii) *Jean il mange.* This is not the case. Again, the child's grammar is not different from the adult's one.

(68) *On la met la robe.* F 27;12
     We put it on the dress.

Second, the examples given so far are also evidence that the children have tense: the distinction between present tense (40), present perfect (42) and immediate future (43) is consistently made.[13]

Additional evidence that verbal morphology has been analyzed by the child comes from negation. It clearly shows that the finite/nonfinite distinction is made from the first occurrence of inflected verbal forms onwards. As in adult French,[14] the negative particle *pas* almost exceptionlessly follows finite verb forms and precedes nonfinite forms, that is, infinitives and past participles (examples (69–70)). Pierce (1989) reports similar findings (for details see Weissenborn, Verrips, & Berman, 1989). We can thus conclude that the finite/nonfinite distinction is systematically made by the child.

(69) a. *L'est pas la.* F 20;08
        He/she's not there.
     b. *Veux pas.* F 22;26
        Don't want.
     c. *Veux pas le mettre.* F 26;11
        Don't want to put it.

(70) a. *Ca marche pas.* P (25;19)
        That doesn't work.
     b. *Pas chercher les voitures.* P (25;19)
        Not to look for the cars.
     c. *Est pas mort.* P (25;19)
        Is not dead.

---

[13]See Meisel (1990) for similar conclusions.

[14]We assume with Emonds (1978) and Pollock (1989) that French is a verb raising language, that is, all finite verbs have to undergo raising to INFL. Thus sentences (ii, iii) are the S-structure and the D-structure of (i) respectively (we ignore the negative particle *ne* that is systematically omitted in colloquial French):

(i) *Marie (n) aime pas Jean*
    Mary doesn't like John

(ii) *Marie [I′ [I present, 3p.sing.] [pas [VP aime- Jean]]*
     Mary   s   not   like- John

(iii) *Marie [I′ [I aime$_i$ + present, 3p.sing] [pas [VP e$_i$ Jean]]*
      Mary   like   +   s   not   John
      (Pollock, 1989)

The position of the negation element *pas* with respect to a verb can thus be taken as a surface structure cue as to whether verb raising has taken place.

Further evidence for the existence of finiteness is related to case assignment. Under the assumption that only a finite INFL can assign Nominative Case, Nominative Case marking should not be available in the null-subject stage in non-*pro*-drop languages such as French and English given the absence of finite INFL at that moment (Kazman, 1988). One would thus predict that both subject clitics and object clitics should be able to occur in subject position. As shown by examples (67–68), subject clitics and object clitics occur at the same time. If, for example, the child were not making a distinction between finite *mange* ("eat") and nonfinite *manger* ("to eat") we would expect to find sentences like the following with dative or accusative *me* ("me") instead of nominative *je* ("I") in subject position:

(71) *Me mange.*
     Me eat.

instead of

(72) *Je mange.*
     I eat.

But errors of this type do not occur.[15]

To summarize the discussion so far, the French data, like the German, are at variance with the predictions of theories in which the development of verbal inflection and the setting of the null-subject parameter are in a trigger relationship.

1.3 Conclusion and General Matters

The French data also bring up the more general question of the relationship between parameters in linguistic theory and parameters in language acquisition. It might be tempting, when we see evidence that French children have acquired a feature associated with a certain setting of a given parameter, but we see at the same time no corresponding switch of the child's grammar to that setting, to take this as evidence that the parameter is incorrectly formulated. We have seen that in Hyams's account of French, [- morphologically uniform] is associated with [- null subject]. But the data from French children show that learners may exhibit this setting yet still operate as if their language is [+ null subject].

The same problem holds for other parameters related to null subjects proposed in linguistic theory, for example, Koster's (1987) formulation of

---

[15]Sentences like (71) have been observed in English during the null subject stage: (i) here me comes (Brown corpus: Adam; from Kazman, 1988)

the *Pro*-drop Parameter or Kayne's (1989) parameter relating null subjects to clitic climbing.

Koster (1987) assumes that movement of a verb to INFL (or COMP) always indicates that the category is a strong governor. He proposes the parametric relationship in (72):

(73) *Pro*-drop occurs if the subject of a sentence is not in the domain of a strong governor.

The prediction is that once children have systematic V-to-I movement, null subjects should disappear. As we have shown, however (cf. examples (69)–(70)), the prediction fails.

Similarly, Kayne (1989) establishes a relationship between the possibility of having (thematic) null subjects and the occurrence of clitic climbing in Romance languages. Thus Italian, a null-subject language, allows for clitic climbing, whereas French, not a null-subject language, does not, as shown in (74) and (75):

(74) *Gianni li vuole vedere.*
     John them wants to-see.

(75) i. **Jean les veut voir.*
        John them wants to-see.
     ii. Jean veut les voir.

This suggests that the occurrence of sentences like (75ii) in the language of the child should indicate that he or she has set the parameter to the adult value. Null subjects should then no longer occur. Again, as shown by our data, this is not the case. Although clitic placement is always correct, as shown in (76), null subjects still occur:

(76) *Je veux l$_i$'ouvrir ça$_i$.*   F (26;11)
     I want it$_i$ open that$_i$

Assuming that there is a direct and unimpeded relationship between a particular parameter in linguistic theory and its role as a trigger in language acquisition may not be correct. There may be other factors which, in the real-time arena of acquisition, prevent the relationship from being as direct as we might have first imagined. These factors may be able to explain discrepancies between expected and actual data, such that the proposed parameter could still be correct. And they may explain other phenomena, not related to the parameter, as well.

This is the approach we will take in the next section. We will show that the parameter-setting model, although looking initially dubious in the cases we have considered, could still be correct in general. We will consider an alternative account of the developmental data of German and French, also under a model that makes use of parameters, including a null-subject parameter. We will show that such an account works, provided it takes into account other factors, in particular, parameter interaction and pragmatic constraints.

2. AN ALTERNATIVE ACCOUNT

If it is not, as we have shown in the preceding discussion, the development of INFL that directly triggers the German or French child to treat his language as a non-null-subject language, could it be that there are other input data that do? And what other factors are involved? Relevant here is Prediction 2, which we reached in the discussion of the German data, repeated here:

PREDICTION 2: If INFL licenses subject *pro* then *pro* should occur in all finite contexts.

Now let us consider, first, the data we have seen. In German as well as French, there was a striking asymmetry between the occurrence of null subjects across structures. Two groups emerge: (1) wh- questions and embedded finite clauses; (2) declarative matrix clauses. In (1) null subjects practically never occur, whereas in (2) they occur freely. This is so from the very beginning of the emergence of these structures.[16]

Now consider the target languages. Whereas genuine null-subject languages, such as Italian, allow null subjects freely in wh-questions and embedded clauses, French and German do not, as (77) through (82) illustrate:

(77) Italian: *Pia a detto che è andata al cinemà.*
Pia has said that (she) has gone to the movies.

(78) French: **Pia a dit qu'est allée au cinéma.*

(79) German: **Pia hat gesagt, dass ins Kino gegangen ist.*

---

[16]These structures are not very frequent at this early stage, especially embedded clauses are relatively rare. Our hypothesis that null subjects are treated differently in these contexts should thus be tested experimentally.

(80) Italian: *Dove è?*
     Where is (he/she/it)?

(81) French: **Où est?*

(82) German: **Wo ist?*

And, recall, we have already seen that German allows null subjects in matrix clauses.

To summarize, there are contexts within a single language in which subjects may be missing, but others where they are required. As such, this points to a more general problem for the learner, a problem of what we might call "ambiguous input." The general problem has been pointed out by Valian (1990a) with respect to any parameter-setting account in which the child is exposed to ambiguous input with respect to the value of a given parameter in a single language.

That children do indeed receive ambiguous input with respect to whether or not their language allows for null subjects results from the fact that, as shown by much of the current work on null subjects in linguistic theory, most languages are not simply $[+/-$ null subject]. Rather, they display varying patterns of occurrence of optional and obligatory thematic, quasi-thematic and expletive subjects (e.g., Huang, 1984; Rizzi, 1986; Rouveret & Sauzet, 1989, Haider, 1987, Cardinaletti, 1990, and the contributions in Jaeggli & Safir, 1989b).

Thus, as we have already seen, German, usually considered a [-null subject] language, allows for missing thematic subjects in verb-second clauses in preverbal position (see example (1)). But whereas an Italian child could safely conclude from an input sentence like (83) that Italian is a language that freely allows for thematic null subjects in all finite contexts, were the German child to draw the same conclusion from the corresponding input data (84), he would end up with the wrong grammar, given that the occurrence of thematic null subjects in German is restricted to the preverbal position in verb-second clauses:

(83) *Guardava la televisione.*
     (He/she) watched TV.

(84) *(Er) sah fern.*

Furthermore, if the expletive pronoun *es* (it) is taken into account, the picture of the distribution of null subjects in German becomes still more complex. That is, expletive *pro* is excluded in the specifier of C position but is *obligatory* in the specifier of INFL position in verb-final and verb-second clauses. This can be seen from examples (85)–(86) taken from Cardinaletti (1990; see also Haider, 1987, Tomaselli 1990):[17]

(85) a. Es /*Pro wird getanzt.
   There was danced.
   b. Es /*pro ist ein Mann gekommen.
   There came a man.
   c. Es /*pro wurde ein Buch gestohlen.
   There was a book stolen.

(86) a. *Ich weiss, dass pro /*es getanzt wurde.*
   I know that (there) was danced.
   b. *Ich weiss, wo pro /*es getanzt wurde.*
   I know where (there) was danced.
   c. *Gestern wurde pro /*es getanzt.*
   Yesterday (there) was danced.[18]

Contrary to German, French and English lack the possibility of freely omitting preverbal thematic subjects, as shown by the unacceptable sentences in (87) through (88), corresponding to the German sentence (84):

(87) * *Regardait la télévision.*

(88) * Was watching television.

But in these languages, too, subjects may occasionally be omitted (see Harris, 1989; Valian, 1990a, b; Radford, personal communication; Roeper & Weissenborn, 1990):[19]

(89) (I) found the book.

(90) (It) seems like it's gonna rain.

---

[17]Tomaselli (1990) explains the distribution of expletive *pro* in German by a parametric difference between German and Italian. In German, COMP is a licensing head, but INFL is not as it is in Italian. COMP only acts as a licenser when the subject does not receive a theta-role. How the child finds out when expletives are obligatorily null, is an open question. The acquisition of experiencer verbs may play a role here.

[18]Similar phenomena can be observed in Italian, a null-subject language, which requires an expletive subject clitic in a sentence with a postverbal subject like the following (taken from Burzio, 1986): (i) C(i)' /*pro *è una lettera nella busta*

[19]In order to evaluate the possible impact of these structures their frequency in the adult input to the German and French child is of interest. Further discussion of this issue will follow.

(91) *(Il) faut pas faire cela.*
(One) should not do this.

The learnability problem that results from the existence of this type of ambiguous input is an example of the "Pendulum Problem" (Randall, 1990). How can parameter setting be kept from staying in limbo or from swinging back and forth between opposite values?

One way to avoid the Pendulum Problem is to assume that for every parameter there is an unambiguous context that allows the child to set the parameter correctly (for pertinent discussion see Roeper & Weissenborn 1990 and Valian, 1990a, b). I want to suggest that for the null-subject parameter it is contexts with a lexical element in CP, either a complementizer or a wh-phrase (but crucially not a verb) that constitute the unambiguous triggering data that allow the child to set the null-subject parameter to its correct value.

Consider the following examples from German and French, which illustrate the contexts:

German

a. Embedded Clauses

(92) *Weil machte machte puppa heia.*   S 28;17
     Because makes makes the doll heia.
     (= because the doll sleeps).

(93) *Weil die weg sind.*   S 29;13
     Because these away are.
     (Because these are gone).

(94) *Weil der Tommy gebissen hat.*   S 29;13
     Because the Tommy bitten has.

(95) *Wenn ich hochheb den.*   B 31;27
     When I lift this.

(96) *Wenn der hier gran (=dran) is.*   B 31;27
     When this here fixed is.

(97) *Wenn der is dunkel.*   B 31;27
     When this is dark.

(98) *Lass mal gucken wo das das is.*   B 32;16
     Let PART see where that that is.

(99) *Weil das so dick is.*   B 32;16
     Because that so thick is.

(100) *Weil ich das wollte.*   H(26;26)
     Because I that wanted.

(101) *Weil ich lust habe zu stehen.*   H(26;29)
     Because I pleasure have to stay.

(102) *Okay wie ich macht hab.*   H(27;15)
     Okay how I made have.

(103) *Ich weiss nicht, wo die rosinen sind.*   H(27;15)
     I know not where the raisins are.

(104) *Ich wartet habe, bis du kommst.*   H(28;13)
     I waited have until you come.

(105) *Weil ich nicht kanne kann.*   H(28;28)
     Because I not the can can.

(106) *Ein auto, wenn ein mann drin sitzt.*   H(29;1)
     A car when a man in-it sits.

b. Wh-questions

(107) *Wo is dine* (=Gardine).   B 27;30
     Where is curtain?

(108) *Wo is ein kugel?*   S 22;20
     Where is a marble?

(109) *Wo is der ball?*   S 22;20
     Where is the ball?

(110) *Was is das?*   S 26;19
     What is that?

(111) *Wo bist du?*   H 24;6
     Where are you?

(112) *Wo bin du?*   H 24;10
      Where are you?

(113) *Warum ich geweint hab?*   H 24;15
      Why I cried have?

(114) *Wo soll ich hinmalen?*   H 29;23
      Where shall I paint?

(115) *Ich weiss nicht wo ist der?*   H 29;23
      I know not where is he?

(116) *Was gibt da?*   S 26;20
      What is there?

(117) *Wo is mein strohhalm mami?*   S 26;20
      Where is my straw, mommy?

French

a. Embedded Clauses

(118) *Faire gros si tu veux.*   P 25;26
      Make a poop if you want.

(119) *Crois que c'est bon.*   P 27;00
      (I) believe that this is good.

(120) *Pour mettre les fleurs on dit que c'est un vase.*   P 27;21
      For t-put the flowers one says that this is a vase.

(121) *Parce que c'est drôle.*   P 30;13
      Because this is funny.

(122) *Parce qu'elle est froide.*   P 30;20
      Because she is cold.

(123) *Parce qu'elle est pas gentille.*   P 30;20
      Because she is not nice.

(124) *Si on fait pas de lumière, ben on voit pas bien.*   P 32;08
      If one makes not light, well one sees not well.

(125) *C'est ça qu'on fait.*   P 32;08
     That's it what one does.

(126) *Parce que tu t'en vas t'es vilaine.*   P 32;08
     Because you leave you are not nice.

b. Wh-questions.

(127) *Où est Kiki?*   F 21;26
     Where is Kiki?

(128) *Où elle est la musique?*   F 22;26
     Where it is the music?

(129) *Où elle est la porte?*   F 22;26
     Where it is the door?

(130) *Où il est le fil?*   P 25;19
     Where it is the cable?

(131) *Où il est le verre?*   P 25;19
     Where it is the glass?

(132) *Comment on fait pour casser les maisons?*   P 25;26
     How one does to break the houses?

(133) *Avec quoi elle va chercher mamie?*   P 26;3
     With what she goes to-get mommy?

The two types of structures have one feature in common: Their CP contains an overt element. In embedded clauses it is a complementizer in C; in wh-questions it is a wh-phrase in Spec. Assume, as we have discussed, that a thematic null subject can be identified either by a topic chain, which requires a null topic position or by a rich INFL (i.e., a +pronominal AGR) (Huang, 1984; Hyams, this volume). If either the head of CP in embedded finite clauses, or the specifier of CP in matrix clauses is lexically filled, then there is no topic position available to which the subject can be moved. Thus it is not possible to form a topic chain and in that way identify a null subject. The only possibility left for having a null subject in these contexts is via a rich INFL.

To put it another way, in these two contexts, lexical material blocks a null subject from being identified from outside the clause by a topic chain, and forces it to be identified from the only other identification possibility, that is, INFL. If INFL, for some other reason, turns out not to be a licit identifier, then a null subject cannot be identified and lexical subjects are required.

The virtual errorlessness of French and German children's use of subjects in these embedded clause and wh-contexts shows that the child must already "know" that identification by a topic is impossible when the CP contains an overt wh-phrase or an overt complementizer. That is, the fact that from their first occurrence in the development of non-null-subject languages, clauses with these elements in CP disallow null subjects clearly shows that by this stage the child obeys formal principles of identification. More specifically, these data indicate that the constraints on topic chain formation as a means of identification for null subjects must be part of the child's grammar from the moment when we find overt wh-phrases and complementizers in CP. If this were not the case, we couldn't explain why coindexation alone would not be sufficient for the child to identify a null subject in the following ungrammatical sentences:

(134) *Pia_i sagt dass e_i ins Kino gegangen ist.
       Pia says that e to the movies gone is.

(135) A: $Hans_i$ hat ein Problem. B: *Was macht e_i nun?
       Hans has a problem. What does e now

The child can now determine whether his or her language has strong or weak INFL and set the identification parameter. The presence of any null subjects in these structures in the input that he or she hears from the adult language will unambiguously tells him or her that a clause-internal identifier must be present. This is what happens in Italian, and does not happen in French or German, since there, the adult input will never exhibit sentences with thematic null subjects in these contexts.

Notice that the Subset Principle holds for these contexts: Unless there is positive evidence to the contrary, lexical thematic subjects are obligatory.[20]

Of course, the parametric choice about whether INFL licenses and identifies *pro* is only relevant after the structures containing overt wh- and complementizers are acquired by children. And this development itself can be seen as the result of an earlier parametric decision. It has been proposed that, unlike German and French, languages such as Chinese or Japanese may lack an overt C-/I-system at S-structure (Fukui, 1986). In these

---

[20]We do not have to claim that there is a default value [-pro] for the null-subject parameter because of the Extended Projection Principle (Chomsky, 1981) that postulates that every clause requires a subject. We assume that this principle is available to the child.

languages, wh-phrases are base-generated *in situ,* overt complementizers are missing and there is no relevant verbal inflection. Thus the child must find out whether the language to be learned has an overt CP, that is, whether the "C-parameter" is + or − . This can be done on the basis of simple input data, namely examples exhibiting, for example, overt wh-movement or overt complementizers. Thus the setting of the INFL-parameter (i.e., whether INFL licenses and identifies *pro*) is directly dependent on the setting of the C-parameter. Only after the first is set, can the child set the second.

The explanation given so far for the distribution of null and lexical subjects in child French and German does not yet explain two things. (1) Why are null subjects occasionally permitted in adult French in matrix clauses? Recall that for German, topic chain formation, as in the adult language, gives the child the input to show that a null subject is licensed here (see example (1)). As we have seen in examples (89–91), however, even in languages such as English or French, typical non-null-subject languages, subjects can nevertheless be omitted in declaratives. This has been attributed to pragmatic factors, and the child's use of null subjects here follows from data that he or she receives in the input.[21]

If children's use is more frequent, then what is still to be acquired, presumably, are aspects of pragmatic knowledge. We will have no more to say about this here.

The second thing to be explained is: (2) Why is there a difference in the degree to which French and German children omit subjects in these matrix declarative clauses (see Tables 12.1 and 12.2 above)?[22] If pragmatics or processing (cp. Bloom, 1989) were solely responsible, we should not find a difference.

It is also not the case here that the difference can be explained by differences in the frequency of these structures in the input of the German and French children. Although German has the general possibility of omitting thematic subjects in V-second clauses, interestingly, the frequency of subject omissions in the input of the German children, under 5%, does not significantly differ from the input of French children.[23]

The difference in these contexts, then, must already be constrained by underlying *structural* differences between German and French. As we have

---

[21]For more discussion of this point, see Roeper and Weissenborn (1990).

[22]It would be desirable to confirm the differences between the proportion of null subject use for French and German with independent measures additional to age; a preliminary analysis of the data for the remaining children listed on page 271 indicates that the difference for P (French) and S (German) does generalize to other child speakers of French and German.

[23]The comparison is based on a count of subjectless declaratives in the first 100 clauses of a number of initial, medial, and final recordings of the German and French children.

said, adult German allows the possibility for *pro* in matrix declaratives, via topic chain formation. But what prevents this type of chain-formation in French?

We can account for the difference syntactically, by relating it to the difference in the position of the finite verb in declarative matrix clauses in the two languages. In French, the verb is in INFL, while in German it is in COMP. This difference in the position of the finite verb in declaratives in the two languages has to be seen as the result of another parametric decision. Languages differ with respect to where the finite verb moves in matrix clauses: to INFL in French and English, to COMP in German, Dutch, and mainland Scandinavian languages (Platzack & Holmberg, 1989). We suggest that this syntactic difference makes the mechanism of topic chain formation available to German but not French. The frequency of subject omissions in matrix clauses, then, could arise from the German child pragmatically overusing the syntactic possibility that the grammar already puts at his or her disposal. (This conclusion depends crucially on the assumption that the clause-initial position is *not* a structure-independent position, contra Valian, 1990a, b). The prediction that follows from these findings would be that languages of the same type as German and French should show comparable differences between subjects in these declarative matrix contexts.[24] The question remains why early French permits null subjects at all. Possibly the existence of null subjects in early French is related to the ambiguity of the input data concerning the existence of WH-movement in French. In adult French the wh-word may be—and frequently is—left *in situ,* as in Chinese:

(136) *Il est allé où?*   He is gone where?

If we assume that the frequency of this type of question delays the establishment of a CP projection in French *and* that the existence of such a node is disjunctive with an IP projection that permits null subjects (as the analysis of Rizzi, 1991, argues; see also Koster, 1986 and Haider, 1988), then the French child may be expected for some period to permit null subjects, but by virtue of a structural analysis different to that used by the German child (a difference in the highest projection for root clauses: IP vs. CP). This analysis does not, however, explain the asymmetry in frequency of null subjects in early German and early French; the frequency might better be explained if one adopts the grammatical analysis just given and also assumes that the indeterminacy in the French data concerning the operation of movement to [Spec, CP] results in an intermediate stage where

---

[24]Thus, Dutch, also a V2 language, should pattern with German. Wevering's (1990) study of Dutch confirms this prediction.

early French has a dual grammatical system. This approach predicts that French should be intermediate between German and English in the proportion of null subjects for comparable stages. I will not develop the consequences of such an approach for the general issue of continuity vs. discontinuity outlined in Chapter 1 (this volume).

To summarize, the preceding discussion has shown that the actual distribution of subject omissions in German and French and their development are explained by assuming that the setting of the licensing and identification parameter interacts with other parameters, that is, the wh-parameter, the C-parameter, and the verb-movement parameter (i.e., V-to-I or V-to-C). Before the identification parameter can be set, these other parameters have to be set, since they are necessary for the child to recognize the wh-questions and embedded clauses needed to set the identification parameter for null subjects. We concluded that frequency differences in subject omissions in declaratives between German and French cannot be explained by pragmatic or processing factors but have to be accounted for by the child's knowledge of structural properties, that is, the landing site, either INFL or COMP, for verb movement in declaratives, which differs in these languages.

3. SUMMARY AND CONCLUSIONS

In the first part of this chapter we discussed a prediction from a number of versions of the null-subject parameter for early child language: The acquisition of the adult properties of INFL should act as a trigger for children to set the null-subject parameter correctly in non-null-subject languages. We showed on the basis of developmental data from German and French that this prediction is not borne out in these two languages. For both languages we found that although the relevant properties of verb inflection had been acquired, subjects were still omitted.

The failure of the prediction to hold in the French and German data invited us to wonder if we should either question the formulations of the parameter, or even the parameter-setting model in general. But we suggested that additional factors are involved in the acquisition process that contribute to the findings.

In Sec. 2 we proposed an alternative parameter-setting account of how French and German are acquired. It explained the apparent lag between the acquisition of INFL and the adult-like use of subjects. The analysis grouped the data into two syntactic contexts: (1) embedded clauses with complementizers or wh-questions; (2) matrix declarative clauses. We showed that in (1), the child's treatment of subjects mirrors the adult's: Subjects in French or German, unlike Italian, are virtually never omitted. Thus we claimed that the child has set the parameter in type (1) contexts from the beginning. For contexts of type (2) we claimed that the difference between the child and adult in both languages is not a syntactic one resulting from a parameter-setting difference, but suggested that it amounts to a lack of pragmatic knowledge. However, pragmatics cannot handle the difference *between* French and German with respect to (2). Rather, we argued that the frequency difference of null subjects that we found here followed from a syntactic difference between the two languages in the position of the finite verb in matrix clauses. The verb in German, being in COMP, allows null subjects to be identified by a topic chain, while the verb in French, being in INFL, does not.

The null-subject parameter should describe the distribution of subjects in a given language. Italian, a [+null-subject] language allows null subjects in both type (1) and type (2) contexts. German allows null subjects in type (2) contexts, but not type (1), appearing to be both a [+null-subject] and [−null-subject] language. The question that arises is, under usual conceptions of the null-subject parameter, how is such a distribution explained?

In this chapter we have discussed two identification possibilities for null subjects: (a) by a topic chain and (b) by a rich INFL. When INFL is a identifier, as in Italian, then null subjects occur in all embedded contexts, as well as matrix contexts. When a topic chain alone is the identifier, as in German, embedded contexts are ruled out; only matrix null subjects are identified. In French null subjects are identified by neither INFL nor a topic chain.

It appears that INFL identification produces a larger set of possible null-subject contexts than topic-chain identification. But this is only a result of another factor, i.e., properties of COMP, which constrain topic chain identification in German. The C-parameter restricts topic-chain identification in German, by virtue of its [+] setting, the setting that also allows complementizers and overt wh-movement into COMP. In Chinese, where the C-parameter is set to [−], these elements are excluded from COMP, and topic chain identification is not restricted, so all types of contexts, embedded as well as matrix clauses, permit null subjects by this possibility. To return to the foregoing question, then, what accounts for the "mixed" null-subject behavior of German is the interaction of the C(OMP)-parameter with the INFL parameter.

We claimed that a third parameter was also involved in the null-subject patterns of German and French. The difference between German and French children's readiness to omit subjects in type (2) contexts (i.e., matrix clause) resulted from the landing site of finite verbs in the two languages. In French, the V-movement parameter is set such that verbs move to INFL, while in German they move to COMP. The COMP position, being available to topic identification, unlike the INFL position, gives German children more freedom to have null subjects in matrix clauses than French children.

The general picture that emerges is that once parameter interaction is considered,[25] child language is much closer to adult language than has been claimed. This seems to be the case for French and German, at least. How true it is of other languages remains to be investigated. We hope to have raised considerations that make these investigations more fruitful. The interesting questions will be where the differences emerge, and how they will ultimately be explained.

ACKNOWLEDGMENTS

I want to thank the following colleagues for comments and suggestions: Josef Bayer, Ruth Berman, Harald Clahsen, David Lebeaux, Andrew Radford, Janet Randall, Tom Roeper, Susan Rothstein, Bonnie Schwartz, Maaike Verrips, and Ken Wexler. Versions of this chapter have been presented at the 14th International Congress of Linguists, Berlin, 1987, the 13th Boston Child Language Development Conference, Boston, 1988, and at the following universities: École des Hautes Études en Sciences Sociales, Paris, Paris VII, Ottawa, Wisconsin, Maryland, Tel Aviv. I thank also the audiences at these various places.

The French data used for this study have been collected by Dominique Bassano, Centre National de Recherche Scientifique, Paris and the author (Child B), by Ulrike Rohde (child F), and Madeleine Léveillé (child P), now in the CHILDES data base. The German data have been collected by Max Miller (1979) (Child S), Christiane von Stutterheim (child H), and myself (child B). I want to thank Ulrike Hurpin, Max Miller, and Christiane von Stutterheim that they made their data available to me.

This research has been partly supported by a grant to the author from the Deutsche Forschungsgemeinschaft and from the German–Israeli Foundation for Scientific Research and Development (GIF).

REFERENCES

Bloom, P. (1989). Why do children omit subjects? *Papers and Reports on Child Language Development, 28,* 57–64.

Borer, H., & Wexler, K. (1988). *The maturation of grammatical principles.* University of California, Irvine, and MIT, Cambridge, MA.

Burzio, L. (1986). *Italian syntax.* Dordrecht, The Netherlands: Reidel.

Cardinaletti, A. (1990). *Es, pro* and sentential arguments in German. *Linguistische Berichte, 126,* 135–164.

Chomsky, N. (1981). *Lectures on government and binding.* Dordrecht, The Netherlands: Foris.

Clahsen, H. (1982). *Spracherwerb in der Kindheit.* Tübingen, Germany: Gunter Narr.

Clahsen, H. (1986). Verb inflections in German child language: Acquisition of agreement markings and the functions they encode. *Linguistics, 26,* 79–121.

---

[25]Nishigaushi and Roeper (1987) also argue for parameter interaction.

Clahsen, H. (1988). *Normale und gestörte Kindersprache.* Amsterdam: John Benjamins.

Clahsen, H. (1991). Constraints on parameter setting. A grammatical analysis of some acquisition stages in German child language. *Language Acquisition, 2.*

Clark, E. (1985). The acquisition of romance with special reference to French. In D. Slobin (Ed.), *The crosslinguistic study of language acquisition* (2 Vols, pp. 687–782). Hillsdale, NJ: Lawrence Erlbaum Associates.

Emonds, J. (1978). The verbal complex V'-V in French. *Linguistic Inquiry, 9,* 155–175.

Fukui, N. (1986). *A theory of category projection and its applications.* Unpublished doctoral dissertation, MIT, Cambridge, MA.

Guilfoyle, E., & Noonan, M. (1988). *Functional categories and language acquisition.* Paper presented at the 13th annual Boston University Conference on Language Development.

Haider, H. (1987). PRO PRO-DROP DROP. Universities of Vienna & Stuttgart.

Haider, H. (1988). Matching projections. In A. Cardinaletti, G. Cinque, & G. Giusti (Eds.), *Constituent structure* (pp. 101–121). Dordrecht: Foris.

Harris, R. (1989). Degree-0 explanation. *Behavioral and Brain Sciences, 12,* 344–345.

Huang, J. (1984). On the distribution and reference of empty pronouns. *Linguistic Inquiry, 15,* 531–574.

Hulk, A. (1987). L'acquisition du français et le paramètre pro-drop. In B. Kampers-Manhe, & C. Vet (Eds.), *Etudes de linguistique française.* Amsterdam: Rodopi.

Hyams, N. (1986). *Language acquisition and the theory of parameters.* Dordrecht, The Netherlands: Reidel.

Hyams, N. M. (1989). The null subject parameter in language acquisition. In O. Jaeggli & K. Safir (Eds.), *The null subject parameter.* Dordrecht, The Netherlands: Kluwer, pp. 215–238.

Jaeggli, O., & Safir, K. (1989a). The null subject parameter and parametric theory. In O. Jaeggli & K. Safir, (Eds.), *The null subject parameter.* Dordrecht, The Netherlands: Reidel, pp. 1–44.

Jaeggli, O., & Safir, K. (Eds.). (1989b). *The null subject parameter.* Dordrecht: Reidel.

Kayne, R. S. (1989). Null subjects and clitic climbing. In: Jaeggli, O. and K. Safir, (Eds.), *The null subject parameter.* Dordrecht, The Netherlands: Reidel, pp. 239–261.

Kazman, R. (1988). *Null arguments and the acquisition of Case and INFL.* Paper presented at the 13th annual Boston University Conference on Language Development.

Koster, J. (1986). *Domains and dynasties.* Dordrecht: Foris.

Koster, J. (1987). *The relation between Pro-Drop, Scrambling, and Verb Movement.* University of Groningen, The Netherlands.

Lebeaux, D. (1988). *Language acquisition and the form of the grammar.* Unpublished doctoral dissertation, University of Massachusetts, Amherst.

Meisel, J. (1990). *INFL-ection: subjects and subject–verb agreement in early child language. Evidence from simultaneous acquisition of two first languages: German and French.* University of Hamburg.

Miller, M. (1979). *The logic of language development in early childhood.* Berlin: Springer.

Mills, A. (1985). The acquisition of German. In D. Slobin (Ed.), *The crosslinguistic study of language acquisition.* Hillsdale, NJ: Lawrence Erlbaum Associates, pp. 141–254.

Nishigaushi, T., & Roeper, T. (1987). Deductive parameters and the growth of empty categories. In T. Roeper & E. Williams (Eds.), *Parameter setting* (pp. 91–121). Dordrecht: Reidel.

Pierce, A. (1989). *On the emergence of syntax: A crosslinguistic study.* Unpublished doctoral dissertation, MIT, Cambridge, MA.

Platzack, C., & Holmberg, A. (1989). The role of AGR and finiteness. *Working Papers in Scandinavian Syntax, 43,* 51–76.

Pollock, J. Y. (1989). Verb movement, UG and the structure of IP. *Linguistic Inquiry, 20,* 365–425.

Radford, A. (1990). *Syntactic theory and the acquisition of English Syntax: The nature of early child grammars of English.* Oxford, England: Blackwell.

Randall, J. (1990). Catapults and pendulums: The mechanics of language acquisition. *Linguistics, 28,* 1381-1406.

Rizzi, L. (1986). Null objects and the theory of pro. *Linguistic Inquiry, 17,* 501-557.

Rizzi, L. (1991). *The development of root null subjects.* Paper presented at the 14th GLOW Colloquium, Leiden.

Roeper, T., & Weissenborn, J. (1990). How to make parameters work. In L. Frazier & J. de Villiers (Eds.), *Language processing and language acquisition.* Dordrecht, The Netherlands: Kluwer, pp. 147-162.

Rothweiler, M. (1989). *Nebensatzerwerb im Deutschen.* Doctoral dissertation, University of Tübingen.

Rouveret, A., & Sauzet, P. (1989). L'approche paramétrique et les langues romanes. In A. Rouveret & P. Sauzet (Eds.), *La structure de la proposition dans les langues Romanes.* Revues des Langues Romanes, *93,* pp V-XI.

Stern, C., & Stern, W. (1928). *Die Kindersprache: Eine psychologische und sprachtheoretische Untersuchung.* Leipzig: Barth.

Tomaselli, A. (1990). COMP⁰ as a licensing head: An argument based on cliticization. In J. Mascaró & M. Nespor, (Eds.), *Grammar in progress. Glow essays for Henk van Riemsdijk.* Dordrecht, The Netherlands: Foris. pp. 433-446.

Tracy, R., Fritzenschaft, A., Gawlitzek-Maiwald, I., & Winkler, S. (1990). *Wege zur komplexen Syntax.* University of Tübingen, Germany.

Valian, V. (1990a). Null subjects: A problem for parameter-setting models of language acquisition. *Cognition, 35,* 105-122.

Valian, V. (1990b). Logical and psychological constraints on the acquisition of syntax. In L. Frazier & J. de Villiers (Eds.), *Language processing and language acquisition* (pp. 119-145). Dordrecht: Kluwer.

Valian, V. (1990c). *Syntactic subjects in the early speech of American and Italian children.* New York: Hunter College.

Verrips, M., & Weissenborn, J. (in preparation). On the relation between the acquisition of verbal inflection and verb movement. To appear in J. Meisel (Ed.), *The acquisition of verb placement: Functional categories and V2 phenomena in language development.* (Studies in Theoretical Psycholinguistics) Dordrecht: Kluwer.

Weissenborn, J. (1990). Functional categories and verb movement: The acquisition of German syntax reconsidered. In M. Rothweiler (Ed.), *Spracherwerb und Grammatik. Lingusitische Untersuchungen zum Erwerb von Syntax und Morphologie.* Linguistische Berichte. Special issue 3/1990, 190-224.

Weissenborn, J., Verrips, M., & Berman, R. (1989). *Negation as a window to the structure of early child language.* Nijmegen, The Netherlands: Max Planck Institut für Psycholinguistik.

Wevering, M. (1990). What's missing in Dutch?. *Papers and Reports on Child Language Development, 29,* 125-132.

13 Comments on Hyams and Weissenborn: On Licensing and Identification

Diane Lillo-Martin
University of Connecticut and Haskins Laboratories

In recent years a number of proposals have been made to account for the distribution of null and overt arguments across a variety of spoken languages. As Hyams and Weissenborn both suggest, these proposals have implications for the analysis of child language development, under the hypothesis that a parameterized theory of language is also a theory of language acquisition. Hence, an accurate theory of why children's early speech seems consistently to allow for null subjects is dependent on an accurate theory of why some adult languages allow null subjects while others do not. In their interesting and informative contributions, Hyams and Weissenborn provide data that will aid in the understanding of both the adult grammars and the explanation of the child's course of development.

THE MORPHOLOGICAL UNIFORMITY ACCOUNT

Hyams adopts the proposal that the theory of null arguments in adult grammars contains at least two parts: a licensing requirement and an identification requirement. Specifically, following Jaeggli and Safir (1989), she proposes that the licensing requirement consists of the Morphological Uniformity Principle. The identification requirement is not specifically given, but from her discussion we can assume three parts to the identification requirement: Identification can be by a c-commanding nominal, by a topic (possibly null) binding a null argument (these two following Huang, 1984), or by AG containing tense. Crucially, if Tense has been moved out of AG (as in some analyses of the Germanic V2 phenomenon), identification is no longer met. As Weissenborn points out, however, this analysis of German leaves unanswered the question of why null arguments are not found in subordinate clauses, in which verbs remain in their clause-final position.

The observation that children's early speech allows null subjects is accounted for under the theory of null arguments that Hyams adopts by assuming that children begin with the following two assumptions: (1) Their language does display Morphological Uniformity; and (2) Their language does allow topic binding of null arguments. For the child learning English, null arguments will be allowed because by assumption (1) the licensing requirement will be met, and because by assumption (2) the identification requirement will be met. However, for the English-learning child both of these assumptions will have to be abandoned. Since the first is determined to be false when the child has acquired English verbal morphology, the second is abandoned because the question of identification is moot if null arguments are not licensed.

However, for the child learning Italian, although the first assumption is true, the second is false. Hyams does not discuss how the Italian-learning child gives up assumption (2). She suggests, in her discussion of the acquisition of American Sign Language (ASL), that there is some grammatical way of taking agreement identification over topic identification, if both are available in a language. However, although both are available in ASL, both are not available in Italian, so presumably the Italian child will need to abandon assumption (2) on the basis of some evidence.[1]

It might thus be necessary to return to a view of assumption (2) as related to an independent parameter, following Huang's original proposal. Huang suggests, following earlier work on Chinese, that Chinese and other languages may be characterized as "Discourse Oriented." Discourse-oriented languages allow topic chaining, by which the topic of a discourse is understood to be the null topic of sentences in that discourse; these sentences may then contain null arguments bound by the null topic. But topic chaining is not the only characteristic of discourse-oriented languages. These languages also display discourse binding of anaphors, topic-comment structures with no gap, and other indications of "topic prominence." According to Huang's analysis, all of these characteristics are captured by one parameter.

If it is empirically correct to maintain these characteristics as a group, it would be more economical to maintain Discourse-oriented versus Sentence-oriented as a separate parameter of grammars, including assumption (2)

---

[1] One reason the child should not go on assuming that both kinds of identification are available in Italian, always choosing agreement identification over topic identification, concerns null objects, to which I will return.

under the [+Discourse Oriented] setting. There would thus be evidence from any of the discourse-oriented characteristics for children to choose the correct parameter setting. However, discourse orientation—and thus, identification of null arguments by topic binding—would then be separate from the licensing requirement on null arguments, and children learning English might be able to learn that English is not discourse-oriented before they have completed morphological learning. Hence, they would not have continued reason to believe English allows null subjects.

Hyams makes a second, more problematical adjustment to Huang's theory, which is necessitated by the claim that English-learning children use null subjects because they have assumed topic binding identification of null arguments. A crucial part of Hyams's argument that missing subjects in early children's speech are a reflex of grammatical development rather than a processing limitation is the observation that only subjects—not objects—are regularly omitted.[2] However, as Huang's analysis requires, both subjects and objects may be null in discourse oriented languages.

Under Huang's analysis, the empty subjects and objects are variables (with the exception of an empty embedded subject; this may be either a variable or a pronominal). Hyams makes the claim that null subjects in early English are [+pronominal, −anaphoric] empty categories, that is, *pro.* As Huang argues, null objects cannot be *pro,* because this would result in a violation of binding conditions. Since null objects are allowed in Chinese, the adult grammar must allow null arguments to be variables, as Huang argues. However, the child, under Hyams's proposal, does not have variable empty categories, so initially null subjects will be allowed, but not null objects. Although Hyams does adopt Huang's proposals for the argument that null objects cannot be *pro,* she apparently does not accept his arguments that null subjects also cannot be *pro.* The same assumptions that rule out empty object *pro* for Huang, that is, that an empty pronoun must be identified by the closest nominal element, will also rule out empty (matrix) subject *pro.*

The issue of null objects can be taken further. Hyams points out that Mazuka, Lust, Wakayama, and Snyder (1986) find a subject–object asymmetry in the occurence of null arguments in early Japanese. In this study, children use null subjects in approximately 50% of the subject–predicate constructions, and null objects in only 17% of the transitive verb constructions. Although the asymmetry is apparent here, it still seems as though the Japanese-learning children are using null objects to a greater extent than the English-learning children in Hyams's study. Hyams (1986, p. 109) claims that the use of null objects in English-speaking children is so rare that it can probably be attributed to performance factors. Further-

---

[2]See Hyams (1986) for a more extensive discussion of this argument.

more, as Hyams points out, "the argument for an early null subject grammar has always been based on the *optionality* of lexical subjects and not on their *frequency*—beyond the obvious need to establish that the phenomenon is indeed systematic." Thus, it seems that Japanese-learning children are optionally using null objects, although with a lower frequency than null subjects.

Why might Japanese-learning children use both null subjects and null objects while English-learning children use only null subjects? One explanation might lie in the fact that adult Japanese, as a Discourse-oriented language, allows both null subjects and null objects. If the information needed to make this parameter setting are abundant, then the Japanese-learning children may be already working on the assumption that both types of null arguments are allowed.[3] However, this explanation then makes it much more unlikely that English-learning children use null subjects because they mistakenly believe English allows topic binding identification of nulls.

Weissenborn presents data from French and German that he takes to pose further problems for Hyams's analysis. German, according to Weissenborn's analysis, is like Chinese in allowing topic binding of null arguments (Huang makes a similar observation). Even if the types of sentences that can exhibit null arguments are more restricted in German than in Chinese, as Weissenborn suggests, it may still be possible to account for the German facts using topic identification. If so, as Weissenborn says, the actual developmental facts of German can be accounted for in Hyams's system by assuming that the German-learning child begins with the same assumptions as the English-learning child, and thus from the beginning identifies null arguments by topic binding. Regardless of the richness of German verbal agreement, Hyams's general analysis of null identification will go through with these changes suggested by Weissenborn.[4] I will return to a discussion of Weissenborn's account of the German developmental facts in the next section.

Weissenborn's French data are harder for Hyams to account for. Apparently, young French-speaking children produce subjectless sentences even after they have analyzed the verb agreement system. This is not predicted by Hyams's account, because for her, the acquisition of verbal morphology in French will prove it not to be morphologically uniform, hence null subjects will be unlicensed. It would thus seem difficult to attribute the final non-*pro*-drop character of French (and, by extension,

---

[3]Similar acquisition data would be expected if the initial setting on the Discourse-oriented vs. Sentence-oriented parameter is Discourse-oriented, regardless of whether the child has had the opportunity to examine this parameter setting.

[4]Recall that agreement identification will not be available in German because of the V2 phenomenon; however, children may use topic-identified null arguments regardless of their state of development with respect to agreement morphology and the V2 rule.

other non-*pro*-drop languages) to the time-consuming learning of agreement morphology. Yet a theory of acquisition is required to explain how children come to have the adult grammar.

TRIGGERING DOMAINS

Weissenborn's alternative analysis maintains a parametric theory of null subjects, but considers specifying the domain in which the data used to trigger a parameter setting can be found. Weissenborn's comments and rich data set bring up problems for Hyams's analysis; his proposal should thus be considered carefully.

Weissenborn proposes that the appropriate domain for triggering data regarding the ability of INFL to identify null subjects is found in embedded clauses with overt complementizers and wh-questions with moved wh-phrases. He asserts that in these domains, unlike matrix declaratives, a topic chain is not available. He suggests that verb movement to COMP, as in German, makes available the topic chain option, while verb movement to INFL, as in French, prohibits it. He further asserts that because German has overt wh-movement, it has fewer options for topic chains than Chinese, a language without syntactic wh-movement. Each of these proposals points to a possible distinction between the types of topic chains to be found cross-linguistically. However, Weissenborn does not develop this analysis syntactically, so it is not clear how to test it with data from other languages. Without knowing why topic chain formation is to be constrained in the way that Weissenborn suggests, one cannot judge how his theory predicts a language should behave with respect to topic chains. Nor does his chapter suggest how a child comes to know whether his or her language allows topic chains, and whatever restrictions must be learned.

A further, more unsettling, uncertainty about Weissenborn's analysis concerns his position on the null subjects used by the youngest children he and others have observed. His proposal points out that children cannot be expected to evaluate a parameter which uses embedded clauses as its triggering domain until a prior parameter regarding the structure of embedded clauses is set. This leads to the possible conclusion that he attributes the early use of null subjects to a child's not yet having set the related C parameter, and hence, not yet having evaluated the null subject parameter. However, he points out that young German- and French-speaking children do appropriately use only overt subjects in these contexts, and he provides examples of such children's utterances, from exactly the same time periods as children's null subject sentences. These facts, and his discussion of the French-speaking children's possible confusion about how to set the C parameter, lead to the conclusion that lateness in setting the C parameter is not what underlies German- and English-speaking children's incorrect uses of null subjects. Rather, these boil down to not yet having learned the pragmatic factors governing use of null subjects in the target languages.

This conclusion is troubling, even aside from the arguments made by Hyams that children's use of null subjects is due to a grammatical, not pragmatic analysis. It is troubling because the children would need to learn pragmatic principles that would produce a retreat from a larger set of options (more null subject sentences) to a smaller set of options (fewer null subject sentences). Retreat usually requires some kind of negative evidence. Although little is known about the acquisition of such pragmatic principles as those required here, it has not been demonstrated that negative evidence is more likely to be available in this domain. Weissenborn does not speculate on how this new acquisition challenge would be accomplished.

NULL ARGUMENTS IN AMERICAN SIGN LANGUAGE

Finally, I would like to comment on the data from the acquisition of ASL which Hyams discusses (see Lillo-Martin, 1986). The main problems for Hyams's analysis of the ASL data are related to the problems that have been mentioned. In my analysis of ASL null arguments, I showed that for the adult grammar, there is a distinct difference between null arguments of verbs that mark agreement (i.e., *pro* null arguments), and null arguments of verbs that do not mark agreement (i.e., variables). The former have pronominal characteristics that the latter do not have. Any alternative theory that is proposed will need to be able to account for this distinction. By allowing *pro* null arguments which are topic identified (rather than agreement identified), Hyams's proposal allows this distinction to be blurred, in contradiction to the syntactic facts.

It is, of course, still possible that children do not make the distinction that adults do, especially while they are still acquiring the verb agreement morphology. If, by making assumptions different from Huang's, Hyams's theory will allow *pro* null subjects identified by topics while disallowing *pro* null objects identified by topics, then her account of the acquisition of ASL might still hold, as long as signing children will eventually discard the *pro* option for the variable. However, two facts from my presentation of the data from ASL-learning children argue against this.

First, the signing children were more like the Japanese-learning children cited herein than English-learning children, in that they used both null subjects and null objects.[5] Furthermore, I distinguished topic-identified early nulls from nonidentified early nulls, using real discourse topics established in the situation. Mostly, the discourse topics which I related to later null arguments were explicit topics, given by the child at the beginning of a story. Thus, just as different syntactic behavior of the two kinds of null arguments led me to the conclusion that *pro* and variable nulls must be distinguished in ASL, different uses by children also lead me to the conclusion that they differentiate null arguments identified by topics from other null arguments.

IDENTIFICATION AND LEARNING

In Hyams's new proposal, she responds to the criticism that her earlier analysis left some null arguments in children's speech unidentified. The same criticism might be applied to the conclusion I come to, since the young signing children are not using overt agreement morphology to identify these other null arguments. I maintain, however, that the particular morphological items which count as identification need to be learned for each language. Presumably, every child assumes the existence of abstract agreement; INFL is present regardless of its morphological realization. Thus, in any language a child must learn whether his or her agreement system — however uniform, however impoverished — identifies null arguments.

This learning stipulation is substantiated by idiosyncratic facts about when various morphologically rich languages allow null arguments. In ASL, as noted, the use of null arguments depends on the actual presence of verb agreement. Certain verbs inflect only for subject, others only for object, others for both subject and object. Null arguments of the *pro* type are allowed when agreement is present. Other idiosyncratic facts relating changes in agreement for particular paradigms with changes in the availability of null arguments can be found in languages such as Arabic (Kenstowicz, 1984), Hebrew (Borer, 1983), and others. Hence even languages which license null arguments generally by verb agreement may impose specific identification requirements, not captured directly by the requirement that AG be in INFL. These requirements must be learned.

Hyams and Weissenborn both provide evidence for the separation of licensing and identification in the description of null-argument constructions and their acquisition. My argument suggests that licensing may come

---

[5]Note that adult ASL has both subject and object agreement, so that both *pro* and variable types of null arguments can be found, depending on the actual presence of agreement morphology.

first in acquisition, since identification (at least for *pro* null arguments) is dependent on the development of an agreement system that may have language-particular idiosyncrasies, and thus take time to learn. Further acquisition data, especially from languages such as German, French, and Chinese, should help to clarify the form of the parameters and the means by which parameter settings are made.

ACKNOWLEDGMENTS

This work was supported in part by NIH grant NIDCD #DC00183. The commentary was based on non-final versions of Hyams's and Weissenborn's chapters.

REFERENCES

Borer, H. (1983). *Parametric syntax*. Dordrecht, The Netherlands: Foris.

Huang, J. (1984). On the distribution and reference of empty pronouns. *Linguistic Inquiry, 15,* 531–574.

Hyams, N. (1986). *Language acquisition and the theory of parameters*. Dordrecht, The Netherlands: Reidel.

Jaeggli, O., & Safir, K. (1989). The null subject parameter and parametric theory. In O. Jaeggli & K. Safir (Eds.), *The null subject parameter*. Dordrecht, The Netherlands: Kluwer.

Kenstowicz, M. (1984). The null subject parameter in modern Arabic dialects. *NELS, 14,* 207–219.

Lillo-Martin, D. (1986). Parameter setting: Evidence from use, acquisition, and breakdown in American Sign Language. Unpublished doctoral dissertation, University of California, San Diego.

Mazuka, R., Lust, B., Wakayama, T., & Snyder, W. (1986). Distinguishing effects of parameters in early syntax acquisition: A cross-linguistic study of Japanese and English. *Papers and Reports on Child Language Development, 25,* 73–82.

Author Index

Subject Index

A

A-bar anaphor, 187
A-bar-binding, 187
ACC-ing constructions, 222, 229, 231, 233
Acquisition mechanisms, 191, 192
Acquisition theory, 191
Active temporal vs. passive temporal conditions, 155–156
Active vs. passive verbs, 83–87, 88, 170–171
Adjectival phrase (ADJ), 218
Adjuncts, 104, 204, 207, 211, 226, 227, 228, 229, 237, 239
  before and *after* complements, 182
  obligatory vs. nonobligatory control, 181–185
  S-, 172, 175–177, 179–187
  temporal, 173–175, 177, 179–181, 183, 185
  VP-, 173, 176, 177–187
  VP-adjunction vs. S-adjunction, 179–187
Adjuncts and control, 174–179, 183, 185–188
  purpose clauses and obligatory control, 176–179
  temporals and nonobligatory control, 174–176
Adults
  vs. children in language acquisition, 1–3, 81
  performance in, 81
Adverbial (adjunct) clauses, 151

AG(reement), 307
Agent, 185–186
Agent-patient roles, 86–87
AGR(eement), 251, 259, 260, 263
American Sign Language (ASL), 252, 260, 261, 302, 306–307
  and null subjects, 263–264
  three major developmental stages in, 263–264
Anaphors, 79, 88, 302
ANOVA, 224, 226
Antecedent, 174, 176
Arb construal, 175
Arbitrary control, 174–175
Argument, 211, 226, 227, 228
Argument structure, 83, 84–86
Argument structure, learning of
  and Attachment Principle, 118–124
  Order Principle, 110–118
  principles as catapults for, 110–131
  and semantic restriction, learning the, 122
Attachment Principle, 103, 107, 122, 123, 131, 134, 142, 144, 146
  and benefactive *for*-dative overgeneralizations, 118–122
  and goal *for*-dative overgeneralizations, 122

B

Backward pronominalizations, 37
Before and *after* complements, 182